BF
575
.A3
A576
1994

Aggressive behavior.

$45.00

DATE			

SOCIAL SCIENCES DIVISION
CHICAGO PUBLIC LIBRARY
400 SOUTH STATE STREET
CHICAGO, IL 60605

BAKER & TAYLOR

AGGRESSIVE BEHAVIOR

CURRENT PERSPECTIVES

THE PLENUM SERIES IN SOCIAL/CLINICAL PSYCHOLOGY
Series Editor: C.R. Snyder

University of Kansas
Lawrence, Kansas

AGGRESSIVE BEHAVIOR
Current Perspectives
Edited by L. Rowell Huesmann

DESIRE FOR CONTROL
Personality, Social, and Clinical Perspectives
Jerry M. Burger

HOW PEOPLE CHANGE
Inside and Outside Therapy
Edited by Rebecca C. Curtis and George Stricker

SELF-DEFEATING BEHAVIORS
Experimental Research, Clinical Impressions, and Practical Implications
Edited by Rebecca C. Curtis

SELF-ESTEEM
The Puzzle of Low Self-Regard
Edited by Roy F. Baumeister

SELF-HANDICAPPING
The Paradox That Isn't
Raymond L. Higgins, C.R. Snyder, and Steven Berglas

THE SELF-KNOWER
A Hero under Control
Robert A. Wicklund and Martina Eckert

A Continuation Order Plan is available for this series. A continuation order will bring delivery of each new volume immediately upon publication. Volumes are billed only upon actual shipment. For further information, please contact the publisher.

AGGRESSIVE BEHAVIOR

CURRENT PERSPECTIVES

EDITED BY

L. ROWELL HUESMANN

University of Michigan
Ann Arbor, Michigan

PLENUM PRESS • NEW YORK AND LONDON

Library of Congress Cataloging-in-Publication Data

Aggressive behavior : current perspectives / edited by L. Rowell Huesmann.
p. cm. -- (The Plenum series in social/clinical psychology)
Includes bibliographical references and index.
ISBN 0-306-44553-0
1. Aggressiveness (Psychology) 2. Violence. I. Huesmann, L. Rowell. II. Series.
[DNLM: 1. Aggression--psychology. 2. Psychological Theory. 3. Social Behavior. 4. Social Problems. 5. Social Behavior Disorders. WM 600 A2662 1994]
BF575.A3A576 1994
155.2'32--dc20
DNLM/DLC
for Library of Congress 93-42186
CIP

ISBN 0-306-44553-0

© 1994 Plenum Press, New York
A Division of Plenum Publishing Corporation
233 Spring Street, New York, N.Y. 10013

All rights reserved

No part of this book may be reproduced, stored in a retrieval system, or transmitted in any form or by any means, electronic, mechanical, photocopying, microfilming, recording, or otherwise, without written permission from the Publisher

Printed in the United States of America

To LEONARD ERON,

teacher, scholar, and friend

SOCIAL SCIENCES DIVISION
CHICAGO PUBLIC LIBRARY
400 SOUTH STATE STREET
CHICAGO, IL 60605

R00859 35963

CONTRIBUTORS

LEONARD BERKOWITZ, Department of Psychology, University of Wisconsin, Madison, Wisconsin 53706

KAJ BJÖRKQVIST, Department of Psychology, Åbo Akademi University, Vasa, Finland

THOMAS J. DISHION, Oregon Social Learning Center, Eugene, Oregon 97401

ERIC F. DUBOW, Department of Psychology, Bowling Green State University, Bowling Green, Ohio 43403

LEONARD D. ERON, Research Center for Group Dynamics, Institute for Social Research, University of Michigan, Ann Arbor, Michigan 48106-1248

DAVID P. FARRINGTON, Institute of Criminology, Cambridge University, Cambridge, United Kingdom

SEYMOUR FESHBACH, Department of Psychology, University of California at Los Angeles, Los Angeles, California 90024

ARNOLD P. GOLDSTEIN, Department of Psychology, Syracuse University, Syracuse, New York 13210

PAMELA C. GRIESLER, Oregon Social Learning Center, Eugene, Oregon 97401

NANCY G. GUERRA, Department of Psychology, University of Illinois at Chicago, Chicago, Illinois 60680

L. ROWELL HUESMANN, Research Center for Group Dynamics, Institute for Social Research, University of Michigan, Ann Arbor, Michigan 48106-1248

KIRSTI M. J. LAGERSPETZ, Department of Psychology, University of Turku, Turku, Finland

JOAN MCCORD, Temple University, Philadelphia, Pennsylvania 19122

LAURIE S. MILLER, Department of Child Psychiatry, New York State Psychiatric Institute, Columbia University, College of Physicians and Surgeons, New York, New York 10032

LARRY NUCCI, Department of Education, University of Illinois at Chicago, Chicago, Illinois 60680

DAN OLWEUS, University of Bergen, Bergen, Norway

GERALD R. PATTERSON, Oregon Social Learning Center, Eugene, Oregon 97401

GRAHAM J. REID, Department of Psychology, Bowling Green State University, Bowling Green, Ohio 43403

PREFACE

The study of human aggressive behavior has traveled through a number of distinct theoretical stages over the course of the past century. First, the conjunction of the animal ethologist's writings on the instinctual basis of aggression converged with Freudian views of the need to aggress to relieve hostility and turn the death wish away from the self. Out of these somewhat anthropomorphic and empirically unvalidated theories emerged the more formal, behaviorally testable frustration-aggression theory as developed by Dollard, Doob, Miller, Mowrer, and Sears. Frustration-aggression theory had its day, but was eventually supplanted by social learning theory, which emphasized the roles of instrumental and, later, observational learning in aggressive behavior. In conjunction with this theoretical evolution, researchers turned more attention to the role of situational and contextual factors in aggression. At the same time the computer, cognitive science, and neuroscience revolutions were leading to a much clearer understanding of the multiple genetic, neuronal, hormonal, and network mechanisms that may influence aggressive behavior. Today these trends have converged to stimulate a reemergence of a focus on internal information processing and cognition in social behavior. In one way or another, all the chapters in this volume reflect this refocusing on cognition in social behavior; however, they were not chosen because they fit that theme.

My main goal in selecting chapters for this book was to present material that includes the best current theoretical work on human aggression. In fact, these chapters do represent the latest thinking of some of the clearest thinkers in the field. But they were also selected to represent the multiple dimensions of the body of work that has been influenced by the man to whom this book is dedicated, Leonard Eron.

Over the course of his almost 50-year career, Eron has contributed substantially both to the rationale and to the empirical database on which aggression theory has grown through its several stages. As a young professor at Yale, after receiving his Ph.D. at Wisconsin, Eron gained considerable attention for his early research on projective testing and on the changes in attitudes and beliefs that educational processes could induce. It was his dissatisfaction with the use of projective tests to assess aggressive behavior, however, that led him into the field of aggression research. As his chapter in this volume reveals, his own transformations in thinking from somewhat Freudian, to social-learning theorist, to social-cognition theorist have been mirrored by the transformations in the field. As the citation for his 1980 APA award for Distinguished Professional Contribution to Knowledge said, "Moving into the experimental study of personality, Eron showed how laboratory apparatus and techniques could be adapted to the study of children's aggression. Far ahead of his colleagues in the field, Eron moved out into the natural environment of the child. He showed through careful longitudinal studies, involving innovative peer-rating measures, that children's aggression was stable over long periods of time, was related to their television-viewing practices, and was related to their parents' use of punitive child-rearing practices."

The chapters in this book are divided into five parts, reflecting five of the major focuses of scholars in the field.

First, in "Emerging Theories of Human Aggression," three chapters are presented that provide theoretical elaborations of the authors' current thinking on aggressive behavior, all of which lean toward social cognition. Eron reviews the trends in theorizing over the past half-century; Guerra and her associates present an integrative view of moral judgment and aggression; and Berkowitz provides a theoretical formulation of how affect and cognitions moderate aggressive behavior.

The three chapters in Part II, "Peers, Sex Roles, and Aggression," describe new theoretical perspectives on the role of gender and peers in children's and adults' aggressive behavior. Dishion and his colleagues provide data in support of their coercion model of peer influences on aggressive behavior; Olweus examines the long-term consequences of being a bully or a victim along with prevention of bullying; and Lagerspetz and Björkqvist challenge the traditional views of male–female differences in aggression.

In Part III, "Environmental Instigation and Mitigation of Aggression," the two chapters focus on a few of the most enduring contextual variables hypothesized to be related to aggression: media violence, stress, and social resources. Huesmann and Miller review the theoretical and empirical basis for the role of media violence in the development of aggression, while Dubow and Reid argue that resource variables, such as social support and social problem-solving skills, are of major importance in mitigating the aggression-stimulating effects of such factors as environmental stress.

In Part IV, "Development of Adult Aggression," the two chapters examine adult aggression and criminality from a developmental perspective, utilizing data from a few of the best-known longitudinal studies in the area. Farrington examines the implications of recent data from his Cambridge study on predicting serious adult aggression, and McCord—using data from her Cambridge–Somerville study—considers the processes through which aggression may be transmitted across generations.

Finally, in Part V, "Group Aggression in Adolescents and Adults," two theories are elaborated to explain how group aggression might evolve out of individual psychological processes. Goldstein considers the alternative theories to account for the violent behavior of adolescent gangs, and Feshbach presents a theory and data in support of the conception that aggression by societies is controlled by psychological processes quite different from those involved in individual aggression.

ACKNOWLEDGMENTS

A number of organizations must be thanked for assisting in the production of this volume. The faculty of the Department of Psychology at the University of Illinois at Chicago stimulated the idea for the volume on the occasion of Eron's retirement. The James McKeen Cattell foundation provided support for me while I was on sabbatical and developing the outline for the book. The National Institute for Mental Health, with its generous support for Eron's and my research over the years, was also a significant factor, as has been the International Society for Research on Aggression, which has provided the conference venue in which most of the authors of these chapters have been able to discuss their ideas. The staff of the Research Center for Group Dynamics at the University of Michigan has provided support in numerous ways.

In editing the manuscripts, I have been assisted by Cheryl-Lynn Podolski at the University of Michigan. In keeping my sanity, I have been assisted by my understanding wife, Penny. I want to thank the authors who have put up with long delays but who produced uniformly high-quality chapters, and, finally, I want to thank Len Eron for 25 years of stimulating collaboration, during which he never lost his sense of humor.

L. R. H.

Ann Arbor, Michigan

CONTENTS

Part IV. Development of Adult Aggression

Part V. Group Aggression in Adolescents and Adults

Part I

EMERGING THEORIES OF HUMAN AGGRESSION

In this section three contemporary theoretical approaches to understanding the psychology of human aggression are developed. All three draw on psychologists' current concerns with the cognitive processes mediating and moderating the emission of aggressive behavior. This does not mean that the role of emotional affect is diminished or that situational factors are considered unimportant. Rather, these theories seek to explain how individual differences in cognitive processes affect the propensity to respond aggressively in similar affective and situational states.

In his opening chapter, Eron reviews the trends in theorizing about aggression since the publication of Dollard, Doob, Miller, Mowrer, and Sears' (1939) book, *Frustration and Aggression*, over 50 years ago. He traces the path of his own thinking about aggression from social learning theory to the current social cognitive theory developed in conjunction with Huesmann.

Guerra and her associates then present a theoretical view of how one can integrate the moral judgment literature with the social cognitive view of aggression. Kohlberg's theory for the development of moral judgment has unfortunately been generally neglected by aggression researchers. Guerra and colleagues propose that self-regulating internal standards, called moral cognitions, are the immediate cognitions through which a child's stages of moral development manifest themselves to affect aggressive behavior.

Finally, Berkowitz provides an exceptionally well-integrated formulation of his associationist theory of how affect interacts with cognitions to moderate and mediate aggressive behavior. He argues that situationally stimulated negative affect is likely to produce associations to hostile thoughts and memories, but—if higher order cognitive processes are engaged that restrain these more primitive associations—then the aggressive behavior may not be emitted.

REFERENCE

Dollard, J., Doob, L. W., Miller, N. E., Mowrer, O. H., & Sears, R. R. (1939), *Frustration and Aggression.* New Haven, CT: Yale University Press.

CHAPTER 1

THEORIES OF AGGRESSION

From Drives to Cognitions

LEONARD D. ERON

FRUSTRATION AND AGGRESSION

The first comprehensive theoretical account of the etiology of aggression which assigned a major role to learning theory was the monograph, *Frustration and Aggression* by Dollard, Doob, Miller, Mowrer, and Sears (1939), a group of psychologists at Yale University. Up until that time most psychologists considered aggression to be instinctual in nature and inherent in human beings as it was in other animal species. Although convinced of the centrality of learning in the development of aggressive behavior, the authors of the monograph did not disagree with the idea that there was a biological basis to aggression. As a matter of fact, they were influenced to a significant degree by the psychoanalytic thinking of that time. For Freud, pleasure seeking and pain avoidance were the basic mechanisms of mental functioning, and frustration occurred when these activities were blocked. The Yale researchers, who were basically behaviorists, proposed, however, to translate the Freudian propositions into more objective behavioral terms which could be put to empirical test. For

LEONARD D. ERON • Research Center for Group Dynamics, Institute for Social Research, University of Michigan, Ann Arbor, Michigan 48106.

Aggressive Behavior: Current Perspectives, edited by L. Rowell Huesmann. Plenum Press, New York, 1994.

example, the Yale group's hypothesis about instigation to injure the frustrator finds a close parallel in Freud's (1915) statement that "if the object is a source of unpleasant feelings . . ." this can eventually lead to "an aggressive inclination against the object . . . an instigation to destroy it" (p. 137).

The premise thus of the frustration–aggression hypothesis is that when people become frustrated (i.e., when their goals are thwarted), they respond aggressively. On the very first page of their monograph the authors state their thesis that "the occurrence of aggressive behavior always presupposes the existence of frustration and, contrariwise, that the existence of frustration always leads to some form of aggression." Aggression was defined by them as "an act whose goal-response is injury to an organism (or organism-surrogate)" (p. 11). This definition implies intent to injure. A similar definition is the one we have used in our own research (1987) to be described later.

The Yale authors went on to specify those factors which determine not only how frustrated an individual will become but also how and when aggression will be expressed. For a review of these factors the interested reader can refer to Dollard et al. (1939) or Berkowitz (1962). The inclusion in the monograph of these causative and concomitant variables provided researchers with an opportunity to test specific aspects of the theory empirically and, as a result, the frustration–aggression hypothesis was subject to much scientific scrutiny, probably as much or more than any other proposition in psychology. This produced a wealth of literature on aggression.

As this literature emerged, however, it became apparent that the frustration–aggression hypothesis, unmodified, was not adequate to explain all aggression. Several specific predictions that were made from this model were not validated (see Bandura, 1973; Parke and Slaby, 1983; Feshbach, 1970 for reviews). For example, a basic premise of the model, that frustration was a necessary precursor to aggression, was questioned by a number of researchers (Buss, 1963; Cohen, 1955; Pastore, 1952). Earlier, Neal Miller himself (1941) had denied the inevitability of aggression as a response to frustration with the statement that, "Frustration produces instigations to a number of different types of responses, one of which is an instigation to some form of aggression" (p. 338).

SOCIAL LEARNING THEORY

These and other studies demonstrating exceptions to the frustration–aggression relation, led to the diminishing influence of this theory, although the research which it instigated has been voluminous. This new and developing research placed a greater emphasis on external environmental cues as elicitors of aggression than it did on inherent or drive factors (see Bandura, 1973; Eron, 1987). With this emphasis on an environmental learning model, rather than one directed by forces within the individual, there was a push to understand aggression in terms of cues, responses, and rewards in addition to or instead of innate or primary drives.

Bandura (1973), for example, proposed that aggressive behavior is *learned* and *maintained* through environmental experiences either directly or vicariously, and that learning of aggression is controlled by reinforcement contingencies and punishment in a fashion similar to the learning of *any* new behaviors (Bandura, 1973, p. 57). For instance, these behaviors may be acquired when an individual attempts a new behavior and is rewarded with a positive outcome. New behaviors will be avoided in the future if those behaviors are punished. Social-learning theory, as Bandura termed his theory, holds that new behaviors may also be acquired vicariously by watching an influential role-model engage in an action which has positive consequences. In my own work I demonstrated back in 1961, that vicarious learning occurs in natural settings as well as in the laboratory, that is, aggressive behaviors are learned by "training" from "various socializing agents, specifically parents, teachers, and peers" (Eron, 1961, p. 296) and also from watching violent models on television.

Inherent in all of these accounts is that external environmental consequences control the acquisition of aggression. The maintenance of aggressive behavior is almost always subject to the principles of reinforcement by the environment. As a rule, behaviors that are reinforced will be repeated; behaviors that are not reinforced will be extinguished. Bandura (1973) points out that according to a social-learning model, aggression is usually seen as being controlled by *positive* reinforcement; in contrast, from a drive model perspective, aggression is usually mediated by *negative* reinforcement or the escape from an aversive situation.

Longitudinal Data

Between 1960 and 1982 my colleagues and I conducted a longitudinal study of a large number of subjects over this 22-year period and found that while some of the results supported social-learning theory, other results were contradictory to this model (Eron, Huesmann, Dubow, Romanoff, & Yarmel, 1987). On the support side, we acquired data showing that when children are exposed to aggressive role-models, the children's aggression will increase. We initially found that when parents punish their children physically, this often serves as a model for future aggression on the part of the child (Eron, 1987; Eron, Walder, & Lefkowitz, 1971). Also, we found that aggressive models on television serve to "teach" children future aggression (Lefkowitz, Eron, Walder, & Huesmann, 1977); this finding offered even more support for the social learning model.

Though these findings support a social-learning position, other elements of the theory were not fully corroborated by this study. For example, our original hypothesis that aggressive children who were punished for their aggressive actions at home would behave less aggressively was based on an early learning theory formulation of Miller who stated that the "strength of inhibition of any act of aggression varies positively with the amount of punishment anticipated to be a consequence of the act" (Miller, 1941, p. 337). We found instead that those children who were punished more behaved more aggressively at school (Eron et al., 1971). Additionally, we found that closeness of identification with the parent was an important mediating variable and that a simple, direct relation between physical punishment and aggression had to be challenged. The relation held up only for boys who were closely identified with their fathers. For those boys who were closely identified with their fathers, the punishment worked the way the fathers intended—when they were punished for aggression by their fathers they tended not to be aggressive. This is what would have been predicted from Hull–Spence theory as explicated by Miller (1941). However, for those youngsters who identified with their fathers only moderately or little, the more they were punished, the more aggressive they became. For them, the instigating quality of the punishment appeared to be more effective than its inhibitory strength. It occurred to us that what might be important is not that the punishment itself occurred with some intensity, perhaps, but rather the interpretation the youngster put on the justification for and appropriateness of that punishment. The identified child might interpret the punishment as justified because of his misbehavior and administered because the parent wanted him to be a good person, just like the father. The unidentified youngster might interpret the punishment as unjustified and as a demonstration of the way adults go about solving interpersonal problems and thus that youngster would model the punitive behavior.

More significantly, upon follow-up 10 years after the original data collection, we found that punishment of aggressive acts at the earlier age was no longer related to current aggression, and instead, other variables like parental nurturance and children's identification with their parents were more important in predicting later aggression (Eron, Huesmann,

Lefkowitz, & Walder, 1974). Because this finding could not be explained by a straight social-learning model, we began to reinterpret our results from a different theoretical standpoint, namely, from a cognitive standpoint.

SOCIAL COGNITIVE THEORY

I and my colleague, Rowell Huesmann (Eron, 1987; Huesmann & Eron, 1984; Huesmann, 1977, 1980, 1982, 1988), as well as a number of other investigators, for example, Bandura (1986), Dodge and Coie (1987), Perry, Perry, and Rasmussen (1986), and Berkowitz (1984) have advocated cognitive models, which build upon the merits of both the frustration-aggression drive theory and the social-learning model. The theories have differed in terms of exactly what is learned, specific behaviors, cue-behavior connections, attitudes, perceptual biases, response biases, or scripts or programs for behavior. They all agree, however, that the way in which the individual perceives and interprets environmental events determines whether he or she will respond with aggression or some other behavior. Bandura also introduced the concept of self-efficacy (1977) which emphasizes how competent the youngster feels in responding in different ways, either aggressive or nonaggressive.

The model that Rowell Huesmann (1977, 1980, 1982, 1988) and I (Eron, 1982, 1987; Huesmann & Eron, 1984) proposed to explain the development of aggression was based on the models of human cognition which had been elaborated in the 1960s and 1970s by information processing theorists. Huesmann hypothesized that social behavior to a great extent is controlled by programs for behavior that have been learned during an individual's early development. These programs are described as cognitive scripts that are stored in memory and are used as guides for behavior and social problem solving. These scripts are learned through observation, reinforcement, and personal experience of situations in which aggression is a salient behavior. As we have pointed out (Huesmann & Eron, 1984), these strategies or scripts become "encoded, rehearsed, stored, and retrieved in much the same way as are other strategies for intellectual behaviors" (p. 244). Once a script has been encoded it is more or less likely to be retrieved in situations that bear some resemblance or relation to the original situation in which the script was encoded. However, not all scripts that are retrieved are translated to overt behavior. Once a script is retrieved, the child evaluates its appropriateness in light of existing internalized norms and also evaluates the likely consequences. Huesmann (1988) maintains that the most important feature of a script's evaluation is the extent to which the sequence is perceived as congruent with the child's self-regulating internal standards for behavior. A child with weak or nonexistent internalized prohibitions against aggression, or one who believes it is normative to behave in this way, is much more likely to use aggressive scripts.

The failure of a child to incorporate appropriate standards will affect the way in which scripts are evaluated and subsequently the way in which he or she interacts with others. Previously I had suggested (1987) that the internalization of appropriate standards is a critical variable that distinguishes aggressive and nonaggressive children. A child's failure to store such standards during critical socialization periods of life could easily lead to learning and using scripts for the expression of aggression. Once crystallized, these scripts and self-regulating standards could produce aggressive behavior with the persistence and stability that a number of studies have revealed. Indeed we have demonstrated that aggressive behavior at age 8 predicts to the extent of criminal behavior by age 30, to both arrests and convictions, to traffic offenses, especially driving while intoxicated, to spouse abuse, to punitiveness toward the subjects' own children, and to self-ratings of the subjects' own behavior and attitudes at age 30 (Huesmann, Eron, Lefkowitz, & Walder, 1984). This consistency supports our contention that aggression is mediated by cognitions that characterize the individual over time and across many situations. Aggression, as a way of interacting with others and solving problems, is learned very early in life and is learned very well. The payoff is very good so that despite occasional or even more frequent punishment it is difficult to unlearn and thus the behavior persists under the regulation of well-established cognitions. This is probably why most interventions and rehabilitation programs instituted in adolescence and young adulthood have been largely unsuccessful.

As described elsewhere (Eron, 1987) my own program of research, at least in the interpretation and implementation of its findings, has followed this route from drives to cognitions. Recent attempts by my associates and me to prevent or reduce aggression and violence with interventions based on behavioral–cognitive methods have met with mixed success (Dubow, Huesmann, & Eron, 1988; Guerra & Slaby, 1990; Huesmann, Eron, Klein, Brice, & Fischer, 1983; Huesmann, Guerra et al., 1991). The same is true of other programs based on similar premises (Kazdin, 1987). The primary reasons for lack of success are the brevity of the programs and their failure to take into account the varying contexts in which aggression and violence are learned and in which they occur. These contexts include the classroom, schools, peer groups, family, and community. The community context is of particular relevance when dealing with inner-city, lower-class, minority children because of the extreme environmental conditions under which they live. The interaction of the learning conditions we have described with the environmental hazards such as poverty and exposure to violence must be taken into account. The developing child learns cognitions and information processing techniques that are adaptive to his or her environmental context. These cognitions and modes of information processing, in turn, influence social behavior in general, and aggression and violent behavior in particular over the course of development.

CONCLUSIONS

In the last 50 years psychologists have progressed from thinking about aggression as a largely innate characteristic which is present in all individuals, both human and animal, to a point of view which emphasizes the learning of aggression as a way of solving interpersonal problems. This is certainly a more optimistic way of looking at the development of destructive behavior since what is learned can be unlearned and new ways of behaving can be adopted. Indeed there are some intervention programs which stem directly from these learning-theoretic ideas and they offer some hope for the mitigation of aggressive antisocial behaviors.

Although the evidence is convincing that learning has an important role in the development of aggressive and violent behavior in children and adults, this does not mean that by itself learning can account for the incidence of such behavior in society. Violent human behavior is multiply determined. The factors involved in its etiology range from genetics, neuroanatomy, endocrinology, and physiology through exogenous substances and firearms to gangs and community influences. No one of these factors by itself can explain much of the variance in the extent and intensity of violent behavior in the population, much less predict who will engage in such behavior. It is only when there is a convergence of a number of variables that aggressive or violent behavior occurs (Eron, 1982). Aggressive behavior does not routinely occur, however, even when these factors do converge. The individual most likely to behave aggressively and violently is one who has been programmed to respond in this way through previous experience and learning. Individuals with given genetic, neuroanatomical, and physiological endowment vary in their likelihood of behaving violently depending on their past experience. Aggressive behavior must somehow have been learned in the past (although not necessarily performed) and incorporated into the individual's repertoire of responses before it can be elicited by some external situation and/or stimulation from within the individual. The conditions most conducive to the learning of aggression seem to be those in which the child is reinforced for his or her own aggression, has many opportunities to observe aggression, and in which the child is the object of aggression. Children growing up under such conditions will come to assume that violent behavior is normative and, therefore, an appropriate response in many interpersonal situations. Such children will continually be rehearsing violent sequences both in actual situations and in fantasy, and will dismiss alternative situations as inappropriate or ineffectual. Moreover, they will encounter many situations in which such responses are easily triggered because of the similarity of cues to the original situation in which the violent response was learned.

REFERENCES

Bandura, A. (1973). *Aggression: A social learning analysis.* Englewood Cliffs, NJ: Prentice-Hall.

Bandura, A. (1977). Self-efficacy: Toward a unifying theory of behavioral change. *Psychological Review, 84,* 191–215.

Bandura, A. (1986). *Social foundation of thought and action: A social cognitive theory.* Englewood Cliffs, NJ: Prentice-Hall.

Berkowitz, L. (1962). *Aggression: A social psychological analysis.* New York: McGraw-Hill.

Berkowitz, L. (1984). Some effects of thoughts on anti and prosocial influences of media events: A cognitive–neoassociation analysis. *Psychological Bulletin, 95,* 410–427.

Buss, A. (1963). Physical aggression in relation to different frustrations. *Journal of Abnormal and Social Psychology, 67,* 1–7.

Cohen, R. (1955). Social norms, arbitrariness of frustration and status of the agent of frustration in the frustration–aggression hypothesis. *Journal of Abnormal and Social Psychology, 51,* 222–226.

Dodge, K. A., & Coie, J. D. (1987). Social-information-processing factors in reactive and proactive aggression in children's peer groups. *Journal of Personality and Social Psychology, 53,* 1146–1158.

Dollard, J., Doob, L. W., Miller, N. E., Mowrer, O. H., & Sears, R. R. (1939). *Frustration and aggression.* New Haven, CT: Yale University Press.

Dubow, E., Huesmann, L. R., & Eron, L. D. (1988). Mitigating aggression and promoting prosocial behavior in aggressive elementary school boys. *Behavior Research and Theory.* 577–581.

Eron, L. D. (1961). Use of theory in developing a design. In L. D. Eron (Ed.), Application of role and learning theories to the study of the development of aggression in children. *Psychology Reports, 9,* 292–334.

Eron, L. D. (1982). Parent–child interaction, television violence and aggression of children. *American Psychologist, 42,* 435–442.

Eron, L. D. (1987). The development of aggressive behavior from the perspective of a developing behaviorism. *American Psychologist, 42,* 435–442.

Eron, L. D., Huesmann, L. R., Dubow, E., Romanoff, R., & Yarmel, P. W. (1987). Aggression and its correlates over 22 years. In D. Crowell, I. M. Evans and C. R. O'Donnell (Eds.), *Childhood aggression and violence*. New York: Plenum.

Eron, L. D., Huesmann, L. R., Lefkowitz, M. M., & Walder, L. O. (1974). How learning conditions in early childhood relate to aggression in late adolescence. *American Journal of Orthopsychiatry, 44*, 412–423.

Eron, L. D., Walder, L. O., & Lefkowitz, M. M. (1971). *Learning of aggression*. Boston: Little, Brown.

Feshbach, S. (1970). Aggression. In P. Mussen (Ed.), *Carmichael's manual of child psychology.* (Vol. 2, pp. 159–259). New York: Wiley.

Freud, S. (1957). Instincts and their vicissitudes. *Standard Edition* (Vol. 14, pp. 109–140). London: Hogarth Press. (Original work published 1915).

Guerra, N. G., & Slaby, R. G. (1990). Cognitive mediators of aggression in adolescent offenders: 2. Intervention. *Developmental Psychology, 26*, 269–277.

Huesmann, L. R. (1977). *Formal models of social behavior.* Paper presented at the meeting of the Society for Experimental Social Psychology, Austin, Texas.

Huesmann, L. R. (1980). *Encoding specificity in observational learning*. Paper presented at a Colloquium at Institute of Psychology, University of Warsaw, Warsaw, Poland.

Huesmann, L. R. (1982). Television violence and aggressive behavior. In D. Pearl, L. Bouthilet & P. Lazar (Eds.), *Television and behavior: Ten years of scientific programs and implications for the 80's.* Washington, DC: U.S. Government Printing Office.

Huesmann, L. R. (1988). An information model for the development of aggression. *Aggressive Behavior, 14*, 13–24.

Huesmann, L. R., & Eron, L. D. (1984). Cognitive processes and the persistence of aggressive behavior. *Aggressive Behavior, 10*, 243–251.

Huesmann, L. R., Eron, L. D., Klein, R., Brice, P., & Fischer, P. (1983). Mitigating the imitation of aggressive behaviors by changing children's attitudes about media violence. *Journal of Personality and Social Psychology, 44*, 899–910.

Huesmann, L. R., Guerra, N. G., Eron, L. D., Miller, L. S., Zelli, A., Wrobleska, J., & Adami, P. (1991). Mitigating the development of aggression in young children by changing their cognitions. *Aggressive Behavior, 17*, 75–76.

Huesmann, L. R., Eron, L. D., Lefkowitz, M. M., & Walder, L. O. (1984). The stability of aggression over time and generations. *Developmental Psychology, 20*, 1120–1134.

Kazdin, A. (1987). Treatment of antisocial behavior in children: Current status and future directions. *Psychological Bulletin, 102*, 187–203.

Lefkowitz, M. M., Eron, L. D. Walder, L. O., & Huesmann, L. R. (1977). *Growing up to be violent: A longitudinal study of the development of aggression*. New York: Pergamon Press.

Miller, N. E. (1941). The frustration–aggression hypothesis. *Psychological Review, 48*, 337–342.

Parke, R. D., & Slaby, R. G. (1983). The development of aggression. In P. H. Mussen (Ed.), *Handbook of child psychology* (4th ed., pp. 547–642). New York: Wiley.

Pastore, N. (1952). The role of arbitrariness in the frustration–aggression hypothesis. *Journal of Abnormal & Social Psychology, 47*, 728–731.

Perry, D. G., Perry, L. C., & Rasmussen, P. (1986). Cognitive social learning mediators of aggression. *Child Development, 57*, 700–711.

Chapter 2

MORAL COGNITION AND CHILDHOOD AGGRESSION

Nancy G. Guerra, Larry Nucci, and L. Rowell Huesmann

Childhood aggression is of great interest because of the impact such behavior has on the welfare of others. Recent advances in understanding the development of children's aggressive behavior have emphasized the role of cognitive factors, since an individual's aggressive behavior is ultimately subject to cognitive control (Dodge, 1986; Huesmann, 1988). Paradoxically, the literature on cognition and aggression has not been informed by the literature on the development of children's moral reasoning. Instead, they have developed in two separate strands that minimally relate to one another. In large part, the lack of connection between these two literatures stems from a paradigmatic clash which has made the integration of research on cognitive correlates of childhood aggression and research on children's moral development problematic. Recent

Nancy G. Guerra • Department of Psychology, University of Illinois at Chicago, Chicago, Illinois 60607. Larry Nucci • Department of Education, University of Illinois at Chicago, Chicago, Illinois 60607. L. Rowell Huesmann • Research Center for Group Dynamics, Institute for Social Research, University of Michigan, Ann Arbor, Michigan 48106-1248.

Aggressive Behavior: Current Perspectives, edited by L. Rowell Huesmann. Plenum Press, New York, 1994.

advances in theory and research in moral development, however, offer the possibility of a rapproachment between these two paradigms.

In this chapter, we will offer an integrated model for research on the relation between children's moral cognition and the development of habitual aggressive behavior. The term *moral cognition* is used to differentiate judgments about moral issues (e.g., issues of harm and fairness) from nonmoral issues (e.g., mathematics). This is distinct from the evaluative use of the word *moral* to confer approbrium. Our proposed model of moral cognition and aggression builds on recent elaborations of the moral development literature which offer new insights into the specific relation between moral cognition and behavior. Because these recent elaborations emphasize how an individual classifies and uses social information when considering complex issues with moral implications, they are also compatible with the social information processing/social cognitive models which have guided most contemporary studies of the cognitive bases of children's aggressive behavior. Our integrated approach affords a way to draw on what has been learned from these two existing strands of research.

First, we will review what has been learned from research on the role of cognition in the development and maintenance of children's aggressive behavior. Next, we will look at extant research on the relation between moral development and aggression, which has emphasized the correlation between moral stage and habitual aggressive behavior (e.g., delinquency). As we will see, the latter provides an inconsistent and conflictual picture of the relation between moral development and aggressive behavior (Blasi, 1980; Turiel & Smetana, 1984). We will then turn to the domain model of moral and social development which posits that situation-specific moral decision making is multifaceted and not simply determined by stage of moral development (Nucci & Nucci, 1982; Nucci, Guerra, & Lee, 1991; Turiel, Hildebrandt, & Wainryb, 1991). As recently pointed out by Saltzstein (1991), the domain model provides a connection between research on moral stage, moral information processing/decision making, and moral action. From this vantage point, we will present an integrated model and some preliminary data which point to a new direction in research on moral cognition and childhood aggression.

THE ROLE OF COGNITION IN CHILDREN'S AGGRESSIVE BEHAVIOR

Aggressive behavior is determined by a variety of factors, such as the biological (e.g., genetics, neuroanatomy, endocrinology); social influence variables (e.g., media violence); social context (e.g., peers, family, school); and environmental conditions (e.g., chronic environmental stress). There has been a plethora of research on each of these factors, although none of them in itself can explain much of the variance in aggressive behavior. Such behavior must somehow be learned (although not necessarily performed) and incorporated into the individual's response repertoire before it is elicited by some external situation or stimulation from within the individual (Eron, 1982). Aggression is both learned and regulated by means of the child's emerging cognitive system. From this perspective, children's cognitions play a central role in the development of aggressive behavior, and play a critical role in maintaining habitual aggressive behavior (Bandura, 1989a; Dodge & Crick, 1990; Eron, 1987; Huesmann, 1988; Huesmann, Guerra, Miller, & Zelli, 1992; Slaby & Guerra, 1988). While aggressive behavior is initially stimulated by a variety of factors, it becomes more stable and consistent over time as children's cognitions become more fully developed and more resistant to change (Eron, 1987; Huesmann et al., 1992).

Recent studies of the specific cognitive factors implicated in the development and maintenance of children's aggression have emerged from two related, but somewhat distinct, research traditions, social information processing theory and social learning/social cognitive theory. Studies which have emphasized social information processing correlates of aggression have focused on the cognitive *processes* children use to interpret and respond to social information in problematic situations. Most of the early work in the area of information processing and children's aggression was derived from an interpersonal, cognitive problem-solving model emphasizing the relation between aggressive behavior and deficits in information processing skills including means–ends thinking, generating solutions, and generating consequences (Shure & Spivack, 1976; Spivack & Shure, 1974).

Subsequent investigations have focused on a broader range of cognitive processes. For example, Dodge (1986) has formulated a five-step sequential model and has proposed that aggressive behavior may result from deficits in processing social information at any or all of the steps. The five sequential steps are: (1) encoding of social cues; (2) representation and interpretation of cues; (3) response search; (4) response decision; and (5) enactment. While a number of studies have suggested that aggressive children differ from nonaggressive children in the way in which they perform some of these cognitive processes (Dodge & Frame, 1992; Dodge, Price, Bachorowski, & Newman, 1990; Huesmann et al., 1992; Slaby & Guerra, 1988), the data do not provide strong support for a generalized *deficit* in information processing. Rather the data suggest that some abnormal or biased styles of processing might contribute to aggressive behavior.

While these models (as applied to the study of children's aggression) have acknowledged the role of "theory-driven" cognitive processes, that is, prior concepts and beliefs which shape how data are viewed, they typically have not examined specific beliefs relevant to the learning of aggressive behavior. This is somewhat surprising in view of the central role that cognitive psychologists ascribe to organized prior knowledge, or schema, in guiding information processing (Shank & Abelson, 1977). Rather, studies of children's beliefs have emerged from the social-learning/social-cognitive tradition (Bandura, 1989a; Guerra & Slaby, 1990; Huesmann et al., 1992), being informed more recently by a growing literature on social schema and aggression (Huesmann, 1988; Mize & Ladd, 1988).

From this perspective, while aggressive behavior is learned through both enactive and observational learning, it is the child's cognitive representation of social interaction that ultimately determines behavior and development. In particular, social learning/social cognitive theory stresses the importance of self-regulatory beliefs in motivating and regulating aggressive behavior (Bandura, 1989b). Two important classes of self-regulatory beliefs are: (1) response–outcome expectancies, and (2) standards of conduct. It has been proposed that children who observe and experience more positive and fewer negative consequences for aggression learn a set of response–outcome expectancies which promote aggressive behavior. Furthermore, on the basis of these anticipated consequences, children also learn to discriminate between acceptable and nonacceptable standards of behavior and to regulate their actions accordingly (Bandura, 1989b; Huesmann, 1988; Perry, Perry, & Boldizar, 1990).

According to social-cognitive theory, cognitive representations of anticipated positive consequences for aggressive behavior serve as motivators of behavior. These positive consequences can include tangible rewards (e.g., desired objects), psychological benefits (e.g., control or dominance over others), self-evaluations (e.g., increased feelings of self-worth), and social reactions (e.g., status among peers). Studies of preadolescent children have shown that aggressive children are more likely than their less aggressive peers to predict that aggressive behavior will result in tangible rewards and termination of aversive behavior toward them by others (Perry, Perry, & Rasmussen, 1986), as well as psychological reinforcement based on control over peers (Boldizar, Perry, & Perry, 1989). Studies of aggressive and delinquent adolescents have shown that they are more likely to believe that aggression results in increased self-esteem and status among peers (Guerra & Slaby, 1990; Slaby & Guerra, 1988).

Similarly, cognitive representations of anticipated negative consequences for aggressive behavior can serve as inhibitors of behavior. These negative consequences may be anticipated for both self and others. Negative consequences for self can include expectations of physical punishment and social disapproval. Negative consequences for others can include harm, injury, and disruption of social relations. Habitual aggressive behavior during adolescence has been found to correlate with lowered expectations of negative consequences for both self (Guerra, 1989) and others (Slaby & Guerra, 1988). In addition to anticipating negative outcomes for aggression, it has also been proposed that aggressive behavior is further influenced by the degree of importance children attach to such outcomes. Several studies have found that aggressive children attach less importance to a range of negative sanctions for aggressive behavior (Guerra & Slaby, 1989; Boldizar et al., 1989).

External sanctions in the form of expected punishment are particularly salient in guiding the behavior of young children (Parke, 1974). While the threat of immediate punishment is quite effective in decreasing aggression, most individuals refrain from behaving aggressively even in the absence of external sanctions. Cognitive representations of expected sanctions provide a more stable and less situationally dependent source of behavior control (Bandura, 1989b). These negative self-generated reactions rely on comparing one's behavior with a set of self-regulatory standards or norms about the acceptability of aggressive behavior. As Perry et al. (1990) note:

> If children see that certain forms of aggression in certain situations and toward certain targets are inappropriate (e.g., physical aggression toward females, or aggression against someone whose frustrating behavior is not intentional), they may avoid acting aggressively under these circumstances for fear of self-censure. (p. 136)

While much has been published about the theoretical link between norms and aggressive behavior (e.g., Bandura, 1989a; Eron, Walder, & Lefkowitz, 1971; Huesmann, 1988), very few empirical studies have directly assessed the relation between normative beliefs about the acceptability of aggression and children's aggressive behavior. For example, Slaby & Guerra (1988) reported that aggressive and delinquent adolescents were more likely than their less aggressive high-school counterparts to endorse beliefs indicating that aggression is an acceptable response across a range of situations. Furthermore, in a subsequent intervention study (Guerra & Slaby, 1990), change in beliefs about the acceptability of aggression was the only cognitive factor directly related to a reduction in posttreatment aggressive behavior. Similarly, Guerra & Nucci (Guerra & Nucci, 1992; Nucci, Guerra, & Lee, 1991) found that adolescents who engage in antisocial behavior (e.g., drug use and aggressive actions) were less likely to judge such behaviors as wrong.

Research with younger children generally has supported these findings, although some studies have reported relatively weak relations, particularly during the early elementary years. For example, in a study of inner-city children from grades 2, 3, and 4, Huesmann et al. (1992) found that approval of aggressive behavior correlated significantly with self-reported aggression of boys and girls but only weakly with peer-nominated aggression, and only for boys. However, in a subsequent study of 1975 elementary school children from grades 2, 3, and 5 from diverse ethnic and socioeconomic backgrounds, children who were rated as aggressive by peers and teachers were significantly more likely to hold beliefs that such aggressive behavior was acceptable (i.e., "OK" or "not wrong") across a range of situations (Huesmann & Guerra, 1993).

These studies suggest that with development, aggressive behavior is increasingly governed by normative standards of acceptable conduct. These standards serve as guides for information processing in different situations, and ultimately influence social behavior. Huesmann (1988) has proposed that this influence also becomes more automatic over time, as children form cognitive representations of sequences of events which occur in well-known situations. For children who view aggression as acceptable, these cognitive representations, or scripts, are more likely to include aggressive responses. While scripts may be used to guide behavior in a controlled manner, producing seemingly reflective behavior, after they are well learned they function in a more automatic fashion, producing seemingly impulsive behavior (Shiffrin & Schneider, 1977).

These well-articulated cognitive models inform us about the relation between cognition and the development of children's aggressive behavior. While beliefs such as response–outcome expectancies and standards of conduct can also be viewed as contributing to moral judgments and may be considered as integral to a comprehensive model of morality (e.g., Bandura, 1991), the focus of the previously discussed research has not been on the uniquely "moral" forms of cognition (Saltzstein, 1991). Furthermore, traditional information-processing/social learning approaches, with their emphasis on procedural knowledge and scripted behavior, cannot adequately account for developmental changes in generalized structures of moral reasoning, nor can they account for the ongoing construction of responses and procedures as a function of the contextual variation in actual life. In contrast, cognitive–developmental research on children's morality (e.g., Piaget 1932/1965; Kohlberg, 1969,

1976) has both differentiated moral from nonmoral forms of cognition, and has emphasized the role of general cognitive structures in generating judgments of right and wrong which guide or direct the construction of responses and procedures in context.

THE RELATION BETWEEN MORAL DEVELOPMENT AND CHILDREN'S AGGRESSIVE BEHAVIOR

Contemporary research on children's moral development has been dominated by cognitive–developmental theory (Piaget 1932/1965; Kohlberg, 1969, 1976). Rather than emphasizing norms, attitudes, or decision-making strategies, the cognitive–developmental approach defines moral cognition in terms of moral judgments or moral reasoning, characterized by justification of actions according to underlying conceptions of justice. The most important function of cognition is seen as the creation of moral meaning (Blasi, 1980). The construction of moral meaning is believed to be dependent on the child's progression through an invariant sequence of stages. Each stage is believed to represent a qualitative transformation in reasoning that reflects movement toward more mature reasoning based on universal moral principles.

Kohlberg (1969, 1976) proposed a six-state typology of moral reasoning. The first two stages represent preconventional thinking, with morality defined in terms of external consequences to self. The third and fourth stages represent conventional reasoning, with morality determined by consideration of the effect of one's actions on others, and by maintenance of the social order. The fifth and sixth stages represent postconventional thinking, where actions are evaluated in terms of moral principles of justice which have validity apart from the persons or society which hold them.

Kohlberg's theory of moral development also differs from social cognitive models in terms of how moral actions are defined. Social cognitive models typically define moral or immoral actions without reference to the actor's reasoning about such behavior. Thus, aggressive behavior is defined as behavior intended to harm another (Eron, 1987), without consideration of how the aggressor may justify such behavior. In contrast, according to cognitive–developmental moral theories, moral action cannot be understood independent of the actor's thoughts about that action—defining an action as moral or immoral requires a direct assessment of the actor's internal moral judgment (Kohlberg & Candee, 1984).

Because moral judgment competence has been viewed as necessary (if not sufficient) for moral action, most of the work derived from cognitive–developmental theory has centered on the analysis of moral reasoning. Early formulations of stage theories offered only vague hypotheses about the relation between moral cognition and action. A particular problem in determining the nature of this relation has been the independence of stage of moral reasoning from the particular action chosen. For instance, in judging a hypothetical moral dilemma, two individuals could both advocate a harmful behavior such as stealing, but, depending on their reasoning, could be classified at two different moral stages. Just as the same behavior can be justified by different moral judgments, the same moral standards can also lead to different behavioral decisions.

More recently, a distinction has been made between "deontic" judgments of what is morally right and "aretaic" judgments of responsibility, which involve a commitment to act on one's deontic judgment. Kohlberg (1984) acknowledged that his stage model applied mostly to deontic judgments. In addition, the concept of substages has been introduced to account for discrepancies in judgment and action. Specifically, at each level, individuals have been found to reason at substage A or substage B. At substage A, people emphasize rules and authority in their decisions within the form of reasoning that is typical of their moral stage. At substage B, justice and welfare concerns are predominant. As Kohlberg and Candee (1984) point out, "Reasoning at the B substage of any structural moral stage approximates formal principles that are fully articulated only at Stage 5. For this reason, the behavior of subjects at Stages 3B and 4B often resembles the behavior of subjects at Stage 5" (p. 52).

Another problem in determining the relation between moral judgment and action centers on the methodology typically used. Empirical analyses of this relation generally involve assessing subjects' stage of moral reasoning by means of their reflective reasoning about a narrow sampling of relatively uncommon and complex moral dilemmas, and correlating their stage scores with their participation in a *different* action presumed to be moral (e.g., participating in demonstrations of free speech) or immoral (e.g., habitual criminal offenses). This methodology seems problematic for at least two reasons. First, level of moral judgment on these dilemmas is compared with a behavior unrelated to the dilemma themes, and which is categorized, a priori, as moral or immoral independent of the actor's reasoning about that particular action. The link to behavior is to assume that global stage score represents a general moral orientation which should be activated across a range of problematic social situations. Second, the level of information included in the hypothetical dilemmas may vary significantly from what is actually available in real life situations. In fact, when information about the likely consequences of different courses of action is presented in hypothetical dilemmas, an increase in the severity of personal consequences corresponds to an increase in justifications based on self-interest (Sobesky, 1983).

Nevertheless, despite both conceptual and methodological problems, a number of empirical studies lend support to the existence of a relation between immature moral reasoning and children's antisocial aggressive behavior. Both Piaget and Kohlberg suggested that "difficult" or "antisocial" children might be delayed in their moral development. In fact, Kohlberg (1958) was one of the first researchers to study this relation. In his dissertation research, he compared a group of nondelinquent boys to a matched group of delinquents. He found that the nondelinquents displayed primarily conventional reasoning (stages 3 and 4), while the delinquents relied mainly on preconventional reasoning (stages 1 and 2). Thus, while nondelinquents tended to consider the effects of one's actions on others, delinquents' concerns centered on concrete and immediate self-interest.

Subsequent studies generally have provided support for the hypothesis that delinquents utilize lower stages of moral reasoning than their nondelinquent counterparts (for reviews see Blasi, 1980; Jurkovic, 1980). The findings are not unequivocal, however, and several limitations have been noted. For example, while delinquents as a group tend to display more preconventional reasoning than nondelinquents, some delinquents display higher stages of reasoning, suggesting that there are also significant differences in moral maturity within delinquent populations. Clearly, delinquent youth represent a heterogeneous group, and actual offenses vary considerably both within and across studies. While some prior studies have reported delayed moral development for subgroups of delinquents displaying deviant personality traits such as psychopathy (e.g., Fodor, 1973), the precise relation between antisocial aggressive behavior and stages of moral reasoning is still unclear.

THE DOMAIN MODEL OF THE DEVELOPMENT OF SOCIAL REASONING

As we have noted, the basis for linking Kohlberg's theory with the study of children's aggression is that the theory purports to offer an analysis of the reasoning process by which people generate decisions pertaining to the right or wrong of actions affecting the welfare of others. According to Kohlberg's theory, the key element in such moral judgments is the structure of the person's justice reasoning (Kohlberg, 1984), that is, whether it is fair in a given situation to inflict harm on another person. Kohlberg recognized, however, that issues of morality (fairness) are rarely isolated in complex situations from other considerations, such as the prudence of a given action, the views of authorities, and prevailing social norms. While Kohlberg is credited with having been one of the first psychologists to have offered a conceptual analysis differentiating moral from nonmoral judgments about social situations (Saltzstein, 1991), his theory of moral development, in keeping with its Kantian and Piagetian roots, holds that morality as justice remains confounded with such considerations of prudence, authority, and convention until the latter stages of development. Only at the level of principled morality, according to Kohlberg (1969), are a person's judgments truly moral (i.e., based on justice principles). In Kohlberg's theory then, we are not provided with a disambiguated analysis of the person's reasoning about harm or fairness, except in very advanced adults. Thus, it is little wonder that stages of moral judgment as defined from this vantage point have provided inconsistent data with respect to children's aggressive and antisocial behavior.

Over the past 15 years an alternative to the Kohlberg paradigm has emerged which may offer a more fine-grained analysis of the multifaceted relationship between aggressive actions and sociomoral judgment. According to the domain theory of social development, concepts of morality (issues of fairness and human welfare), convention (consensually determined norms that maintain social structure), and personal issues (areas of perspective and privacy, actions that impinge primarily on the self) are structured within distinct conceptual and developmental frameworks (Nucci, 1981; Smetana, 1982; Turiel, 1983). More recently, Tisak and Turiel (1984) have identified an additional category, prudential, to describe concepts about those personal acts that are potentially harmful to the self. Each of these aspects of social understanding emerges from a distinctive facet of the individual's social interactions; each has an identifiable and distinct structure; and each follows its own developmental trajectory (see Helwig, Tisak, & Turiel, 1990; and Turiel, Killen, & Helwig, 1987 for comprehensive reviews). While reasoning within each social domain forms a differentiated structured whole, contextualized social judgments may invoke knowledge from more than one domain, resulting in judgments reflecting input and/or coordination across knowledge systems (Turiel, 1983; Turiel & Smetana, 1984). Interpretations of judgment-action relations that vary with context are unlikely, then, to be explained through a straightforward analysis of development in a single social reasoning dimension such as morality. Instead such analyses would require an investigation of the individual's decision making based on a reading of the social situation in moral and/or nonmoral terms, including the situational and intrapersonal sources of bias that would heighten or diminish the salience of the moral aspect of multifaceted social situations.

Our current understanding of the domain nature of social knowledge affords a reinterpretation of Kohlberg's stages of moral development as an approximation of the age-related changes in the development of cross-domain coordinations. For example, stage 4 (conventional) moral reasoning, as described in the Kohlberg system, reflects the emergence in middle to late adolescence of understandings in the *conventional* domain that social norms are constitutive of social systems. Although these age-typical integrations are captured by Kohlberg's stage descriptions, they do not represent the full range of sociomoral decision-making patterns that individuals present. For example, as we noted earlier, research conducted by the Kohlberg group itself (Kohlberg, 1984) shows that individuals at all points in development may respond to moral dilemmas from a perspective of either rules and authority (substage A), or justice and welfare (substage B). From the domain point of view, such within-stage variation can be accounted for only by recognizing that the tasks used by Kohlberg to assess moral development generate reasoning employing knowledge from more than one conceptual system.

The utility of applying domain theory to the study of complex issues involving potential harm to persons has been demonstrated through several recent studies. In one study, Smetana (1982) found that pregnant women's decisions regarding whether or not to engage in an abortion were largely determined by whether the action was viewed by the women as a moral issue entailing the taking of another human life, or as a matter of personal discretion with no interpersonal moral consequences. In her study, Smetana also obtained Kohlberg moral stage scores for subjects' judgments about abortion as well as their reasoning on standard Kohlberg dilemmas. What she found was that, for those women who viewed abortion as a moral issue, the stage scores they obtained on standard moral dilemmas were highly correlated with the stage scores they obtained regarding abortion. For women who viewed abortion as a personal issue, however, their stage scores on the standard moral dilemmas were uncorrelated with their stage scores on the abortion dilemma. Smetana interpreted these results as indicating that the moral stage scores on abortion were valid only for those women who viewed abortion as a moral issue.

Another study, which investigated the relation between domain of social judgment and actions involving potential harm to persons, examined adolescents' reasoning about drug use (Nucci, Guerra, & Lee, 1991). In that study, 9th and 12th grade students were asked to rate the harmfulness and wrongness of various forms of substance use, and to indicate whether use of a given drug was an issue of interpersonal harm (morality), a matter of social convention, personal choice, or prudence. These subjects were also asked, through an anonymous questionnaire, to indicate their own degree of drug use.

Regardless of their own level of drug use, few subjects viewed drug use in moral terms (i.e., concern over potential harm to others). Rather, the overwhelming tendency was for subjects to view drug use as a matter of personal discretion or prudence. This tendency to view drug use as a personal issue was significantly more prevalent among high drug users. These high drug users also tended to view the behavior as less harmful and less wrong. In contrast, low drug users were most likely to view the behavior in terms of prudential concerns, although a small number of these low-use subjects considered the moral implications of this behavior. These findings suggest that individuals generally do not spontaneously consider the interpersonal consequences of the harm caused by drug use (Berkowitz, Guerra, & Nucci, 1991). They also suggest that the tendency to engage in drug use is a function of its placement in the personal domain.

Employing a similar methodology, Guerra and Nucci (1992) examined the relation between 9th and 12th grade student's self-reported delinquency and their judgments of the harmfulness and wrongness of prototypical moral (e.g., hitting and hurting another person), conventional (e.g., calling a teacher by her first name), personal (e.g., maintaining the privacy of one's diary), and prudential (e.g., riding a motorcycle without a helmet) issues. Subjects were also asked to indicate whether a given action was an issue of morality, social convention, personal choice, or prudence. Compared to nondelinquents, delinquent youth were significantly less likely to view moral issues as wrong and harmful, and were more likely to classify such issues as matters of personal choice. There were no significant differences in the ways in which delinquent and nondelinquent subjects treated nonmoral issues. These preliminary findings suggest that the tendency to engage in aggressive and delinquent behavior is also a function of its domain placement, and that more aggressive individuals can be characterized by an overextension of the personal domain.

AN INTEGRATIVE MODEL OF THE RELATION BETWEEN MORAL COGNITION AND AGGRESSION

These and other studies from the domain perspective indicate that understanding the relation between sociomoral judgments and aggression requires: (1) attention to how the person understands the nonmoral as well as moral aspects of situations, and (2) knowledge of individual and contextual factors which impact the reading of situations in moral or nonmoral terms. Various integrative models have been proposed for linking the development of moral reasoning with nonmoral components of judgment to address the issue of the relation between moral reasoning and behavior (Berkowitz, Guerra, & Nucci, 1991; Gerson & Damon, 1978; Rest, 1984; Turiel & Smetana, 1984). None of these, however, provides a framework for integrating information-processing/social learning research on the cognitive correlates of children's aggression with a domain analysis of the development of children's social and moral judgments. We will now turn to a preliminary model which integrates these two paradigms. First, let us specify four assumptions of this model.

Assumption 1: Knowledge is structured in discrete knowledge systems that correspond to fundamentally and qualitatively differing aspects of individual–environment interactions. As we have discussed previously, the conceptual and developmental systems that have been identified that pertain to aggression are the moral, conventional, and personal domains. This is distinct from the Kohlbergian differentiation hypothesis in which moral development entails the progressive differentiation of the moral from the nonmoral such that the nonmoral receives little attention. The Kohlbergian perspective provides no theoretical basis for examining interactions between moral and nonmoral knowledge systems in contextualized judgments.

Assumption 2: Understanding within each knowledge system or domain undergoes structural changes with age. We assume that there are also structural changes in how individuals organize knowledge and that these changes are not simply the result of an expanded knowledge base or an improvement in strategy use. Thus, this assumption differs from information-processing accounts (e.g., Darley & Schultz, 1990) of the relation between knowledge systems and moral judgment in that we also assume structural changes as a function of development within each knowledge system rather than an increased sophistication of accessing information.

Assumption 3: Decisions in context are a function of the coordination of contextually generated information across domains. This coordination is a func-

tion of the levels of development within accessed domains. As Turiel & Smetana (1984) have noted, these coordinations can vary in complexity as a function of the degree to which knowledge systems are emphasized or deemphasized in context. They can also vary in relation to individual differences in the weight attached to the many decisional components of complex situations. Furthermore, in familiar day-to-day situations, coordination of contextually generated information should proceed with relative automaticity.

Assumption 4: Actions in context may solely entail the automatic implementation of procedural knowledge (scripts) or may involve reflective engagement of structural knowledge. These aspects of knowledge are reciprocally implicated and cogenerative. That is, development within a given domain is generated out of reflections on the outcomes of behaviors and the procedures that led to them. Transformations in social knowledge structure enable the generation of more sophisticated procedures which, in turn, through reflection, enable the construction of more developed structures. Actions in context do not necessarily, however, engage the reflective process, particularly under conditions of heightened affective arousal. Indeed it has been proposed that affect functions to reduce an individual's cognitive workload by "selecting" procedures in most situations (e.g., Brown, 1987). Thus, while the procedures in use imply a particular minimum level of developmental sophistication, they may not necessarily reflect the person's highest level of sophistication and may not necessarily generate developmental change. Moral judgment, as opposed to procedurally driven behavior, requires the engagement of reflection.

CONTEXTUALIZED JUDGMENTS AND AGGRESSIVE BEHAVIOR

Drawing on these assumptions, we propose that aggressive actions are directed by judgments which may draw primarily from the moral knowledge system or may entail reasoning from the personal or conventional domains, although preliminary studies suggest that aggressive behavior may be characterized by an overextension of the personal domain. The resulting judgments will be a function of the degree to which various knowledge systems are invoked *and* the level of development within those systems. We also propose that these judgments should become highly routine in nature, to the point where behavior appears relatively automatic and insensitive to the unique features of each situation. Factors that determine which knowledge systems are utilized in decision making stem from many sources, including: (1) the person's self-guiding beliefs; (2) the person's interpretative biases; and (3) the salience of situational cues.

We use the term *self-guiding beliefs* to refer to those beliefs which provide guides for behavior based on justifications for specific actions. From a social–cognitive perspective, these beliefs include both evaluative (i.e., right or wrong) and informational (i.e., potential consequences) concepts. For example, if parents strongly believe it is inappropriate to spank a child under any circumstances (evaluative) because spanking is harmful (informational), their decisions should reflect these moral concerns. In contrast, believing that violence is acceptable (evaluative) because victims don't really suffer (informational) would reduce the likelihood that moral considerations would be engaged when harming another. Similarly, if a teenage boy believes that it is okay to hit other boys because everyone in his social group does it and approves of it, his decisions related to hitting other boys should primarily invoke social conventional reasoning.

Within the moral developmental literature, recent investigations have also highlighted the importance of a person's "informational assumptions," or understanding of the relevant facts (whether they are correct or not) regarding a given phenomenon which bear on their interpretation of the *impact* of given actions (Wainryb, 1991). These assumptions may reflect characteristic beliefs (e.g., stereotypes) or situation-specific interpretation of cues. While informational assumptions do not determine moral judgments, evidence suggests that they affect the meaning given to an act and thereby affect the understanding of moral issues. For example, in Wainryb's (1991) investigation of adult's beliefs about corporal punishment, she found that procorporal punishment parents held the view that this behavior was all right because it was a highly effective, educative act rather than one of unprovoked harm. When such parents were presented with information that spanking is no more effective than other methods of disciplining children, significant numbers of these parents shifted in their view of corporal punishment and maintained that it was not all right for parents to engage in the behavior. Conversely, when parents who maintained that it was wrong to engage in corporal punishment were presented with information that experts had found spanking to be the most efficient method to teach young children, there was a tendency for such parents to shift toward a view that corporal punishment would be all right.

The term *interpretive biases* refers to an individual's tendency to place multidimensional issues into particular judgment categories. From an information-processing perspective, these biases should produce selective attention to certain cues as well as potential distortions of these cues. For example, a traditional conservative male might read all situations of gender bias in terms of social convention rather than as involving moral issues of equity and fairness. There are two important sources of these biases: (1) intrapersonal factors such as mood states, personality, needs, self-definition, and attributional style, and (2) sociocultural influences.

Stable intrapersonal factors such as personality and self-definition can affect the relative salience of different judgment categories. For instance, less empathic individuals would be less likely to interpret complex situations as a matter of others' welfare. In contrast, individuals who consider "being a moral person" to be part of their essential self should be particularly aware of the moral issues imbedded in interpersonal situations (Blasi, 1984). Factors such as mood states may be relatively stable and represent physiological predispositions or relatively transient. Stable mood states should promote relatively enduring interpretative biases while transient mood states may temporarily alter the salience of judgment categories.

Sociocultural influence refers not only to the larger cultural framework but also to specific sources of bias stemming from salient reference groups (e.g., family, peers, school, religion). Social contexts vary markedly in the degree to which they emphasize personal gains, conventional standards, or moral concerns. Just as religious training fosters a bias toward interpreting events in moral terms, juvenile gangs turn morality upside down by reframing it as a matter of social convention defined by gang standards.

The impact of social context on interpretative bias was demonstrated in a recent study by Nucci and Weber (1991). In this study, they divided students into three discussion groups which met once a week for 4 weeks. During these groups, students discussed issues that were primarily moral, conventional, or both moral and conventional. Throughout the course of these weekly discussions, one group was directed to treat all issues in terms of moral concerns of fairness and human welfare; a second group was directed to treat all issues as matters of social convention and social order, and the third group was directed to treat moral issues from a moral perspective, conventional issues from a conventional perspective, and to coordinate moral and conventional perspectives of multifaceted issues. Following this intervention, students were asked to write their views about the values issues contained in an incident which had both moral and conventional features. Findings were that subjects who had been in the moral only group subordinated complex issues to moral concerns, and subjects in the convention only group subordinated complex issues to matters of norms organization. Only the third group spontaneously looked at tures of issues and attempted to coordinate them. As this benign and short-term treatment illustrates, social groups can b ential in framing the meaning individuals will give to social situ ions.

Situational cues further direct which domain system will be involved in a decision to engage in aggressive actions. For instance, cues that focus attention on perceived dissimilarities between an aggressor and his or her victim will reduce the likelihood of moral engagement (Bandura, 1989a). Similarly, portraying victims as inferior through verbal derogation or outgroup affiliation minimizes the activation of a moral orientation, a technique which is used by both juvenile gangs and countries at war. Conversely, situational cues depicting a victim's suffering should activate moral concerns. Turiel's (1983) analysis of the Milgram studies provides a good example of how specific conditions can shift people from a conventional to moral orientation, and how this orientation is correlated with individual's willingness to engage in harm.

SUMMARY

We propose that the generation of moral behavior involves a multicomponent decision-making process. One step consists of coordinating intrapersonal factors and situational cues vis-à-vis the reading of a given situation in nonmoral or moral terms. This step is similar to the social information processing components of encoding and interpreting cues, although we assume that in familiar day-to-day situations this process becomes routine, so that domain placement is accomplished with little thought, although novel circumstances may engage the reflective process. We are not, however, suggesting that behavior is merely an artifact of domain placement. In fact, two individuals might both evaluate a situation in terms of morality, yet respond very differently.

As we have discussed, understanding within each domain also undergoes developmental changes, and individuals should display differences in their level of reasoning within each domain as well as differences in their corresponding normative understanding of appropriate behavior. Individuals search for and decide on a response based, in part, on their judgments regarding the appropriateness of that response. In familiar situations, individuals develop a repertoire of likely response procedures or scripts which are both consistent with their cognitive interpretation of similar types of situations, and subject to modification in accordance with their level of structural understanding. Furthermore, an individual's level of reasoning within a domain may also increase the salience of that domain. For instance, a person who thinks it is very wrong to hit others because all people deserve respect might display a heightened sensitivity to the moral characteristics of any situation involving potential harm to others and might develop a repertoire of highly prosocial scripts.

Because this chapter has focused primarily on cognition, we have not discussed the role of response skills in aggressive behavior. It is clear that a child may read a situation in terms of morality and decide on a corresponding course of action, yet lack the response skills to perform an appropriate behavior. For instance, a child who is used to behaving aggressively may be sensitized, through intervention, to the moral implications of a conflict resolution situation, decide to compromise with his or her peer, yet lack the specific social skills to engage in a social interaction sequence involving compromise and reciprocal exchange. Thus, moral behavior also requires certain performance competencies.

Our model has several implications for prevention and intervention to reduce childhood aggression. We suggest that the relation between moral cognition and aggression is complex, and that intervention efforts should focus on at least three components of this relation. First, interventions should increase the salience of the morality dimensions of social interactions. Second, interventions should promote the development of more sophisticated moral reasoning structures which focus on internal sanctions for causing harm to others. Finally, children should be encouraged to develop and practice behavioral repertoires which include prosocial responses and which can be engaged automatically in real-life social interactions.

REFERENCES

Bandura, A. (1989). Self-regulation of motivation and action through internal standards and goal systems. In L. A. Pervin (Ed.), *Goal concepts in personality and social psychology* (pp. 19–85). Hillsdale, NJ: Lawrence Erlbaum.

Bandura, A. (1991). Social cognitive theory of moral thought and action. In W. M. Kurtines & J. L. Gewirtz (Eds.), *Moral behavior and development: Advances in theory, research, and applications* (Vol. 1, pp. 45–103). Hillsdale, NJ: Lawrence Erlbaum.

Berkowitz, M. W., Guerra, N. G., & Nucci, L. (1991). Sociomoral development and drug and alcohol abuse. In W. M. Kurtines & J. L. Gewirtz (Eds.). *Handbook of moral behavior and development* (Vol. 3, pp. 35–54). Hillsdale, NJ: Lawrence Erlbaum.

Blasi, A. (1980). Bridging moral cognition and moral action: A critical review of the literature. *Psychological Bulletin, 88,* 1–45.

Blasi, A. (1984). Moral identity: Its role in moral functioning. In W. M. Kurtines & J. L. Gewirtz (Eds.), *Morality, moral behavior, and moral development* (pp. 128–139). New York: Wiley Interscience.

Boldizar, J. P., Perry, D. G., & Perry, L. (1989). Outcome values and aggression. *Child Development, 60,* 571–579.

Brown, T. (1987). Values and affectivity. *The Genetic Epistemologist, 15,* 29–32.

Darley, J. M., & Shultz, T. R. (1990). Moral rules: Their content and acquisition. *Annual Review of Psychology, 41,* 525–556.

Dodge, K. A. (1986). A social information processing model of social competence in children. In M. Perlmutter (Ed.), *Minnesota Symposia on Child Psychology* (Vol. 18, pp. 77–125). Hillsdale, NJ: Lawrence Erlbaum.

Dodge, K. A., & Crick, N. R. (1990). Social information-processing bases of aggressive behavior in children. *Personality & Social Psychology Bulletin, 16,* 8–22.

Dodge, K. A., & Frame, C. L. (1982). Social cognitive biases and deficits in aggressive boys. *Child Development, 53,* 620–635.

Dodge, K. A., Price, J. M., Bachorowski, J., & Newman, J. P. (1990). Hostile attributional biases in severely aggressive adolescents. *Journal of Abnormal Psychology, 99,* 385–392.

Eron, L. D. (1982). Parent-child interaction, television violence, and aggression of children. *American Psychologist, 37,* 197–211.

Eron, L. D. (1987). The development of aggressive behavior from the perspective of a developing behaviorism. *American Psychologist, 42,* 435–442.

Eron, L. D., Walder, L. O., & Lefkowitz, M. M. (1971). *The learning of aggression in children.* Boston: Little, Brown.

Fodor, E. M. (1973). Moral development and parent behavior antecedents in adolescent psychopaths. *Journal of Genetic Psychology, 122,* 37–43.

Gerson, R., & Damon, W. (1978). Moral understanding and children's conduct. In W. Damon (Ed.), *New directions for child development* (Vol. 1, pp. 41–60). San Francisco: Jossey-Bass.

Guerra, N. G., & Slaby, R. G. (1989). Evaluative factors in social problem solving by aggressive boys. *Journal of Abnormal Child Psychology, 17,* 277–289.

Guerra, N. G., & Slaby, R. G. (1990). Cognitive mediators of aggression in adolescent offenders: II. Intervention. *Developmental Psychology, 26,* 269–277.

Guerra, N. G., & Nucci, L. (1992). *Delinquent behavior as an overextension of the personal domain.* Manuscript submitted for publication.

Helwig, C., Tisak, M., & Turiel, E. (1990). Children's social reasoning in context. *Child Development, 61,* 2068–2078.

Huesmann, L. R. (1988). An information-processing model for the development of aggression. *Aggressive Behavior, 14,* 13–24.

Huesmann, L. R., Guerra, N. G., Miller, L. S., & Zelli, A. (1992). The role of social norms in the development of aggressive behavior. In A. Fraczek & H. Zumkley (Eds.), *Socialization and aggression* (pp. 139–152). New York/Heidelberg: Springer-Verlag.

Jurkovic, G. J. (1980). The juvenile delinquent as a moral philosopher: A structural-developmental perspective. *Psychological Bulletin, 88,* 709–727.

Kohlberg, L. (1958). *The development of modes of moral thinking and choice in the years ten to sixteen.* Unpublished doctoral dissertation, University of Chicago.

Kohlberg, L. (1969). Stage and sequence: The cognitive–developmental approach to socialization. In D. A. Goslin (Ed.), *Handbook of socialization theory and research* (pp. 347–480). Chicago: Rand McNally.

Kohlberg, L. (1976). Moral stages and moralization. In T. Lickona (Ed.), *Moral development and behavior* (pp. 31–53). New York: Holt, Rinehart, & Winston.

Kohlberg, L. (1984). *Essays on moral development:* Vol. 2. *The psychology of moral development.* San Francisco: Harper & Row.

Kohlberg, L., & Candee, D. (1984). The relation of moral judgment to moral action. In

W. M. Kurtines & J. L. Gewirtz (Eds.), *Morality, moral behavior, and moral development* (pp. 52–73). New York: Wiley Interscience.

Mize, J., & Ladd, G. (1988). Predicting preschoolers' peer behavior and status from their interpersonal strategies: A comparison of verbal and enactive responses to hypothetical social dilemmas. *Developmental Psychology, 24,* 782–788.

Nucci, L. (1981). Conceptions of personal issues: A domain distinct from moral or societal concepts. *Child Development, 52,* 114–121.

Nucci, L., & Nucci, M. S. (1982). Children's responses to moral and social-conventional transgressions in free-play settings. *Child Development, 53,* 1337–1342.

Nucci, L., Guerra, N., & Lee, J. (1991). Adolescent judgments of the personal, prudential, and normative aspects of drug usage. *Developmental Psychology, 27,* 841–848.

Nucci, L., & Weber, E. (1991). The domain approach to values education: From theory to practice. In W. M. Kurtines & J. L. Gewirtz (Eds.), *Handbook of moral behavior and development* (Vol. 3, pp. 252–266). Hillsdale, NJ: Lawrence Erlbaum.

Parke, R. (1974). Rules, roles, and resistance to deviation: Recent advances in punishment, discipline, and self-control. In A. D. Pick (Ed.), *Minnesota symposia on child psychology* (Vol. 8, pp. 11–143). Minneapolis: University of Minnesota Press.

Perry, D. G., Perry, L. C., & Boldizar, J. P. (1990). Learning of aggression. In M. Lewis & S. Miller (Eds.), *Handbook of developmental psychopathology* (pp. 135–146). New York: Plenum.

Perry, D. G., Perry, L. D., & Rasmussen, P. (1986). Cognitive social learning mediators of aggression. *Child Development, 57,* 700–711.

Piaget, J. (1965). *The moral judgment of the child.* London: Routledge & Kegan Paul. (Original work published 1932).

Rest, J. R. (1984). The major components of morality. In W. M. Kurtines & J. L. Gewirtz (Eds.). *Morality, moral behavior, and moral development* (pp. 24–38). New York: Wiley Interscience.

Saltzstein, H. (1991). Why are nonprototypical events so difficult, and what are the implications for social-developmental psychology? In E. Turiel, C. Hildebrant, & C. Wainryb (Eds.), Judging social issues. *Monographs for the Society for Research in Child Development* (Vol. 56, pp. 104–117).

Shank, R. C., & Abelson, R. (1977). *Scripts, plans, goals and understanding.* Hillsdale, NJ: Lawrence Erlbaum.

Shiffrin, R. M., & Schneider, W. (1977). Controlled and automatic human information processing: II. Perceptual learning, automatic attending, and general theory. *Psychological Review, 84,* 127–190.

Shure, M. B., & Spivack, G. (1976). *Problem-solving techniques in childrearing.* San Francisco: Jossey-Bass.

Slaby, R. G., & Guerra, N. G. (1988). Cognitive mediators of aggression in adolescent offenders: I. Assessment. *Developmental Psychology, 24,* 580–588.

Smetana, J. (1982). *Concepts of self and morality: Women's reasoning about abortion.* New York: Praeger.

Sobesky, W. E. (1983). The effects of situational factors on moral judgments. *Child Development, 54,* 575–584.

Spivack, G., & Shure, M. B. (1974). *Social adjustment of young children.* San Francisco: Jossey-Bass.

Tisak, M., & Turiel, E. (1984). Children's conceptions of moral and prudential rules. *Child Development, 55,* 1030–1039.

Turiel, E. (1983). *The development of social knowledge: Morality and convention.* Cambridge: Cambridge University Press.

Turiel, E., Hildebrant, C., & Wainryb, C. (1991). Judging social issues. *Monographs for the Society for Research in Child Development* (Vol. 56, pp. 1–103).

Turiel, E., Killen, M., & Helwig, C. (1987). Morality: Its structure, functions, and vagaries. In J. Kagan & S. Lamb (Eds.), *The emergence of moral concepts in young children* (pp. 155–244). Chicago: University of Chicago Press.

Turiel, E., & Smetana, J. G. (1984). Social knowledge and action: The coordination of domains. In W. M. Kurtines & J. L. Gewirtz (Eds.), *Morality, moral behavior, and moral development* (pp. 261–282). New York: Wiley Interscience.

Wainryb, C. (1991). Understanding differences in moral judgments: The role of informational assumptions. *Child Development, 62,* 840–851.

CHAPTER 3

IS SOMETHING MISSING?

Some Observations Prompted by the Cognitive–Neoassociationist View of Anger and Emotional Aggression

LEONARD BERKOWITZ

Any really close and thorough examination of the psychological research into the origins of anger and emotional aggression must leave the thoughtful reader somewhat dissatisfied. The literature presents us with occasional inconsistencies and unexpected findings that most of the investigators seem not to have noticed and certainly have not addressed as they focus on the more usual research results. In my view any really adequate account of anger and emotional aggression must deal with these apparent exceptions to the general rule and show how they can be explained by the theoretical scheme. Only then, I believe, will we have a truly far-ranging theory. Hoping to assist in the development of this comprehensive formulation, I will first highlight these matters that seem to be almost entirely neglected by most contemporary analyses of anger, and I will then offer a general theoretical model that can accommodate

---

LEONARD BERKOWITZ • Department of Psychology, University of Wisconsin, Madison, Wisconsin 53706.

Aggressive Behavior: Current Perspectives, edited by L. Rowell Huesmann. Plenum Press, New York, 1994.

both the seeming exceptions and the much more frequently reported research results.

Before proceeding with this discussion, however, I should note that the present chapter is concerned exclusively with emotional (not instrumental) aggression, behavior aimed at the verbal or physical injury of a target, that is instigated by some circumstance that arouses negative feelings. Correspondingly, the term *anger* as used here refers to an experience, the person's feelings when he or she is inclined to assault someone verbally or physically.

FINDINGS USUALLY LEFT UNEXPLAINED

The Conventional Account

A common theme runs through the results obtained in the conventional studies of emotion—investigations in which the participants are basically asked to describe the occasions on which they have become (or are likely to become) angry. Although their findings at times differ in detail, many of these studies conclude that anger arises primarily when someone is wronged. A brief sampling of this research will suffice.

Guided by his attribution theory analysis of emotions but also supported by his questionnaire studies, Weiner (e.g., Weiner, Graham, & Chandler, 1982) tells us that people are apt to become angry when (1) they had an unhappy experience that (2) they attribute to (3) someone or something external to themselves, who (4) could have controlled what had happened. Smith and Ellsworth (1985) have reported results in accord with Weiner's formulation. Many people in their sample did tend to believe angering situations could have been controlled by the responsible external agent.

Other investigators employing the questionnaire paradigm go somewhat further along these lines and contend that the angering agent is typically seen as not only responsible for the occurrence but also as having violated a widely shared social rule. As one example, Averill's (1982, 1983) examination of reported angering incidents noted that in the great majority of these instances the instigator was viewed as having had control over what happened. But more than this, he concluded from his data that anger is an accusation of having been mistreated, and he maintained that this held for frustrations. Summarizing the answers given him by the majority of his respondents, Averill argued that most persons become angry when they are frustrated only to the degree that they regard the frustrater's behavior as unjustified. Moreover, according to Averill, laboratory studies have also found that "it is primarily arbitrary (unwarranted) frustrations that arouse subjects to anger and/or aggression."

Scherer, Walbott, and Summerfield (1986) reached much the same conclusion in their study of people from seven west European countries and Israel. "Most of the [reported] antecedents of anger . . . centered around situations in which somebody had violated an explicit norm or rule or where the person answering the questionnaire felt unjustly or unfairly treated by others" (p. 59).

Other traditional investigators accept this general line of thought but hold that angry persons also have other beliefs about the provocative situation. For Lazarus (e.g., Lazarus & Smith, 1989), they supposedly became angry only to the extent that they appraised the negative event as personally significant, and perhaps also thought they were able to cope with or do something about the evocative situation. Stein and Levine (1989) placed even more emphasis on this latter perception as being necessary for anger arousal.

Clearly, then, even with the variations in detail, these conventional studies all generally agree that the basic requirement for anger arousal is the perception of having been deliberately wronged in some way. Social psychologists following the Schachter and Singer (1962) two-factor theory of emotion would share this view, even though their analysis is presumably based on laboratory-tested theory rather than subjective reports. From their perspective, events are not intrinsically pleasant or unpleasant in themselves but become affectively positive or negative only as a result of how they are construed. When people are frustrated, for example, their failure to attain the goal they desire supposedly creates only a diffuse and undifferentiated emotional arousal. What specific feelings they experience and what actions they undertake are said to depend on their interpretation of their internal sensations. According to the latest and most popular version of this formulation, the label the aroused individuals give to their sensations is determined by their belief as to what had caused these feelings. And so, here too it is held that the afflicted persons will regard themselves as angry, and thus will feel anger, only if they think their frustrator had intentionally and wrongly prevented them from getting what they wanted.

Neglected Observations

No one doubts that people's construals can determine how they will react to frustrations or other occurrences that produce feelings, or that they are especially likely to become angry when they think they had been intentionally mistreated. My question is whether this perception is as necessary for the creation of anger and emotional aggression as is widely believed. A growing body of evidence, all too often disregarded by most emotion researchers, indicates that anger can arise and emotional assaults take place even when the aroused persons had not been afflicted by controllable events aimed at them personally in a manner contrary to social norms.

Exceptions in the Self-Report Studies

Some of this neglected evidence comes from the research cited earlier. In a number of these studies a minority of the respondents indicated that they become angry at times even when they are not deliberately affronted. Averill's (1982, 1983) data are illustrative. Two out of five respondents in his sample reported having been angered by another person's action even when that behavior had not been socially improper, and 12% also said that the instigating behavior had been justified (Averill, 1983, p. 1150). Similarly, in the previously mentioned investigation conducted by Scherer et al. (1986), some of the participants in each of the countries sampled indicated they had been angered by such unpleasant occurrences as inconveniences, the receipt of bad news, someone's death, and even temporary separations (cf. p. 82). We are not told whether the participants believed they had been deliberately mistreated in all of these cases, but it seems likely that there were no perceived norm violations in at least some of these instances.

Exceptions in the Research into the Aggressive Consequences of Frustrations

Besides neglecting these relatively few cases in their own investigations, the conventional researchers seem to have totally disregarded the laboratory experiments demonstrating that, contrary to Averill's above quoted statement, even nonarbitrary frustrations can incite subjects to anger or aggression (Berkowitz, 1989). Several of these studies are especially noteworthy.

In one of them, not reported in my 1989 literature survey, Walters and Brown (1963) showed that children who were intermittently reinforced for punching a Bobo doll subsequently were most apt to display realistic aggression not appropriate to the situation while in a game with another youngster. More important for us here, though, is the significant effect for frustration within the intermittent reinforcement condition. The experimenter told all of the children they would see an exciting movie and, to fulfill this promise, started showing the film before the subjects played the final game. In half of the cases, however, the projector supposedly broke down during the movie so the participants could not see how the exciting story ended. These thwarted children were the most assaultive of all during the game that followed. Inclined to be aggressive because of their prior training, they readily exhibited the aggressive tendencies generated by the frustration, even though this event was ostensibly accidental and not aimed at them personally and surely could not be seen as a norm violation.

While the subjects' previous learning experience had undoubtedly increased the likelihood of aggressive responses to the thwarting (Bandura, 1973; Davitz, 1952), other research with animals as well as human infants and adults indicates this prior learning is not necessary for the aggression to occur. At the human level, as just one example, Campos, Barrett, Lamb, Goldsmith, and Stenberg (1983) frustrated infants by restraining their arms and legs and found that the babies then tended to display angerlike facial expressions. The researchers proposed that restraints of this type are inborn elicitors of anger.

Geen (1968) has also provided suggestive evidence. In his experiment university subjects were individually first either reinforced or not for behaving aggressively in a training session and then were required to complete a jigsaw puzzle in the presence of another student (the experimenter's accomplice). Most of the subjects were frustrated by being unable to complete the puzzle, either because (1) the confederate deliberately interfered with their work (i.e., the thwarting was externally and wrongly produced), or (2) unknown to them, the puzzle actually was insoluble so that it seemed they themselves were responsible for their failure to get the job done (i.e., the frustration was internally caused and not socially unjustified). Then, soon afterwards, each subject was given a series of opportunities to shock the other student.

Of particular interest to us here are the results with this aggression measure in the condition in which the subjects had not previously been rewarded for aggression: While the externally thwarted people administered the most severe shocks over the series of trials, even the participants who were themselves responsible for their failure to complete the puzzle were more punitive to the confederate than the nonfrustrated "controls." Their inability to reach their goal had made them aggressively inclined even though they had not previously been taught that aggression was permissible in the present situation.

These indications of a frustration-generated instigation to aggression do not mean, of course, that every barrier to goal attainment leads to an open assault on an available target. My review of the frustration–aggression literature has acknowledged the occasional failure to find a significant increase in aggression after an unexpected nonfulfillment of some desire. But again, any truly comprehensive account of emotional aggression must be able to explain these inconsistencies as well. Why do some frustrations give rise to overt attacks on a target whereas other thwartings do not seem to have the same effect?

Exceptions in Studies of the Effects of High Temperatures

There are still other unfortunate omissions in the conventional discussions of anger and emotional aggression but I will here single out only one of them: the research into the aggression-enhancing effects of unpleasantly high temperatures. It is now quite well established through both field and laboratory research that people exposed to uncomfortable heat are more likely to be assaultive than they otherwise would have been in more comfortable surroundings (Anderson, 1989; Baron, 1977; Bell & Baron, 1990).

Some of the field studies investigated the effects of unusually hot weather on the urban disorders of the 1960s. Goranson and King (cited in Berkowitz, 1982), Baron and Ransberger (1978), and Carlsmith and Anderson (1979) have concluded that the urban riots that racked many American cities in this period were especially likely to arise on exceptionally hot days and then tended to diminish in intensity when the weather cooled.

Anderson (1989) has now generalized this finding much further. In his careful review of the relevant research, he noted that violent crimes and spouse abuse tend to increase when the temperature is unusually and unpleasantly high. As Anderson has also emphasized, this jump in the rate of violent offenses cannot be explained away as being merely the result of greater interpersonal contacts on hot days, because comparable findings have been obtained in laboratory experiments in which social contacts remain constant. The best known of these experiments were carried out by Griffitt (1970) and Baron (1977). Employing a variety of aggression measures, these researchers demonstrated that laboratory subjects placed in uncomfortably hot rooms expressed greater hostility and displayed stronger aggression to a stranger than did their counterparts exposed to normal room temperatures.

Why the Neglect of These Findings?

There does not seem to be any one reason why the conventional emotion researchers have failed to give these findings any consideration. Many of them might claim they are dealing mainly with emotional experience (i.e., felt anger) rather than overt behavior, so that the laboratory experiments employing behavioral measures are not relevant to their interests. Contrary to such a simple contention, however, a number of the investigators in this camp actually have discussed behavioral effects (e.g., Averill, 1982, 1983; Frijda, 1986) and it is tacitly if not always explicitly recognized that action does fall within the domain of emotion research. But perhaps more important, several of the studies just cited did investigate the subjects' emotional experiences, and their results have also been neglected.

A better explanation can be found, I think, in the conventional researchers' methodological and theoretical biases. Many of them believe laboratory experiments are inadequate or even suspect for their purposes, and they insist that their particular research interests are best satisfied by asking ordinary people about their emotional experiences (i.e., Averill, 1983; Scherer et al., 1986). While this is not the place to debate the advantages and shortcomings of laboratory versus self-report procedures, I should note that the subjects' accounts are all too susceptible to the types of errors and distortions noted by Nisbett and Wilson (1977). The subjects' descriptions of what happened or is likely to occur in an emotion-arousing incident are too easily influenced by their desires to present themselves in the best possible light and also their laypersons' theories about emotion (which may or may not be accurate). Few of the conventional emotion researchers seem to recognize these problems.

This failure to confront the possible shortcomings of questionnaire and interview studies is probably basically due to the conventional researchers' overriding preference for purely cognitive and even rationalistic explanations of emotion. Believing from the start that appraisals-attributions-construals are virtually the only determinants of emotional reactions, they see no difficulty in employing methodologies that will generally support their suppositions. Nonetheless, as I tried to show earlier, even with these possibly biasing research procedures, there seem to be important exceptions to their theoretical propositions in their own investigations.

AN INTEGRATING PERSPECTIVE: THE COGNITIVE–NEOASSOCIATIONISTIC APPROACH

As I indicated at the start of this chapter, I believe that a truly comprehensive account of anger and emotional aggression must explain why some people at least become angry and assaultive even when they are not personally and deliberately affronted. The present chapter attempts such an explanation. More than this, however, it assumes that the same underlying processes operate when the precipitating event is a controllable misdeed, as when people are afflicted by unpleasant happenings that are no one's fault. These processes, the model proposes, are both associative and cognitive in nature, with the relatively basic and automatic "bottom up" associative processes presumably being dominant at the outset and the higher order "top down" cognitive processes theoretically becoming much more important as the person attends to and thinks about what is happening. Because of the recognition of both sets of processes, I believe it is entirely appropriate to regard the present analysis as taking a cognitive–neoassociationistic stance.

Several ideas are central to this particular perspective. The first of these, in fundamental agreement with other theoretical formulations (e.g., Bower, 1981; Bower & Cohen, 1982; Lang, 1979, 1984; Leventhal, 1980), holds that emotional states are best regarded as an associative network in which specific types of feelings, physiological reactions, motor responses, and thoughts and memories are all linked together to a greater or lesser extent. Since angry feelings are associated with hostile thoughts, certain types of physiological reactions, and aggression-related expressive-motor tendencies, we can properly speak of an anger–aggression network (or syndrome), although it is important to remember that these connections can differ in strength and are often relatively weak. In common with the other formulations, the present model also assumes that the activation of any one of these components in the given network will activate the other parts in proportion to their degree of association. Thus, the recall of earlier occasions in which the individual was extremely angry often evokes hostile ideas, angry feelings, and even anger/aggression-related expressive-motor tendencies, at least to some extent, because of these associative interconnections.

There are two other key notions, however, that are not shared by the other network conceptions, one involving the anger/aggression-activating influence of negative affect and the other having to do with changes in the emotional state with thought and time. I will have something to say about both of these ideas although the first one, more central to the present paper, will be given greater attention.

Negative Affect-Anger/Aggression Associations

As Figure 1 indicates, the cognitive–neoassociationistic model posits a sequence of stages in the generation of anger and emotional aggres-

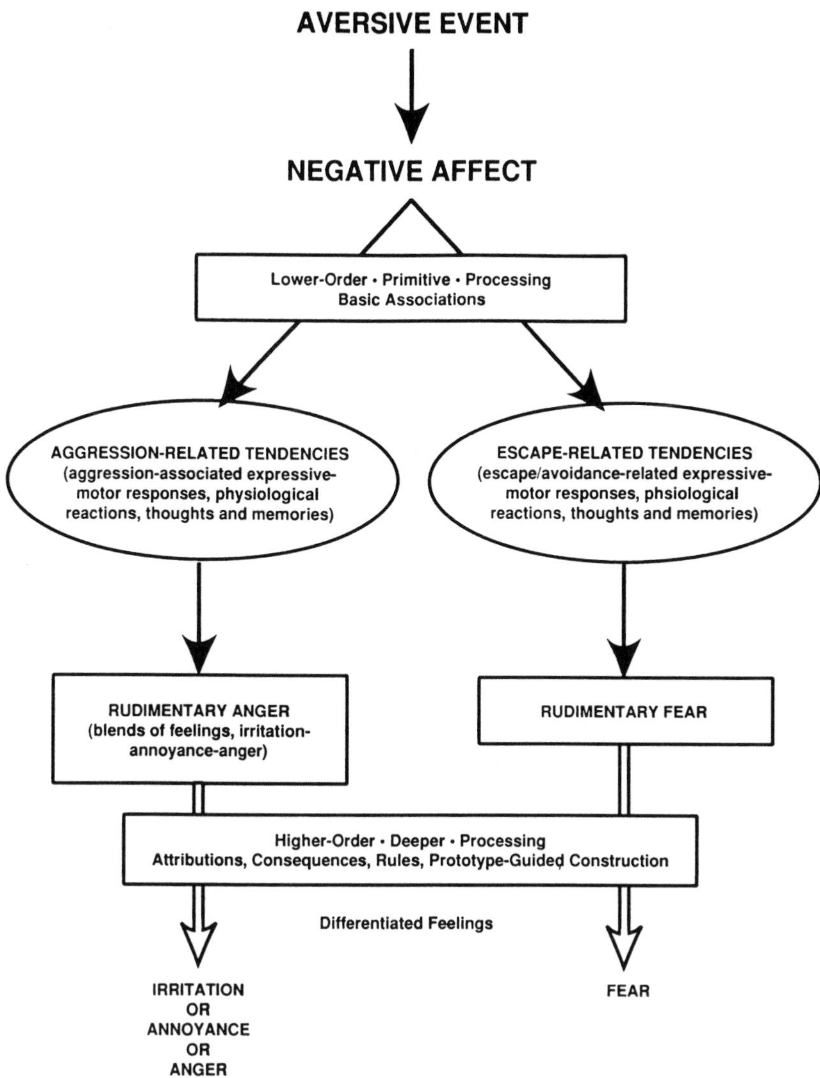

FIGURE 1. An outline of the cognitive–neoassociationistic model.

sion, with relatively primitive associations being dominant at the outset. Because of presumed "built-in" linkages in many animal species, including humans, I suggest, the negative affect produced by an aversive event initially activates at least two different emotional networks at the same time: one dealing with the escape–avoidance (or "flight") syndrome and the other involving the anger–aggression (or "fight") network. In other words, the unpleasant feelings generated by an aversive event presumably give rise at first to *both* flight and fight tendencies, not one or the other, although a host of factors, genetic, learning, and situational, can determine which of these tendencies is dominant at any one time. But even when the afflicted animals or humans would rather flee than fight, they presumably are also somewhat aggressively inclined. As can also be seen in the figure, the model proposes that the anger experience stems from the awareness of the physiological, motoric, and cognitive changes associated with the aggressive tendencies, whereas the fear experience grows out of the awareness of the escape/avoidance-linked physiological, expressive-motor, and cognitive changes.

I will here concentrate on the negative affect–anger/aggression linkage since it is this connection that is the focus of the present chapter. My thesis (Berkowitz, 1983, 1989, 1990, 1993) is a simple but sweeping one: All of the anger/aggression-generating instances noted in this paper, whether they had to do with an intentional misdeed or an accidental thwarting, were unpleasant, and it is this displeasure that produced the felt anger and aggressive reactions.

Why Attributions Matter

Appraisals and attributions are important, according to this argument, largely (but not only, as I will argue later) because they help determine the intensity of the negative affect evoked by the aversive event. People obviously are far more unhappy when they believe that someone has deliberately and wrongly kept them from satisfying their desires than when they think this failure was only inadvertent, and consequently, because of the stronger displeasure, the former perception will usually activate the anger–aggression network more strongly. But as I also noted, we are sometimes bothered even by chance mishaps, and so, even unfortunate and unintended frustrations can produce aggressive reactions (Berkowitz, 1989). Nonetheless, every failure to reach a wanted goal is not equally unpleasant. Some thwartings are not especially disturbing, perhaps because the goal is not particularly attractive or because the barrier to goal attainment arises before the person anticipates the pleasures of reaching the objective. Thus, while there are many reasons why the inability to fulfill one's desires does not always lead to an open attack on some available target, on at least some of these nonaggressive occasions the frustration may not be particularly unpleasant.

Does All Negative Affect Have the Same Effect?

My working assumption for the time being is that virtually any kind of negative affect can activate the anger–aggression network as long as this feeling is intense enough. Particular types of affect, however, such as unpleasant feelings of agitation, might be especially likely to prime this emotional syndrome. Be this as it may, existing research indicates that an impressively broad variety of negative occurrences can generate aggressive inclinations (Berkowitz, 1983, 1989, 1990, 1993). Only a few of these conditions will be discussed here.

Aversive Environmental Conditions

I have already mentioned the aggression-producing effects of frustrations and unpleasantly high temperatures. To add to the list, both naturalistic and experimental research has shown that atmospheric pollution and foul odors can also promote violence. Laboratory experiments by Rotton and his associates (Rotton, Barry, Frey, & Soler, 1978; Rotton, Frey, Barry, Milligan, & Fitzpatrick, 1979) demonstrated this using odors as the aversive stimulation. Subjects exposed to foul smells rated themselves as feeling more "aggressive" and also were more punitive to a fellow student than their counterparts breathing normal air. Judging from the findings reported by Zillmann, Baron, and Tamborini (1981), in a study using cigarette smoke as the annoying pollutant, this increased hostility-aggression occurs even when the attacked target cannot be blamed for the unpleasantness. Then, proceeding to a correlational analysis of naturalistic archival data, Rotton and Frey (1985) showed that the rate of violent crimes in an area tends to increase when air pollution rises.

An experiment by Berkowitz, Cochran, and Embree (1981) has extended these findings by indicating that painful cold can also incite aggression and that the aim of this assault is to do harm. University women kept one hand in a tank of water that was either very cold or at a warmer room temperature as they evaluated a fellow student's answers to a series of business problems. In these evaluations they could deliver either rewards (nickels) or punishments (blasts of noise). Half of the subjects had been informed beforehand that any punishment they administered would help the problem solver (by motivating her to do better), whereas the others were told punishment would hurt (by interfering with the other student's performance). As can be seen in Figure 2, the subjects in the warmer water condition did not want to harm the

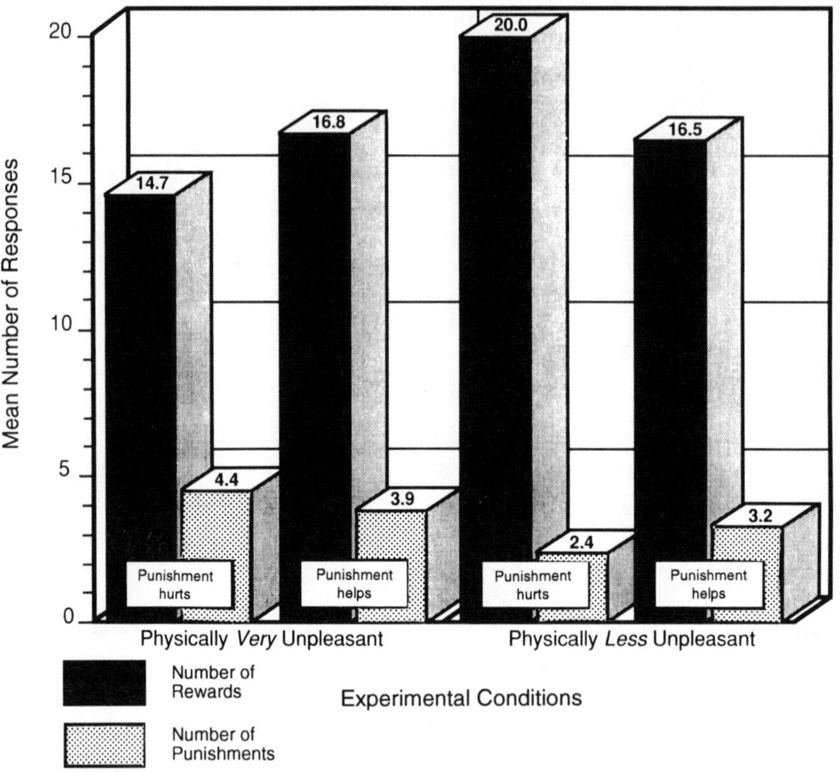

FIGURE 2. The rewards and punishments given as a function of the physical unpleasantness of the situation and whether punishment would help or hurt the target.

other student and gave her the most rewards and fewest punishments when they thought their punishment would hurt. By contrast, the women exposed to the very cold water were much less intent on not injuring their partner. In comparison to the other groups, they gave the problem solver the fewest rewards and most punishments when they had been informed their punishment would be hurtful. The pain these latter subjects felt had evidently activated a relatively strong desire to harm someone even when the available target was not responsible for their suffering and their punishment could not alleviate their distress.

Depression and Sadness

In the cases just described it is fairly easy to think of the afflicted persons as feeling irritable and/or annoyed. The present formulation suggests, however, that negative feelings not usually said to be irritating or annoying can also activate the anger–aggression syndrome. We can see this, for example, in the frequent clinical reports of depressed or sad people exhibiting outbursts of temper and aggression (Abraham, 1968; Berkowitz, 1983, 1993; Blumberg & Izard, 1986). Much more often than our everyday conceptions of sadness and depression would lead us to expect, those who are unhappy with themselves or who have suffered a serious loss are susceptible to uncontrolled explosions of rage. As a matter of fact, these outbursts can be so frequent, as Blumberg and Izard (1986) noted, that they sometimes keep others from recognizing the underlying depression: "the emotion of anger may motivate the impulsive, aggressive, or acting-out behavior that sometimes conceals some of the traditional signs of depression" (p. 856).

Our common conceptions are right in one respect. These unhappy persons usually do not engage in planned and effortful aggression. Rather, as the above cited quotation indicates, they seem much more apt to be impulsive in their displays of anger and aggression. The Poznanski and Zrull (1970) study of highly depressed children provides further support. "Frequently," they observed, "the aggression [the youngsters carried out] was violent and explosive, occurring in short outbursts" (p. 13).

Clinicians have speculated about the origin of this association between depression and aggression, usually suggesting that the depression is aggression turned inward, that is, the aggression produced the depression (Abraham, 1968). The present formulation raises another possibility. Many depressives are hostile toward themselves (Blumberg & Izard, 1986). But nevertheless, in quite a few of these cases the depressed feelings could have activated the anger and emotional aggression.

Some of the evidence for this causal direction comes from laboratory studies testing the learned helplessness analysis of depression. As Miller and Norman (1979) pointed out, in a number of these experiments the subjects exposed to the helplessness training became relatively depressed as expected, but they also rated themselves as angry and even expressed hostility toward others. Supporting findings also come from experiments creating temporary depressive feelings by means of the Velten mood-induction procedure. In two of these investigations (Finman & Berkowitz, 1989; Hynan & Gush, 1986) the strongest aggression was displayed by those persons who (1) were made depressed, and (2) gave relatively little thought to what they were doing because of their personalities and also because they had to react quickly. Feeling depressed, they were inclined to be aggressive but revealed this urge only impulsively when they did not think much about their actions.

Also contrary to our usual notions of how people act when they are emotionally upset, even sadness can lead to anger. It is by no means unusual for grieving persons mourning the loss of a loved one to burst out in a fit of temper. Indeed, these displays of anger and aggression are frequent enough that Rosenblatt, Jackson, and Walsh (1972) commented, "it is not uncommon for people who are bereaved to be angry and even to engage in violent acts" (p. 271). Some of these aggression-exhibiting mourners could become extremely agitated but even less severe sadness can also produce anger. According to Wickless and Kirsch (1988), when their respondents said they felt sad they were also likely to report having felt angry as well. More important, though, a multivariate analysis showed that the sense of loss, which was the primary determinant of the sad feelings, also contributed to the anger over and above any sense of having been wronged. An unhappy loss apparently could create anger even when the loss was not believed to be morally improper.

Conventional emotion theorists confronted by these observations typically explain the anger in attributional terms: The afflicted persons supposedly blame their loss on someone or something. In their minds they presumably think they have been wronged by God, Heaven or Fate. Observations published by Termine and Izard (1988) indicate that sadness can give rise to anger even without these attributions. In their experiment mothers deliberately exhibited the facial expressions of either joy or sadness while their 9-month-old infants played with toys. The mothers' displayed sadness caused the babies to show both sadness and anger in their own facial reactions—and it is unlikely that the infants' exhibited anger stemmed from any attributions of blame. Termine and Izard explained their results by proposing, in agreement with the present formulation, that "the emotions of sadness and anger are dynamically related . . . and that situations or conditions eliciting sadness frequently elicit anger" (pp. 227–228).

Negative Affect Associations with Thoughts and Memories

The associative network model of the anger–aggression syndrome does more than posit that negative affect produced angry feelings and aggressive inclinations. It also maintains that those who are feeling bad for one reason or another are also likely to have hostile thoughts and memories.

There are relatively few direct tests of this thesis in the experimental literature but some studies have obtained supporting results. In one of these, Rule, Taylor, and Dobbs (1987) found that subjects placed in unpleasantly hot rooms were much more likely to use aggression-related ideas in completing stories of an emotional nature than were their more comfortable counterparts. Monteith, Berkowitz, Kruglanski, and Blair (cited in Berkowitz, 1990) obtained comparable findings in a study establishing differences in the participants' degree of muscular discomfort. While the male and female subjects were either very uncomfortable or not (because their extended nondominant arm was either physically supported or not for the entire period), they were asked to talk about how they would feel in an imagined situation that was either neutral in nature or was emotional (either aggressive or anxiety-provoking). In general, the highly uncomfortable participants talking about either of the two emotional incidents were more apt to mention angry feelings than their more comfortable controls (see Table 1). Of particular interest, within the imagined anxiety situation there was a significant interaction between discomfort level and the frequency of references to fear or anger. Relative to the more comfortable participants, the pained subjects had a drop in the number of times they mentioned being afraid and an increase in the number of anger references.

A second experiment by the same authors suggests that hostility-related memories are also primed by negative affect. Again using the extended arm procedure to establish either high or low discomfort, the women in this study were asked to recall a significant incident with a person they knew (either their mother or their boyfriend or someone about whom they did not have any strong feelings) as they held their arm out. Over all target persons, the pained women were more likely

TABLE 1. Effects of Fist Clench and Recalled Incident on Reported Feelings

	Nature of recalled incident					
	Angry		Sad		Neutral	
	Hand position					
Mood index	Clench	No fist	Clench	No fist	Clench	No fist
Anger	6.3[a]	4.7[b]	2.7[cd]	3.6[bc]	2.0[d]	2.4[d]
Depression/ sadness	3.3[ab]	2.3[b]	2.4[b]	4.1[a]	2.1[b]	2.0[b]
Anxiety	2.5[a]	2.2[a]	2.3[a]	3.4[a]	3.0[a]	2.3[a]

Note: The scores reported are the adjusted means on the respective indices holding constant the premanipulation scores. In each row considered separately, cells not having a common superscript are significantly different.
Source: Berkowitz, 1990.

than the control subjects to mention being in conflict during the recalled situation, although this difference was least when they were talking about their mother (see Berkowitz, 1990, Table 2).

In sum, then, available research has yielded findings in accord with the cognitive–neoassociationistic formulation of anger and emotional aggression. Negative affect often promotes angry feelings and aggressive inclinations and also tends to bring hostile thoughts and memories to mind.

Self-Regulation of the Affect-Activated Syndrome

Despite this evidence, however, it is obvious that people do not always show anger and become assaultive when they are feeling bad. According to the cognitive–neoassociationistic analysis, these seeming exceptions come about because of the intervention of higher order cognitive processes that operate to restrain or even alter the initial, more primitive reactions to the negative affect.

This type of cognitive intervention, I suggest, actually is fairly common. Evidence from various psychological domains indicates that associative processes are typically dominant when the person engages in unattended and highly routine activities, but that more cognitively controlled executive or supervisory mechanisms come more strongly into operation as attention is given to what is happening (Norman & Shallice, 1986). This observation can be applied to the consequences of unpleasant feelings. Since the display of anger and aggression is usually frowned on, and emotionally aroused persons frequently believe it is wrong to attack someone who had not been responsible for their felt distress, the relatively primitive, association-engendered emotional aggression is most likely to be exhibited openly when cognitive controls are not in operation, that is, when the afflicted persons are not fully aware of what they are doing. Moreover, these aroused people should be much more apt to regulate and possibly even inhibit this emotional reaction when they pay attention to their feelings and the events before them.

Findings from five separate experiments by Troccoli and myself (e.g., Berkowitz, 1990; Berkowitz & Troccoli, 1990) are consistent with this reasoning. In one of these reported by Berkowitz and Troccoli (1990), university women individually heard a job applicant talk about herself while they were experiencing either severe or little discomfort (because their extended arm was either unsupported or resting on a table). Equally important, half of the subjects in both conditions were then led to be highly aware of their feelings (by asking them to rate their feelings at the time), whereas the others were distracted by giving them an extraneous task (thinking of word associations). Immediately afterwards, when all of the women indicated their impressions of the job applicant's personal qualities, only those who had *not* previously attended to their feelings showed negative evaluations in accord with their negative affect; the more uncomfortable they had been, the more negative qualities they attributed to the applicant. By contrast, those who had rated their negative feelings and thus had attended to them, were particularly likely to have regulated their reactions; in this case, the more uncomfortable the subjects had been, the *more favorable* was their evaluation of the applicant. Figure 3 summarizes this interactive effect of "Felt Unpleasantness" and "Attention to Feelings" on anger in the data obtained by Berkowitz and Troccoli (1990).

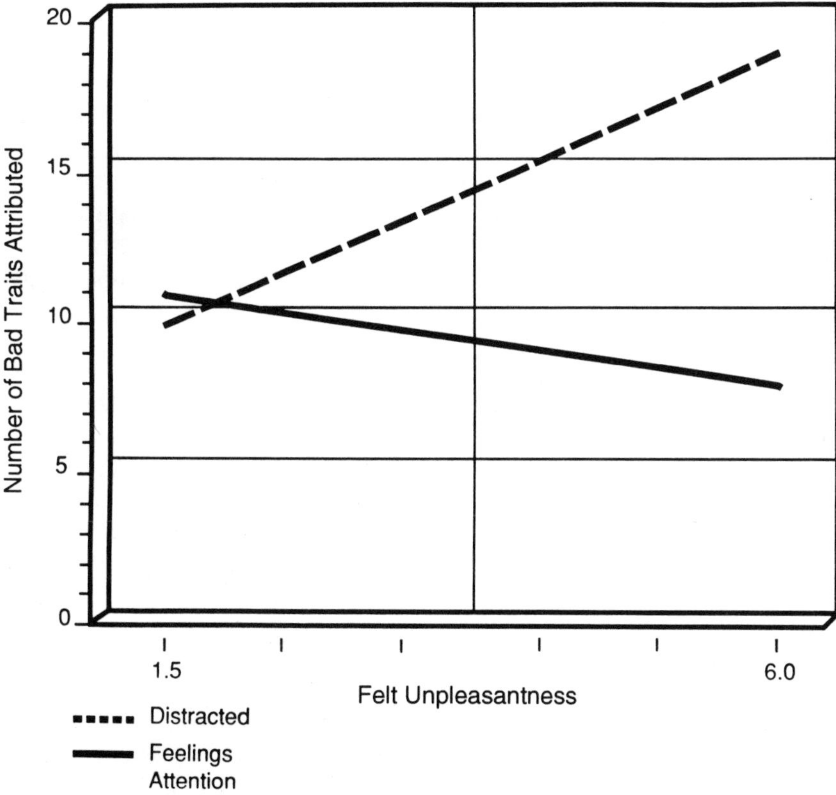

FIGURE 3. The relation between the felt unpleasantness of the situation and the number of bad traits assigned to the target as a function of the subjects' direction of attention.

Yet another experiment by the same researchers testifies to the generality of this attention-activated self-control phenomenon. Using the cold stressor procedure to create differences in physical discomfort, the subjects (male students this time) individually kept one hand in a tank of water that was either very cold (7° C) or at a more comfortable room temperature (23° C) as they listened to another man's autobiographical statement. Differences in the subjects' attention to their feelings were established by then having them rate either their feelings (high attention to oneself) or the personal qualities of other students (low attention to oneself). Immediately after this the subjects indicated their impressions of the target on the basis of his autobiographical statement.

Despite the differences in subject gender and experimental procedure, the results were similar to those obtained in the preceding study. Only the men whose attention had been directed outward (in this case to other students' personal qualities) expressed negative evaluations of the target in accord with their negative feelings. Being distracted, the automatic, negative affect-engendered hostility was expressed with relative ease. On the other hand, and as before, those subjects whose attention was focused on themselves (because they had to rate their feelings) tended to control the impact of their negative feelings on their expressed judgments so that they were *more favorable* to the target when they were in pain than when they were not so uncomfortable. Thinking it was wrong to be critical of the target under the circumstances, their awareness of their feelings enabled them to control the anger–aggression effects activated by their negative affect.

Construction of the More Elaborate Emotional Experience

Higher order cognitive processing which occurs after the initial, relatively primitive associative reactions can also help shape the person's later emotional experience. According to the cognitive–neoassociationistic model, and in basic agreement with Leventhal's (1980) formulation, the mind constructs the more highly developed and differentiated emotional experience by bringing together various types of information. In this process the afflicted persons consider their appraisals, attributions, and construals much as the conventional emotion theorists propose, but they also take into account their internal sensations and the thoughts and memories that have been primed by both the external situation and their internal affect. Furthermore, the way in which they integrate all this information is presumably guided by their prototypic conceptions of what emotions they might be experiencing under the p[illegible] ditions.

It could be that the aroused persons are especially likely [illegible] perception of themselves as angry if they are experiencing [illegible] agitated unpleasant feelings, because such feelings are a central feature of the anger prototype. I also suspect that the anger construction at this time is facilitated by the availability of specific targets for aggression. Much as the Schachter two-factor theory of emotion (Schachter & Singer, 1962) suggests, the suffering persons may well think of themselves as angry if particular targets are present on whom they can focus their activated hostile ideas and thus blame these targets for their affliction.

While very few experiments bear directly on this analysis, Eunkyung Jo and I have obtained suggestive evidence consistent with parts of this reasoning. Findings reported by Shaver, Schwartz, Kirson, and O'Connor (1987), as well as several other investigators, indicate that the prototypic conception of anger includes a relatively intense sense of physiological arousal, muscular tightness throughout much of the body, and tendencies to frown and clench one's fists. The sadness prototype, by contrast, encompasses feelings of being tired, low in energy, moving slowly, and having a slumped, drooping posture. Jo and I therefore attempted to induce physical sensations in our subjects that were in accord with one or the other of these prototypes, and then sought to determine if the subjects would combine these sensations with other types of appropriate emotional information available to them at the time so that the relevant emotional feelings would be intensified.

The first of these studies has been summarized elsewhere (Berkowitz, 1990, pp. 498–499). A second unpublished experiment has explored this phenomenon further. As in the earlier study, the subjects were asked to recall a particular kind of emotional incident, one that had been either angering, sad, or neutral in nature. As they talked about the occurrence for 3 minutes, one group of subjects in these three conditions clenched their fists on a hand dynamometer at a relatively weak, 2 kg force level, while the others only placed an open hand on the dynamometer. Then, at the end of the period, the subjects rated their feelings at that time.

As Table 1 shows, the condition means on our two main emotion indices, those for anger and sadness, are in line with our theoretical expectations. Those who were thinking (and talking) about the angering incident as they clenched a fist—thus combining two anger-related "inputs"—reported feeling the strongest anger, significantly greater than the rated anger in any other group. But on the other hand, a clenched fist tended to lessen the felt sadness activated by the recall (and telling) of the sad incident, presumably because this muscular tension was incompatible with the sadness prototype. All in all, then, the subjects in these two experiments apparently had combined different types of information to the degree that the information was compatible with their presumed conception of the dominant emotion they were experiencing.

Once the final emotional experience is constructed in this manner, it could influence subsequent behavior. I suspect the formed self-perception serves as a filter to inhibit thoughts, memories, and even action tendencies that are incompatible with this perception.

CONCLUSION

This paper is not intended to be a sweeping critique of conventional cognitive theories of emotion. Indeed, as the last section of this chapter should have made clear, I believe these formulations have considerable validity. My contention, however, is that they are incomplete. In particular, they fail to give adequate attention to the important part played by "bottom up" automatic associative processes in producing emotional reactions, especially in the display of anger and emotional aggression. Perhaps because of their underlying assumption of the fundamental rationality and purposiveness of all significant human actions, the conventional analyses of anger and aggression have not adequately recognized the extent to which people can feel irritated, annoyed, and even angry at times simply because they have been inconvenienced or exposed to uncomfortable conditions. Nor have these analyses acknowledged the degree to which emotionally aroused persons sometimes strike out in blind rage at available targets, doing more injury than they had consciously intended and occasionally even attacking innocent parties who cannot possibly be blamed for their felt displeasure. According to the present approach, we must refer to associative processes if we are to account for these occurrences. But thoughts do matter and cognitions can also be very important in the formation and display of the anger–aggression syndrome. The cognitive–neoassociationistic model says that cognitions become increasingly influential as the aroused individuals attend to their feelings and actions. Maybe this means that people in general, and not only emotion theorists, must learn how their emotional behavior can be affected by involuntary reactions to their unpleasant feelings so that, with this increased awareness, they can exert greater control over their responses to other persons when they are not feeling well.

REFERENCES

Abraham, K. (1968). Notes on the psychoanalytic investigation and treatment of manic-depressive insanity and allied conditions. In W. Gaylin (Ed.), *The meaning of despair.* New York: Science House.

Anderson, C. A. (1989). Temperature and aggression: Ubiquitous effects of heat on occurrence of human violence. *Psychological Bulletin, 106,* 74–96.

Averill, J. (1982). *Anger and aggression: An essay on emotion.* New York: Springer-Verlag.

Averill, J. (1983). Studies on anger and aggression: Implications for theories of emotion. *American Psychologist, 38,* 1145–1160.

Bandura, A. (1973). *Aggression: A social learning analysis.* Englewood Cliffs, NJ: Prentice-Hall.

Baron, R. A. (1977). *Human aggression.* New York: Plenum.

Baron, R. A., & Ransberger, V. M. (1978). Ambient temperature and the occurrence of collective violence: The "long hot summer" revisited. *Journal of Personality and Social Psychology, 36,* 351–360.

Bell, P. A., & Baron, R. A. (1990). Affect and aggression. In B. S. Moore & A. M. Isen (Eds.), *Affect and social behavior* (pp. 64–88). Cambridge/New York: Cambridge University Press.

Berkowitz, L. (1982). Aversive conditions as stimuli to aggression. In L. Berkowitz (Ed.), Advances in experimental social psychology (Vol. 15, pp. 249–288). New York: Academic Press.

Berkowitz, L. (1983). Aversively stimulated aggression: Some parallels and differences in research with animals and humans. *American Psychologist, 38,* 1135–1144.

Berkowitz, L. (1989). Frustration-aggression hypothesis: Examination and reformulation. *Psychological Bulletin, 106,* 59–73.

Berkowitz, L. (1990). On the formation and regulation of anger and aggression: A cognitive–neoassociationistic analysis. *American Psychologist, 45,* 494–503.

Berkowitz, L. (1993). *Aggression: Its causes, consequences, and control.* New York: McGraw-Hill.

Berkowitz, L., Cochran, S., & Embree, M. (1981). Physical pain and the goal of aversively stimulated aggression. *Journal of Personality and Social Psychology, 40,* 687–700.

Berkowitz, L., & Troccoli, B. T. (1990). Feelings, direction of attention, and expressed evaluations of others. *Cognition and Emotion, 4,* 305–325.

Blumberg, S. H., & Izard, C. E. (1986). Discriminating patterns of emotions in 10- and 11-year-old children's anxiety and depression. *Journal of Personality and Social Psychology, 51,* 852–857.

Bower, G. H. (1981). Mood and memory. *American Psychologist, 36,* 129–148.

Bower, G. H., & Cohen, P. (1982). Emotional influences in memory and thinking: Data and theory. In S. Fiske & M. Clark (Eds.), *Affect and social cognition.* Hillsdale, NJ: Lawrence Erlbaum.

Campos, J. J., Barrett, K. C., Lamb, M. E., Goldsmith, H. H., & Stenberg, C. (1983). Socioemotional development. In P. Mussen (Ed.), *Handbook of child psychology* (Vol. 2, pp. 783–915). (4th ed). New York: Wiley.

Carlsmith, J. M., & Anderson, C. A. (1979). Ambient temperature and the occurrence of collective violence: A new analysis. *Journal of Personality and Social Psychology, 37*, 337–344.

Davitz, J. R. (1952). The effects of previous training on postfrustration behavior. *Journal of Abnormal and Social Psychology, 47*, 309–315.

Finman, R., & Berkowitz, L. (1989). Some factors influencing the effect of depressed mood on anger and overt hostility toward another. *Journal of Research in Personality, 23*, 70–84.

Frijda, N. H. (1986). *The emotions*. Cambridge/New York: Cambridge University Press.

Geen, R. G. (1968). Effects of frustration, attack, and prior training in aggressiveness upon aggressive behavior. *Journal of Personality and Social Psychology, 9*, 316–321.

Griffitt, W. (1970). Environmental effects on interpersonal affective behavior: Ambient effective temperature and attraction. *Journal of Personality and Social Psychology, 15*, 240–244.

Hynan, D. J., & Grush, J. E. (1986). Effects of impulsivity, depression, provocation, and time on aggressive behavior. *Journal of Research in Personality, 20*, 158–171.

Lang, P. J. (1979). A bio-informational theory of emotional imagery. *Psychophysiology, 16*, 495–512.

Lang, P. J. (1984). Cognition in emotion: Concept and action. In C. E. Izard, J. Kagan, & R.)B. Zajonc (Eds.), *Emotions, cognition and behavior* (pp. 192–226). Cambridge/New York: Cambridge University Press.

Lazarus, R. & Smith, C. A. (1988). Knowledge and appraisal in the cognition-emotion relationship. *Cognition and Emotion, 2*, 281–300.

Leventhal, H. (1980). Toward a comprehensive theory of emotion. In L. Berkowitz (Ed.), *Advances in Experimental Social Psychology* (Vol. 13, pp. 139–207). New York: Academic Press.

Miller, I., & Norman, W. (1979). Learned helplessness in humans: A review and attribution theory model. *Psychological Bulletin, 86*, 93–118.

Nisbett, R. E., & Wilson, T. D. (1977). Telling more than we can know: Verbal reports on mental processes. *Psychological Review, 84*, 231–259.

Norman, D. A., & Shallice, T. (1986). Attention to action: Willed and automatic control of behavior. In R. J. Davidson, G. E. Schwartz, & D. Shapiro (Eds.), *Consciousness and self-regulation* (Vol. 4, pp. 1–18). New York: Plenum.

Poznanski, E., & Zrull, J. P. (1970). Childhood depression: Clinical characteristics of overtly depressed children. *Archives of General Psychiatry, 23*, 8–15.

Rosenblatt, P. C., Jackson, D. A., & Walsh, R. P. (1972). Coping with anger and aggression in mourning. *Omega: Journal of Death and Dying, 3*, 271–284.

Rotton, J., Barry, T., Frey, J., Soler, E. (1978). Air pollution and interpersonal attraction. *Journal of Applied Social Psychology, 8*, 57–71.

Rotton, J., & Frey, J. (1985). Air pollution, weather, and violent crime: Concomitant time-series analysis of archival data. *Journal of Personality and Social Psychology, 49*, 1207–1220.

Rotton, J., Frey, J., Barry, T., Milligan, M., & Fitzpatrick, M. (1979). The air pollution experience and physical aggression. *Journal of Applied Social Psychology, 9*, 397–412.

Rule, B. G., Taylor, B., & Dobbs, A. R. (1987). Priming effects of heat on aggressive thoughts. *Social Cognition, 5*, 131–144.

Schachter, S., & Singer, J. (1962). Cognitive, social, and physiological determinants of emotional state. *Psychological Review, 65*, 379–399.

Scherer, K. R., Wallbott, H. G., & Summerfield, A. B. (1986). *Experiencing emotion: A cross-cultural study.* Cambridge/New York: Cambridge University Press.

Shaver, P., Schwartz, J., Kirson, D., & O'Connor, C. (1987). Emotion knowledge: Further exploration of a prototype approach. *Journal of Personality and Social Psychology, 52,* 1061–1086.

Smith, C. A., & Ellsworth, P. C. (1985). Patterns of cognitive appraisal in emotion. *Journal of Personality and Social Psychology, 48,* 813–838.

Stein, N. L., & Levine, L. J. (1989). The causal organization of emotional knowledge. *Cognition and Emotion, 3,* 343–378.

Termine, N. T., & Izard, C. E. (1988). Infants' responses to their mothers' expressions of joy and sadness. *Developmental Psychology, 24,* 223–229.

Walters, R. H., & Brown, M. (1963). Studies of reinforcement of aggression. III. Transfer of responses to an interpersonal situation. *Child Development, 34,* 563–571.

Weiner, B., Graham, S., & Chandler, C. (1982). Pity, anger, and guilt: An attributional analysis. *Personality & Social Psychology Bulletin, 8,* 226–232.

Wickless, C., & Kirsch, I. (1988). Cognitive correlates of anger, anxiety, and sadness. *Cognitive Therapy & Research, 12,* 367–377.

Zillmann, D., Baron, R., & Tamborini, R. (1981). Social costs of smoking: Effects of tobacco smoke on hostile behavior. *Journal of Applied Social Psychology, 11,* 548–561.

Part II

PEERS, SEX ROLES, AND AGGRESSION

The three chapters in this part advance our understanding of how peer relations and gender affect the development of aggression.

It has been well established that associating with delinquent peers is one of the best predictors of delinquent behavior in youth. In Chapter 4, Dishion and his associates present a "confluence" theory to reconcile this empirical fact with other data showing that antisocial children are disliked by peers and that antisocial children are often the product of parents with ineffective behavior management skills. They propose that the coercive family management practices these children experience produce behaviors that lead them into associations with deviant peers and rejections by other peers which in turn reinforce their antisocial tendencies.

In Chapter 5 Olweus explores the extent to which patterns of peer bullying and victimization persist from childhood into young adulthood and explores the consequences for the bully and victim. Using data from his massive Norwegian study, Olweus argues that there are long-term deleterious consequences both for the child who is pegged as a bully and the child who is pegged as a "whipping boy" by his or her peers. He also presents data suggesting that appropriate interventions can mitigate these effects.

It has been an accepted premise of almost all aggression researchers that males are more aggressive than females. In the final chapter in this section, however, Lagerspetz and Bjorkqvist suggest that such a conclusion has depended greatly on the common definition of aggression as a physical act that injures or irritates another. In fact, they propose, females may simply be aggressive in other ways. They back up this theorizing with some very compelling developmental data.

Chapter 4

PEER ADAPTATIONS IN THE DEVELOPMENT OF ANTISOCIAL BEHAVIOR

A Confluence Model

Thomas J. Dishion, Gerald R. Patterson, and Pamela C. Griesler

INTRODUCTION

Overview

Findings from research on antisocial children present a paradox. Studies reveal that the antisocial child is disliked by peers (Coie & Kupersmidt, 1983; Dishion, 1990; Dodge, 1983), and lacks critical social, academic, and problem-solving skills (Dishion, Loeber, Stouthamer-Loeber, & Patterson, 1984; Freedman, Rosenthal, Donahue, Schlundt, & McFall, 1978; Patterson, 1982). The social skill deficits are not surprising, given that antisocial behavior in childhood is also associated with coercive parent-

Thomas J. Dishion, Gerald R. Patterson, and Pamela C. Griesler • Oregon Social Learning Center, Eugene, Oregon 97401.

Aggressive Behavior: Current Perspectives, edited by L. Rowell Huesmann. Plenum Press, New York, 1994.

ing (Patterson, 1986), and generally poor family management practices (Loeber & Dishion, 1983; McCord, McCord, & Howard, 1963; Patterson, Reid, & Dishion, 1992; West & Farrington, 1973). These findings paint a picture of a child or adolescent who has difficulties getting along with people.

On the other hand, the strongest correlate of adolescent problem behavior is associating with deviant peers, including both substance use (Dishion, Reid, & Patterson, 1988; Elliott, Huizinga, & Ageton, 1985; Huba & Bentler, 1982, 1983; Kandel, 1973) and delinquency (Elliott, Huizinga, & Ageton, 1985; Patterson & Dishion, 1985). In fact, if one were to count sheer number of friends, antisocial adolescents tend to report larger peer networks (Andrews, Dishion, & Patterson, in press) than more normative children. Indeed, some investigators have noted that delinquent behavior is a team activity (Gold, 1970). Clearly, antisocial behavior is not disruptive to the formation of all relationships, and may, in fact, actually facilitate the formation of some friendships.

The task of this chapter is to attempt an integration of two sets of seemingly contradictory findings within a social learning framework. A confluence model is used that relates three levels of peer adaptation to a child's antisocial behavior over time from age 10 to 14. Longitudinal data from the Oregon Youth Study (OYS) are used (Capaldi & Patterson, 1987; Patterson, Reid, & Dishion, 1992), including 2 cohorts of 100 boys each, who were assessed at ages 9 to 10, 11 to 12, and 13 to 14.

Previous research on the OYS boys has confirmed the hypothesis that childhood aggression can be considered a specific subset of a larger response class referred to as antisocial. Behaviors such as lying, stealing, and fighting tend to come in a package and are highly intercorrelated (Patterson et al., 1992). The theoretical importance of considering antisocial behavior as a single response class is the hypothesis which states that while these behaviors are topographically dissimilar (e.g., lying, fighting), they are functionally equivalent (Patterson, 1974). Within a social interactional view, antisocial behavior patterns are maintained within the context of moment-by-moment interpersonal exchanges (Cairns, 1979; Patterson & Reid, 1984). Much of our model development to date has focused on the role of family interaction in generating antisocial child behavior within the context of what has been referred to as coercive family processes (Patterson, 1982). For those youngsters who start on the antisocial trajectory early, we think that coercive family interactions provide the foundation for a potentially antisocial lifestyle.

THE COERCION MODEL

Patterson (1982) has conceptualized parenting as a set of highly interrelated skills referred to as family management, including discipline, monitoring, problem solving, and positive reinforcement. Parent disciplinary practices appear to be especially critical to the development of antisocial behavior in early to middle childhood, and parent monitoring is critical to adolescent onset via the child's association with deviant peers.

In the context of ineffective parent discipline, child coercive behaviors are a means for turning off the aversive intrusions by other family members. This form of negative reinforcement involves three steps. First, the parent makes a demand that is experienced as aversive by the child. Second, the child's noxious response (whine, yell, etc.) is experienced as aversive by the parent. If the parent relinquishes, following the child's coercive behavior, and the child stops his or her aversive behavior, both the parent and child have been subtly changed through negative reinforcement (Patterson, 1982). The parents will more likely give up their demands in the future when the child becomes aversive. Of course, the child will then become more aversive each time a parent makes a demand. Typically, neither parent nor child is consciously aware of the insidious training program underway in the family. It is the repetition of such parent–child exchanges that are associated with the child's frequency, seriousness, and cross-setting consistency in his or her antisocial behavior (Loeber & Dishion, 1984; Patterson et al., 1992). Consistent with the coercion model, a meta-analysis of longitudinal studies on the prediction of adolescent delinquency revealed that among the best predictors are harsh, erratic, and lax family management (Loeber & Dishion, 1983).

Coercive family processes are thought to train a pattern of responding in the child that spills over into other settings such as school. The child uses these settings to further support an antisocial pattern. Inattentiveness and noncompliance establishes the child as "a problem" in the school setting, concomitant with disapproval and rejection that vitiates the child's sense of unfairness and failure (Patterson, Reid, & Dishion, 1992). We think the chain of reactions within the peer domain has important and unique relevance to the child's long-term adjustment.

PEER CONFLUENCE

Confluence refers to the emergence of child characteristics in the context of friendship. The confluence model describes the influence of peers on antisocial behavior in respect to three aspects of peer adaptation: (1) acceptance from the peer group at school; (2) friendship selection; (3) friendship interaction with respect to interpersonal interaction and deviancy training (Buss, 1987). As will be discussed, these three aspects of peer adaptation are seen as highly interrelated. As shown in Figure 1, peer rejection leads to the reduced availability of potential friends. Moreover, the friends that are available may also be antisocial and, therefore, reinforce existing predispositions.

Like the merging of streams into a larger river, a host of ecological factors account for where the streams come together, if they do, and how far the river continues. In regard to children's friendships, ecological factors such as neighborhoods, schools, communities, classrooms, and so on may affect with whom children become friends. For example, policies of tracking children according to ability levels would induce the development of friendships among children who are alike with respect to academic skills (Kellam, 1990). Similarly, children's friendships may be well established prior to the first grade, where children from the same neighborhood may become friends and display similar characteristics on the first day of school. The confluence model proposes that a combination of the child's individual behaviors and ecological factors determine his or her friendship networks.

Peer Reactions

Research associating peer experiences with antisocial behavior has focused on peer rejection as a consequence of antisocial behavior rather than an antecedent (e.g., Coie & Kupersmidt, 1983; Dodge, 1983). In these studies, rejection of the antisocial child by the conventional peer group (i.e., peers sharing a classroom) is assessed by summarizing peer nominations for each child on items such as "kids who I like" and "kids who I don't like." A social preference score (number of liked / number of disliked nominations) is derived, as well as categorical groupings such as Rejected, Average, Popular, Controversial, and Neglected (Coie, Dodge, & Coppotelli, 1982, Peery, 1979). The definition of the rejected child stimulated a plethora of studies on children's social behavior associated with rejection. It is well established that rejection shows temporal stability (Coie et al., 1982; Coie & Dodge, 1988), is negatively correlated with academic skills (Dishion, 1990), is associated with negative parenting practices (Putallaz, 1987; Dishion, 1990), depression (Patterson & Stoolmiller, in press), and loneliness (Asher & Wheeler, 1985).

In a recent analysis of analogue study data, Coie, Dodge, Terry, and Wright (1991) found rejected children more likely to engage in reactive

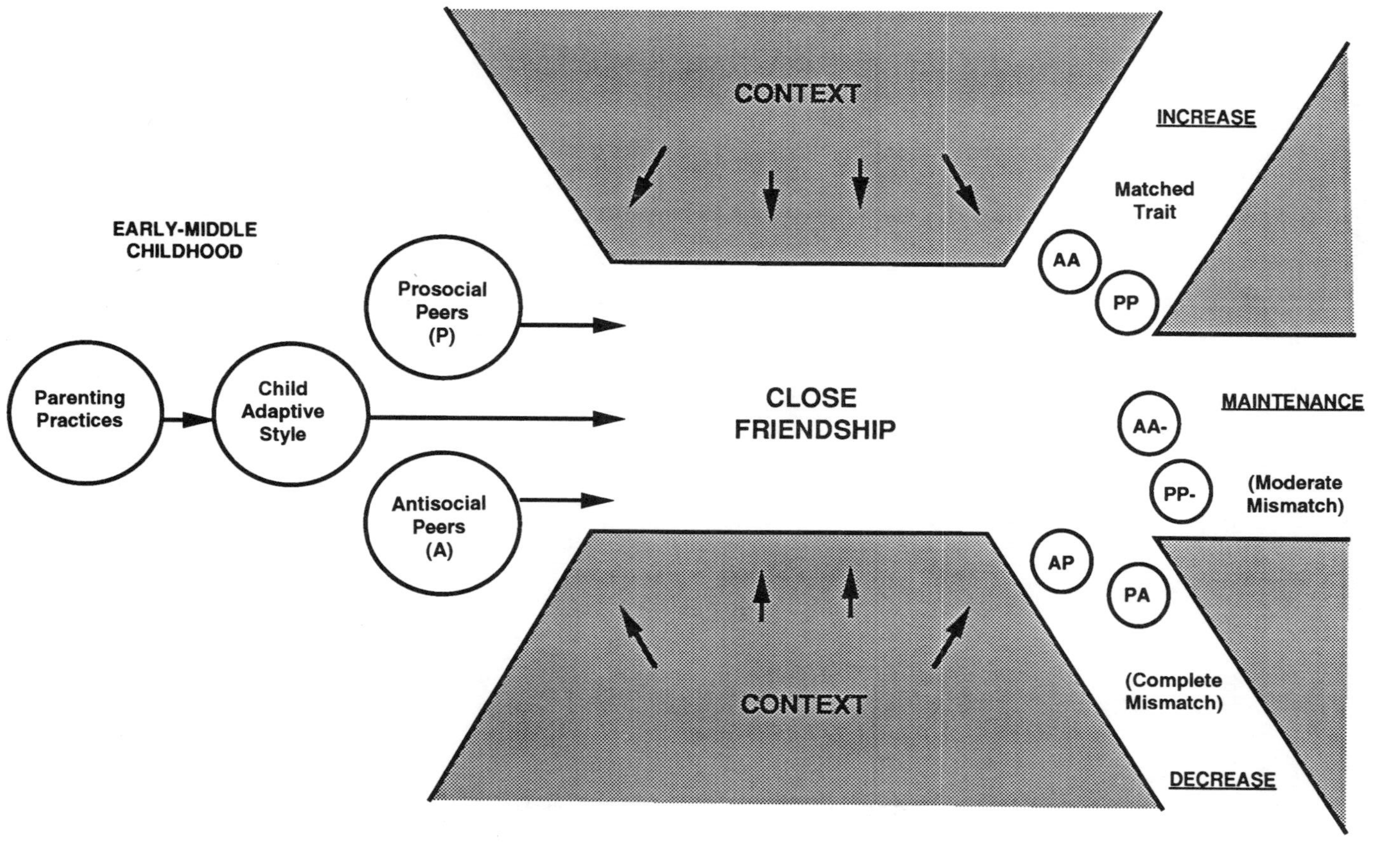

FIGURE 1. The behavioral trait confluence metaphor.

and instrumental aggression when interacting with peers. In their earlier analogue research, it was found that the emergence of peer rejection with unfamiliar peers paralleled the expression of the child's behavior in the group (Coie & Kupersmidt, 1983; Dodge, 1983).

Virtually every study on the social behavior of rejected children supports a strong link between antisocial behavior and rejection by the conventional peer group in school settings. Coie and Koeppl (1990) later concluded that intervention studies attempting to prevent or reduce peer rejection have neglected to include interventions aimed at reducing antisocial behavior as a means to that end.

Peer Selection

It is a myth that the peer rejected child has no friends. Parker and Asher (1989, April) reported that 54% of the low-accepted children had reciprocating best friends *within their classroom,* and these friends were of similar sociometric status to their own. In many respects the quality of the relationships among low-accepted children were similar to those of popular children, except there was a tendency for low-accepted children to report less effectiveness in conflict resolution, show less intimate exchange, less loyalty, and little helping/sharing. Unfortunately this study did not distinguish between Neglected and Rejected children.

In a study of peer companionship, Kupersmidt, Griesler, and Patterson (1990) reported findings similar to the Parker and Asher (1989) investigation. Though rejected children had smaller peer networks, as compared to sociometrically popular, average, and controversial children, 40% of these rejected children had at least one reciprocating companion. Also, in this study, aggressive children reported having as many school and neighborhood companions as their nonaggressive peers.

The most striking findings related to the social stature of aggressive and rejected children are reported by Cairns, Cairns, Neckerman, Ferguson, and Gariepy (1989). Like most studies, Cairns et al. found that aggressive children were more likely to be rejected than other children. An interview measure of the classroom social networks revealed, however, that aggressive children were as likely as anyone to be a member of the main social clusters. Moreover, there was a tendency for aggressive children to prefer other aggressive children as friends. Ladd (1983) examined the playground social networks of low-status children and found they interacted more often with other low-status children or with children who were younger. Moreover, in a study of children's neighborhood friendships, Kurdek and Lillie (1985) found that rejected children were not socially isolated and had as many playmates as sociometrically average children.

Dishion (1987) examined the nominations of the OYS boys specific to their sociometric status using a Peery (1979) classification system. It was found that there was a statistically reliable tendency for rejected children to nominate other rejected children as friends, despite the massive bias toward nominating popular children as friends by all sociometric groups. Longitudinal analyses of the same OYS boys, from age 10 to 12, revealed a link between peer rejection at age 10 and involvement with antisocial peers by age 12 (Dishion, Patterson, Stoolmiller, & Skinner, 1991). Within a multivariate analysis of poor peer relations, academic skill deficits and low parent monitoring combined to account for subsequent child involvement with antisocial peers. Among all the predictors, however, the boy's antisocial behavior and involvement with antisocial peers at age 10 were the best predictors of membership in a deviant peer group by age 12.

Patterson, Littman, and Bricker (1967) suggested the "shopping" metaphor to describe the process leading to the formation of deviant peer groups. In the course of their daily lives, individuals shop while interacting with others and develop relationships with people who provide rich levels of reinforcement. It is a given that rejection by peers goes along with receiving low rates of social reinforcement from peers as well as relatively high rates of punishment from peers (Hartup, Glazer, & Charlesworth, 1967). At times, the process may be purposeful and planned as implied by the shopping metaphor. The majority of the time, however, we think of this as a gradual, almost haphazard search process, often entirely unintentional, until, unexpectedly, one experiences the pleasant sensation of "hitting it off." Research on the development of friendships reveals that one of the best predictors of children successfully "hitting it off" is by establishing a common-ground activity (Gottman, 1983). Children with similar demographic characteristics, behavior, history, and verbal rules are most likely to be successful in "hitting it off" with another peer. Causal observation of interactions at parties revealed the most animated (reinforcing) discussions going on among individuals with some common-ground experiences to discuss.

Kandel (1978, 1986) and Cohen (1977) discussed the process as *homophily,* a term which refers to the tendency for people to be attracted to others similar to themselves. Since there are so many dimensions upon which common ground can be established, it is hypothesized that success in hitting it off is only problematic, where similar individuals are more likely than not to become friends. For the antisocial children, we hypothesize that the common ground that forms the foundation of their relationship is rule-breaking. To assess the role of misbehavior in the relationship of antisocial children, one must consider how such behavior plays out in the moment by moment interchanges within such friendships.

Friendship Interaction

It is hypothesized that shopping does not stop once the friendship is established. As the relationship progresses, there is a gradual merging of social characteristics of the individuals within a dyad (Figure 2). The individual, gradually and over time, repeats behaviors that were reinforced by the partner and decreases behaviors that are punished or ignored. It is hypothesized that this process does not necessarily entail the direct shaping of behavior within interpersonal contingencies but, rather is described as rule-governed (Hayes & Hayes, 1989; Skinner, 1989). The reaction of the listener to description of past or future antisocial behavior results in rich information regarding what behaviors might lead to the friend's approval or disapproval. It is the relative rate of reinforcement that determines the gradual shift in each member's behavior within the relationship. Because of the reinforcing properties of friendships within adolescence, parents are often surprised by how different their teenagers are when they are with their friends. Many values, of course, are established within such friendships. When the values are antisocial, we refer to the above process as deviancy training. We think this process explains Kandel's (1986) and Cohen's (1977) finding that

FIGURE 2. Confluence of individual characteristics into dyadic traits.

individuals within adolescent cliques tend to get more similar over the course of a school year, or they break up.

The coercion model suggests that antisocial children would have more difficulty in friendship, due primarily to their use of abrasive interactions learned within the family. As Buss (1987) points out, established relationships elicit manipulation and control practices by the members. The interactional tactics used may vary in respect to skillfulness.

A study by Bierman and McCauley (1987) found that rejected children described their friends as containing both positive and negative characteristics. Although rejected children reported a larger proportion of negative social exchanges in their interactions with peers, they also reported as much positive interaction and as many friends as their more socially accepted peers. Rejected children reported more hostile behavior from the peer group, viewed themselves as having more aggressive interchanges with peers, but also reported having mixed friends and being participants with peers in different activities.

Observational research on antisocial children's peer interactions paints a similar picture, showing few differences in positive behavior and consistent differences in negative behavior. Raush (1965), for example, found that "hyperaggressive" children were most different from normal children with respect to their levels of aggressive behavior. Walker, Shinn, O'Neill, and Ramsey (1987) found the differences in positive peer playground behavior between antisocial and normal OYS boys to be negligible. In contrast, antisocial boys showed almost twice the level of negative play behavior.

Less research has examined how antisocial children interact with their close friends. In looking at interactions within adolescent friendships, Panella and Hengeler (1986) found no *observed* differences in the friendship processes between conduct disordered boys, anxious-withdrawn boys, and well-adjusted boys. Minor differences were obtained, however, on coders' global impressions of social competence. Dishion, Andrews, and Crosby (in press) looked at the interactions of the OYS boys in problem-solving discussions with their best friends. There was a correlation between the boy's use of directives and their level of antisocial behavior. As one might expect, the use of directives was negatively correlated with the boy's low relationship satisfaction as well as the probability that the friendship would break up within a year.

Summary

In general, it appears that the coercive behavior of the child undermines their acceptance in the conventional peer group. Many antisocial children have close friends, however, and a combination of factors seems to lead to their selection of other antisocial children, including similarity in behavior, rejection by the peer group, academic skill deficits, and poor parental monitoring. Antisocial talk may be the common ground that elicits positive reinforcement within those relationships and these successful friendships result in increased similarity over time. Findings suggest that successful adaptations within the deviant peer group will result in continuation or increase in the child's antisocial behavior.

We will compare the profiles of OYS antisocial boys with the normal boys in respect to their observed interactions with peers on the playground at age 10, interactions with their best friend at age 14, and their general peer relations at these two time periods. We then break the sample into groups based on their antisocial behavior at ages 10, 12, and 14.

Specifically we hypothesize:

1. *Coercion hypothesis:* For interactions on the playground as well as with a friend, negative interpersonal exchanges with peers will differentiate antisocial boys from normal boys, but the rates of positive exchanges will be roughly equivalent.
2. *Deviancy training hypothesis:* Friendship dyads of antisocial boys display higher rates of antisocial and substance use talk than normal dyads, even in videotaped problem-solving tasks. Furthermore, deviancy training will be correlated with the course of antisocial behavior over time.
3. *Parallel continuity hypothesis:* It is expected that the antisocial trajectories of boys from middle childhood to adolescence will be roughly parallel to the above defined negative peer experiences, supporting the hypothesis that children's antisocial patterns are embedded and maintained within pathogenic peer environments.

METHODS

Sample

The present study includes a community sample of 206 at-risk boys aged 13 to 14 who form two cohorts in the Oregon Youth Study that is researching the development of antisocial behavior in males (Patterson, 1986). Using the Hollingshead (1975) Index of Socioeconomic Status, more than 50% of the boys' families were of working class or below when the boys were 10, with approximately 25% middle class and 20% unemployed (Capaldi & Patterson, 1989).

At ages 10, 12, and 14, the boys and their families completed an intensive assessment which focused on family management practices, peer relations, and antisocial behavior. Assessments of peer adjustment were most intensive at ages 10 and 14; and only those measures were included in this study. The assessment battery consisted of multiple respondents (e.g., parents', teachers', and boys' self-report) as well as multiple methods (observations, interviews, and daily telephone reports). At age 14, the boys were asked to bring a friend with whom they spent the most time (combining the parents' report with the study boys' report) to the research center. Two hundred and two of the original 206 boys completed the assessments at age 14 (98% retention rate). Of the 202 boys, 184 were able to identify a friend for the peer interaction task or agreed to participate in this assessment (89% retention rate).

Subsample Selection

Two subsamples of 40 boys each were observed on the playground and also completed the assessment described above. Of the 80 boys, 40 were selected as antisocial at age 9 to 10 and 40 were selected as normal. The specifics of the selection procedures are reported in detail by Walker et al. (1987). The 40 antisocial boys were at the most extreme on the antisocial construct score, which consisted of parent, teacher, and child report of antisocial behavior at age 9 to 10. After selecting the 40 most extreme in antisocial behavior from the two cohorts of 206 boys, 40 additional boys were randomly selected to define a subsample of nonantisocial boys.

Construct Development

Constructs representing a multiagent/multisetting measurement technique were created by a standard procedure of the OYS. A theoretical approach using a priori construct indicators which are empirically refined with item, correlational, and principal components analyses was employed to create the antisocial, peer acceptance, and peer antisocial behavior constructs. This approach is described in detail by Capaldi and Patterson (1989). In this approach, the following steps and criteria were implemented.

1. Indicator scales were assessed for internal consistency. Scales

with Chronbach alphas above .60, and items with at least .20 item-total correlations were retained.
2. Indicators correlating reliably ($p < .05$) with at least one other construct indicator were retained.
3. Indicators producing standardized factor loading above .30 in a principal components analysis were retained.

Indicator scales meeting these criteria were standardized into scores and calculated as construct scores represented by the mean of the indicator Z scores. These scores represented the outcome of the construct development process described above. The psychometric properties of each of the scores can be found in Capaldi and Patterson (1993) or in other specified research reports.

Child Antisocial at Ages 10, 12, 14

Parent- and teacher-reports of antisocial items on the Child Behavior Checklist (Achenbach & Edelbrock, 1983) were included as construct indicators. Also included as construct indicators were telephone interviews with the boys in which they were asked about both overt (e.g., argue with adult, scream or yell, swear, disobey parents) and covert (e.g., tell a lie, trouble at school, stealing) behaviors that occurred within 24 hours prior to the telephone interview.

Antisocial Trajectories

The boys were classified into four groups by using the multiagent construct of Child Antisocial Behavior (.5 standard deviations above the mean) assessed at ages 10, 12, and 14:

1. Chronically antisocial, at-risk at ages 10, 12, and 14 ($n = 30$);
2. Late starter, above .5 standard deviations at age 14 but not age 10 ($n = 20$);
3. Desister, above .5 standard deviations at age 10 but not age 14 ($n = 16$); and
4. Never antisocial, below .5 standard deviations at ages 10, 12, and 14 ($n = 117$).[1]

Constructs of peer adjustment used in subsequent analyses are listed below, along with the methods used to define each. All but the peer relations measures relied on multimethod and multiagent constructs as

[1] A small ($n = 23$) subgroup of boys did not fall within any of these groups and therefore were excluded from the analyses.

described above. The details of the scoring and scaling procedures used are detailed in the appendix to this chapter.

1. Sociometric status and social preference (age 10): Peers.
2. Social preference (age 14): Teachers.
3. Peer antisocial behavior (age 10, 14): Parent, teacher, child.
4. Antisocial talk (age 14): Observations and coder impressions.
5. Interpersonal abrasiveness (age 14): Observations and coder impressions.

RESULTS

Coercion Hypothesis

The following set of analyses tested the idea that antisocial boys are distinguishable from normal boys by virtue of their coercive adaptations with their peer group, and later, within their friendships in adolescence. It is believed that a coercive interpersonal style leads to rejection by conventional peers and antisocial boys' subsequent involvement with antisocial peers. The Walker et al. (1987) subsample was used for these analyses. Figure 3 shows the mean Z scores for the boys within each group on construct scores of social preference and antisocial peers at age 10 and 14. These mean Z scores represent relative standing compared to others in the full sample of 206 boys. One can see that chronically antisocial boys continually find themselves disliked by the peer group at large, primarily in the school setting. The friendships that do develop are primarily with other antisocial peers. Over the course of four years (middle childhood through early adolescence), the chronically antisocial boys, as a group, are one-half of a standard deviation below the mean on peer social preferences. The continuity in their difficulty with peers is particularly notable considering the changes in measurement approaches used at the two time points, with peer nominations of social preference defining the construct at age 10 and teacher and parent ratings defining the construct at age 14. Even more pronounced is the difference in profiles for association with antisocial peers, where the antisocial subsample are at least one standard deviation above the mean at both ages 10 and 14, as compared to the normal boys who are at least one-half of a standard deviation below the mean.

A basic tenet of the coercion theory is that children who are trained within the family interaction to use aversive behavior to terminate unpleasant demands made by parents will use this approach with peers.

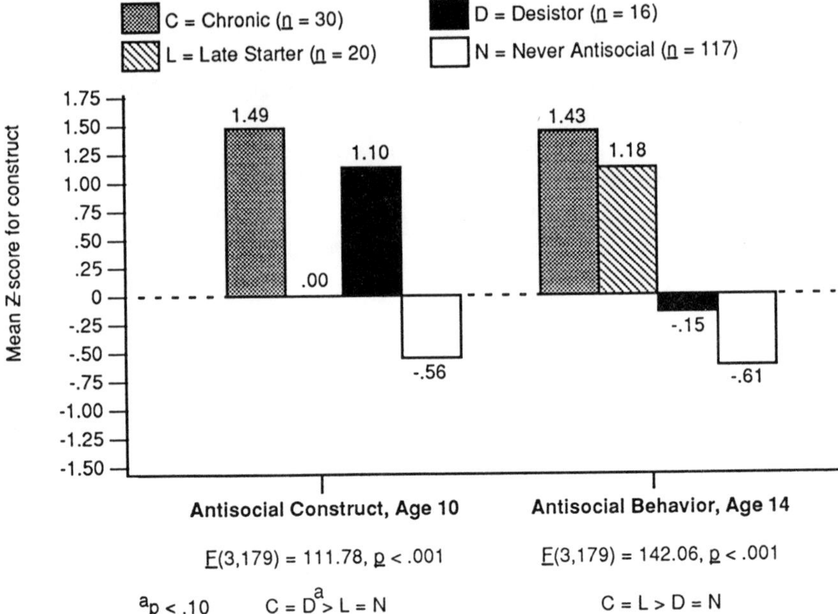

FIGURE 3. Mean Z-Scores from age 10 to 14 on global constructs of boys' peer adjustment.

Walker et al. (1987), based on observations of the OYS subsamples of boys on the playground, reported that antisocial boys at age 10 were not dramatically different than their normal agemates in respect to most activities and positive peer interaction (see Table 1). However, the antisocial boys showed twice the rates of negative behavior on the playground when interacting with peers. It is understandable, therefore, that these boys at age 10 also received twice the rate of negative behavior from peers on the playground compared to the normal boys.

Current analyses of the OYS subsample data also provided information with respect to boys' interpersonal behavior with their close friends at age 14. The quality of the exchanges was evaluated on four observation scores (Directives, Negative Engagement, Converse, and Positive Engagement) as presented in Table 2. One can see that the only difference between the antisocial and normal boys by age 14 is, again, in negative behavior. The antisocial boys showed a higher rate of negative engagement and use more directives than the normal boys. A high rate of directives in a friendship context would be experienced as unpleasant and is indicative of relatively unskilled control tactics. Coder impressions of a boy's social skills and use of obnoxious behavior also discriminates well

TABLE 1. Observations of Boys' Play at Recess at Age 10

Activity	Antisocial	Not antisocial
	(n = 40)	(n = 40)
Free play	33.6	26.1
	(18.9)	(19.2)
Structured activities*	36.6	52.0
	(28.4)	(30.3)
Parallel play	19.8	15.3
	(13.1)	(14.3)
Alone	7.3	5.4
	(6.8)	(9.2)
Interaction Scores		
Total positive	38.4	44.1
by study boy	(13.5)	(17.8)
Total negative*	9.9	4.1
by study boy	(10.7)	(5.2)
Total positive	31.3	33.8
by peers	(12.8)	(15.0)
Total negative*	8.10	3.42
by peers	(8.0)	(3.4)

*$p < .01$.
Adapted from Shinn, Ramsey, Walker, Steiber, & O'Neill, 1987.

TABLE 2. Quality of Observed Interactions with a Close Friend at Age 13–14 for Boys Identified as Antisocial and Normal at Age 9–10

Behavior with friend at age 13–14	Status as antisocial (n = 36)		Age 9–10 normal (n = 37)	
Peer Process Code Rate per Minute				
Positive engagement	2.72	(1.49)	2.54	(1.34)
Negative Engagement*	.53	(.53)	.34	(.33)
Converse	5.56	(1.32)	5.71	(1.31)
Directives*	.27	(.23)	.16	(.16)
Z Score Coder Impressions				
Socially skilled*	−.34	(1.08)	.32	(.99)
Noxious*	.39	(1.19)	−.23	(.94)
Interpersonal Abrasiveness Construct*	.42	(1.28)	−.31	(.80)

*$p < .05$ one-way ANOVA between groups.

between the antisocial and normal boys with their friends as does the Interpersonal Abrasiveness construct. A boy's use of negative behavior within intimate relationships is consistent with the coercion model.

Deviancy Training

It was hypothesized that by adolescence the friendships of the antisocial boys, compared to the normal boys, would be organized around their antisocial talk. That is, antisocial behavior provides the common ground on which the relationship is based. As of this writing, we can only address the level of antisocial talk across the two groups of boys. Later research will focus on the extent to which antisocial talk elicits more reinforcement within friendships of antisocial boys.

As expected, Table 3 establishes that the content of conversation within the friendships of antisocial boys is clearly more deviant than that of normal boys. When counting the number of times the antisocial quali-

TABLE 3. Deviancy Training in Observed Interactions with Close Friends at Age 13–14 for Boys Identified as Antisocial and Normal at Age 9–10

Behavior with friend at age 13–14	Status at age 9–10			
(Peer process code rate per minute)	Antisocial (n = 36)		Normal (n = 37)	
	$\bar{X}$	(SD)	$\bar{X}$	(SD)
Antisocial talk*	1.77	(1.84)	1.04	(.94)
Z Score Coder Impressions				
Substance use talk*	.48	(1.52)	−.24	(.41)
Endorse antisocial talk*	.34	(1.17)	−.28	(.82)
Z score deviancy training construct*	.47	(1.47)	−.28	(.64)
Dyad Duration[a]				
Antisocial talk*	344.	(305.4)	94.1	(115.8)
Normative talk	855.	(285.1)	1165.2	(222.3)
Dyad Probability Reinforce				
Antisocial talk	.40	(.23)	.36	(.29)
Normative talk*	.43	(.29)	.64	(.20)
Relative rate of reinforcement for antisocial talk*	1.80	(2.11)	.67	(.54)

[a] As of this writing only Cohort 2 has been coded with the Topic Code.
*$p < .05$ one-way ANOVA between groups.

fier switch was used in the two different types of dyads, it went on 1.77 times-per-minute when the antisocial boys were talking with their close friends, compared to 1.04 times-per-minute in the normal boys' dyads. The effect is quite clear when looking at the coder impressions of the content of the boys' talk, where the antisocial boys were nearly a half standard deviation above the cohort mean on talk supporting substance use and delinquent behavior. Inspection of the mean Z scores for the Deviancy Training construct indicates that the antisocial boys were much higher compared to their normal agemates. This deviancy training effect is particularly strong when one considers that these groups were formed based on the boy's behavior when they were age 10.

As noted below, there is significant change from age 10 to 14 in the OYS boys' antisocial talk. We now turn to the question of the extent to which these peer adjustment indices parallel the boy's antisocial trajectories from age 10 to 14, grouped as chronic, desister, late starters, and never antisocial.

Parallel Continuity

These analyses focus on the extent the above peer adjustment indices at age 10 and 14 are prognostic of the course of antisocial behavior over the same time span. The boys' social preference and contact with antisocial peers at age 10 were examined relative to the stability of their antisocial behavior (Figure 4). Overall, the difference between the four groups was statistically reliable on the social preference score, with the chronic group reliably lower on social preference at age 10 than the late starter group. Examination of the construct score for antisocial peers shows that the chronic and desister groups were quite high compared to the late starter and never antisocial groups, and the late starter group was practically at the mean for this sample. The omnibus f-test revealed statistically reliable differences between the four groups, and the planned comparison t-test showed that the chronic group was at significantly greater risk for contact with deviant peers at age 10 than the late starters.

To complement these analyses, the boy's sociometric status at age 10 was cross-tabulated with his chronicity status. The scoring protocol described by Coie et al. (1982) was followed for this analysis. The symmetric uncertainty coefficient (.10) showed a statistically reliable relationship between these two nominal classifications ($T = 3.50$, $p < .001$). Eighty percent of the rejected boys were at some time above a half of a standard deviation on the antisocial construct. The opposite trend was observed for the popular boys, where very few of these boys showed

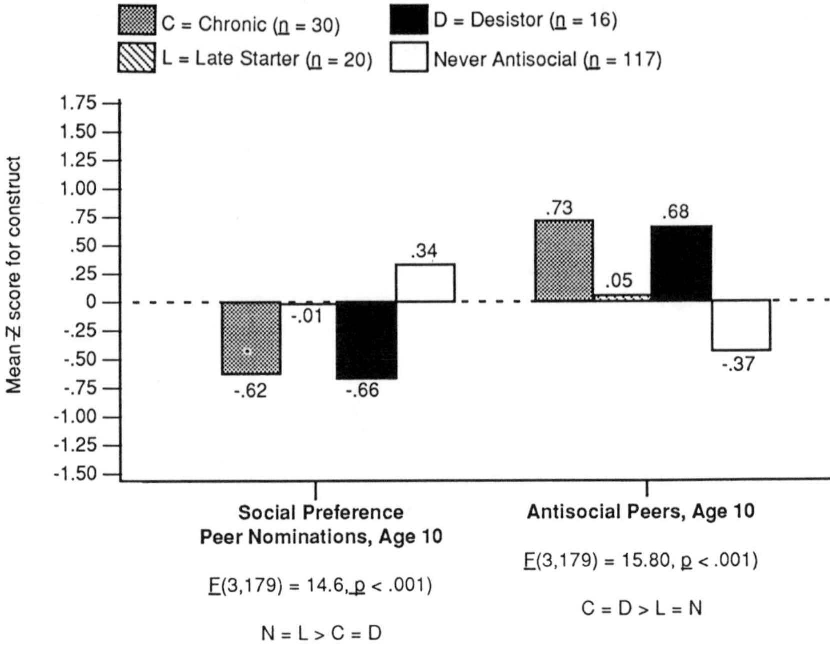

FIGURE 4. Global measures of peer adjustment by age 10 by chronicity status.

any evidence of antisocial behavior between the ages of 10 to 14. Table 4 shows that boys defined as chronic and desisters were roughly equivalent in respect to the percent rejected in fourth grade, with 43% of the desisters and 33% of the chronics rejected.

At age 14, we relied on teacher ratings as an indicator of social preference for the boys in the four groups (see Figure 5). Again, in adolescence, the four groups were statistically different on social preference in the school setting. At age 14, the chronic group appears to have more difficulty in peer relations than the late starters or desisters. Contact with deviant peers was again related to boys' stability of antisocial behavior. At age 14, the chronic group was one standard deviation above the mean on the peer antisocial construct and was at significantly greater risk than the desister group. In contrast, the late starters, who were *not at risk* on deviant peer exposure at age 10, were more than one standard deviation above the mean on the peer antisocial behavior construct at age 13 to 14. The omnibus f-test revealed significant differences between the four groups on contact with deviant peers.

The above analyses referred to the standing of the four groups with

TABLE 4. Stability of Boys' Antisocial Behavior (Age 10–14) and Sociometric Status at Age 10 (.5 standard deviations above the mean on Antisocial Construct)

	Sociometric status at age 10					
	Rejected	Neglected	Average	Controversial	Popular	
Antisocial age 10, 12, 14 (chronics)	10 (33%)	3	12	3	2	30
Antisocial age 14 only (late starters)	3 (15%)	2	14	0	1	20
Antisocial age 10 only (desisters)	7 (44%)	0	6	0	3	16
Never antisocial	5 (04%)	7	79	4	22	117
	25 (13.7%)	12 (6.6%)	111 (60.7%)	7 (3.8%)	28 (15.3%)	183

Symmetric uncertainty coefficient = .10.
$T = 3.50$, $p < .001$

respect to the general peer environment. The analyses that followed were specific to each boy's interactions with a selected friend with whom the boy typically spent most of his time. Figure 6 shows the mean Z scores across the four groups on the deviancy training and interpersonal abrasiveness constructs. The groups were significantly different on both constructs, although the planned comparisons revealed that the chronic group displayed more deviancy training than the desisters, this effect was marginally significant ($p < .10$). Inspection of the mean profiles revealed a tendency for the late starter group to be more engaged in deviancy training and showed greater interpersonal abrasiveness than all other groups, a trend that was not hypothesized or tested within the planned comparisons. The interpersonal abrasiveness of the late starter group was somewhat inconsistent with the results of all other analyses that showed these boys to be reasonably adjusted with peers at age 10 and rated by teachers as having reliably better peer relations than the chronic group at age 14.

To take into account the intercorrelations among the various predictors and to determine the patterns of peer experiences that distinguish the four groups of boys, a discriminant function analysis was computed using the four groups as the dependent variable. The continuous con-

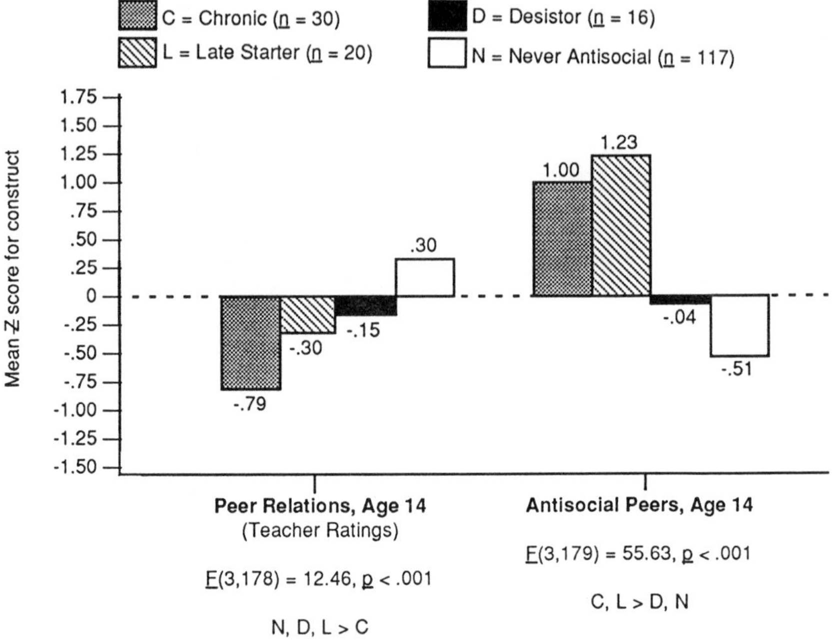

FIGURE 5. Global measures of peer adjustment by age 14 by chronicity status.

structs shown in Figures 3 through 6 were entered into the discriminant function analysis as independent variables. A boy's antisocial behavior at age 10 was also entered to determine the extent to which the boy's initial level of antisocial behavior was associated with continuity over time. In this way, the effect of peers could be assessed when controlling for the severity of antisocial behavior.

The results of this analysis produced two statistically significant discriminant functions which are shown in Table 5. Labels were provided for these functions based on the pattern of correlations observed between each of the independent variables and the discriminant functions.

The first discriminant function was highly significant, yielding a canonical correlation of .83 between the independent and dependent variables. This function was labeled *initial deviance* because contact with antisocial peers and the child's level of antisocial behavior at age 10 were significantly correlated with this function. Also correlated with the first discriminant function is contact with antisocial peers at age 14. At the bottom of Table 5, the group centroids are provided to indicate the

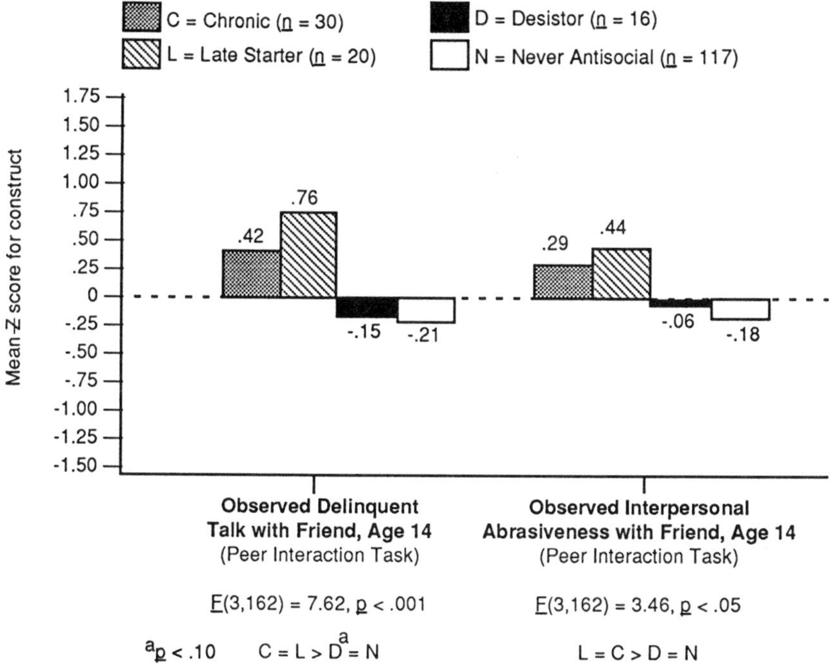

FIGURE 6. Observed behavior with best friend at age 14 by chronicity status.

overall placement of each group in each discriminant function. As can be seen from the group centroids, the chronic group loaded highest on the initial deviance function, followed second by the desister group.

The second discriminant function was labeled as *late starting*. Deviancy training and association with antisocial peers at age 14 correlated positively with this function as did interpersonal abrasiveness with a friend. The late starter group, as expected, loaded highest on this dimension and the desister group the lowest. The second discriminant function produced a statistically significant canonical correlation of .64 which was found between the independent and dependent variable and on the second canonical variate.

A coherent picture emerges by considering this multivariate analysis of the covariation between peers and stability in antisocial behavior. In general, it appears that chronicity in antisocial behavior can be predicted relatively well from the child's level of antisocial behavior and involvement with antisocial peers in middle childhood. Deviant peer associations seemed to be relatively synchronous with antisocial behavior, ebbing and flowing with the child's level of antisocial behavior. The

TABLE 5. Multivariate Profiles Associated with Antisocial Behavior Temporal Patterns

Structure matrix (correlations with discriminant functions)	Function 1 Initial deviance	Function 2 Antisocial peers in adolescent
Age 10		
Antisocial behavior	.91*	.27
Peer social preference	−.33	.16
Antisocial peers	.35*	−.06
Age 14		
Observed abrasiveness	−.13	.19*
Observed antisocial talk	.18	.23*
Antisocial peers	.62	.68*
Peer relations	.29	−.10
Group centroids		
Chronic antisocial (n = 27)	2.72	−.09
Late starter (n = 18)	.68	2.11
Early starting desister (n = 18)	1.61	−1.41
Never antisocial (n = 105)	−1.05	−.14
Summary statistics for discriminant functions		
Canonical correlation	.83	.64
Wilk's lambda	$p < .001$	$p < .001$

late starter group, for example, was the most extreme on the second discriminant function, which primarily described later involvement with a deviant peer group. Of course, even with these longitudinal data, cause and effect are impossible to disentangle.

CONCLUSIONS AND IMPLICATIONS

Friendship and Deviancy

It is paradoxical to claim that friendships contribute to antisocial behavior. This statement is inconsistent with the preconception that antisocial people are essentially unlikable and unskilled people. These analyses suggest, at the very least, that antisocial boys have rich friendship networks that contain many of the positive features of any friendship: compliments, support, laughter, and mutual enjoyment. These data suggest that skill deficits may not be the most constructive frame for understanding the relationships of antisocial people, in comparison to normal people. We agree with Meichenbaum (1979) that you cannot fully understand a process by focusing on what it is not. Research on skill deficits does not yield information regarding the developmental process leading to maladaptive outcomes.

The confluence model is offered as a process explaining the emergence of an individual's dispositions into a dyadic trait. The model is based on the shopping process which leads youths to engage in relationships that maximize interpersonal payoffs. The process is thought to be experiential; we rarely rationally select those with whom we become intimate (i.e., many false positive and negative errors). Although we may "intentionally" target individuals for intimacy, the relationship is not established until it "feels right." Conversely, there are many with whom we become friends (or marry) that we never purposely targeted. Children and adults "hit it off" when they establish common-ground activities or discussions. Based on these pleasant interpersonal events, we continue and repeat behavior that promotes the relationship. The two individuals meld over time, depending on the exclusivity of the relationship (i.e., network density) and the relative ease with which the common-ground activities are pursued by both participants. It is predicted that individuals sharing common interests, history, and interpersonal patterns (similar or complimentary) have the highest potential for establishing friendships in which the boys become more similar over time in some respects. Antisocial children, therefore, will most likely become friends with others who are also antisocial, and their adaptations are associated with developing an antisocial life-style (West & Farrington, 1977).

The empirical documentation of the unique impact of friendships on socialization remains elusive. We suggest that three hurdles were climbed by the research reported in this chapter. First, research has extended the coercion model (Patterson, 1982) to show that antisocial boys use twice the level of aversive behavior with peers in school at age 10 and with their close friends at age 14. As expected, these boys experienced rejection by conventional peers from middle childhood through adolescence.

Second, this research has shown that involvement with antisocial friends begins early, is well underway by age 10, and shows parallel continuity with antisocial behavior on into adolescence. This essentially means that the course of the boys' antisocial behavior was parallel to their involvement with deviant peers.

Third, this research has identified that the "shopping" process within friendships could be readily identified by observing boys at age

14 with their best friends. Boys with a history of antisocial behavior were in relationships that engaged in relatively high levels of deviant talk, including substance use and antisocial activities, even under videotaped conditions. More research is needed to test the hypothesis that differential positive reactions to deviant talk in some relationships account for the rule-governed characteristics of chronic antisocial behavior (Wolfgang, Figlio, & Sellin, 1972).

It would be a mistake to overemphasize the role of peers in the development of antisocial behavior and not include parenting practices in this development. As well established by previous studies, it is the parent's repetition of predominantly inconsistent, harsh, and ineffective discipline practices that provides a training ground for the child's development of the coercion adaptation. It is coercive behavior that underlies failure with peers that ultimately leads to the boy's embeddedness within a deviant peer group. It is the major tenet of the coercion model that the coercive interpersonal style is developed primarily within the family (Patterson et al., 1992).

Parents are also key players in monitoring and establishing children's friendships. We cite research that demonstrates the high correlation between poor parent monitoring and a boy's involvement with deviant peers. Parents are critical as managers of the their children's relationships (MacDonald & Parke, 1984; Parke & Bhavgari, 1988). Directly, parents involve their children in activities that develop friendships, select neighborhoods and communities, and develop relationships with other adults who have children of similar ages with whom their children become friends. Parents may directly coach their children in dealing with peer relationship problems. In fact, videotaped materials have been developed to assist parents in identifying peer relationship problems and model constructive approaches to coach their children through these difficulties (Dishion & Kavanagh, 1991). Parents, after all, are the only adults in a child's life who have information regarding their children's adaptation among peers across all relevant settings. It is assumed that parents remain critical to the development and progression of antisocial behavior through late adolescence or when the child moves from his or her family of origin.

Applied Implications

One hopes that developmental models of antisocial behavior would have some utility for prevention and intervention. The family-based model is corroborated by the fact that the most promising intervention approach for children with conduct problems appears to be parent training (Kazdin, 1987; Patterson, Dishion, & Chamberlain, in press).

Interventions aimed at remediating the social skill deficits of antisocial children have been primarily disappointing (Kazdin, 1987). From the data reported in this chapter, one would think that antisocial children's social behavior may well fit within the interpersonal niche of their friendship cliques. Although "deficits" may be identified, the child is not likely to be experiencing relational problems. It seems, from the Kazdin review, that the most promising peer-focused intervention is simply to increase the at-risk child's positive exchanges with a wider range of peers, particularly prosocial peers. The major problem appears to be reducing the negative behavior of antisocial children with their peers and promoting reinforcement, within peer groups, for prosocial behavior. In the elementary school years, classwide interventions, such as the Good Behavior Game (e.g., Barrish, Saunders, & Wolf, 1969; Dolan et al., in press; Medland & Stachnik, 1972) that decrease negative behaviors, are important. Cooperative learning strategies (Johnson & Johnson, 1986) for teaching in schools have been shown to result in positive gains in skill acquisition for all learners as well as improvements in social acceptance for at-risk children. Strategies such as these can be applied to school environments by school professionals to engineer the peer environments that do not actively support behavior harmful to others.

It is recommended, therefore, that peer-focused interventions consider the networking of children with their peers as a clinical target. Such an approach demands stepping out of the clinical setting and working within the environmental context of children in settings such as the school or neighborhood. This concern is more consonant with a prevention focus rather than a treatment focus, as such efforts become unwieldy when taken for individual, troubled children.

We also recognize that factors not considered in the present research may be particularly promising to such an effort. For example, the parent's monitoring of the child's time with peers and peer networks may prevent the child from becoming overly committed to a deviant peer group (Dishion et al., 1991; Snyder, Dishion, & Patterson, 1986). Characteristics of the neighborhood and the school may also influence the child's exposure to a deviant peer group. Rutter (1978) found the school to be a strong effect in the incidence of conduct disorders. We find variability among schools in the density of the boy's antisocial peers in this study. For example, in the first cohort, there was a range between .50 standard deviations above-the-mean to −.50 below-the-mean in the aggregated antisocial peer construct for each of the seven schools. In this sense, some neighborhoods and corresponding school settings place an enormous demand on the monitoring practices of parents and the management practices of teachers and adult school personnel who attempt to minimize the mutual reinforcement of problem behavior among at-risk children. At this point, creativity, innovation, resources, and an understanding of the existing strengths within high-risk settings are needed to design intervention packages that buttress adults' efforts to have a healthy impact on children's social development.

APPENDIX: SCORING AND SCALING PROCEDURES

Sociometric Status (Age 10)

The scoring approach described by Coie et al. (1982) was used to ascertain the continuous measures of social impact, social preference, as well as the categorical measure of sociometric status. To remain consistent with this approach, only the following two nomination items were used, "kids you like as friends" and "kids you don't want to be friends with." These two items were standardized by classroom. The social preference score consisted of a difference score on "liked as friends" and "don't want to be friends with" standardized items. The social impact score represents the sum of nominations on both these items which reflected the extent to which each boy was both liked and disliked. The following five sociometric groups were formulated by using the scoring criteria described by Coie et al. (1982): (1) rejected (high social impact and low social preference); (2) controversial (high social impact, ambivalent social preference); (3) neglected (low social impact and low social preference); (4) popular (high social impact and high social preference); and (5) average (all other boys). The average classification is consistent with research by Coie and Dodge (1988), in which children formerly defined as having "undetermined" sociometric status are combined with the average group. Using this algorithm, there were 30 rejected boys, 14 controversial boys, 11 neglected boys, 27 popular boys, and 124 average boys across the two cohorts.

Social Preference at Age 14

Since conventional measures of the boys' sociometric status were unavailable at age 13 to 14, a composite score was formulated based on teacher-, parent-, and child-report indices. Teacher report consisted of items ("doesn't get along with other pupils, gets teased, not liked") from the Teacher version of the Child Behavior Checklist (CBC) (Achenback & Edelbrock, 1986) and the Walker-McConnell Peer Interaction scale (Walker & McConnell, 1988). The parent-report indicator aggregated items similar to the teacher items. Walker-McConnell Peer Interaction scale adapted for parents, and items from the peer relations questionnaire ("feels kids don't like him, other kids pick on him"). The child's report consists of items describing peer support (e.g., "friends sense when I am upset, friends encourage me to talk about difficulties, I tell my friends about my problems, friends ask when I'm bothered"), and the child's general perception of peers in the neighborhood and school are rated on a series of bipolar adjectives (fair/unfair, nice/mean, warm/cold, friendly/unfriendly, good/bad, kind/cruel, honest/dishonest).

Peer Antisocial Behavior at Age 10

This construct at age 10 consisted of the parent, teacher, and child report on peer antisocial behavior. The Child Interview Indicator included the following items concerning how many of his friends had:

1. Cheated on school tests.
2. Ruined or damaged other people's things on purpose.
3. Stolen something worth less than five dollars.
4. Hit or threatened to hit someone without a reason.
5. Broken into someplace like a car or building to steal something.
6. Stolen something worth more than $50.
7. Made suggestions of illegal activity.

The items for each scale were standardized and averaged to yield a peer delinquency and peer drug use indicator. These two indicators were then standardized and averaged to yield an overall child-report indicator of deviant peers.

The parent report consisted of an item from the Child Behavior Checklist (Achenback & Edelbrock, 1981), that asks how often the child "hangs out with others who get into trouble," and a similar item from a parent-report questionnaire developed by the research staff which asks how often the child "hangs out with children who steal."

The Child Behavior Checklist completed by teachers included an item on how often the child "hangs out with children who get into trouble," which served as the third indicator for this construct.

Peer Antisocial Behavior at Age 14

A similar measurement strategy was used for assessing this construct at age 14, although an effort was made to expand the assessment of peer antisocial behavior at this age. The expanded list of items consisting of the boys' reports of antisocial peer activity are the following:

My friends

1. Get into many fights.
2. Don't like schoolwork.
3. Get into trouble a lot.
4. Don't get along with adults.
5. Are kids who get into trouble and are daring.

Items added to the one-item from the age 10 construct ("Hangs around with others who get into trouble") from the Teacher CBC at age 14 included:

1. How often does this student associate with kids who misbehave at school?
2. Does the student associate with kids who steal or vandalize?
3. Does the student associate with kids who get into fights?

Three items comprised the parent-report indicator of Peer Antisocial Behavior including, "Hangs around with others who get into trouble (parent CBC)"; "Does he hang out with kids who steal?"; and "Has he been with a friend or group of friends who were setting fires?" These three items were considered insufficient to test for internal consistency.

Peer Interaction Task

When the OYS boys were 13 to 14 years old, they were asked to bring a close friend to Oregon Social Learning Center (OSLC) to videotape a peer problem-solving task. The Peer Interaction Task (PIT) was designed to elicit a wide range of interactive behaviors between the participating boys and their friends. The task was based on the work of Panella and Henggeler (1966), combined with a format for assessing family problem-solving used by Forgatch, Fetrow, and Lathrop (1985). During the family interview, the boys were asked to nominate "a child with whom you spend the most amount of time" to participate with them in the study. The boys' parents were also asked to give the name of a peer with whom their child spent most of his time. Parent nominations and child nominations were compared, and peers were selected to participate if they were nominated by the study child and confirmed by his parent(s).

The selected dyads came to the research center and participated in the PIT. The boys were videotaped during a 25-minute session in which they were asked to:

1. Plan an activity together (something they could potentially do together within the next week).
2. Solve a problem that occurred between the subject child and his parents within the last month.
3. Solve a problem that occurred between another peer and the subject child within the last month.
4. Solve a problem that occurred between the participating peer and his parents within the last month.
5. Solve a problem that occurred between the participating peer and another peer within the last month.

Each portion of the observation session lasted approximately 5 minutes.

The resulting videotaped interactions were coded by a set of observers (unaware of the adjustment status of the boys) using the Peer Process Code (PPC) (Dishion et al., 1989). The PPC is a microsocial coding system which records peer interaction in real time, capturing the interpersonal content and affective valence of the discussion. The PPC was also designed to assess the antisocial nature of the boys' discussion by using an "antisocial qualifier" switch. The qualifier switch was turned on when either boy in the PIT suggested or described illegal behavior, and turned off following five seconds of discussion that did not involve illegal behavior.

The coders also completed global impression ratings of the interactions following the work of Weinrott, Reid, Bauske, and Brummett (1981).

Interobserver reliability on the PPC is established through the constant monitoring of coders. Coders were considered reliable based on minimum percent agreement, scores above .75, and consistent kappas over .56%. Ten percent (18) of the videotaped, friend dyadic interactions were randomly selected to be coded independently by two observers. Reliability between the two observers was determined by comparing the moment-by-moment entries using a six-second "window of agreement." For each reliability session, one observer was randomly selected, post hoc, as the calibrator and the other, the reliability coder. For agreement to be recorded, the reliability coder must have made the same code entry as the calibrator with a six-second window of error. Using this approach, we found 86.4% agreement on the content of the code (basic code category) and 73.4% on the affective valence and a overall weighted Kappa (Cohen, 1960) of .69 on the combined content and valence of each entry. The percent of agreement on the antisocial qualifier switch was 94.1%, with a Kappa of .56.

All codes with the Peer Process Code were collapsed into four a priori clusters: positive engagement, negative engagement, directives, and converse. Two construct scores (delinquent talk and interpersonal abrasiveness) were developed from the PIT by combining direct observation scores with coder global impressions. Rate-per-minute scores were used as indicators of the boy's observed behavior during the PIT, reflecting the number of times the boys were observed engaging in the targeted behavior every minute during the 25-minute videotaped session.

Delinquent Talk at Age 14

This score reflects the frequency with which the target child discussed or suggested antisocial or illegal activity with his friend in the PIT (Dishion, Andrews, & Crosby, in press). Because the behavior of the study boy and his friend was so highly intercorrelated, a dyad score was created. Three indicators were combined to form this score. The coding system used for these videotaped interactions provided a qualifier switch (i.e., antisocial talk) for whenever the child discussed or suggested antisocial activity. On an impression inventory, the coders were asked to rate the extent to which the study boy and his friend discussed or suggested a variety of delinquent activities or substance use. Coder impressions of the boys' endorsement of delinquent and substance use activity comprised separate indicators for the Delinquent Talk construct. The relation between each of the indicators on this construct and the boy's antisocial behavior was individually considered as well.

Interpersonal Skill at Age 14

This score was also formulated by combining coder impressions and observed behavior (Dishion, Andrews, & Patterson, in press). Coder impressions were used to assess the social skillfulness and competence of the boys and obnoxious and irritating behavior displayed during the task. Direct observation measures consisted of: (1) the rate-per-minute of directives of the study child to his friend; (2) the rate-per-minute of negative engagement (e.g., verbal attacks, hits) to his friend; and (3) the rate-per-minute of converse in neutral affective valence, representing calm conversation. The construct was scored so that high scores reflected positive social skills. Therefore, the coder impressions of obnoxious behavior, the boys' use of directives and social aggression, were weighted negatively to create the Interpersonal Abrasiveness construct.

Acknowledgments

Preparation of this chapter was supported by grants to Dr. Gerald R. Patterson (MH 37940, Center for Studies of Antisocial and Violent Behavior, NIMH, U.S. PHS.) and Dr. Thomas J. Dishion (DA07031, National Institute of Drug Abuse, U.S. PHS.). The following colleagues read a previous draft of this chapter and provided useful feedback: R. Huesmann, D. Capaldi, B. Fagot, M. Stoolmiller, and D. Andrews. In addition, Carol Kimball is appreciated for her assistance in manuscript preparation. This research would not have been possible but for the consistent support and cooperation of the local school districts as coordinated through Mr. Robert Lady, Dr. Robert Hammond, and Dr. Charles Stevens.

REFERENCES

Achenbach, T. M., & Edelbrock, C. (1981). Behavioral problems and competencies reported by parents of normal and disturbed children aged four through sixteen. *Monographs of the Society for Research in Child Development, 46,* (Serial No. 188).

Achenback, T. M., & Edelbrock, C. (1983). *Manual for the child behavior checklist and revised child behavior profile.* Burlington, VT: University of Vermont Press.

Achenbach, T. M., & Edelbrock, C. S. (1986). *Manual for the teacher's report form and teacher version of the child behavior profile.* Burlington, VT: University of Vermont.

Asher, S. R., & Wheeler, V. A. (1985). Children's loneliness: A comparison of rejected and neglected peer status. *Journal of Consulting and Clinical Psychology, 53,* 500–505.

Barrish, H. H., Saunders, M., & Wolff, M. M. (1969). Good behavior game: Effects of individual contingencies for group consequences on disruptive behavior in a classroom. *Journal of Applied Behavior Analysis, 2,* 119–124.

Bierman, K. L., & McCauley, E. (1987). Children's descriptions of their peer interactions: Useful information for clinical and child assessment. *Journal of Consulting and Clinical Psychology, 16,* 9–18.

Buss, D. M. (1987). Selection, evocation, and manipulation. *Journal of Personality and Social Psychology, 53,* 1214–1221.

Cairns, R. B. (1979). *Social development: The origins and plasticity of interchanges.* San Francisco: W. H. Freeman.

Cairns, R. B., Cairns, B. D., Neckerman, H. J., Ferguson, L. L., & Gariepy, J. L. (1989). Growth and aggression: I. Childhood to early adolescence. *Developmental Psychology, 25,* 320–330.

Capaldi, D. M., & Patterson, G. R. (1987). An approach to the problem of recruitment and retention rates for longitudinal research. *Behavioral Assessment, 9,* 169–177.

Capaldi, D. M., Patterson, G. R. (1989). *Psychometric properties of fourteen latent constructs from the Oregon youth study.* New York: Springer-Verlag.

Capaldi, D. M., & Patterson, G. R. (1991). The relation of parental transitions to boys' adjustment problems: I. A test of a linear hypothesis, and II. Mothers at-risk for transitions and unskilled parenting. *Developmental Psychology, 27,* 489–504.

Capaldi, D. M., & Patterson, G. R. (1993). *Is violence a selective trajectory or part of deviant life style?* Oregon Social Learning Center, Eugene, OR. Manuscript in preparation.

Cohen, J. A. (1960). A coefficient of agreement for nominal scales. *Educational and Psychological Measurement, 20,* 37–46.

Cohen, J. M. (1977). Sources of peer group homogeneity, *Sociology of Education, 50,* 227–241.

Coie, J. D., & Dodge, K. (1988). Multiple sources of data on social behavior and social status in the school: A cross-age comparison, *Child Development, 59,* 815–829.

Coie, J. D., Dodge, K. A., & Coppotelli, H. (1982). Dimensions and types of social status: A cross-age perspective. *Developmental Psychology, 18,* 557–570.

Coie, J. D., Dodge, K. A., Terry, R., & Wright, V. (1991). The role of aggression in peer relations: An analysis of aggression in boys' playgroups. *Child Development, 62,* 812–826.

Coie, J. D., Koeppl, G. K. (1990). Adapting intervention to the problems of aggressive and disruptive rejected children. In S. R. Asher & J. D. Coie (Eds.), *Peer rejection in childhood* (pp. 309–338). New York: Cambridge University Press.

Coie, J. D., & Kupersmidt, J. B. (1983). A behavioral analysis of emerging social status in boys groups. *Child Development, 54,* 1400–1416.

Dishion, T. J. (1987, June). *A developmental model for peer relations: Middle childhood correlates and one-year sequelae.* Unpublished doctoral dissertation. Eugene, OR: University of Oregon.

Dishion, T. J. (1990). Peer context of child and adolescent troublesome behavior. In P. Leone (Ed.), *Understanding troubled and troublesome youth* (pp. 128–154). Beverly Hills, CA: Sage Publications.

Dishion, T. J., Andrews, D. W., & Crosby, L. (in press). Adolescent boys and their friends in early adolescence: I. Relationship characteristics, quality, and interactional process. *Child Development.*

Dishion, T. J., Andrews, D., & Patterson, G. R. (in preparation). *The microsocial friendship interactions of adolescent boys and their relation to problem behavior.*

Dishion, T. J., Crosby, L., Rusby, J. C., Shane, D., Patterson, G. R., & Baker, J. (1989). *Peer process code: multidimensional system for observing adolescent peer interaction.* Unpublished training manual. Eugene, OR: Oregon Social Learning Center.

Dishion, T. J., & Kavanagh, K. (1991, November). *Secondary prevention with at-risk middle school youth: A social interactional approach.* Workshop presented at the Association for Advancement of Behavior Therapy, New York, NY.

Dishion, J. R., Loeber, R., Stouthamer-Loeber, M., & Patterson, G. R. (1984). Skill deficits and male adolescent delinquency. *Journal of Abnormal Child Psychology, 12,* 37–54.

Dishion, T. J., & Patterson, G. R. (in press). Early screening for early adolescent problem behavior: A multiple gating strategy. In M. Singer & L. Singer (Eds.), *Handbook for screening adolescents at psychosocial risk* (pp. 375–399). Lexington MA: Lexington Books.

Dishion, T. J., Patterson, G. R., Stoolmiller, M., & Skinner, M. L. (1991). Family, school, and behavioral antecedents to early adolescent involvement with antisocial peers. *Developmental Psychology, 27,* 172–180.

Dishion, T. J., Reid, J. B., & Patterson, G. R. (1988). Empirical guidelines for a family intervention for adolescent drug use. In R. H. Coombs (Ed.), *The family context of adolescent drug use* (pp. 181–216). Binghamton, NY: Haworth.

Dodge, K. A. (1983). Behavioral antecedents: A peer social status. *Child Development, 54,* 1386–1399.

Dolan, L. J., Kellam, S. G., Brown, C. H., Werthamer-Larsson, L., Rebok, G. W., Mayer, L. S., Turkkan, J. S., & Laudoff, J. (in press). An early classroom-based preventive intervention aimed at aggressive and shy behaviors: Impact at the end of first grade. *American Journal of Community Psychology.*

Elliott, D. S., Huizinga, D., & Ageton, S. S. (1985). *Explaining Delinquency and Drug Use.* Beverly Hills, CA: Sage Publications.

Farrington, D. P., & West, D. J. (1971). A comparison between early delinquents and young aggressives. *British Journal of Criminology, II,* 341–358.

Forgatch, M. S., Fetrow, B., & Lathrop, M. (1985). *Solving problems in family interaction.* Unpublished training manual. Eugene, OR: Oregon Social Learning Center.

Freedman, B. J., Rosenthal, L., Donahue, L. P. Jr., Schlundt, D. G., & McFall, R. M. (1978). A social-behavioral analysis of skill deficits in delinquent and nondelinquent adolescent boys. *Journal of Consulting and Clinical Psychology, 46,* 1448–1462.

Gold, M. (1970). *Delinquent behavior in an American city.* Belmont, CA: Brooks/Cole.

Gottman, J. M. (1983). How children become friends. *Society for Research in Child Development, 48,* (Monograph Series No. 201).

Hartup, W. W. (1990). Peer relations in early and middle childhood. IN V. B. Van Hasselt & M. Hersen (Eds.), *Handbook of social development: A lifespan perspective.* New York: Plenum.

Hartup, W. W., Glazer, J. A., & Charlesworth, R. (1967). Peer reinforcement and sociometric status. *Child Development, 38,* 1017–1024.

Hayes, S. C., & Hayes, L. J. (1989). The verbal action of the listener as a basis for rule-governance. In S. C. Hayes (Ed.), *Rule-governed behavior: Cognition, contingencies, and instructional control* (pp. 153–190). New York: Plenum.

Hollingshead, A. B. (1975). *Four factor index of social status.* Unpublished manuscript. New Haven, CT: Yale University, Department of Sociology.

Huba, G. J., & Bentler, P. M. (1982). A developmental theory of drug use: Derivation and assessment of a causal modeling approach. *Life-Span Development and Behavior, 4,* 147–203.

Huba, G. J., & Bentler, P. M. (1983). Causal models of the development of law abidance and its relationship to psychosocial factors and drug use. In W. S. Laufer & J. M. Day (Eds.), *Personality theory, moral development, and criminal behavior* (pp. 165–215). Lexington, MA: Lexington Books.

Johnson, R. T., & Johnson, D. W. (1983). Effects of cooperative and individualistic experiences on social development. *Exceptional Children, 49,* 323–329.

Kandel, D. B. (1973). Adolescent marijuana use: Role of parents and peers. *Science, 181,* 1067–1070.

Kandel, D. B. (1978). Homophily, selection, and socialization in adolescent friendships. *American Journal of Sociology, 84,* 427–436.

Kandel, D. B. (1982). Epidemiological and psychosocial perspectives on adolescent drug use. *Journal of the American Academy of Child Psychiatry, 21,* 328–347.

Kandel, D. B. (1986). Process of peer influence on adolescence. In R. K. Silbereisen (Ed.), *Development as action in context* (pp. 33–52). Berlin, Germany: Springer-Verlag.

Kazdin, A. (1987). Treatment of antisocial behavior in children: Current status and future directions. *Psychological Bulletin, 102,* 187–203.

Kellam, S. G. (1990). Developmental epidemiological framework for family research on depression and aggression. In G. R. Patterson (Ed.), *Depression and aggression in family interaction* (pp. 11–48). Hillsdale, N.J.: Lawrence Erlbaum Associates.

Kupersmidt, J. B., Griesler, P. C., & Patterson, C. T. (1990). Socioeconomic status, aggression, and affiliation patterns of peers. Unpublished manuscript. Chapel Hill, N.C.: Department of Psychology, University of North Carolina.

Kurdek, L. A., Lillie, R. (1985). The relation between classroom social status and classmate likability, compromising skill, temperament, and neighborhood social interactions. *Journal of Applied Developmental Psychology, 66,* 239–242.

Ladd, G. W. (1983). Social networks of popular, average, and rejected children in school settings. *Merrill-Palmer Quarterly, 29,* 283–307.

Loeber, R. (1982). The stability of antisocial and delinquent child behavior: A review. *Child Development, 53,* 1431–1446.

Loeber, R., & Dishion, T. J. (1983). Early predictors of male delinquency: A review. *Psychological Bulletin, 94,* 68–98.

Loeber, R., & Dishion, T. J. (1984). Boys who fight at home and in school: Family conditions influencing cross-setting consistency. *Journal of Consulting and Clinical Psychology, 52,* 759–768.

MacDonald, K., & Parke, R. (1984). Bridging the gap: Parent–child play interaction and peer interactive competence. *Child Development, 55,* 1265–1277.

McCord, W., McCord, J. A., & Howard, A. (1963) Family interaction as antecedent to the direction of male aggressiveness. *Journal of Abnormal and Social Psychology, 66,* 239–242.

Medland, M. B., & Stachnik, T. J. (1972). Good-behavior game: A replication and systematic analysis. *Journal of Applied Behavior Analysis, 5,* 45–51.

Meichenbaum, D. (1979). Cognitive-behavioral modifications: Future directions. In P. Sjoden, S. Bates, & W. S. Dockens (Eds.), *Trends in behavior therapy.* New York: Academic Press.

Olweus, D. (1979). Stability of Aggressive reaction patterns in males: A review. *Psychological Bulletin, 86,* 852–875.

Panella, D., & Henggeler, S. W. (1986). Peer interactions of conduct-disordered, anxious-withdrawn, and well-adjusted black adolescents. *Journal of Abnormal Child Psychology, 14,* 1–11.

Parke, R., & Bhavnagri, N. P. (1988). Parents as managers of children's peer relationships. In D. Belle (Ed.), *Children's social networks and social supports* (pp. 33–55). New York: John Wiley.

Parker, J. G., & Asher, S. R. (1989, April). *Peer relations and social adjustment: Are friendship and group acceptance distinct domains?* Paper presented at the biennial meeting of the Society for Research in Child Development, Kansas City, MO.

Patterson, G. R. (1974). Interventions for boys with conduct problems: Multiple settings, treatments, and criteria. *Journal of Consulting and Clinical Psychology, 42,* 471–481.

Patterson, G. R. (1982). *A Social Learning Approach: III. Coercive Family Process.* Eugene, OR: Castalia.

Patterson, G. R. (1986). Performance models for antisocial boys. *American Psychologist, 41,* 432–444.

Patterson, G. R., & Dishion, T. J. (1985). Contributions of families and peers to delinquency. *Criminology, 23,* 63–79.

Patterson, G. R., Dishion, T. J., & Chamberlain, P. (in press). Outcomes and methodological issues relating to the treatment of antisocial children. In T. R. Giles (Ed.), *Effective psychotherapy: A handbook of comparative research.* New York: Plenum.

Patterson, G. R., Littman, R. A., & Bricker, W. (1967). Assertive behavior in children: A step toward a theory of aggression. *Monographs of the Society for Research in Child Development, 32,* No. 5 (Serial No. 113).

Patterson, G. R., & Reid, J. B. (1984). Social interactional processes within the family: The study of moment-by-moment family transactions in which human social development is imbedded. *Journal of Applied Developmental Psychology, 5,* 237–262.

Patterson, G. R., Reid, J. B., & Dishion, T. J. (1992). *Antisocial Boys.* Eugene, OR: Castalia Press.

Patterson, G. R., & Stoolmiller, M. (in press). Replications of a dual failure model for boys' depressed mood. *Journal of Consulting and Clinical Psychology.*

Peery, J. C. (1979). Popular, amiable, isolated, rejected: A reconceptualization of sociometric status in preschool children. *Child Development, 50,* 1231–1234.

Putallaz, M. (1987). Maternal behavior and children's sociometric status. *Child Development, 58,* 324–340.

Putallaz, M., & Gottman, J. M. (1979). Social skills and group acceptance. In S. R. Asher & J. M. Gottman (Eds.), *The development of children's friendships* (pp. 116–149). Cambridge: Cambridge University Press.

Putallaz, M., & Gottman, J. (1981). An interactional model for children's entry into peer groups. *Child Development, 52,* 986–994.

Raush, H. L. (1965). Interaction sequences. *Journal of Personality and Social Psychology, 2,* 487–499.

Rutter, M. (1978). Family, area, and school influences in the genesis of conduct disorders. In L. A. Hersov, M. Berger, & D. Schaffer (Eds.), *Childhood and Adolescence* (pp. 95–114). Oxford, England: Pergamon Press.

Shinn, M. R., Ramsey, E., Walker, H. M., Steiber, H., & O'Neill, R. E. (1987). Antisocial behavior in school settings: Initial differences in at-risk and normal population. *Journal of Special Education, 21,* 69–84.

Skinner, B. F. (1989). The behavior of the listener. In S. C. Hayes (Ed.), *Rule-governed behavior: Cognition, contingencies and instructional control* (pp. 85–96). New York: Plenum.

Snyder, J., Dishion, T. J., & Patterson, G. R. (1986). Determinants and consequences of associating with deviant peers during preadolescence and adolescence. *Journal of Early Adolescence, 6,* 29–43.

Walker, H. M., & McConnell, S. R. (1988). *Walker-McConnell scale of social competence and school adjustment,* Austin, TX: Pro-Ed.

Walker, H. M., Shinn, M. R., O'Neill, R. E., & Ramsey, E. (1987). A longitudinal assessment of the development of antisocial behavior in boys: Rationale, methodology, and first year results. *Remedial and Special Education, 8,* 7–16.

Weinrott, M. R., Reid, J. B., Bauske, B. W., & Brummett, B. (1981). Supplementing naturalistic observations with observer impressions. *Behavioral Assessment, 3,* 151–159.

West, D. J., & Farrington, D. P. (1973). *Who becomes delinquent?* London, England: Heinemann Educational Books, Ltd.

West, D. J., & Farrington, D. P. (1977). *The delinquent way of life.* London, England: Heinemann Educational Books, Ltd.

Wolfgang, M. E., Figlio, R., & Stellin, T. (1972). *Delinquency in a birth cohort.* Chicago: University of Chicago Press.

CHAPTER 5

BULLYING AT SCHOOL

Long-Term Outcomes for the Victims and an Effective School-Based Intervention Program

DAN OLWEUS

INTRODUCTION

Bullying among schoolchildren is certainly a very old phenomenon. The fact that some children are frequently and systematically harassed and attacked by other children has been described in literary works, and many adults have personal experience of it from their own school days. Though many are acquainted with the bully/victim problem, it was not until fairly recently, in the early 1970s, that efforts were made to study it systematically (Olweus, 1973a, 1978). For a considerable time, these attempts were largely confined to Scandinavia. In the 1980s and early 1990s, however, bullying among schoolchildren has received some public attention in Japan, England, Australia, the United States, and other countries. There are now clear indications of an increasing societal as well as research interest into bully/victim problems in several parts of the world.

DAN OLWEUS • Department of Psychosocial Science, University of Bergen, Bergen, 5007, Norway.

Aggressive Behavior: Current Perspectives, edited by L. Rowell Huesmann. Plenum Press, New York, 1994.

In the first part of this chapter I report on a study that examines the possible long-term consequences of regular bullying or victimization by peers in school. The latter part of the chapter is mainly concerned with the effects of the school-based antibullying intervention program that we developed and evaluated in 42 schools in Norway. (For more details about these studies, see Olweus, 1993b, for the first study, Olweus, 1991, for the second.) Before embarking on these studies, however, I will give a brief definition of what I mean by the terms *bullying* or *victimization.* In addition, I will report some prevalence data and briefly provide a profile of typical victims and bullies as a general background. (For more comprehensive overviews, see Olweus, 1978, 1984, 1991, 1993a).

A DEFINITION OF BULLYING

I define bullying or victimization in the following general way: A person is being bullied or victimized when he or she is exposed, repeatedly and over time, to negative actions on the part of one or more other persons.

The meaning of the expression *negative actions* must be further defined. It is a negative action when someone intentionally inflicts, or attempts to inflict, injury or discomfort upon another—basically what is implied in the definition of aggressive behavior (Olweus, 1973b). Negative actions can be carried out by physical contact, by words, or in other ways, such as making faces or obscene gestures or refusing to comply with another person's wishes.

It must be stressed that the terms *bullying* or *victimization* are not (or should not be) used when two persons of approximately the same strength (physical or psychological) are fighting or quarrelling. In order to use the term *bullying,* there should be an *imbalance in strength* (*an asymmetric power relationship*): The person who is exposed to the negative actions has difficulty in defending him or herself and is somewhat helpless against the harasser or harassers.

It is useful to distinguish between *direct bullying/victimization*—with relatively open attacks on the victim—and *indirect bullying/victimization* in the form of social isolation and exclusion from a group. It is important to pay attention also to the second, less visible form of victimization.

In the present chapter the expressions *bullying, victimization,* and *bully/victim problems* are used synonymously.

PREVALENCE OF BULLYING

In connection with a nationwide campaign against bully/victim problems in Norwegian comprehensive schools (all primary and junior high schools in Norway), launched by the Ministry of Education in 1983, data were collected with my Bullying Questionnaire[1] from more than 700 schools from all over Norway (Olweus, 1985, 1986, 1991, 1993a).

On the basis of this survey, one can estimate that some 84,000 students, or 15% of the total population of Norwegian comprehensive schools (568,000 in 1983–1984), were involved in bully/victim problems with some regularity—as bullies or victims (autumn 1983). This percentage represents one student out of seven. Approximately 9%, or 52,000 students, were victims, and 41,000, or 7%, bullied other students less or more frequently. Some 9,000 students were both victims and bullies.

It can thus be stated that *bullying is a considerable problem in Norwegian comprehensive schools,* a problem that affects a very large number of students. Data from other countries such as Sweden (Olweus, 1986), Finland (Lagerspetz, Björkqvist, Berts, & King, 1982), Britain (Smith, 1989; Whitney & Smith, 1991), United States (Perry, Kuşel, & Perry, 1988), and Canada (Ziegler & Rosenstein-Manner, 1991) indicate that this problem exists also outside Norway and with similar or even higher prevalence rates.

CHARACTERISTICS OF TYPICAL VICTIMS AND BULLIES

The picture of the typical victim emerging from research is relatively unambiguous (Olweus, 1978, 1984, 1993a). Victims of bullying are more anxious and insecure than students in general. They are often cautious, sensitive, and quiet. When attacked by other students, they commonly react with crying (at least in the lower grades) and withdrawal. They have a negative view of themselves and their situation. They often look upon themselves as failures and feel stupid, ashamed, and unattractive. Further, victims are lonely and abandoned at school. As a rule, they don't have a single good friend in their class. They are not aggressive or teasing in their behavior; accordingly one cannot explain the bullying as

[1] There is an (expanded) English version of the Bullying Questionnaire (one version for grades 1–4, and another for grades 5–9 and higher grades). For more information, see Footnote 2 and write to Dan Olweus, University of Bergen, Oysteinsgate 3, N-5007 Bergen, Norway.

a consequence of the victims themselves being provocative to their peers. If they are boys, they are likely to be physically weaker than their peers.

In summary, the behavior and attitude of the victims seem to signal to others that they are insecure and worthless individuals who will not retaliate if they are attacked or insulted. A slightly different way of describing typical victims is to say that they are characterized by *an anxious reaction pattern combined* (in the case of boys) *with physical weakness*.

This is a sketch of the most common type of victim, whom I have called *the passive or submissive victim*. There is also another, smaller group of victims, *the provocative victims*, who are characterized by a combination of both anxious and aggressive reaction patterns (see Olweus [1978] for more information about this kind of victim).

A distinctive characteristic of *typical bullies* is their aggression toward peers; this is implied in the definition of a bully. They are, however, often also aggressive toward teachers, parents, and siblings. Generally, they have a more positive attitude to violence and the use of violence than students in general. They are often characterized by impulsivity and strong needs to dominate others. They have little empathy with victims of bullying. If they are boys, they are likely to be physically stronger than their peers, and their victims in particular.

In contrast to a fairly common assumption among psychologists and psychiatrists, we have found no indicators that the aggressive bullies (boys) are anxious and insecure under a tough surface. Data based on several samples and using both direct and indirect methods such as projective techniques and hormonal assays all point in the same direction: The bullies have unusually little anxiety and insecurity or are roughly average on such dimensions (Olweus, 1981, 1984). And they do not suffer from poor self-esteem.

In summary, the typical bullies can be described as having an aggressive reaction pattern combined (in the case of boys) with physical strength.

Bullying can also be viewed as a component of a more general conduct-disordered, antisocial, and rule-breaking behavior pattern. From this perspective, it is natural to predict that youngsters who are aggressive and bully others in school run a clearly increased risk of later engaging in other problem behaviors such as criminality and alcohol abuse. Several recent studies confirm this general prediction (Huesmann & Eron, 1984, in press; Loeber & Dishion, 1983; Magnusson, Stattin, & Duner, 1983; Stattin & Magnusson, 1989).

In our own follow-up studies we have also found strong support for this view. Approximately 60% of boys who were characterized as bullies in grades 6 through 9 had at least one conviction by the age of 24. Even more dramatically, as many as 35 to 40% of the former bullies had three or more convictions at this age while this was true of only 10% of the control boys (those who were neither bullies nor victims in grades 6–9). Thus, as young adults the former school bullies had a fourfold increase in the level of relatively serious, recidivist criminality, as documented in the official criminal records.

It should be mentioned that the former victims had an average or somewhat below average level of criminality in young adulthood.

STUDY 1: LONG-TERM OUTCOMES OF BULLYING BY PEERS IN SCHOOL

To be regularly harassed and bullied by peers in school is no doubt a very unpleasant experience which may seriously affect the mental health and well-being of the victim. It seems fairly obvious that bullying by peers should have negative effects on the victim in the short term (Olweus, 1993a). But will the negative effects remain even several years after the bullying has ended?

Almost nothing is known about the long-term development of children who have been victimized during a sizable period of their school life. Will the reaction patterns associated with their victim status at school be found again if we study them several years later, for example, in young adulthood? Are these individuals still socially withdrawn and isolated, maybe even harassed by their working or student companions? Or, have they recovered in most respects after they have escaped the straitjacket of companionship forced upon them in comprehensive school, and they can choose their social environments more freely? Or, does the painful experience of being victimized over long periods of time leave certain scars on the adult personality even if the former victims seem to function well in most respects? These and related issues are explored herein drawing from a follow-up study of young men at age 23, some of whom had been victims of bullying and harassment by peers for a period of at least three years, from grade 6 through grade 9.

Methodology

The *subjects* of this study were 87 men who were approximately 23 years at follow-up in the winter of 1982 to 1983. All of them had participated in an assessment in grade 9 when they were 16, and for the overwhelming majority, data were also available from grade 6.

The 87 subjects of the follow-up sample consisted of the following three groups:

1. A largely representative sample of 64 subjects which included six former victims and five former bullies (Olweus, 1980a; Olweus, Mattsson, Schalling, & Löw, 1980, 1988);
2. A selection of 11 additional former victims. The total number of former victims in the study was thus 17. These boys can be considered to be among the most severely victimized boys in the representative cohort of 276 boys to which they belonged;
3. A selection of 12 additional former bullies. Accordingly, the total number of former bullies was also 17. These boys were among the most pronounced bullies in the cohort (representing about 6% of the total *n* of 276).

For the purposes of the present analyses only the following two groups were used: The group of 17 former victims and the representative sample of 58 subjects (64 minus the six former victims). Due to missing data on some of the variables, the actual number of subjects in the present analyses were 15 and 56, respectively.

To be defined as a victim in grade 6 or 9, a subject had to fulfill the following two criteria:

1. He had to have been nominated by at least one of the main class teachers as a victim (according to a specified definition); and
2. He had to have received an average score of one standard deviation or more above the mean of the total distribution (for approximately 275 boys) on at least one of two peer rating variables, aggression target and degree of unpopularity. (The average of these two variables defined the peer rating variable *degree of victimization by peers* to be used in subsequent analyses; for additional details, see Olweus [1993b].)

The stability of victimization status over time was quite high. In actual fact, 16 of the total group of 17 victims in the present study qualified as victims in both grades 6 and grade 9. Assuming continuity over the interval covered, they had thus been exposed to fairly severe bullying and harassment for a very long period of time. In addition to having the typical characteristics described above, the habitual victims were also found to have elevated levels of the stress hormone adrenaline at age 16 in comparison with the control boys.

At follow-up, the subjects of this study completed a number of questionnaires designed to tap various dimensions of assumed relevance: Scales for being directly harassed (e.g., "Others are fairly often mean and nasty to me"); for being indirectly harassed (social isolation, loneliness); for social anxiety (shyness, social-evaluative concerns); emotionality-worrying in achievement-related situations, involvement in antisocial activities, several dimensions of aggression (assertiveness) and aggression inhibition, frustration tolerance, neuroticism and extraversion (slightly abbreviated versions of the Eysenck scales; Eysenck & Eysenck [1975]), global self-esteem (7 items from Rosenberg's scale; Rosenberg, 1979) and depression (9 items from Beck's scale; Beck, Ward, Mendelsohn, Mock, & Erbaugh, [1961]). Most of the items had a 6-point Likert format. The internal-consistency (alpha) reliabilities of the scales were generally quite satisfactory, in most cases lying in the .80 to .95 range.

In one of the questionnaires, the subjects were asked to look back to the year they were in grade 9 and to assess (retrospectively), among other things, the degree to which they had been exposed to direct and indirect bullying and harassment by peers. The five items covering these domains were combined into one scale.

Several samples of blood and urine were also collected from the subjects at two different periods, about eight weeks apart. These samples were used for the assessment of several hormones including adrenaline, noradrenaline, testosterone, and cortisol.

It was considered appropriate to focus the present analyses not only on significance testing but also on effect sizes (in this context I used the standardized mean difference measure *d* defined as the difference between the means of the two groups divided by the standard deviation of the nonvictim or "control" group [Cohen, 1977]). One reason for this strategy is that we are mainly concerned here with exploring possible causal relationships and mechanisms, and from this perspective effect size measures give better information about the relationships of interest than tests of significance. Correlation (Pearson) and regression analyses were also used.

Results and Discussion

Lack of Continuity in Victimization

The first important result to report is an absence of relationship between indicators of victimization in school and data on both direct and indirect harassment in young adulthood. The point-biserial correlation between being directly harassed in young adulthood (alpha = .91) and victim/nonvictim status in grades 6 through 9 (group membership) was only .06 (n.s.). The corresponding correlation for being indirectly harassed (alpha = .84) was .15 (n.s.). Similarly, the product-moment correlations of these two adult harassment variables with the peer rating variable, degree of victimization by peers, averaged across grades 6 and 9, were .07 and .18 (both n.s.). The fact that a boy had been regularly victimized by his peers in school for a long period of time was thus basically unrelated to (self-reported) later harassment and social isolation. Obviously, the experience of victimization in school did not seem to increase the boy's probability of being victimized in young adulthood.

Considering this finding, one might wonder if the experience of being bullied and victimized in school had been so painful to many former victims that they had simply come to deny or repress any indications that they were being victimized as young adults. This hypothesis, however, could be safely ruled out by means of the retrospective data. Here we found substantial correlations between the retrospective estimates of degree of direct/indirect harassment in grade 9 and victim/nonvictim status (r = .42) as well as degree of victimization in grade 9 as measured by the peer ratings (r = .58). These findings show that a considerable proportion of the subjects had a fairly realistic view of their peer relationships in school seven years earlier. The "denial/repression hypothesis" was thus not a viable explanation of the lack of association between degree of harassment in school and in young adulthood.

One might also wonder if the lack of association was a consequence of the fact that different methods of assessment were used at the two time points: The categorization of the subjects as victims and nonvictims in school was based on a combination of teacher nominations and peer ratings, whereas the adult measure of harassment was derived from self-reports. Accordingly, one could argue that use of "noncongruent" assessment techniques, which partly sample different aspects of the phenomena under consideration, might lead to a substantial underestimate of the "true relationship."

Fortunately, this possibility could be checked within the present study since self-report data on degree of victimization/harassment in school were also available. Four 6-point questionnaire items (such as "Other boys are nasty to me," and "I feel lonely and abandoned at school") which were part of the assessment battery in both grade 6 and grade 9, were combined into a composite averaged across grades (alpha = .84). This composite correlated .42 with concurrent victim/nonvictim status and .61 with the peer rating variable degree of victimization by peers (the correlation within the victim group was even higher, .73). Accordingly, the composite must be considered a valid and meaningful self-report indicator of victimization/harassment in school.

When this scale of self-reported victimization in school was correlated with the adult measures of harassment, the results were very much the same as those obtained with the "other-based" measure of victimization in school: The correlation with being directly harassed in young adulthood was .05 (the corresponding value for victim/nonvictim status in school was .06, above), whereas the correlation with being indirectly harassed was .16 (and the corresponding value for victim/nonvictim status was .15, above). Obviously, use of "congruent" methods of assessment would not lead to a different conclusion.

To sum up, the lack of association between victim/nonvictim status in school and degree of harassment in young adulthood could not be explained as a consequence of denial/repression or of "noncongruence" of methods of assessment. In all probability, then, the lack of a relation was a reflection of reality (I am also basing this judgment on the substantial correlation of degree of adult harassment with concurrent levels of depression and self-esteem, reported below).

Long-Term Effects of Victimization

In spite of the fact that the former victims were no more harassed or socially isolated than the control boys as young adults, they had clearly higher levels of depression, or maybe depressive tendencies, and a more negative view of themselves (poorer self-esteem) at age 23. On the somewhat abbreviated, but highly reliable Beck scale of depression (alpha = .87), the *t*-value for the mean difference between the victim and nonvictim groups was 2.77 ($p < .01$ on a two-tailed test) and the effect size *d* a substantial .87 (a "large" effect size according to Cohen [1977]). The point–biserial correlation between group membership and the depression scale was .32. For the equally reliable Rosenberg scale of global self-esteem (also somewhat abbreviated; alpha = .89) the *t*-value was 2.28 ($p = .03$ on a two-tailed test) and the value of *d* .70. The corresponding point–biserial correlation amounted to .26.

To get a better understanding of how to interpret these results, a more elaborate analysis of the data is required. The key variables and relationships in terms of correlation coefficients are shown in Figure 1 with the Beck scale of depression as the "ultimate" dependent variable.

Three of the variables in the figure have already been discussed and we note the approximately zero correlation between victim/nonvictim status during the school period and later degree of direct harassment. The fourth variable in the graph is a scale that was derived through factor analysis of a Q-sort inventory used in both grade 6 and grade 9. The factorially derived scale consists of 12 items. and was interpreted to reflect feelings of maladjustment, anxiety, and personal inadequacy (Ol-

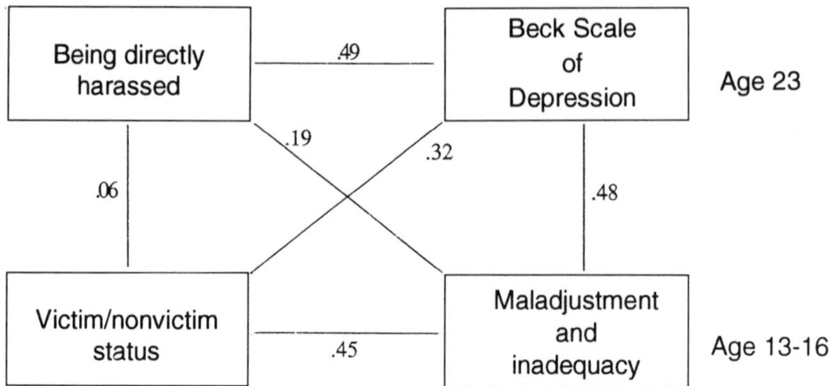

FIGURE 1. Overview of relations (Pearson correlations) among key variables at age 13–16 and age 23 (n = 71).

weus, 1978). The reaction patterns covered by this dimension can be assumed to be precursors of later depressive tendencies and this assumption was supported by the fairly substantial correlation of .48 between this scale (averaged over grade 6 and grade 9) and the Beck scale 7 to 10 years later. The reliability of the scale can be estimated at .92.

The basic starting point for interpretation of the results is the finding that the former victims had higher levels of depressive tendencies than nonvictims in young adulthood (alternatively, the correlation of .32 in Figure 1 of victim/nonvictim status with later depressive tendencies). This difference or correlation can clearly not be a consequence of different levels of concurrent harassment, since the former victims and nonvictims did not differ in that respect at age 23, as discussed under point A (and as evidenced in the .06 correlation in Figure 1). So, even though there is a substantial correlation between level of contemporaneous harassment and depressive tendencies (r = .49), this relation is not linked to former victim/nonvictim status.

Accordingly, one has to look more closely at the relation with the variables in the right-hand part of the figure. Generally, it seems reasonable to assume that there should be *no direct effect* (in a causal–analytic sense) of former victim/nonvictim status on depressive tendencies which were measured at a much later point in time (7–10 years later). If there were an effect, it would much more likely be *an indirect one*, with marked, relatively immediate (direct) effects which were in some way "internalized" and manifested (also) later in life as a predisposition to react with depressive tendencies.

Applying this reasoning to the data in Figure 1, one would expect that most of the effect of victim/nonvictim status on depressive tendencies was mediated via the concurrent variable *maladjustment* and inadequacy. Such a mechanism would also largely account for the cross-lagged correlation of .32, making it close to zero in a path-analytic framework. This is actually what happens if the Beck scale is regressed on maladjustment and inadequacy and victim/nonvictim status: The cross-lagged standardized path coefficient becomes almost zero ($\beta = .13$, n.s.) whereas the path from maladjustment and inadequacy is .42 (and highly significant).

The pattern of relations discussed thus far is certainly consistent with an assumption of an indirect causal effect of victimization in school on later depressive tendencies. Before drawing conclusions along these lines, however, one should also consider the possibility of a causal relationship in the opposite direction, from feelings of maladjustment and depression to victimization/harassment.

Although there are indications (as discussed above) that a boy's early psychological characteristics (in addition to physical weakness and child-rearing variables) affect his probability of being victimized, the present data covering somewhat later periods and more anxiety/depression-related characteristics do not seem to support the idea of a causal relationship in this direction. In particular, since the maladjustment and inadequacy variable (a proxy for depressive tendencies) shows considerable continuity with later depressive tendencies, it would seem intuitively reasonable to expect some degree of continuity also for the victimization/harassment variable (rather than the obtained zero-correlation), *if* there were a causal relation as postulated.

In contrast, the substantial continuity of the depression-related variables can be partly accounted for by an "indirect-effect" mechanism as discussed above, if we assume that victimization/harassment exerts a causal influence on the depression-related variables. It should be added that part of the continuity of the depression-related variables is probably explained by the continuing influence of other factors not included in the model.

All in all, the above results support the view that the major causal influence is from victimization to depression-related variables, and not the other way around. This interpretation is strengthened by a consideration of the nature of the peer relationships concerned. As mentioned, the victims tend to be physically weaker than their peers and are typically nonaggressive and nonprovocative. Accordingly, it is very reasonable to assume that they simply fall prey to harassment and dominance on the part of other, more aggressive students (bullies, in particular).

And naturally, the humiliating and hostile treatment they are exposed to is likely to affect their self-evaluations and levels of anxiety/depression.

Further support of this reasoning is gained through examination of the relation between degree of victimization in grades 6 through 9 and level of depressive tendencies at age 23 *within the victim group.* In this group, there was a substantial .54 ($p < .02$) correlation of degree of victimization with later depressive tendencies. Although it is possible that chance has played some role in producing the amazingly high correlation in the relatively homogenous victim group, it should be emphasized that the result was not due to one or two extreme outliers; the scatterplot displayed an essentially linear and fairly regular pattern. This within-group correlation becomes even more impressive when one considers the fact that the two variables involved were derived from completely different sources of data—peer ratings and self-reports, respectively—thereby precluding the possibility that the correlation was inflated due to potentially shared method variance.

Taken together, all of this evidence indicates a pattern of causal relationships among the variables as portrayed in Figure 2. Victimization in school (victim status) leads concurrently to heightened depression-related tendencies which continue to be elevated 7 to 10 years later, even though the former victims are no more harassed than their controls at that point in time. Depressive tendencies at age 23 are also affected by concurrent (adult) harassment, but the degree of such harassment is not related to earlier victim status. It is worth noting that the correlation between the two adult measures may be somewhat inflated due to

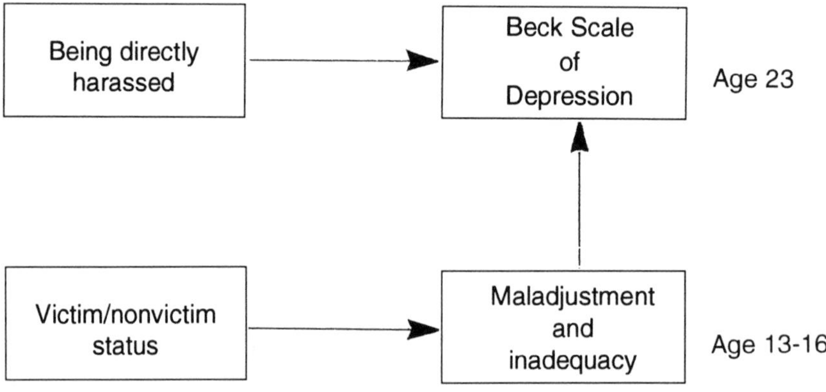

FIGURE 2. Major causal relations among key variables at age 13–16 and age 23.

shared method variance, since they were both derived from self-reports.

It should be added that an analysis parallel to that presented above was conducted with Beck's depression scale replaced by Rosenberg's scale of global self-esteem and the maladjustment inadequacy scale exchanged with a scale of poor self-esteem in grades 6 to 9. The latter a priori defined scale consisted of nine items, five of which where included in the factorially derived maladjustment and inadequacy scale (Olweus, 1978, Appendix). The correlation of this scale with scores on the Rosenberg scale collected 7 to 10 years later was .56, whereas its correlation with concurrent victim/nonvictim status was .36 (and the cross-lagged correlation of victim/nonvictim status with the Rosenberg scale was .26, as previously reported). The relations among these variables were thus very similar to those displayed in Figure 1 and were given a very similar interpretation.

Nondeviant Development on Several Dimensions

On several adult dimensions on which it would be natural to expect differences between former victims and nonvictims, considering their situation and characteristics in grades 6 to 9, there were basically no differences. These dimensions included social anxiety (shyness, social–evaluative concerns), emotionality-worrying, different forms of aggression/assertiveness and aggression inhibition, and neuroticism (several of these dimensions correlated .40–.50 with similar dimensions assessed in grades 6–9). In contrast to the findings from grade 9, the victims also did not have elevated levels of the stress hormone adrenaline (in spite of a correlation around .70 for the group as a whole between adrenaline levels at age 16 and 23, respectively), nor were they more introverted than the controls at 23. In accordance with expectations, however, the former victims had been somewhat less involved in criminal activities, both according to self-reports and official records.

Summary of Study 1 and Major Implications

Methodological Adequacy

Before summarizing the findings of this study and pointing out major implications, I would like to emphasize that the results were based on a relatively limited number of subjects. This fact should make us regard the conclusions to be drawn as somewhat tentative and in need of replication. At the same time, it should be underscored that the findings obtained presented a conceptually very meaningful and coherent pattern, in addition to being quite consistent across two distinct but theoretically and empirically related "ultimate" dependent variables, depressive tendencies and global self-esteem. Also, the victim group was well delineated and its members had no doubt been exposed to fairly severe bullying and harassment for several years. Finally, the quality of the data was quite good according to standard psychometric criteria. These aspects of the study should lead to an increased confidence in the conclusions that were reached.

Lack of Continuity in Victimization

A major finding was the absence of a relation between victim/nonvictim status in grades 6 through 9 and the highly reliable measure of harassment at age 23. The retrospective data showed the lack of correlation not to be an effect of denial/repression. In all probability, this lack of continuity is an indication that the subjects, after having left school, had considerably greater freedom to choose their own social and physical environments. In this way, the former victims had succeeded in escaping later harassment and victimization to approximately the same degree as their peers. This finding is, of course, encouraging, though our reactions should be mitigated by the lasting negative effects of earlier victimization, to be discussed below.

It should be added that the lack of continuity with victimization as measured at age 23 does not preclude the possibility that a former school victim could have an increased probability of being victimized under more circumscribed conditions, for example, in a marital relationship.

Situation-Related Strain Rather than Personality Disturbance

Another finding was that the former victims had "recovered" or scored in the normal range (like the controls) on several "internalizing" dimensions at age 23: They were no longer particularly anxious, inhibited, introverted, or nonassertive in interactions with others, nor were there indications that they had elevated stress levels. This pattern of results implies that a good deal of the anxiety-related/internalizing characteristics of the victims as measured during the school years were situationally determined, that is, relatively transient effects of the harsh treatment they were exposed to from aggressive peers.

A related implication is that a considerable proportion of the school victims cannot be characterized as having a "disturbed" or pathological personality. As already discussed, boys who get victimized are likely to have certain previctim characteristics, but many of them would probably function reasonably well if they were not exposed to repeated bullying and harassment over long periods of time. The elevated levels of anxiety and stress that we could register in the school years, were thus more a reflection of situation-related strain than of a relatively permanent personality disturbance.

In a similar vein, the "normal" adult outcome with regard to peer relationships and social interaction (according to self-reports) would seem to suggest that the victims were not lacking in social skills (Asher & Coie, 1990; Ladd, 1985). Or, if they were deficient in such skills in the school period, these problems were not serious enough to prevent normal development in the area of social interaction in young adulthood.

Implications for Intervention

All of this evidence supports the view that intervention efforts in this domain should not be primarily focused on changing the reactions and characteristics of the victims but rather the behavior and attitudes of the social environment, in particular the aggressive bullies (see below). Such a view does not preclude installment of intervention measures specifically designed for the victims: Such measures may help the victims make the harassment stop more quickly and may have good effects on their self-perceptions.

A further implication of the preceding analyses is that the high stability of individual differences in victimization over the junior high school years is largely a reflection of the stability of the social environment (Olweus, 1977, 1979, 1980b), in particular, the continuing influence of aggressive bullies and their followers. Although it has been shown (and will be shown below) that it is possible to achieve dramatic reductions in bully/victim problems with a suitable intervention program, and it is my conviction that such problems should largely be solved through a "restructuring of the social environment" (Olweus, 1991, 1993a), the results obtained suggest that a well-planned change of environment may sometimes be helpful to victims. Among other things, victims might benefit from interacting with other peer groups than that of their own class, for example, in connection with sports or musical activities. Also, if an identified bully/victim problem in a class does not seem to be solvable, in spite of serious efforts, it may be useful as a last resort to move the victim to a different class or even school. It must be stressed, however, that such changes of environment should be carefully planned if they are to be successful (Olweus, 1986, 1993a).

The Negative Long-Term Effects

Even though the former victims seemed to function well in a number of respects as young adults, there were two dimensions on which they clearly differed from their peers, depressive tendencies and poor self-esteem. The elevated levels on these dimensions can be interpreted as a consequence of earlier persistent victimization which had marked effects on the self-system or personality of some proportion of the young victims; in all probability, they had gradually come to take over the social environment's (the dominant peers') negative evaluations of themselves as worthless and inadequate individuals (Olweus, 1991, p. 423). These negative self-perceptions, which also imply an increased vulnerability to depressive reactions, tended to become internalized and "cemented" within the individuals. From a different perspective, one can say that these perceptions and reaction tendencies had gradually become "functionally autonomous" (Allport, 1937), "living a life of their own" independent of their original, immediate causes.

We don't have data available to assess accurately how serious the depression-related problems of the victim group were from a clinical point of view. It is reasonable to believe, however, that they were serious enough to deprive some proportion of the victims of considerable joy and satisfaction with their lives and generally, to worsen the quality of their existence. In addition, it is quite possible that the full consequences of the increased vulnerability of the victims will become evident only at a somewhat higher age. These results make it urgent for school authorities and parents to intervene against bully/victim problems not only to stop the current suffering of the victims (Olweus, 1991, 1993a) but also because of the long-term sequelae for these individuals (as well as for the bullies; see above).

Peer Rejection as a Predictor of Later Outcomes

It is also natural to connect the findings of the present study with some of the results and research issues from the peer relationships literature. In this area, much attention has been directed to the phenomenon of peer rejection, in part on the assumption that peer rejection may have a causal effect on later adjustment, for example, by making rejected-aggressive children more delinquent or criminal than peers who are aggressive but not rejected (Asher & Coie, 1990; Parker & Asher, 1987).

There have been few longitudinal studies in which it has been possible to test this assumption adequately (Kupersmidt, Coie, & Dodge, 1990; Olweus, 1989a). The empirical evidence obtained so far, however, has produced mixed or negative results (Kupersmidt et al., 1990). My own study (Olweus, 1989a), for example, failed to show that aggressive-rejected (unpopular) grade 6 through 9 boys had a worse long-term outcome than their nonrejected aggressive peers. In one of the two samples analyzed ($n = 276$ and $n_2 = 195$), there were even indications that aggressive-rejected boys were better off than their nonrejected counterparts. In this study, the long-term outcome was indexed by number of officially registered criminal offenses up to age 23.

Whereas much attention has been directed at the connection between rejection and aggression, recent peer relationships research has shown very little interest in the combination of rejection and social withdrawal. In part, this may stem from the fact that it is only quite recently that the heterogeneity of the rejected group has been documented within this research tradition (French, 1988). Considering the present data from this perspective, our results clearly indicate the rejection in the form of victimization combined with social withdrawal and passivity, has negative long-term effects on depressive tendencies and self-esteem.

The Causal Role of Victimization in Depression/Suicide

It can be added that victimization/harassment by peers in school appears to be a factor whose causal role in the development of depressive reaction patterns in adolescents and young adults has been much neglected. Since it is known that a considerable proportion of young people who actually commit or attempt to commit suicide, are depressed (Sudak, Ford, & Roshforth, 1984), it is by extension likely that victimization/harassment may also be an important causal factor in suicidal behavior. Incidentally, it is worth noting that the nationwide campaign against bully/victim problems in Norwegian schools, launched by the Ministry of Education, was initiated after it had been discovered that three 10 to 14-year-old boys had committed suicide as a consequence of severe bullying and harassment by peers (Olweus, 1991, 1993a).

STUDY 2: EFFECTS OF A SCHOOL-BASED INTERVENTION PROGRAM AGAINST BULLYING

Against this background, it is now appropriate to briefly describe the effects of the intervention program that we developed in connection with the campaign against bully/victim problems in Norwegian schools. The major goals of the program were to reduce as much as possible existing bully/victim problems and to prevent the development of new problems. The main components of the program, which was aimed at teachers and parents as well as students, were the following:

1. A 32-page booklet for school personnel describing what is known about bully/victim problems (or rather, what was known in 1983) and giving detailed suggestions about what teachers and the school could do to counteract and prevent the problems (Olweus & Roland, 1983). Efforts were also made to dispel common myths about the nature and causes of bully/victim problems which might interfere with an adequate handling of them. This booklet was distributed free of charge to all primary and junior high schools in Norway.
2. A 4-page folder with information and advice to parents of victims and bullies as well as "ordinary" children. This folder was distributed by the schools to all families in Norway with school-age children (also free of charge).
3. A 20-minute videocassette showing episodes from the everyday lives of two bullied children, a 10-year-old boy and a 14-year-old girl. This cassette could be bought or rented at a highly subsidized price.
4. A short questionnaire designed to obtain information about different aspects of bully/victim problems in the school, including frequency, and the readiness of teachers and students to interfere with the problems. The anonymous questionnaire was completed by the students individually (in class). Registration of the level and nature of bully/victim problems in the school was thought to serve as a starting point for active interventions on the part of both school and parents. The results on prevalence of bully/victim problems presented earlier in this chapter were based on information collected with this questionnaire.[2]

Another "component" was added to the program as used in Bergen, the city in which the evaluation of the effects of the intervention program took place. Approximately 15 months after the program was

[2] The updated "package" related to the intervention program against bully/victim problems consists of the Bullying Questionnaire for the measurement of bully/victim problems (above and Footnote 1), a copy of a small book *Bullying at school—what we know and what we can do* (Olweus, 1993a), which describes in detail the program and its implementation, and a 20-minute videocassette (with English subtitles; for European or North American current). These materials are copyrighted, which implies certain restrictions on their use. For more information, please write to the author at the address given in Footnote 1, p. 99.

first offered to the schools (in early October 1983) we gave, in a 2-hour meeting with the staff, individual feedback information to each of the 42 schools participating in the study (Manger & Olweus, 1985). This information, derived from the students' responses to the questionnaire in 1983, focused on the level of problems and the social environment's reactions to the problems in the particular school as related to data from comparable schools obtained in the nationwide survey (October 1983). At the same time, the main principles of the program and the major procedures for intervention were presented and discussed with the staff. Since we know from experience that many (Norwegian) teachers have somewhat distorted views of the characteristics of bullying students, particular emphasis was placed on a discussion of this topic and on appropriate ways of handling bullying behavior. Finally, the teachers rated different aspects of the program, in particular its feasibility and potential efficacy. Generally, this addition to the program as well as the program itself were quite favorably received by the teachers, as expressed in their ratings.

Subjects and Design

Space limitations prevent detailed presentation of methodological information including sampling scheme, definition of measuring instruments and variables, and significance tests. Only summary descriptions and main results will be provided in this context (for more details, see Olweus [1991], Olweus & Alsaker [1991]).

Evaluation of the effects of the intervention program is based on data from approximately 2500 students originally belonging to 112 grade 4 through 7 classes in 42 primary and junior high schools in Bergen (modal ages at Time 1 were 11, 12,, 13, and 14 years respectively). Each of the four grade/age cohorts consisted of 600 to 700 subjects with a roughly equal distribution of boys and girls. The first data collection (Time 1) took place in late May (and early June) 1983, approximately four months before the initiation of the campaign. New measurements were taken in May 1984 (Time 2) and may 1985 (Time 3).

Statistical Analyses

Since classes rather than students were the basic sampling units (with students nested within classes), it was considered important to choose a data analytic strategy that reflected the basic features of the design. Accordingly, data were analyzed with analysis of variance (ANOVA) with students nested within classes nested within schools nested within times/occasions (Time 1 versus Time 2, Time 1 versus Time 3). Sex of the subjects was crossed with times, schools (within times), and classes (within schools). Since several of the cohorts figured in two comparisons, the analyses had to be conducted separately for each combination of cohorts (for further information, see Olweus [1991]; Olweus & Alsaker [1991]).

For several of the variables (or derivatives of them such as percentages), less refined analyses with t-tests and chi square were also carried out. The findings from these analyses were in general agreement with those obtained in the ANOVAs.

Properties of the outcome variables analyzed are discussed elsewhere in some detail (Olweus, 1991). Generally, it was concluded that the evidence available attests to the adequacy and validity of the data employed.

Results

Results for the self-report variables "Being exposed to direct bullying" and "Bullying other students" are presented separately for boys and girls in Figures 3 through 6. (Due to space limitations, only the results for these two variables are shown graphically. See Olweus [1991] for a more complete presentation.) Since the design of the study is relatively complex, a few words about how to read the figures are in order.

The panel to the left shows the effects after 8 months of intervention, while the one to the right displays the results after 20 months. The upper curves (designated *before*) show the base line data (Time 1) for the relevant cohorts (the grade 5, grade 6, and grade 7 cohorts in the left panel and the grade 6 and grade 7 cohorts in the right). The lower curves (designated *after*) display data collected at Time 2 (after 8 months of intervention) in the panel to the left and at Time 3 (after 20 months of intervention) in the right-hand panel for the age-equivalent cohorts (the grade 4, grade 5, grade 6 cohorts at Time 2 and the grade 4 and grade 5 cohorts at Time 3).

The *main findings* of the analyses can be summarized as follows:

- There were marked reductions in the levels of bully/victim problems for the periods studied, 8 and 20 months of intervention respectively. By and large, reductions were obtained for both boys and girls and across all cohorts compared. For the longer time period the effects persisted in the case of "Being exposed to direct bullying" and "Being exposed to indirect bullying" and were strengthened for the variable "Bullying other students."

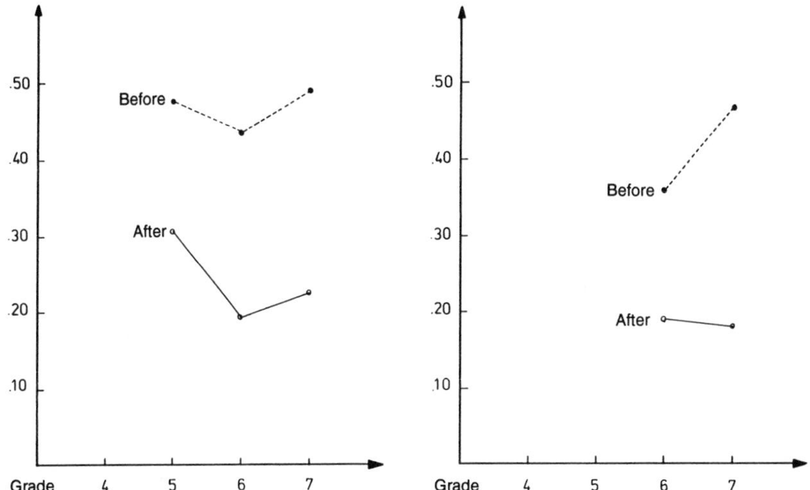

FIGURE 3. Effects of intervention program on "Being exposed to direct bullying" for boys. Panel to the left shows effects after 8 months of intervention, and panel to the right displays results after 20 months of intervention. Upper curves (designated Before) show base line data (Time 1), and the lower curves (designated After) display data collected at Time 2 in the left panel and at Time 3 in the panel to the right.

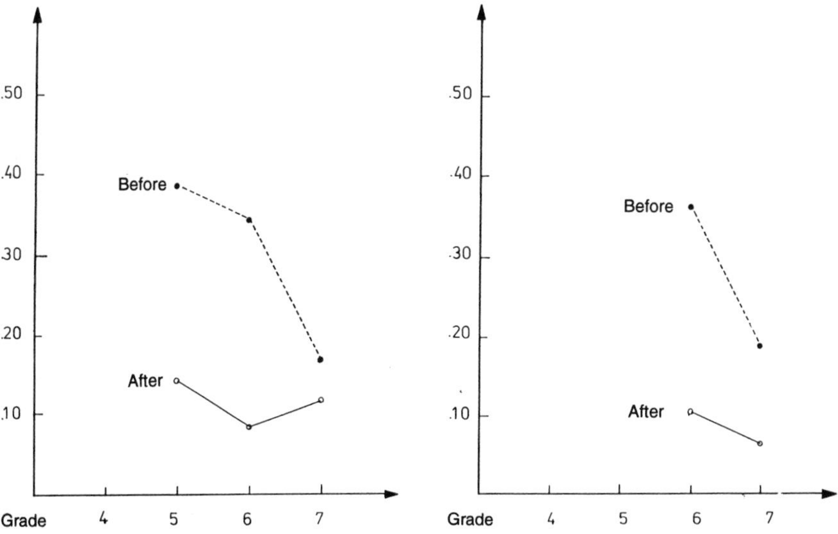

FIGURE 4. Effects of intervention program on "Being exposed to direct bullying" for girls. See Figure 3 for explanation of the figure.

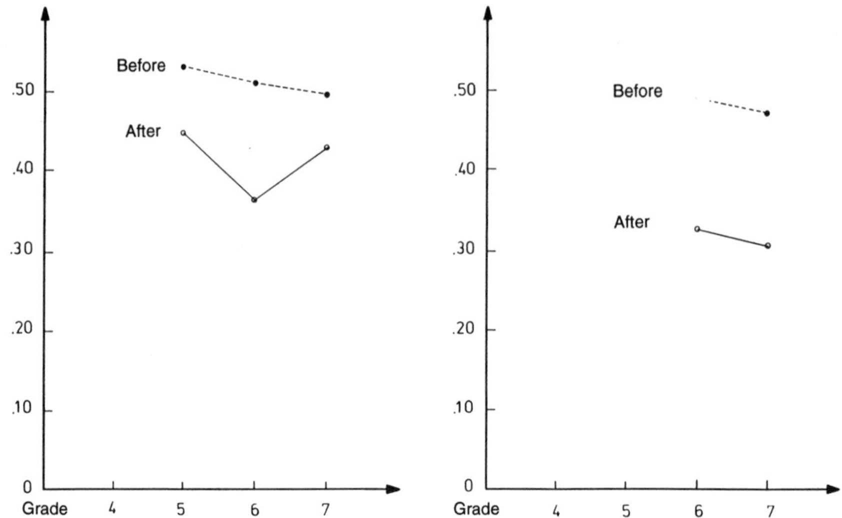

FIGURE 5. Effects of intervention program on "Bullying other students" for boys. See Figure 3 for explanation of the figure.

- Similar reductions were obtained for the aggregated peer rating variables—"Number of students being bullied in the class" and "Number of students in the class bullying other students." There was thus consensual agreement in the classes that bully/victim problems had decreased during the periods studied.
- In terms of percentages of students reporting being bullied or bullying others "now and then" or more frequently, the reductions amounted to approximately 50% or more in most comparisons.
- There was no displacement of bullying from the school premises to the trip to and from school. There were reductions or no changes on measures of bully/victim problems on the way to and from school.
- There was also a reduction in general antisocial behavior such as vandalism, fighting, theft, and truancy. (For the grade 6 comparisons the effects were marginal for both time periods.)
- In addition we could observe marked improvement as regards various aspects of the "social climate" of the class: improved order and discipline, more positive social relationships, and a more positive attitude to schoolwork and the school.
- At the same time, there was an increase in student satisfaction with school life as reflected in "liking recess time."
- There was not only a reduction in already existing victimization

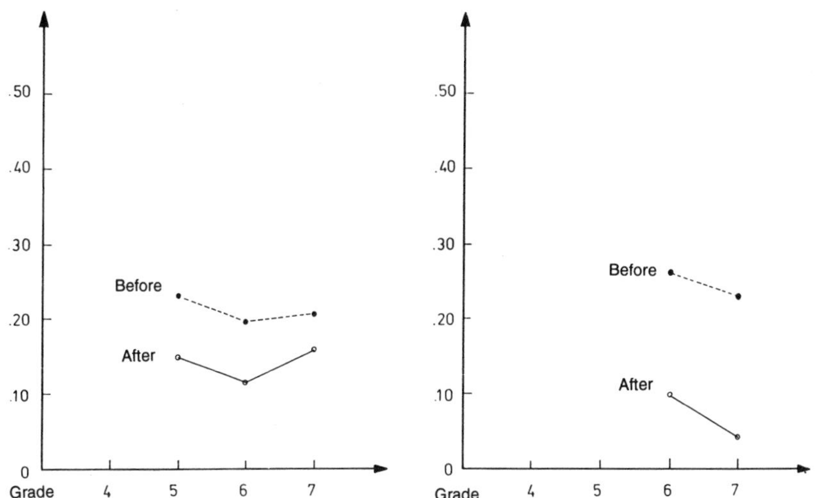

FIGURE 6. Effects of intervention program on "Bullying other students" for girls. (See Figure 3 for explanation of the figure).

problems, but also a reduction in the number (and percentage) of *new* victims. The program had thus both primary and secondary prevention effects (Cowen, 1984; Olweus, 1989b).

In the majority of comparisons for which reductions were reported above, the differences between baseline and postintervention measurements were highly significant or significant (in spite of the fact that many of them were based on single items).

Quality of Data and Possible Alternative Interpretations

It is beyond the scope of this chapter to discuss in detail the quality of the data collected and the possibility of alternative interpretations of the findings (with one exception, see below). An extensive discussion of these matters can be found elsewhere (Olweus, 1991). In that context, the following main conclusions were reached:

- Self-reports, which were implicated in most of the analyses conducted so far, are in fact the best data source for the purposes of this study. (It should be noted, however, that largely parallel results were obtained for the peer rating variables mentioned above and for teacher ratings of bully/victim problems at the class level; in the latter case, however, the effects were somewhat weaker.)

- It is very difficult to explain the results obtained as a consequence of (a) underreporting by the students; (b) gradual changes in the students' attitudes to bully/victim problems; (c) repeated measurement; and (d) concomitant changes in other factors.

With regard to the last point (d), however, some additional discussion is in order. In particular, one must also consider the possibility that the reported changes in the dependent variables mainly reflected "general time trends", that is, historical societal changes that happened to coincide with the intervention. For several reasons, this is a highly unlikely explanation.

First, examining official Norwegian data for various forms of criminality and suicidal behavior (which are the kinds of data for which possible general time trends can be assessed in this context; the relevance of this examination is based on the fact that these dimensions are likely to be correlated with bullying behavior and being victimized, respectively), there are no clear indications of a decline from 1983 to 1985. Rather, the curves remain essentially constant or show a slight to moderate increase for these years (see *Stortingsmelding nr.23. 1991–92*, for criminality, and Rettersstøl, 1990, for suicide).

Second, while all of the reported changes can be meaningfully linked to operation of the intervention program, it is highly unlikely that such a broad range of largely parallel changes (in not strongly correlated variables such as bullying/victimization, more general antisocial behavior, satisfaction with school life, and the social climate of the class) would be a "consequence of" a common time trend (due to unknown causes). Also, the relative abruptness of the changes in all of these variables (with marked changes within less than one year) speaks against a time trend interpretation. In this context, it should also be mentioned that a number of variables that were not expected to decline as a result of the intervention program, including extraversion and impulsivity, remained essentially unchanged.

Third, the reported changes showed, by and large, a meaningful pattern with the most marked changes for the directly targeted dimensions (being bullied, bullying others) and smaller changes for more indirectly targeted behavior patterns (e.g. the social climate dimensions).

In sum, all of these findings and arguments make a time trend interpretation highly unlikely.

In addition, a clear "dosage-response" relationship (r = .51, n = 80) has been established in preliminary analyses at the class level (which is the natural unit of analysis in this case): Those classes that showed larger reductions in bully/victim problems had implemented three presumably essential components of the intervention program (including establishment of class rules against bullying and use of class meetings) to a greater extent than those with smaller changes (additional information on these analyses can be found in Olweus & Alsaker, 1991). This finding certainly provides corroborating evidence for the effects of the intervention program.

All in all, it can be *concluded that the reductions in bully/victim problems and the changes in associated behavior patterns described above were likely to be mainly a consequence of the intervention program and not of some other "irrelevant" factor.*

Brief Comments

The reported effects of the intervention program must be considered quite positive in particular since most previous attempts to systematically reduce aggressive and antisocial behavior in preadolescents/adolescents have been relatively unsuccessful (Dumas, 1989; Gottfredson, 1987; Kazdin, 1987). The importance of the results is also accentuated by the fact that there has been a highly disturbing increase in the prevalence of violence and other antisocial behavior in most industrialized societies in the last decades. In the Scandinavian countries, for instance, various forms of recorded criminality have typically increased by 400 to 500% since the 1950s (and these increases cannot, or only to a very small degree, be explained as a consequence of changes in risk of detection).

As mentioned above, we can estimate that approximately 80,000 students in Norwegian comprehensive schools were involved in bully/victim problems in 1983. On the basis of the reported results the following conclusion can be drawn: *If all comprehensive schools in Norway used the intervention program in the way it was used in Bergen, the number of students involved in bully/victim problems might be reduced to 40,000 or less in a relatively short period.* Effective use of the intervention program would also result in lower levels of theft, vandalism, and other antisocial behavior which would save society large amounts of money. In all probability, it would also improve classroom discipline and other aspects of the "social climate" of the class and the school.

BASIC PRINCIPLES

Having reported the main goals and components of the intervention program as well as some of its effects it is now natural to present its underlying principles and major subgoals.

The intervention program is built around a limited set of key principles derived chiefly from research on the development and modification of the implicated problem behaviors, in particular aggressive behavior. It is considered important to try to create a school, and ideally, also a home environment characterized by warmth, positive interest, and involvement from adults on the one hand and firm limits to unacceptable behavior on the other. Third, in cases of violations of limits and rules, nonhostile, nonphysical sanctions should be consistently applied. Implied in the latter two principles is also a certain degree of monitoring and surveillance of the students' activities in and out of school (Patterson, 1986). Finally, adults are supposed to act in an authoritative manner at least in some respects.

The first three of these principles largely represent the opposite of the child-rearing dimensions that have been found in our research to be important in the development of an aggressive personality pattern (Eron, Walder, & Lefkowitz, 1971; Olweus, 1980a): negativism on the part of the primary caretaker, permissiveness and lack of clear limits, and use of power–assertive methods. In a sense, the present intervention program is based on an authoritative adult–child interaction, or child-rearing model (Baumrind, 1967) applied to the school setting.

The principles listed above can be translated into a number of specific measures to be used at the school, class, and individual levels. It is considered important to work on all of these levels, if possible. Space limitations prevent a description of the various measures suggested but such an account can be found in a small book designed for teachers and parents (Olweus, 1993a). Figure 7 lists a set of core components which are considered, on the basis of statistical analyses and our experience with the program, to be particularly important in any implementation of the program (see Olweus, 1993a).

With regard to implementation and execution, the program is mainly based on a utilization of the existing social environment: teacher and other school personnel, students, and parents. Non-mental-health professionals thus play a major role in the desired *"restructuring of the social environment."* Experts such as school psychologists and social workers also serve important functions such as planning and coordinating, counselling teacher and parent groups, and handling more serious cases.

It may be added that the intervention program has been evaluated by more than 1000 Norwegian and Swedish teachers. In short, their reactions have generally been quite favorable, indicating among other things that the teachers see the proposed principles and measures as useful and realistic.

General Prerequisites
Awareness and involvement on the part of adults

Measures at the School Level
Questionnaire survey
School conference day
Better supervision during recess
Meeting staff—parents (PTA meeting)

Measures at the Class Level
Class rules against bullying
Class meetings

Measures at the Individual Level
Serious talks with bullies and victims
Serious talks with parents of involved students
Teacher and parent use of imagination

FIGURE 7. Overview of core components of the antibullying intervention program at the school, class, and individual levels.

SOME POSSIBLE REASONS FOR PROGRAM EFFECTIVENESS

In this concluding section, I would like to discuss briefly some of my personal views about why the intervention program has been effective. I will present my comments in six main points:

1. First, I think it is important to emphasize generally that the intervention program rests on a sound knowledge base (cf. Cowen, 1984). Over the years, we have devoted a considerable amount of time in testing via empirical research a number of more or less popular conceptions or hypotheses about the causes and mechanisms behind bully/victim problems. As shown elsewhere (Olweus, 1978, 1991), several of these conceptions have proven to be "myths" with no or little empirical support. In this way, it has been possible to avoid at least some "false leads" about how to reduce or prevent bully/victim problems in school (by avoiding intervention efforts, for example, that focus on external deviations in the victims, anxiety and poor self-esteem in the bullies, or on reducing class or school size).

At the same time, research-based knowledge has been accumulating about the causes and mechanisms involved in bully/victim problems as well as in the two broader categories of "adjustment reactions" of which these problems form a part: aggressive, conduct-disordered, externalizing reaction patterns and anxious, withdrawn, internalizing reaction patterns, respectively. We have tried to build a good deal of this knowledge into the program. As stated above, several of the principles underlying the program are directly derived from research on the development and modification of the implicated problem behaviors.

2. An additional reason for the relative efficacy of the program probably lies in its *direct focus on the relevant behaviors and associated norms* (e.g., "we don't accept bullying in our school and will see to it that it comes to an end") rather than on some assumed underlying or mediating mechanism.

Implied in the above is also a view of aggressive behavior that differs in important respects from several contemporary approaches. Many present-day researchers and clinicians seem to have the understanding that aggressive children usually share society's and the school's values and norms about appropriate behavior and are basically interested in conforming to them. However, due to such personal characteristics as lack of conflict-management capacities, cognitive or behavior (social) deficits, or a poor self-image, they are believed to be unable to do so.

Though I recognize that a certain proportion of aggressive children may have skills deficits or poor self-esteem (which may or may not show up as statistically significant differences in group comparisons), I do not think there is much evidence to support the hypothesis that these factors actually cause aggressive behavior (or at least are major causal factors [cf. Dumas, 1989]). In my own approach, I stress the view that a good deal of aggressive behavior, and in particular bullying, can be seen as "self-initiated behavior" with the deliberate aim of inflicting pain and discomfort, of dominating and oppressing others, and of obtaining tangible and prestigious rewards through coercion. In this view, bullying behavior is not primarily seen as a consequence of lack of skills or abilities but rather as *a function of "deviant" motivations and habits.* It is more a question of what the aggressors want to do and are used to doing than what they are able to do. In line with this view, major foci of the present intervention program are the bullying behavior itself and its "opportunity structure" (opportunities to bully others with associated expected positive or negative consequences), to borrow a term from criminology.

3. Related to the above formulations is the fact that program participants are encouraged via the program to *take a clear stance against bullying behavior:* "Bullying is not tolerated in our class/school." The program also makes clear the power relationships in that regard: The adults are in charge and have the authority (and responsibility) to stop such behavior.

It is also important, however, to make the students take a clear stance. This can be done, for example, in the context of the development of class rules (norms) against bullying as well as in follow-up discussions at class meetings.

While the program stresses the importance of repudiating bullying behavior, it also makes it clear that such repudiation should not be made in a harsh, hostile, or punitive way. Consistent use of nonhostile, noncorporal sanctions in cases of rule violations is an important part of the intervention program. At the same time, it is considered essential to develop a class/school climate characterized by warmth and involvement.

4. Another presumably important aspect of the program is that it is directed toward the school as "system" and works simultaneously at several levels: the school, the class, and the individual levels. In addition, it is highly desirable to get the students' parents involved, although less control over this is possible. In this way, measures used at different levels and in different settings can support each other and will result, under favorable conditions, in consistent "messages" from most of the students' social environment. This approach also makes it possible to achieve a certain degree of collective commitment to the program, in particular on the part of the adults at school. If these possibilities are adequately realized, the program is likely to have powerful effects which may also generalize from one setting to another.

From a somewhat different perspective it may be said that the program is both environment- or systems-oriented and person-oriented. Although its main focus is on the environment or the system ("a restructuring of the social environment"), it also contains person-oriented components (e.g., serious talks with the students involved in an identified bully/victim problem and their parents). It is likely that the combination of these two approaches is better than either alone.

5. The positive effects of the intervention, and in particular their maintenance, are likely to be related to the fact that the program is built to achieve not only relatively immediate, more or less short-lived effects on already existing bully/victim problems. It is also designed to prevent the development of new problems and the reemergence of earlier problems. It is reasonable to assume that bully/victim problems may occur whenever several children are together without adequate adult "supervision." Accordingly, it is of great importance for the school to have a constant readiness to detect such problems and to counteract them effectively. For example, by use of class rules against bullying in combination with regular class meetings, problems can be discovered at an early stage before they have become ingrained or have taken a dramatic turn. In this way, these and similar mechanisms built into the program are

likely to prevent the emergence of new problems and the reemergence of problems from earlier periods. They may also have preventive effects, for example, through changing class or school norms and the nature of the interactions among students.

6. Finally, there are several advantages to formulating the problems to be targeted in the intervention as bully/victim problems and not in some other way such as problems with aggressive and antisocial behavior or conduct disorder problems.

In the first place, by conceptualizing it as a bully/victim problem, the aggressive behavior is placed or anchored in a social context: The recipient of the aggression, the victim, comes into focus in addition to the aggressor. In this way, the repeated humiliation and suffering of the victim are brought into the foreground. This serves an important function in justifying use of the program.

To a considerable degree, installment of the program is in fact legitimized by the suffering of the victims, that is, by reference to the immediate, current situation and not to possible long-term effects on the aggressive, antisocial students. Future beneficial effects for the bullies may perhaps occur, but in trying to use such effects as an argument for an intervention program, one is usually met (at least in more sophisticated quarters) with the problem of "false positives" (individuals who are predicted to have a "deviant" outcome but who in fact become "nondeviant" over time). As is well known from research, a sizable proportion of aggressive antisocial children and youths will "normalize" when they grow older and will not turn delinquent or criminal (or whatever outcome is expected) in the absence of any systematic intervention. Since there is usually no way of knowing with suitable accuracy which students will become "false positives" (or "true positives"), this may make it difficult to argue for the necessity of installing an intervention program, at least if it is person-oriented.

These problems are nicely avoided when the main justification of the program lies in the current suffering of the victims as in the present antibullying program. Here the possible long-term changes of the bullies, though highly desirable, are not the key argument for use of the program, they only serve as accessory justification.

By focusing on bully/victim problems, it is usually also relatively *easy to reach consensual agreement* among teachers, parents and (the majority of) students that such problems should not be tolerated in the class or the school: Psychologically and physically stronger students must not be allowed to harass and humiliate weaker and more anxious students. For several reasons, it may be much more difficult to come to consensus about the desirability of counteracting aggressive or antisocial behavior in general.

Though it is certainly important to address bully/victim problems for their own sake, it should be noted that the program had beneficial effects also with regard to other forms of antisocial or conduct-disordered behavior such as vandalism and truancy. In addition, it increased the students' satisfaction with school life and was probably conducive to improved classroom discipline. In this way, bully/victim problems can be regarded as *a nice entry point* for dealing with several other major problems that plague present-day schools.

Related to the last point is the fact that many components and activities of the program (e.g., class rules against bullying, regular class meetings, role-playing, better recess supervision, PTA meetings) are aimed at the total population of students, not only at particularly targeted, "deviant" or at-risk children. Due to this "universal" orientation, the necessity of deciding which students will and will not be involved or focused on in the program—and possible stigmatization problems—are partly avoided. The program may not only reduce and prevent undesirable behaviors and attitudes; it is also likely to generally improve social relationships (as evidenced, for example, in a better social climate of the class) and to enhance prosocial behavior. In this way, the present program shares some of the features of what has been called "mental health promoting" programs (Peters, 1990).

All in all, the above characteristics of the program may make it not only acceptable but often even attractive to the staff of the school (and to many parents). Formulating the problems in this way is likely to make schools more willing to "take ownership of the problems" and to recognize that it is primarily their responsibility to do something about them. Again, if the problems were conceptualized in a different way, for instance, in terms of conduct disorders, schools would be more inclined to disengage themselves from responsibility for the problems and to regard their solution as a task for the child psychiatrist or school psychologist. In sum, the way in which a problem is conceptualized, formulated, and presented to the school has important implications for the school's readiness to do something about it.

CONCLUSION

Though what has been presented in this chapter about the effects of the intervention program only represents the first stages of analysis, the basic message of our findings is quite clear: It is definitely possible to reduce substantially bully/victim problems in school and related problem behaviors with a suitable intervention program. And such a program need not be costly in terms of money or time. Whether these problems will be tackled or not no longer depends on whether we have the knowledge necessary to achieve desirable changes. It is much more a matter of our willingness to involve ourselves and to use the existing knowledge to counteract the problems.

ACKNOWLEDGMENTS

The research reported was supported by grants from the William T. Grant Foundation, the Norwegian Research Council for Social Research (NAVF), the Swedish Delegation for Social Research (DSF), and, in earlier phases, from the Norwegian Ministry of Education (KUD) for which the author is grateful.

REFERENCES

Allport, G. W. (1937). The functional autonomy of motives. *American Journal of Psychology, 50,* 141–156.

Asher, S. R., & Coie, J. D. (Eds.). (1990). *Peer rejection in childhood.* New York: Cambridge University Press.

Baumrind, D. (1967). Child care practices anteceding three patterns of preschool behavior. *Genetic Psychology Monographs, 75,* 43–88.

Beck, A. T., Ward, C. H., Mendelson, M., Mock, J., & Erbaugh, J. (1961). An inventory for measuring depression. *Archives of General Psychiatry, 4,* 561–571.

Cohen, J. (1977). *Statistical power analysis for the behavioral sciences* (rev. ed.). New York: Academic Press.

Cowen, E. L. (1984). A general structural model for primary program development in mental health. *Personnel and Guidance Journal, 62,* 485–490.

Dumas, J. E. (1989). Treating antisocial behavior in children: Child and family approaches. *Clinical Psychology Review, 9,* 197–222.

Eron, L. D., Walder, L. O., & Lefkowitz, M. M. (1971). *Learning of aggression in children.* Boston: Little, Brown.

Eysenck, S. B. G., & Eysenck, H. J. (1975). *Manual of the Eysenck Personality Questionnaire.* London: University of London Press.

French, D. C. (1988). Heterogeneity of peer-rejected boys: Aggressive and nonaggressive subtypes. *Child Development, 59,* 976–985.

Gottfredson, G. D. (1987). Peer group interventions to reduce the risk of delinquent behavior: A selective review and a new evaluation. *Criminology, 25,* 187–203.

Huesmann, L. R., & Eron, L. D. (1984). Cognitive processes and the persistence of aggressive behavior. *Aggressive Behavior, 10,* 243–251.

Huesmann, L. R., & Eron, L. D. (in press). Childhood aggression and adult criminality. In J. McCord (Ed.), *Advances in criminological theory: Crime facts, fictions, and theory.* New Brunswick, NJ: Transaction Publishers.

Kazdin, A. E. (1987). Treatment of antisocial behavior in children: Current status and future directions. *Psychological Bulletin, 102,* 187–203.

Kupersmidt, J. B., Coie, J. D., & Dodge, K. A. (1990). The role of poor peer relationships in the development of disorder. In S. R. Asher & J. D. Coie (Eds.), *Peer rejection in childhood* (pp. 217–249). New York: Cambridge University Press.

Ladd, G. W. (1985). Documenting the effect of social skill training with children: Process and outcome assessment. In B. H. Schneider, K. H. Rubin, & J. E. Ledingham (Eds.), *Children's peer relations: Issues in assessment and intervention* (pp. 243–269). New York: Springer.

Lagerspetz, K. M., Björkqvist, K., Berts, M., & King, E. (1982). Group aggression among school children in three schools. *Scandinavian Journal of Psychology, 23*, 45–52.

Loeber, R., & Dishion, T. (1983). Early predictors of male delinquency: A review. *Psychological Bulletin, 94*, 69–99.

Magnusson, D., Stattin, H., & Dunér, A. (1983). Aggression and criminality in a longitudinal perspective. In K. T. Van Dusen & S. A. Mednick (Eds.), *Prospective studies of crime and delinquency.* Boston: Kluwer-Nijhoff.

Manger, T., & Olweus, D. (1985). Tilbakemelding til skulane. *Norsk Skoleblad* (Oslo, Norway), *35*, 20–22.

Olweus, D. (1973a). *Hackkycklingar och översittare: Forskning om skolmobbning*. Stockholm: Almqvist & Wiksell.

Olweus, D. (1973b). Personality and aggression. In J. K. Cole & D. D. Jensen (Eds.), *Nebraska symposium on motivation, 1972* (Vol. 20, pp. 261–321). Lincoln: University of Nebraska Press.

Olweus, D. (1977). Aggression and peer acceptance in adolescent boys: Two short-term longitudinal studies of ratings. *Child development, 48*, 1301–1313.

Olweus, D. (1978). *Aggression in the schools: Bullies and whipping boys.* Washington, DC: Hemisphere (Wiley).

Olweus, D. (1979). Stability of aggressive reaction patterns in males: A review. *Psychological Bulletin, 86*, 852–875.

Olweus, D. (1980a). Familial and temperamental determinants of aggressive behavior in adolescent boys: A causal analysis. *Developmental Psychology, 16*, 644–660.

Olweus, D. (1980b). The consistency issue in personality psychology revisited—with special reference to aggression. *British Journal of Social and Clinical Psychology, 19*, 377–390.

Olweus, D. (1981). Bullying among school-boys. In N. Cantwell (Ed.), *Children and violence.* Stockholm: Akademilitteratur.

Olweus, D. (1984). Aggressors and their victims: Bullying at school. In N. Frude, & H. Gault (Eds.), *Disruptive behavior in schools.* New York: Wiley.

Olweus, D. (1985). 80 000 barn er innblandet i mobbing. *Norsk Skoleblad* (Oslo, Norway), *35*, 18–23.

Olweus, D. (1986). *Mobbning—vad vi vet och vad vi kan göra.* Stockholm: Liber.

Olweus, D. (April, 1989a). *Peer relationship problems: Conceptual issues and a successful intervention program against bully/victim problems.* Paper presented at the biannial meeting of the Society for Research in Child Development, Kansas City, U.S.A.

Olweus, D. (1989b). Prevalence and incidence in the study of antisocial behavior: Definitions and measurement. In M. Klein (Ed.), *Cross-national research in self-reported crime and delinquency* (pp. 187–201). Dordrecht, The Netherlands: Kluwer.

Olweus, D. (1991). Bully/victim problems among schoolchildren: Basic facts and effects of a school based intervention program. In D. Pepler & K. H. Rubin (Eds.), *The development and treatment of childhood aggression* (pp. 411–448). Hillsdale, N.J.: Erlbaum.

Olweus, D. (1993a). *Bullying at school: What we know and what we can do.* Oxford: Blackwell Publishers.

Olweus, D. (1993b). Victimization by peers: Antecedents and long-term outcomes. In K. H. Rubin & J. B. Asendorf (Eds.), *Social withdrawal, inhibition, and shyness in childhood* (pp. 315–341). Chicago: University of Chicago Press.

Olweus, D., & Alsaker, F. D. (1991). Assessing change in a cohort longitudinal study with hierarchical data. In D. Magnusson, L. Bergman, G. Rudinger, & B. Törestad (Eds.), *Problems and methods in longitudinal research* (pp. 107–132). New York: Cambridge University Press.

Olweus, D., Mattsson, Å., Schalling, D., & Löw, H. (1980). Testosterone, aggression, physical, and personality dimensions in normal adolescent males. *Psychosomatic Medicine, 42,* 253–269.

Olweus, D., Mattsson, Å., Schalling, D., & Löw, H. (1988). Circulating testosterone levels and aggression in adolescent males: A causal analysis. *Psychosomatic Medicine, 50,* 261–272.

Olweus, D., & Roland, E. (1983). *Mobbing—bakgrunn og tiltak.* Oslo, Norway: Kirke- og undervisningsdepartementet.

Parker, J. G., & Asher, S. R. (1987). Peer relations and later personal adjustment: Are low-accepted children at risk? *Psychological Bulletin, 102,* 357–389.

Patterson, G. R. (1986). Performance models for antisocial boys. *American Psychologist, 41,* 432–444.

Perry, D. G., Kusel, S. J., & Perry, L. C. (1988). Victims of peer aggression. *Developmental Psychology, 24,* 807–814.

Peters, R. DeV. (1990). Adolescent mental health promotion: Policy and practice. In McMahon, R. J., & Peters, R. DeV. (Eds.), *Behavior disorders of adolescence.* New York: Plenum Press.

Retterstøl, N. (1990). *Selvmord.* Oslo: Universitetsforlaget.

Rosenberg, M. (1979). *Conceiving the self.* New York: Basic Books.

Smith, P. (1989). *The silent nightmare: Bullying and victimization in school peer groups.* Paper presented at the meeting of the British Psychological Society, London, England.

Stattin, H., & Magnusson, D. (1989). The role of early aggressive behavior in the frequency, seriousness, and types of later crime. *Journal of Consulting and Clinical Psychology, 57,* 710–718.

Stortingsmelding nr.23. 1991–92. (1992). Om kriminalitetens bekjempande og forebygging. Oslo: Justis- og politidepartementet.

Sudak, H. S., Ford, A. B., & Rosforth, N. B. (1984). *Suicide in the young.* Boston: John Wright.

Whitney, I., & Smith, P. K. (1991). *A survey of the nature and extent of bullying in junior/middle and secondary schools.* Manuscript. University of Sheffield, England.

Ziegler, S., & Rosenstein-Manner, M. (1991). *Bullying at school: Toronto in an international context* (Report No. 196). Toronto: Toronto Board of Education, Research Services.

CHAPTER 6

INDIRECT AGGRESSION IN BOYS AND GIRLS

KIRSTI M. J. LAGERSPETZ AND KAJ BJÖRKQVIST

INTRODUCTION

RESEARCH ON AGGRESSION IN FEMALES

Traditionally, men and boys have been regarded as more aggressive than women and girls. This is supported by the fact that, with few exceptions, males are more aggressive than females in most animal species. A review of these issues was presented by Moyer (1977). In humans, there is evidence for a higher level of physical aggression in males than in females. Criminal statistics show that men outnumber women as perpetrators of physical violence in all societies. Women are also aggressive, however, and researchers in different fields have started to pay attention to the forms of female aggression. For instance, anthropologists have described violence committed by women in different cultures (Burbank, 1987; Cook, 1992; Fry, 1992; Glazer, 1992; Schuster, 1983). Female aggression is found in all regions of the world in a great variety of forms.

KIRSTI M. J. LAGERSPETZ • Department of Psychology, University of Turku, Turku, Finland. KAJ BJÖRKQVIST • Department of Psychology, Åbo Akademi University, Vasa, Finland.

Aggressive Behavior: Current Perspectives, edited by L. Rowell Huesmann. Plenum Press, New York, 1994.

Reviews have usually found males to score higher on measures of aggression than females (Frodi, Macaulay, & Thome, 1977; Frost & Averill, 1982; Huesmann & Eron, 1986; Huesmann, Eron, Lefkowitz, & Walder, 1984; Lambert, 1985; Maccoby & Jacklin, 1974; Rauste-von Wright, 1989; White, 1983). It is true, however, that the difference between the sexes appears more clearly in some conditions and situations than in others. Recent reviews are more careful in their claims about sex differences than previous ones.

All human behavior is, however, regulated and formed by cultural factors. Accordingly, the difference in aggressiveness between the sexes has been attributed to their social roles, in addition to or instead of biological factors. Physical aggression is conceived of primarily as a male characteristic in many cultures. Unfortunately, the socialization process works in the same direction as the assumed biological differences; that is, it encourages and even idealizes aggression and violence in males, but discourages females from direct aggressive confrontation and violent behavior. It is therefore difficult to distinguish between biological and social effects in the causation of sex differences in aggression.

Björkqvist, Ekman, & Lagerspetz (1982) carried out a study of self-images and ideal self-images of 12-to-14-year-old boys and girls, rated as bullies and victims by their peers. A comparison of the self-images on these two levels showed that girls who were bullies wished that they were less domineering than they were, but aggressive boys wanted to be still more domineering than they were in reality. This result can be seen as reflecting the idealization of aggression in the case of males, but not in the case of females, in Western culture. The aggressive girls obviously felt that they were domineering and that this was at variance with their own ideals, whereas the aggressive boys felt comfortable with their own domineering behavior, which corresponded to what they felt was expected of them. The idealization of aggression among boys, but not among girls, was also found by Rauste-von Wright (1989).

In an international follow-up study in six countries (Huesmann & Eron 1986), the self-ratings of boys correlated positively with their peer-rated aggression in most countries and samples, but for girls, the correlations between self-ratings and peer-ratings were generally poor. This result may reflect the difficulty a girl has in admitting that she is aggressive, and in thinking about and analyzing her own aggressive reactions. Her peers may still conceive of her as aggressive, even when she does not conceive of herself in that way.

Direct aggression with females as perpetrators may depend, in relative terms, more than its male counterpart on the situation than on norms of behavior. This suggestion is based on findings that females are likely to react aggressively, similarly to males, if the setting seems to call for it. Females will be aggressive, for instance, if they are provoked, or if the aggression is seen by them to be justified in the situation, but typically they will not show as much unprovoked aggression as males do (Frodi et al., 1977; Lambert, 1985). This fact may well be due to culturally determined sex roles in regard to aggression.

Pulkkinen (1987) suggests that the behavior of males tends to be more of the offensive type, whereas that of females is confined more to the defensive type. The distinction between offensive and defensive aggression is, however, problematic due to the fact that what should be regarded as a provocation is not self-evident. There is also evidence suggesting that women do not become provoked as easily as men. According to Zillman (1979), women are more effective in minimizing the provocations and in handling annoyance in other ways than by counteraggression. Zillman thinks that the conflict solution strategies used by women are often more efficient than those used by men, since the latter often lead to an escalation of the conflict.

The sex of the target has also been found to influence aggression. Males are aggressive more frequently and more intensively toward other males than toward females (Pitkänen, 1973; DeTurck, 1987). For females, the influence of the target changes with age. Preschool girls are more severely aggressive toward boys than toward girls (Miller, Donaher, & Forbes, 1986), whereas college girls claimed in self-reports that they use direct aggression more toward girls of the same age than toward boys (DeTurck, 1987).

It has been commonly believed that males use more physical aggression while females use more verbal aggression. Reviews of the research show, however, that males are verbally as aggressive, and often even exceed females in this respect (Hyde, 1984).

Indirect Aggression

If direct aggression is discouraged in females, it is likely that they instead resort to indirect forms of aggression. This would show only in measurements indicating indirect instead of direct aggression. The common feature of this type of aggression is that the aggressor can stay unidentified and thereby avoid both counterattack from the aggressor and disapproval from the rest of the community. According to Buss (1961, p. 8), "indirect aggression may be verbal (spreading nasty gossip) or physical (a man sets fire to his neighbor's home)." Measurement techniques usually do not detect indirect aggression precisely because it is indirect, and the perpetrator will disguise her or his aggression, or refrain completely from aggressive behavior if she or he is aware of being observed. If asked about one's own aggression in a questionnaire, the person who uses indirect forms of aggression would typically also be expected to deny being aggressive.

A typical feature of psychological follow-up studies is that aggression in females is found to be less stable than in males (Huesmann et al., 1984; Huesmann & Eron, 1986; Olweus, 1984; Pulkkinen, 1987). A reason for this state of affairs may be that the type of behavior measured is more typical of males than of females. The items used in these tests of aggression, whether they are based on questionnaires, peer nominations, observations in field studies, or in experimental contests, measure almost exclusively direct, offensive aggression. Although some items of indirect aggression may be included in the questionnaires, the measures principally tap behavior that may be typical of male but not of female aggression. Accordingly, the total aggression score of a person, male or female, will be based on the prevalence of this type of behavior.

Kagan and Moss (1984) differentiate between *homotypic* and *heterotypic* continuity of personality traits. A trait is said to be homotypic if the same behavior (e.g., the display of direct offensive aggression) continues for many years, resulting in high stability in repeated measurements. When a trait is heterotypic, the trait (e.g., aggression) is exhibited in different ways during the different age periods. Aggression previously shown directly, may later be exhibited in other forms, for instance in disguised or indirect forms. The outcome is low stability, when measurements with the same instrument are repeated.

In a developmental study with children aged 6 to 12 years, Rotenberg (1984) found that indirect retaliation in aggressive encounters became more common with age. This suggests that indirect aggression may be a more "advanced" behavior than is direct aggression.

In younger girls, direct forms of aggression, both physical and verbal, are perhaps the most common type of hostile behavior. During adolescence, however, aggression may shift into indirect expressions in girls but perhaps not yet in boys, whose social skills develop later. If this is the case, low stability measures for female, but not for male aggression will be found. Stable overt, direct aggression among girls seems to be deviant according to the norms of Western culture. Evidence of this comes from a study that seemingly contradicts the findings of less stability of aggression in girls: the follow-up was performed by Cairns, Perrin, & Cairns (1985). These authors found that a group of 10 extremely aggressive girls (according to nominations by peers and teachers), maintained stable positions in terms of aggression, to a greater extent than an all-boy group of the same size. The behavior rated was direct, overt aggression. Girls engaging in this type of behavior were, as the authors themselves conclude (p. 239), distinctive relative to unselected girls. Aggressive behavior patterns which are atypical for the gender can perhaps be expected to remain more stable. Being statistically "abnormal," they may represent a kind of behavioral "disturbance" which is maintained by complicated personality dynamics, and not easily changed. The 10 most aggressive boys, on the other hand, obviously represented the upper end of the normal distribution, and accordingly lost their positions more easily.

Friendship Patterns

Girls' friendships are more intimate and emotional than those of the boys, and the expression of personal feelings is more common and more free (Mazur, 1989). Cairns et al. (1985) also studied the social structure of boys' and girls' groups in junior high school. The girls' friendship groups were smaller, pairs were more common among the girls, and there was higher agreement than among boys about who belonged to which group. The boys tended to have larger and looser groups, with less clear boundaries. It would be expected that a tight social structure, like the one which girls tend to have, would offer more possibilities to use social relations as a vehicle for indirect aggression.

An Investigation of Indirect Aggression among Girls

Our research group decided to investigate the prevalence and development of indirect aggressive strategies in both sexes. The studies were conducted amongst schoolchildren of varying ages. The age of the groups studied were 8 to 9 years (here referred to as the 8-year-old age group, or cohort); 11 to 12 years (here referred to as the 11-year-old cohort); 15 to 16 years (here referred to as the 15-year-old cohort); and 18 to 19 years (here referred to as the 18-year-old cohort). Group sizes, and numbers of boys and girls in each group, are presented in Table 1.

The studies are reported in more detail in the following articles (Björkqvist, Lagerspetz, and Kaukiainen, 1992; Björkqvist, Österman, and Kaukiainen, 1992; Kaukiainen, Lagerspetz, Björkqvist, and Jokila (submitted); Lagerspetz, Björkqvist, and Peltonen, 1988).

Although anger is not the same as aggression, it is the emotion most commonly connected with aggression. (For an analysis of the relationship between anger and aggression, see Averill [1982].) Aggression is usually defined as a response the intent of which is to injure another organism. Aggression is the kind of behavior which an angry person will most typically engage in.

To find out about the prevalence of indirect aggression among the

TABLE 1. Sample Sizes in the Four Cohorts

Age group	Boys	Girls	Total	Classes	Schools
8	40	45	85	5	3
11	78	89	167	7	4
15	73	74	147	5	4
18	87	118	205	8	4
Total	278	326	604	25	10*

*The participating schools in the different age groups were in some cases the same ones.

subjects, we asked them to describe what each one of the other boys or girls in the class does when they are angry at some of their peers. Boys rated boys and girls rated girls, except for the oldest cohort (the 18-year-olds), in which peers of the opposite sex also were rated. In addition, all subjects rated their own behavior.

We asked each child to rate his or her classmates on fixed behavior options, that is, ways in which they might harm the person they were angry with. The options were derived from preinterviews with students of the same age as the actual subjects. Both direct forms of agonistic behavior (like yelling, hitting, pushing) and indirect ones (spreading false rumors about the person, making friends with somebody else in revenge, etc.) were included. In some cohorts, a smaller sample was additionally interviewed about their own behavior when angry, as well as about that of their peers. The validity of this measurement was thus based on two criteria: (1) the behavior was carried out when the perpetrator was angry; (2) the behavior was likely to harm the target person. One may, accordingly, be reasonably confident that the actions constituted forms of aggression. Our hypothesis was that girls would show more indirect, while boys more direct aggression.

Since indirect aggression is mostly carried out in a social setting, we thought that the subjects might use the social structure as a vehicle of their aggression. The friendship patterns of the class were accordingly investigated with methods roughly similar to those designed by Cairns et al. (1985). Our hypothesis was that a tight friendship structure would be connected with the use of indirect methods, whereas a loose structure would favor the use of direct aggression.

The subjects gave answers to the following questions: (1) Who in your class are friends? (mention groups or pairs). (2) Are there students in your class who do not belong to any group or pair? What are their names? (3) Do you have good friends in the class? If so, who are they? A student was counted as belonging to a group category (group, pair, or loner) if 30% of the classmates rated him or her accordingly.

RESULTS

The Questionnaires and the Interviews

Because of the different levels of student maturity, the same items could not be used with all age groups, but the items were constructed on basis of preinterviews with some students from each cohort. The questionnaire for the 8-year-olds was quite simple. The questionnaire for the older cohorts contained descriptions of more complicated behaviors and situations. The final questionnaire for the 8-year-old cohort consisted of only 12 items; for the 11-year-old age group there were 18 items, and both the 15- and 18-year-old cohorts had 34 items in their questionnaire. Only nine items were identical for all cohorts. The questionnaires are presented in full in Björkqvist, Lagerspetz, and Kaukiainen (1992), and in Kaukiainen, Lagerspetz, Björkqvist, and Jokila (submitted). The most recent version of our Direct–Indirect Aggression Scales is presented in Björkqvist, Österman, and Kaukiainen (1992).

All items used for the 11-year-old cohorts are presented in Table 2, in combination with a comparison of the means of the two sexes (Lagerspetz, Björkqvist, & Peltonen 1988). As presented in the table, the boys tended to employ direct aggression, while the girls used significantly more indirect than direct forms of aggression.

In the interviews, with the 14 boys and 15 girls of this cohort, the girls described interesting kinds of indirect aggression, like writing anonymous letters about the girl they were angry at; criticizing the clothes of the girl they were angry at; making their friend jealous by associating with somebody else; and revealing secrets about herself which the other girl had told them in confidence. These were things that they claimed other girls did. When asked about what they did themselves, they usually mentioned that they "just go away" or "do nothing." Indirect aggression is obviously a difficult thing to recognize in oneself, although it is easy to describe in others. This fact was also revealed by the low correlations between self-ratings and peer ratings in the case of indirect aggression (see below).

Boys claimed to become angry more often than girls did (or admitted). When the 11-year-olds were asked about duration of anger, the girls considered their anger to last longer than did the boys, who usually mentioned durations of a few minutes, the time of a break between two lessons, the course of a single lesson, at any rate, less than a day. There was greater variation in the duration mentioned by girls, but on average, it was longer than among the boys ($\chi^2(2) = 6.50$, $p < .05$). According to two girls, a person could be angry with another for "either one minute or for the rest of her life."

TABLE 2. Behavior when Angry. Means and Significant Differences between Peer Ratings of Boys and Girls in the 11-Year-Old Cohort

Behavior	Girls Mean *(sd)*	Boys Mean *(sd)*	*t*	*p*<
Direct Aggression				
Kicks or hits	0.41 *(0.40)*	1.12 *(0.60)*	9.02	.001
Trips	0.23 *(0.28)*	0.83 *(0.56)*	9.04	.001
Shoves	0.64 *(0.46)*	1.16 *(0.56)*	6.59	.001
Takes things	0.45 *(0.36)*	0.84 *(0.54)*	5.56	.001
Argues	1.33 *(0.48)*	1.05 *(0.40)*	4.10	.001
Swears	0.74 *(0.56)*	1.19 *(0.63)*	4.90	.001
Calls names	1.03 *(0.55)*	1.19 *(0.53)*	1.89	.10
Abuses	1.09 *(0.56)*	0.96 *(0.51)*	1.59	n.s.
Indirect Aggression				
Tells untruth behind the back	1.32 *(0.55)*	0.84 *(0.44)*	6.11	.001
Starts being somebody else's friend as revenge	0.90 *(0.48)*	0.65 *(0.39)*	3.64	.001
Tries to get the other on his or her side	1.07 *(0.57)*	0.70 *(0.37)*	4.91	.001
Says to others: "Let's not be with him or her."	0.82 *(0.48)*	0.63 *(0.33)*	3.09	.01
Takes revenge in play	0.71 *(0.45)*	0.75 *(0.41)*	0.66	n.s.
Peaceful Means				
Talks to clarify	1.32 *(0.46)*	1.01 *(0.41)*	4.54	.001
Forgets all about it	1.44 *(0.41)*	1.31 *(0.31)*	2.36	.05
Tells teacher or parent	0.56 *(0.49)*	0.52 *(0.47)*	0.44	n.s.
Withdrawal				
Sulks	1.17 *(0.48)*	0.67 *(0.38)*	7.27	.001
Acts as if didn't know the other	0.83 *(0.37)*	0.36 *(0.27)*	9.28	.001

Summed Variables of Direct and Indirect Aggression

In order to reduce the variables and to find out how the items grouped together, factor analyses were performed. On the basis of these, summed variables were constructed. This procedure resulted in three summed variables of peer estimated behavior when angry for the 8- and 11-year-old cohorts: *direct aggression, indirect aggression,* and *peace-*

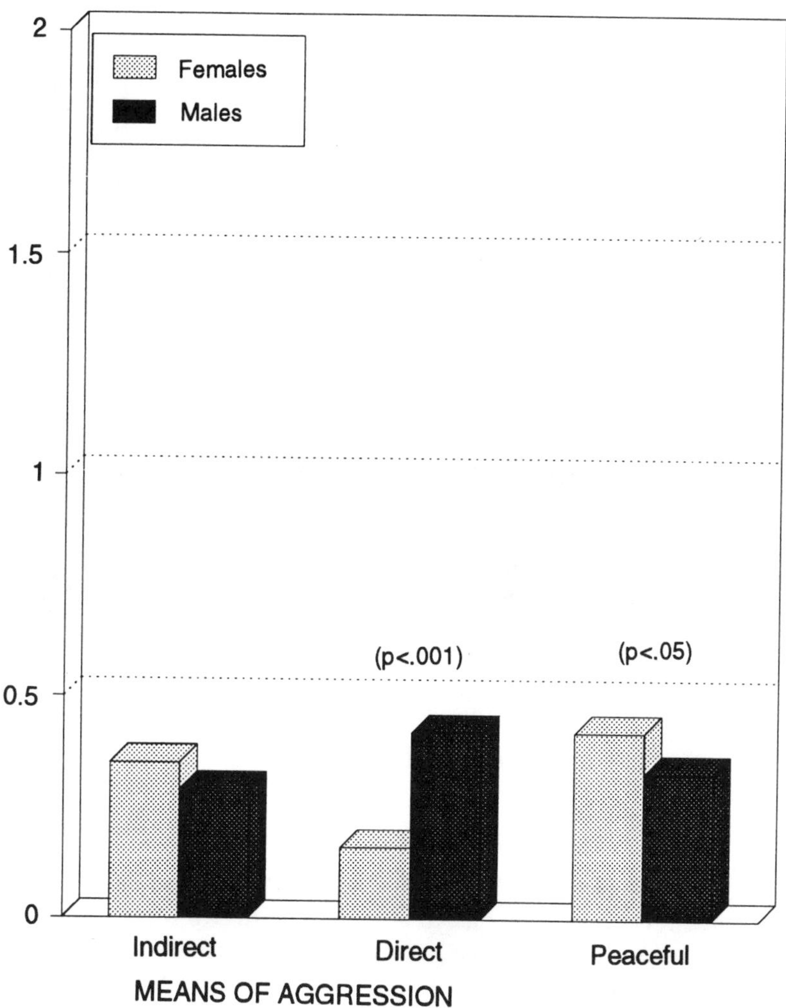

FIGURE 1. Peer-estimated behavior when angry, 8-year-old subjects.

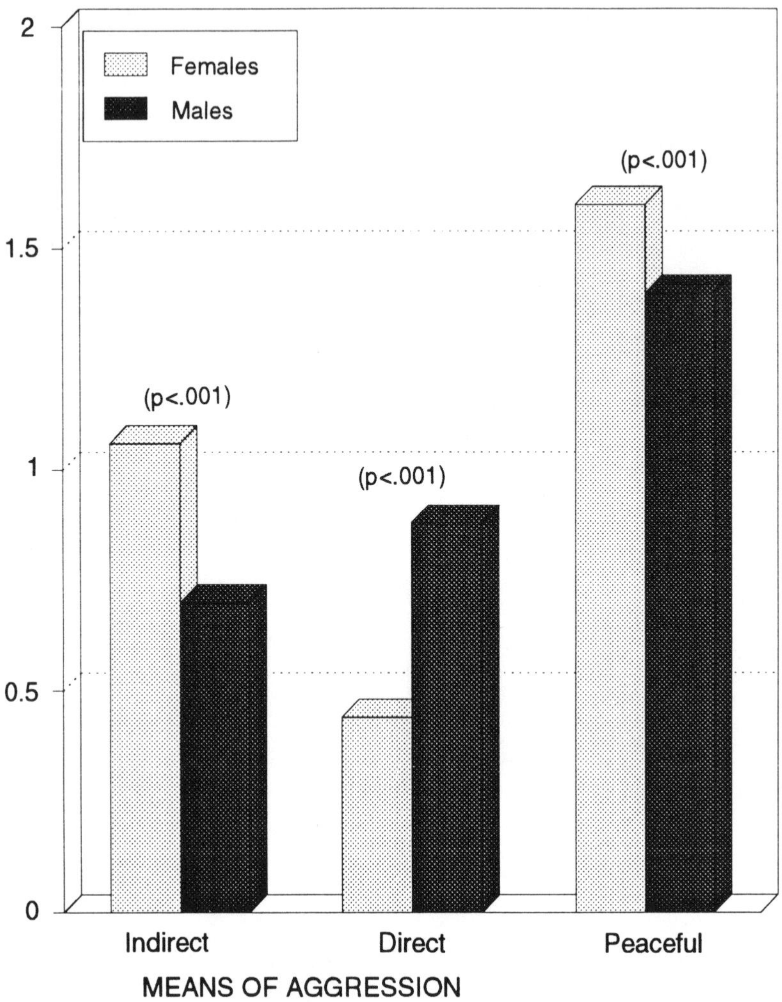

FIGURE 2. Peer-estimated behavior when angry, 11-year-old subjects.

ful means of problem solving. In the case of the 15- and 18-year-old age groups, direct aggression had to be divided into two separate subscales: *physical aggression,* and (direct) *verbal aggression.* The internal consistencies of these summed variables are presented in Lagerspetz, Björkqvist, and Peltonen (1988), Björkqvist, Lagerspetz, and Kaukiainen (1992), and Kaukiainen et al. (submitted).

Figures 1 to 4 show the means of the summed variables of peer

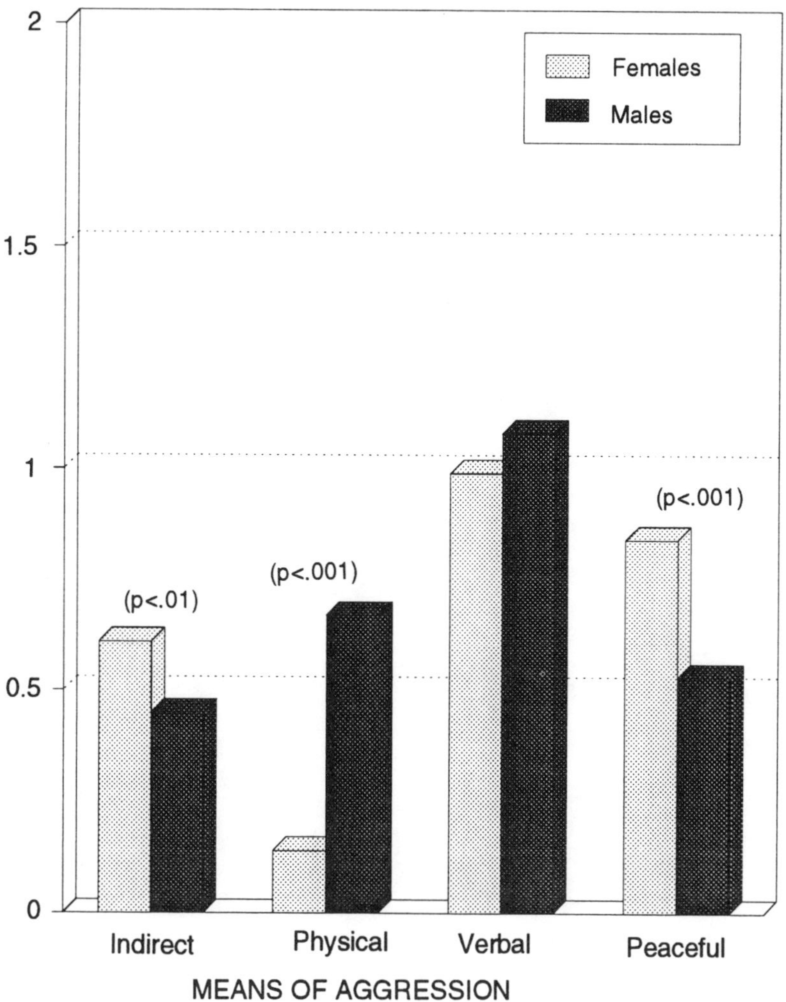

FIGURE 3. Peer-estimated behavior when angry, 15-year-old subjects.

estimated behavior when angry in the four age groups, for boys and girls respectively.

The use of indirect aggression, and of withdrawal and peaceful means were more common among the girls than among the boys in all cohorts, with the exception of the youngest one (the 8-year-olds), in which girls did not yet use significantly more indirect aggression than the boys. The behavior of boys, in all age groups, was characterized by

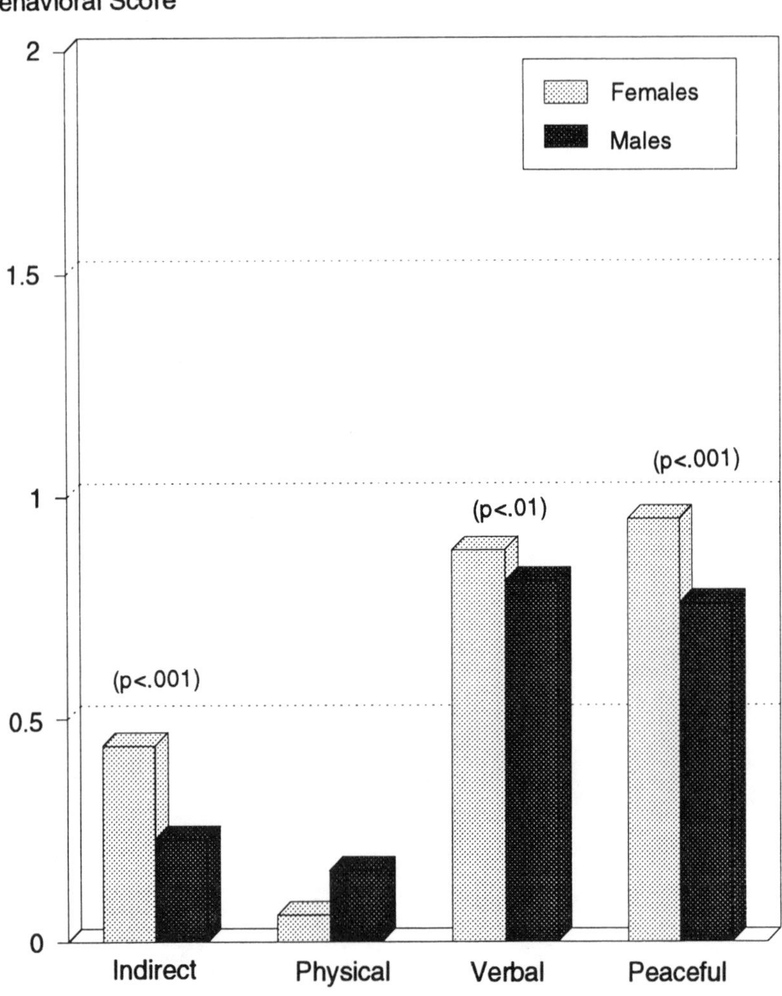

FIGURE 4. Peer-estimated behavior when angry, 18-year-old subjects.

direct forms of aggression and physical aggression. It seems as if indirect aggression was not yet fully developed among the youngest girls, who showed generally less aggression than boys of the same age. It is conceivable that some degree of social maturation is required for a skillful use of indirect aggression.

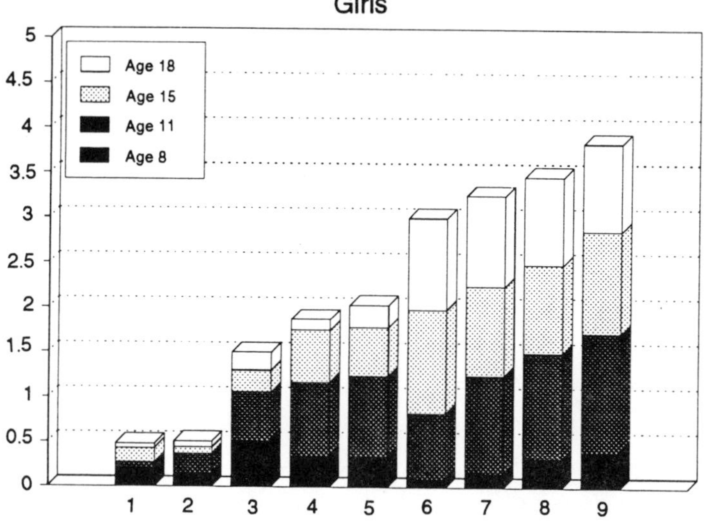

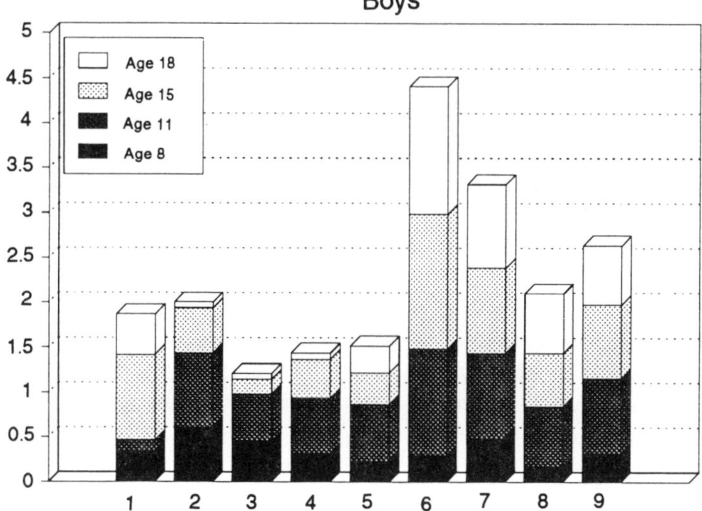

1. Shoves
2. Kicks
3. Tells teacher
4. Says to others: "Let's not be with her/him!"
5. Starts being somebody else's friend as revenge
6. Swears
7. Abuses
8. Sulks
9. Gossips

FIGURE 5. Developmental trends in aggressive styles. Peer-estimated styles of aggression in four age groups (8-, 11-, 15-, & 18-year-old subjects).

Developmental Trends

As already mentioned, nine items were identical for all age cohorts, and they thus allow for comparisons between age groups. They are presented in Figure 5.

The 11-year-old cohort appears to be the most aggressive one (or at least is estimated to be), since it shows the highest figures for most forms of aggressive behavior in both sexes, with the exception of swearing in the case of boys. Swearing, which is not necessarily always a form of aggression, showed the highest prevalence in the age of 15.

Self-Rated and Peer-Rated Aggression

Correlations between self- and peer ratings with respect to indirect and direct aggression were calculated. In the case of the 11-year-old cohort, the correlations were lower for indirect than for direct aggression (.34, $p < .001$; and .60, $p < .001$, respectively), both sexes included. They were lower for the girls (.23, $p < .01$ for indirect and .29, $p < .05$ for direct aggression) than for the boys (.24, $p < 0.1$ for indirect and .63, $p < .001$ for direct aggression) (Lagerspetz, Björkqvist, & Peltonen, 1988). The correlations were thus (1) lower for indirect than for direct aggression, and (2) lower for girls than for boys.

In the 8-year-old cohort, correlations between self- and peer estimations were not significant, with the exception of individual items (boys *shoving*, .29 $p < .05$, and girls *calling names*, .29, $p < .05$).

In the case of the 18-year-old cohort, peer and self-ratings of indirect aggression did not correlate significantly for either sex. In regard to direct aggression, however, the correlations were significant both for boys and girls. The obvious conclusion is that it is difficult to perceive, or admit, indirect aggression as part of one's own behavioral repertoire, although it can be observed by one's peers.

The Friendship Patterns of the Class

The estimated sizes of the friendship groups did not differ between the two genders in the youngest cohort (the 8-year-olds). In all, 23% of the relationships mentioned were pairs, groups with three members were mentioned by 15% of the children, and groups with four or more members were mentioned by 8%.

In the 11-year-old age group, however, the size of the friendship groups was somewhat larger for boys than for girls; more pair relationships were mentioned by the girls, and the boys mentioned more groups with more than four members. The most remarkable gender difference was that the boys were not able to classify the friendship groups as clearly as the girls did. Only 66.9% of the boys were assessed as belonging to a clearly defined category (i.e., in a group, or as a "loner"), whereas as many as 95.3% of the girls were clearly classified by their peers ($\chi^2(1) = 16.55$, $p < .001$) (Lagerspetz, Björkqvist, & Peltonen, 1988).

In the 15-year-old cohort, significantly more of the girls reported being in pairs than the boys (Björkqvist, Lagerspetz, & Kaukiainen, 1992). Another novelty in this cohort was that a few friendship groups including members of both sexes existed. More students were mentioned as "loners" than in the 11-year-old cohort of Lagerspetz et al. (1988) (Table 3).

Among the 18-year-olds, the groups of the girls were smaller than those of the boys. The girls also favored pairs more than the boys did. The girls' groups seemed to be more clearly defined, and tighter than those of the boys. Only 5.9% of the girls belonged to the category of "loners," whereas a fifth of the boys (20.7%) were categorized as not belonging to any group by their peers.

The Target of Aggression

The 18-year-olds were also asked about being angry at members of the other sex, as well as at persons of their own sex. Both boys and girls rated that they became angry at individuals of the same sex more often than at members of the opposite sex. The sex of the rater did not influence this result significantly. (see Figure 6). In contrast to the other means of behavior when angry, "withdrawal" was assessed as being

TABLE 3. Numbers of Pupils of Both Sexes, within the 15-Year-Old Cohort, Estimated by at Least 30% of Peers as Members of Friendship Groups of Different Sizes

	Boys		Girls	
Group size	%	*N*	%	*N*
Alone	40	29	20	15
Group of two	16	12	49	36
Group of three	16	12	12	9
Four or more	27	20	19	14

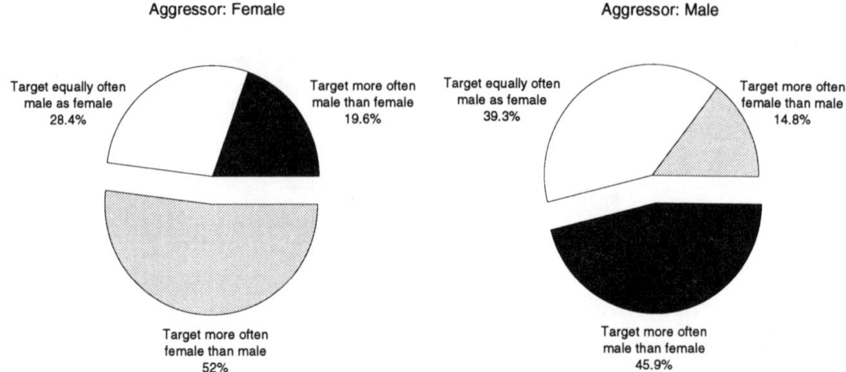

FIGURE 6. The gender of the target for aggression (18-year-old subjects).

used mostly with female opponents. Boys especially claimed to use this kind of behavior toward girls. In addition to aggressiveness, chivalry also belongs to the male role in the society (Eagly & Crowley, 1986). The result may reflect this tendency.

Boys Rating Girls and Girls Rating Boys

In the three younger cohorts, only students of the same sex were rated by the subjects. In the case of the 18-year-old cohort, the procedure was, however, extended also to the opposite sex. The sex of the rater influenced the ratings of all kinds of aggression in a remarkable way: members of both sexes rated the opposite sex to use indirect aggression more than the within-sex estimations showed.

DISCUSSION

The boys of the present investigation were rated as becoming angry more often than the girls. They also engaged more in direct aggression, especially in physical aggression. The most remarkable finding was, however, the extensive use of indirect aggression among the girls. The low correlations between self-ratings and peer ratings for indirect aggression, and the results of the interviews, showed that the perpetrator may not want to admit to (or is perhaps even not herself aware of) her own aggressive behavior. The self- and peer ratings of indirect aggression by boys did not correlate as highly as those of direct aggression. It is obviously easier to admit being overtly aggressive than to see oneself as intriguing and scheming, as a person is obliged to say if she or he admits to indirect aggression. Furthermore, indirect aggression is easier to "explain away" to both oneself and to others. For example, if you write a letter describing "what kind of person" your friend "really" is, you can say that you are just telling the truth and not being aggressive. The girls also exceeded boys in dealing with conflicts by negotiation, withdrawal, and other peaceful means.

In a study by Rotenberg (1984), indirect retaliation to aggression was found to be more common in older than in younger children. Avoidance of direct offensive aggression may be seen as a mark of social maturation, because it characterizes adult social life as compared to the life of children. In that respect, the use of indirect aggression and of the nonaggressive ways of conflict-solving behavior might be seen to reflect girls' earlier social maturation.

The results of this investigation present a rather cruel and ruthless picture of the social life of girls. Adult social life is, however, also cruel, and the girls are "practicing" for it earlier than the boys, who still practice more immature conflict strategies. In adult social relations, direct aggression is more or less prohibited, but indirect aggression becomes "tuned down" or "refined" by sanctions against too obvious forms of it. The same types of behavior exhibited rather crudely by the girls of this study may, in principle, be discerned in adult relations. And indeed, the modes of aggression became more diversified in the older cohort as compared to the younger ones. Furthermore, the girls of the youngest cohort had not yet "discovered" the use of indirect aggression to any great extent, but they simply displayed generally less aggression than the boys. The girls of this age were also "nicer" than the boys, using peaceful means to a greater extent.

One may speculate that since indirect aggression has always been the strategy of oppressed groups in the society, it is natural for females to use it when they mature socially. Girls may even be "forced" to mature earlier in order to be able to use these types of strategies. The friendship ratings showed more disagreement among the boys than among the girls about the correct location of individuals in the peer groups, and in the friendship categories. Among the girls, the unanimity of the raters showed that they had clear ideas about who belonged to which group or pair, and who were loners. The groups of the girls were also smaller, there were more pairs, that is, cases of only two girls being close friends. This kind of social structure is likely to make the friendships emotionally more important for the participants than a looser constellation does. When the friendships are tight and the other peers know about them, there are more possibilities for a manipulative use of the social relations in indirectly harming others.

The 11-year-old cohort was found to be the most aggressive one, when most of the nine items were compared. This was especially true of the girls' display of indirect aggression. Also in the older cohorts, however, indirect aggressive strategies were more typical of the girls than of the boys.

A matter for further study is the question whether males later "catch up," and start to use indirect means of aggression as much as females do. Or, are backbiting, gossiping, and manipulative behavior still more typical female strategies during adult life? In Western society, adult males have been responsible for most of the serious physical aggression. However, males do not function in isolation from their social background. Women have traditionally supported the fighters, not least by keeping the hostilities between families and other groups alive through the use of indirect aggression. It is conceivable, however, that the changing roles of women and men in society will also change roles and norms of the sexes with respect to aggression in the future.

Acknowledgments

Our thanks are due to the Council of Social Sciences, Academy of Finland for financial support. We are also grateful to Ari Kaukiainen, Tarja Peltonen, Riikka Ketola, Markku Jokila and Karin Österman who participated in different ways in this study.

REFERENCES

Averill, J. R. (1982). *Anger and aggression. An essay on emotion.* New York: Springer Verlag.

Björkqvist, K., Ekman, K., & Lagerspetz, K. M. J. (1982). Bullies and victims: Their ego-picture, ideal ego-picture, and normative ego-picture. *Scandinavian Journal of Psychology, 23,* 281–290.

Björkqvist, K., Lagerspetz, K. M. J., & Kaukiainen, A. (1992). Do girls manipulate and boys fight? Developmental trends in direct and indirect aggression. *Aggressive Behavior, 18,* 117–127.

Björkqvist, K., Österman, K., & Kaukiainen, A. (1992). The development of direct and indirect aggressive strategies in males and females. In: K. Björkqvist, & P. Niemelä (Eds.), *Of mice and women: Aspects of female aggression* (pp. 51–64). Orlando, FL: Academic Press.

Burbank, V. K. (1987). Female aggression in cross-cultural perspective. *Behavior Science Research, 21,* 1–4.

Buss, A. (1961). *The psychology of aggression.* New York: John Wiley.

Cairns, R. B., Perrin, J. E., & Cairns, B. D. (1985). Social structure and social cognition in early adolescence: Affiliative patterns. *Journal of Early Adolescence, 5,* 339–355.

Cook, K. (1992). Matrifocality and female aggression in Margeriteño society. In: K. Björkqvist, & P. Niemelä (Eds.), *Of mice and women: Aspects of female aggression* (pp. 000–000). Orlando, FL: Academic Press.

DeTurck, M. (1987). When communication fails: Physical aggression as a compliance-gaining strategy. *Communication Monographs, 54,* 106–111.

Eagly, A. H., & Crowley, M. (1986). Gender and helping behavior: A meta-analytic review of the social psychological literature. *Psychological Bulletin, 100,* 283–308.

Frodi, A., Macaulay, J., & Thome, P. R. (1977). Are women always less aggressive than men? A review of the experimental literature. *Psychological Bulletin, 84,* 634–660.

Frost, W. D., & Averill, T. R. (1982). Difference between men and women in the everyday experience of anger. In: J. R. Averill (Ed.), Anger and aggression: An essay on emotion. (pp. 281–316). New York: Springer-Verlag.

Fry, D. (1992). Gender and aggression among the Zapotec of Oaxaca. In: K. Björkqvist, & P. Niemelä (Eds.), *Of mice and women: Aspects of female aggression* (pp. 187–199). Orlando, FL: Academic Press.

Glazer, I. M. (1992). Interfemale aggression and resource scarcity in a cross-cultural perspective. In: K. Björkqvist, & P. Niemelä (Eds.), *Of mice and women: Aspects of female aggression* (pp. 163–171). Orlando, FL: Academic Press.

Huesmann, L. R., & Eron, L. D. (1986). *Television and the aggressive child: A cross-national comparison.* Hillsdale, NJ: Lawrence Erlbaum.

Huesmann, L. R., Eron, L. D., Lefkowitz, M. M., & Walder, O. (1984). Stability of aggression over time and generations. *Developmental Psychology, 20,* 1120–1134.

Hyde, J. S. (1984). How large are gender differences in aggression? A developmental meta-analysis. *Developmental Psychology, 2,* 722–736.

Kagan, J., & Moss, H. A. (1984). *Birth to maturity.* Orlando, FL: Yale University Press.

Kaukiainen, A., Lagerspetz, K. M. J., Björkqvist, K., & Jokila, M. Sex differences in aggressiveness in late adolescence. Submitted to *Aggressive Behavior.*

Lagerspetz, M. J., Björkqvist, K., & Peltonen, T. (1988). Is indirect aggression typical of females? Gender differences in aggressiveness in 11- to 12-year-old children. *Aggressive Behavior, 14,* 403–414.

Lambert, W. E. (1985). What happens to children when they act aggressively in six cultures? In: F. R. Brush & J. B. Overmeier (Eds.), *Affect, conditioning, and cognition: Essays on the determinants of behavior* (pp. 325–339). Hillsdale, NJ: Lawrence Erlbaum.

Maccoby, E. E., & Jacklin, C. N. (1974). *The psychology of sex differences.* Stanford, CA: Stanford University Press.

Mazur, E. (1989). Predicting gender differences in same-sex friendships from affiliation motive and value. *Psychology of Women Quarterly, 13,* 277–291.

Miller, P., Donaher, D., & Forbes, D. (1986). Sex related strategies for coping with interpersonal conflict in children aged five to seven. *Developmental Psychology, 22,* 543–549.

Moyer, K. E. (1977). *The psychobiology of aggression.* New York: Harper & Row.

Olweus, D. (1984). Development of stable aggressive reaction patterns in males. In: D. C. Blanchard (Ed.), *Advances in the study of aggression* (Vol. 1, pp. 000–000). Orlando, FL: Academic Press.

Pitkären, L. (1973). An aggression machine I-II. *Scandinavian Journal of Psychology, 14,* 56–74.

Pulkkinen, L. (1987). Offensive and defensive aggression in humans: A longitudinal perspective. *Aggressive Behavior, 9,* 197–212.

Rauste-von Wright, M. (1989). Physical and verbal aggression in peer groups among Finnish adolescent boys and girls. *International Journal of Behavioral Development, 12,* 473–484.

Rotenberg, K. J. (1984). Causes, intensity, motives, and consequences of children's anger from self-reports. *Journal of Genetic Psychology, 146,* 101–106.

Schuster, I. M. (1984). Women's aggression: An African case study. *Aggressive Behavior, 9,* 319–331.

Zillman, D. (1979). *Hostility and aggression.* Hillsdale, NJ: Lawrence Erlbaum.

Part III

ENVIRONMENTAL INSTIGATION AND MITIGATION OF AGGRESSION

In the first chapter in this part, Huesmann and Miller provide an overview of the longitudinal research on media violence and aggression conducted over the past 25 years. They place this research in the framework of social–cognitive theories of aggressive behavior and show how dramatic media violence can exert its effect on behavior through multiple psychological processes. In particular, they argue that media violence can have long-term effects through a variety of observational learning processes. At the same time, media violence can produce short-term effects by cuing cognitive schema that promote aggressive behavior.

The second chapter, by Dubow and Reid, investigates how the social resources available to an adolescent may mitigate the aggression-stimulating effects of environmental variables such as stress. These authors argue that social support and social skills make children more resilient to developing aggressive styles of behavior in response to environmental stress.

CHAPTER 7

LONG-TERM EFFECTS OF REPEATED EXPOSURE TO MEDIA VIOLENCE IN CHILDHOOD

L. ROWELL HUESMANN AND LAURIE S. MILLER

INTRODUCTION

About a quarter of a century ago, a young American radical, Stokely Carmichael, commented that violence was as American as apple pie! At least in terms of prevalence, nothing much seems to have changed since that time. The frequency of violence directed by one human being at another was appallingly high then and is appallingly high now. The United States is not the most violent society in the world. That distinction belongs to some of the less developed countries ravaged by wars, terrorism, drug battles, and general lawlessness. Nor is violence as endemic now as it has been during many of the last 20 centuries. Among

L. ROWELL HUESMANN • Research Center for Group Dynamics, Institute for Social Research, University of Michigan, Ann Arbor, Michigan 48106-1248. LAURIE S. MILLER • Department of Child Psychiatry, New York State Psychiatric Institute, Columbia University, College of Physicians and Surgeons, New York, New York 10032.

Aggressive Behavior: Current Perspectives, edited by L. Rowell Huesmann. Plenum Press, New York, 1994.

the highly developed Western societies, however, the United States has scored at the top for the past several decades on most objective measures of interpersonal violence. For example, homicides in the United States rose from an overall rate of about 5 per 100,000 to 10 per 100,000 between World War II and the 1980s and have remained at about that level. Of course, the rate in some inner-city ghettos may be 10 times this rate (100/100,000) and the rate for certain age cohorts may be 3 times this rate (e.g., 30/100,000 for males 18 to 24). In comparison, no other highly developed Western society has a rate much above 3 per 100,000 and most are below 1 per 100,000. Rates at these levels are cause enough for concern and also reflect increases since World War II, but the sustained rates in the United States are a national tragedy. In some urban areas of the United States the most common cause of death for young males is now homicide.

The dramatic increase in interpersonal violence in the past century has occurred at the same time as other dramatic changes in life-styles produced by the great technological revolutions of the 20th century. Among the most notable of these for child development has been the introduction of the mass visual media into children's everyday life. When two highly salient events cooccur, it is common to hypothesize a causal relation between them; so it is not surprising that speculation about the role of media violence in stimulating violent behavior has been prevalent ever since motion pictures depicting violent acts first were distributed. With the advent of television in the early 1950s the speculation advanced to the point of theorizing, and the first studies were initiated. Since then, the question of whether media violence somehow promotes violence in society has been a constant, major topic of concern to communication researchers, psychologists, and policymakers. As a result, a large body of scientific literature on the topic has emerged.

The scientific studies fall into three major categories. First, there are the experimental studies in which exposure of children to scenes of violence is manipulated and the short-term changes in the children's behavior are evaluated. These experiments have been linked together under the rubric of "laboratory research" whether or not they have been executed in a laboratory or classroom. These studies have clearly shown that exposing children to visual portrayals of dramatic violence causes at least some of the children to behave more aggressively immediately afterwards. Second, there have been static observational field studies in which aggressive behavior and exposure to media violence are assessed in samples of children in their home and school environments. These studies have demonstrated that children who behave more aggressively on the average watch and prefer to watch more violent TV shows and movies. Finally, there are the longitudinal field studies in which children's exposure to media violence and their actual aggressive behavior are assessed at two or more points in their lives. These are the kind of studies that our research group has focused on over the past 30 years. In many respects they are now the most crucial studies because they allow researchers to assess most directly the practical significance of the established relation between media violence and aggression.

On the basis of these empirical studies one can probably dismiss the notion that the current level of interpersonal violence in the United States and other Western nations is solely due to or even primarily due to the long-term exposure of our youth to scenes of violence in the dramatic media. Indeed, few serious students of aggressive behavior would have ever suggested such an hypothesis. More to the point, the existing empirical studies do provide support for the conjecture that the current level of interpersonal violence in our societies has been *boosted* by the long-term effects of many persons' childhood exposure to a steady diet of dramatic media violence. This thesis is supported most directly with a review and analysis of longitudinal studies of real children growing up to be real adults. Since one cannot analyze those studies in a theoretical vacuum, we must begin with a review of the relevant psychological theory and also attend to the more traditional laboratory experiments that have been used to test aspects of this theory. Only then can we turn to a review of the relevant longitudinal studies.

AGGRESSIVE BEHAVIOR

Let us begin, however, with a definition of aggressive and violent behavior. Some harmful events are violent without being manifestations of aggressive behavior; for example, automobile accidents. We are not interested in that kind of violent event in this chapter. We are interested in behaviors by one individual that are intended to injure or irritate another individual. Such behaviors are called aggressive behaviors (Eron, Walder, & Lefkowitz, 1971). Excluded from this class of behaviors are assertive actions that are commonly called "aggressive" (e.g., aggressive salespeople or executives).

Multiple Causes and Early Onset

Two of the clearest conclusions one can draw about human aggressive behavior from the existing research is that severe aggressive acts are most often the product of multiple causes and that characteristically aggressive people first display their abnormal behavior at a very early age.

Individual differences in social behavior related to aggression (e.g., early temperament) are apparent before age 2 (Kagan, 1988). By age 6, a number of children have adopted aggressive patterns of behavior in their interactions with others (Parke & Slaby, 1983). From that point on the extent of aggressive behavior in children tends to increase into adolescence. By age 8, children are characteristically more or less aggressive over a variety of situations; and aggression becomes a relatively stable characteristic of the individual youngster that predicts adult aggression (Ensminger, Kellam, & Rubin, 1983; Farrington, 1982, 1990; Huesmann, Eron, Lefkowitz, & Walder, 1984; Loeber & Dishion, 1983; Magnusson, Duner, & Zetterblom, 1975; Moffitt, 1990; Olweus, 1979; Robins & Ratcliff, 1980; Spivack, 1983). The more aggressive child becomes the more aggressive adult.

The existing research also suggests that childhood aggression is most often a product of a number of interacting factors: genetic, perinatal, physiological, familial, and learning. In fact, it seems most likely that severe antisocial aggressive behavior occurs only when there is a convergence of many of these factors.

The evidence for a heritable predisposition to aggression has accumulated in recent years. Adoption studies in Scandinavia, where subjects are easily tracked over several decades, show more concordance between adults' antisocial and aggressive behavior and their natural parents' behaviors than with their adoptive parents' behaviors (Cloninger & Gottesman, 1987; Mednick, Gabrielli, & Hutchings, 1984). In fact, both twin and adoption studies now provide compelling evidence that many personality characteristics tied to social behavior are influenced by heredity (Bouchard, 1984; Loehlin, Willerman, & Horn, 1985; Rowe, 1987; Rushton, Fulker, Neale, Nias, & Eysenck, 1986). While the methodologies of many studies in this area are necessarily complex and open to criticism, the evidence that there is a substantial heritable predisposition to aggression now seems compelling. That does not mean, of course, that situational and environmental variables are unimportant. On the basis of extrapolations from the animal literature, it seems quite probable that a heritable predisposition to aggression manifests itself in characteristic early social interactions. The animal literature also suggests that early interactions of an appropriate type can greatly mitigate the genetic predisposition to aggression. Lagerspetz and Lagerspetz (1971), for example, have shown that selective breeding for aggression can produce highly aggressive strains of mice in just a few generations. But the extent to which even mice from the most aggressive strain (after

30 generations) will evidence aggression as adults depends on their early social interactions with other mice (Lagerspetz & Sandnabba, 1982). Mice who are predisposed to be aggressive but who are raised in an environment in which "prosocial" behavior is rewarded, do not evidence such strong aggressive tendencies. Genetic predispositions interact with an organism's early learning experiences.

It also seems likely that the effects of specific chronic neurophysiological deficits that promote aggression, and the effects of neurotoxins (such as lead) and central nervous system (CNS) trauma (such as blows to the head) interact with the early environment to affect childhood and ultimately adult aggressive behavior. The evidence for the involvement of neurophysiological abnormalities in some cases of severe aggression is strong (Lewis, Moy, Jackson, Aaronson, Restifo, Serra, & Simos, 1985; Moyer, 1976; Nachson & Denno, 1987; Pontius, 1984). Less extreme individual differences in aggression sometimes seem to be related to naturally occurring variations in hormones such as testosterone, estrogen, and progesterone (Dalton, 1977; Olweus, Mattsson, Schalling, & Low, 1988). Individual differences in characteristic heart rates have also been linked to individual differences in adolescent aggression (Raine & Jones, 1987) and also to the differences in early childhood temperament that are related to aggression.

It has also been demonstrated that the effects on aggressive behavior of individual differences in neurophysiology are exacerbated and mitigated by both a child's early learning experiences and situational factors in the person's environment. For example, Olweus' (Olweus, Mattsson, Schalling, & Low, 1988) data suggest that a high testosterone adolescent would only be prone to behave aggressively in situations in which he was strongly provoked. In many cases of extreme aggressive reactions linked to neurophysiological deficits, the responses have been triggered by situational factors producing stress or early experiences that promoted aggression.

More generally, the existing research suggests that habitual aggressive behavior in young humans is to a great extent learned from the child's early interactions with the environment (Bandura, 1973; Berkowitz, 1974; Eron, Walder, & Lefkowitz, 1971; Huesmann, Eron, Lefkowitz, & Walder, 1984). While genetic and physiological factors may predispose a child toward aggression, it is the child's early learning experience that molds him or her into one who behaves more or less aggressively.

What are the key elements of the child's environment that promote the development of aggressive behavior? One must distinguish between instigators that motivate or cue aggressive responses and indirectly affect learning, and those components of the child's environment that more directly mold the child's responses to these stimuli and socialize the child. An environment rich with environmental deprivations, frustrations, and provocations is one in which habitual aggression readily develops as the high level of aggression in our urban ghettos attests. The elements that are more important theoretically in socializing the child and in determining individual differences in learned responses, however, are the child's family, peers, and cultural surroundings, including exposure to television and movies.

The Socialization Process for Children

As part of the socialization process, children are expected to adopt society's rules, attitudes, values, and norms. Throughout development, children are directed to think and behave in ways that are consistent with cultural standards. These standards are viewed as the essential regulators that lead children to develop patterns of behaviors and ways of interacting with others (Damon, 1983).

The socialization process requires children to learn to inhibit antisocial behavior and to display acceptable behavior. The process involves helping children to regulate and control their own behavior and to chose behavior that is appropriate to the situation.

Parents are traditionally thought of as the primary agents of socialization early in children's lives. Appropriate behavior is taught by parents' encouragement of acceptable behavior and discouragement of behavior that is unacceptable. Additionally, parents teach their children through direct tuition and modeling of appropriate behaviors. Although parents can have great influence over their children, their standards for behavior are not simply accepted and adopted because children are not passsive recipients of social information (Bell & Harper, 1977). Children are active agents in creating the social experiences that influence their development. They participate in determining the nature of their social relations, bringing their own individual characteristics to the interactions in which they engage. Therefore, the process of interaction between the child and others in the child's social environment has bidirectional effects, changing both the child and those with whom the child interacts.

Although parents usually serve as the main socializing agents for young children, early in a child's development other sources of information can influence the socialization process. For example, peers become increasingly important in influencing a child's social development, as do the media (e.g., television, movies, videogames) and other adults (i.e., teachers and extended family members).

Because of the malleability of behavior in young children and the relative intractability of aggressive and violent dispositions once they have developed, it is important that theories concerning the influence of media violence on habitual aggressive behavior focus on exposure to media violence and aggression and antisocial behavior in preadolescent children. As we have argued above, individual differences during this period are influenced, of course, by factors with earlier loci of effect, such as genetics; but the major issue of interest is how, during early childhood, individual differences in the propensity for aggressive behavior develop as a consequence of the child's interaction with his or her environment. What are the dimensions and parameters of the socialization processes that lead to these individual differences? Through what psychological process does the influence of this early socialization process extend into adulthood? These are key issues for an understanding of the long-term effects of exposure to media violence.

Cognitive Processes and the Learning of Aggression

Bandura (1977, 1986) has perhaps had the greatest influence on researchers' theorizing about how media violence influences social behavior. According to Bandura's cognitive/social learning theory, one way that the different sources (i.e., parents, peers, television, teachers) influence children is by serving as models for behavior (Bandura, 1977). The modeling process proposed by Bandura is based on research in cognitive psychology and hypothesizes a complex interaction of *cognitive* subprocesses that determine whether or not, and to what degree modeling takes place. In order for a modeled event to be performed, it must proceed through the four subprocesses of attention, retention, reproduction, and motivation (Bandura, 1977). According to Bandura, children do not learn patterns of interacting by copying specific behaviors. In fact, children older than 2 years of age are unlikely to learn behaviors from "pure" imitation. Instead, as they develop, children observe many behaviors from a variety of sources. According to Bandura's more recent formulations (Bandura, 1986), children not only adopt specific behaviors modeled by others but they also tend to adopt evaluative standards employed by these models. Bandura argues that these standards can be established by direct tuition, by other's reactions to one's behavior, and by observing the self-evaluative standards modeled by others. Therefore, beyond modeling specific behaviors, a child may pattern his or her thoughts, feelings, and actions after another person who serves as a model (Bandura, 1986). It is assumed that a child who consistently exhibits certain behaviors may have generalized beliefs that represent adopted standards of conduct or values that support the use of these behaviors (Bandura, 1986; Huesmann & Eron, 1984). In other words, a child's social behavior is controlled to a great extent by these standards for behavior which may be learned from a variety of sources.

The cognitive structures that guide the child's behavior, are a central component in Bandura's formulation of the socialization process. In recent years, a number of other theorists, drawing both on Bandura's social learning theory and research in cognitive psychology, have offered theories that implicate the child's cognitions in the learning and maintenance of aggressive habits. These models put the stress primarily on cognitive processes and the steps through which a child must proceed in order to react appropriately, competently, and nonaggressively to a social situation or stimulus. Among the most influential of these have been the revised formulation from Bandura himself (1986), the neoassociationist perspective of Berkowitz (1984, 1988), and the information processing theory put forth by Huesmann (1982, 1988; Huesmann & Eron, 1984).

According to Bandura's (1986) recent formulation, social behavior comes under the control of internal self-regulating processes. What is important is the cognitive evaluation of events taking place in the child's environment, how the child interprets these events, and how competent he/she feels in responding in different ways. These cognitions provide a basis for stability of behavior tendencies across a variety of situations. Internalized standards are developed from information conveyed by a variety of sources of social influence. Children are exposed to many opportunities in which they may observe the self-evaluative standards of others, one of which is through the media. As Bandura asserts, in many aspects of living, televised vicarious influence has supplanted the primacy of direct experience. "Whether it be through patterns, values, attitudes, or styles of behavior, life increasingly models the media" (1989, p. 89). Berkowitz, on the other hand, has emphasized the importance of enduring associations in explaining stable behavioral tendencies. Aggression is an aversively stimulated behavior. An aversive event produces negative affect which is associated in most people with "expressive-motor reactions, feelings, thoughts, and memories that are associated with both flight and fight tendencies. . ." (Berkowitz, 1988, p. 8). A variety of factors—genetic, learned, and situational—affects the strengths of the flight and fight tendencies. The stronger tendency wins out, and, if it is fight, the emotional experience is interpreted as anger. Attributions about the behavior may occur later as a "controlled" cognitive process, but the generation of the behavior and the associated anger is relatively "automatic."[1] Huesmann (1988; Huesmann & Eron, 1984) has viewed the child as a processor of information who develops programs called "scripts" to guide social behavior. Once scripts are firmly established they may be automatically executed, and the child's responses may seem to be "unthinking" even though they are the product of a complex set of cognitive processes. The more aggressive child, according to Huesmann (1988), is one who learns, retains, retrieves, and utilizes more aggressive scripts.

All of these approaches have the common theme that the child's cognitions play a key role in maintaining the stability of aggressive behavior over time and situation subject to the moderating or exacerbating influence of other predisposing factors. In the remainder of this review we will focus on Huesmann's script theory as the framework for understanding the long-term effects of media violence as revealed in longitudinal studies. It should be noted, however, that many of the same predictions would obtain from Bandura's or Berkowitz's theories.

Script Theory and Learning from Media Violence

Of all these cognitive approaches, the information processing script theory developed by Huesmann (1988) is most directly intended to explain the stability of aggressive tendencies over time and the role of media violence in promoting aggressive behavior. Huesmann's theory adopts the premise that social behavior is controlled to a great extent by programs for behavior that are established during a person's early development. These programs can be described as cognitive scripts (Abelson, 1981) that are stored in a person's memory and are used as guides for behavior and social problem solving. A script suggests what events are to happen in the environment, how the person should behave in response to these events, and what the likely outcome of those behaviors would be. It is presumed that while scripts are first being established they influence the child's behavior through "controlled" mental processes (Schneider & Shriffrin, 1977; see footnote 1), but these processes become "automatic" as the child matures. Correspondingly, scripts that persist in a child's repertoire, as they are rehearsed, enacted,

[1] The terms *controlled* and *automatic* are technical terms developed by cognitive psychologists to describe different modes of mental processing (Schneider & Shriffrin, 1977). Automatic processes are mental processes that operate very rapidly with a person having little awareness of the mental operations involved (e.g., reading). Controlled processes operate much more slowly, and a person is much more aware that they are "controlling" the mental operations (e.g., mental arithmetic).

and generate consequences, become increasingly more resistant to modification.

According to Huesmann, the process through which scripts are formed is a learning process involving both *observational and enactive* components. The primary learning process is one in which the child observes sequences of behavior by others and encodes these sequences into a cognitive script. This is observational learning. The secondary learning process occurs when the child utilizes this script to guide his or her own behavior and is reinforced (positively or negatively) for the resulting response. This is enactive learning. Both learning processes may alter the structure of a script, affect the strength with which it is encoded, and its connections to other elements in the child's cognitive schema. Cognitive rehearsal of a script will also strengthen its encoding and connectedness. Furthermore, through a process of cognitive abstraction, subsets of learned scripts may be converted into more general scripts that provide overall guiding principles for social behavior. Thus, the scripts that guide the child into "childish" aggressive behavior form the basis for a set of more general scripts guiding the adult into adult "aggressive" behavior.

It is clear that, according to this theory, the child's observation of dramatic or real violence in childhood could contribute to the construction of lasting cognitive structures that would affect the child's behavior in childhood and when he or she was grown. The theory suggests, however, that the role for adult exposure to media violence in the learning of aggressive behavior is limited. Scripts for social behavior may still be learned during adulthood, but we adopt the developmental perspective that scripts learned early are the most influential. In practical terms this means that the theory predicts little relation between adult aggression and an adult's exposure to media violence but a significant relation between childhood exposure and childhood aggression. Furthermore, childhood exposure to media violence should be related to adult aggression to the extent that childhood aggression is related to adult aggression.

EXPERIMENTAL STUDIES OF TV VIOLENCE AND AGGRESSION

While the focus of this chapter is on longitudinal field studies of media violence and aggression, one cannot properly interpret such studies without placing them in the context of the true experiments and static field studies that have been conducted on this topic. Causal hypotheses can never be tested as well in field settings as in true experiments. Since the reality of a child's life can never be captured very well in a laboratory setting, it is important to examine each in the context of the other.

In contrived experimental settings, children exposed to violent behavior on film or TV usually behave more aggressively immediately afterwards. Large numbers of laboratory and field experiments have demonstrated this fact over the past quarter-century (see reviews by Comstock, 1980; Geen, 1983, 1990; Geen & Thomas, 1986). Such results obtain both for aggression directed at inanimate objects (e.g., "Bobo" dolls) and for aggression directed at peers (Bjorkqvist, 1985; Josephson, 1987). For example, Josephson found that for boys the combination of having viewed a recent violent film and then being exposed to a distinctive cue that had been present in the film was particularly potent in stimulating aggression toward their peers in a natural setting. The role of distinctive cues in theories of how aggression is stimulated by media violence have been studied by Berkowitz (1983) and Huesmann (1986). The effects of violent TV or films on the affective responses that mediate aggression have also been clearly demonstrated with valid experiments. For example, Bushman and Geen (1990) demonstrated that violent videotapes elicit both aggressive cognitions and higher systolic blood pressure in college students. It is also true that in the laboratory, children can be taught to be less aggressive by showing them films with prosocial models (Eron & Huesmann, 1986; Pitkannen-Pulkkinen, 1979). These short-term effects are not limited to children but have been observed in teenagers and adults, particularly when the dependent measures reflect attitudes or opinions rather than behaviors (Malamuth & Donnerstein, 1982). In these well-controlled laboratory studies there can be no doubt that it is the children's observation of the scenes of violence that is *causing* the changes in behavior. Some critics would dismiss these studies completely as "artificial" approximations to life (Freedman, 1984) and focus only on field studies. But such a position is not defensible in light of the complementary nature of experimental and nonexperimental research in this area (Huesmann, Eron, Berkowitz, & Chaffee, 1991).

STATIC OBSERVATIONAL STUDIES OF TV VIOLENCE AND AGGRESSION

The demonstration of a relation between the observation of media violence and the commission of aggressive behavior has not been limited to the laboratory. Evidence from field studies over the past 20 years has led most reviewers to conclude that a child's current aggressiveness and the amount of TV and film violence the child is regularly watching are positively related to some degree. More aggressive children watch more violent television. (Andison, 1977; Bachrach, 1986; Belson, 1978; Chaffee, 1972; Comstock, 1980; Eron, 1963; Eysenck & Nias, 1978; Hearold, 1979; Eron, Huesmann, Lefkowitz, & Walder, 1972; Huesmann, Eron, Lefkowitz, & Walder, 1973; Huesmann, 1982; Huesmann & Eron, 1986; Huesmann, Lagerspetz, & Eron, 1984; Lefkowitz, Eron, Walder, & Huesmann, 1977; Leyens, Parke, Camino, & Berkowitz, 1975; Loye, Gorney, & Steele, 1977; Milavsky, Kessler, Stipp, & Rubens, 1982; Parke, Berkowitz, Leyens, West, & Sebastian, 1977; Singer & Singer, 1981; Stein & Friedrich, 1972; Williams, 1978). This relation is not strong by the standards used in the measurement of intellectual abilities, and varies as a function of environmental, familial, cognitive, and TV programming variables. The relation is usually statistically significant, however, and substantial by the standards of personality measurement with children. Correlations of the magnitude usually obtained in the field can have real social significance (Rosenthal, 1986). Moreover, the relation is highly replicable even across researchers who disagree about the reasons (e.g., Huesmann, Lagerspetz, & Eron, 1984; Milavsky, Kessler, Stipp, & Rubens, 1982) and across countries (Huesmann & Eron, 1986). In contrast, significant correlations between aggression and adults' concurrent violence viewing have been observed only rarely in the field.

LONGITUDINAL OBSERVATIONAL STUDIES OF TV VIOLENCE

Let us summarize the most relevant points we have made so far. Existing longitudinal studies of aggression have established with some clarity that childhood aggression is predictive of adult aggression and antisocial behavior. Existing static field studies of media violence have established that exposure to media violence and childhood aggression are correlated. Existing true experiments done in the laboratory and field have established that exposure to dramatic scenes of violence on TV can cause a child to behave more aggressively immediately afterwards. The question that remains, then, is whether childhood exposure to media violence relates to aggression in later life. Yet, this is a critical issue for the media violence-aggression research. Most of that research has associated childhood aggression with childhood exposure to violence. Such childhood aggression is predictive of adult criminality. Therefore, if exposure to media violence is an important precursor of aggressive behavior, children's TV habits should be expected to be predictive of adult antisocial behavior as well. Furthermore, just as not all children who are exposed to media violence display childhood aggression, it is likely that not all children who may learn to be more aggressive from viewing violence will behave more aggressively as adults. A variety of environmental, cultural, familial, and cognitive differences might exacerbate or mitigate the lasting effect of exposure to violence. These factors need to be identified. In the remainder of this chapter we discuss several longitudinal field studies that address this issue.

One cannot challenge the validity of the conclusion that exposure to media violence caused children to behave more aggressively in the true experiments described above. The experimental methodology assures the validity of the conclusion. Nor can one challenge the conclusion from the static field studies that more aggressive children watch and prefer more TV violence. Again the conclusion is appropriate for the methodology employed and the results uncovered. Taken together, these results also clearly suggest that media violence would play a causal role in stimulating real life aggression. It is impossible, however, to conclusively tease apart cause and effect with certainty in even the best longitudinal observational studies. Without the control that true experiments provide, causal conclusions are very risky. Nevertheless, appropriate multivariate analyses of data from longitudinal observational studies can suggest whether a causal effect is plausible.

The thesis of this chapter is that the available longitudinal data on the whole suggest that a causal effect is likely, particularly in the context of the cognitive–developmental theory of aggression outlined above. Specifically, the most plausible hypothesis is that habitual exposure to violent television programs teaches children aggressive habits which are maintained well into adulthood. More specifically, as described above, we hypothesize that the observed relation between exposure to media violence and aggressive behavior later in life by the viewer is the product of multiple psychological processes operating simultaneously, but that the key process involves a cycle of observational and enactive learning. Children may imitate specific violent behaviors they see on TV. But, more importantly, they store in their memories general "scripts" for aggressive behavior abstracted from whole sets of violent scenes. To repeat, by "script" we mean a cognitive representation of a program for behavior. Scripts can neither be observed nor directly measured, but they serve as useful hypothetical constructs for explaining behavior. We believe that social behavior is controlled to a great extent by such scripts which are usually learned quite early in life. Once learned, they are resistant to change, providing a mechanism through which early exposure to scenes of media violence can influence later behavior. Scripts may be triggered into action by the occurrence of a particular type of social problem or by the presence of a cue associated with the script. Thus, once aggressive scripts have been incorporated into a child's repertoire, new scenes of violence, either in the media or in the environment, may trigger the use of a previously learned aggressive script as well as providing material for new scripts. To the extent that the scripts are rehearsed and utilized to guide behavior, the scripts become more firmly entrenched.

The relation between media violence and aggression quite probably involves other cognitive processes as well. Violent scenes may change children's attitudes about violence, and may change children's emotional responsiveness to violence (Malamuth & Briere, 1986; Rule & Ferguson, 1986). Numerous intervening environmental, cognitive, and programming variables seem to affect these processes (Huesmann et al., 1984), and aggression itself may stimulate violence viewing through its effect on the child's social environment and cognitions. More aggressive children, ostracized by their peers, may find justification for their behavior in the scenes of violence that characterize the media's representation of life. Thus, the susceptible child may become enmeshed in a continuous cycle of violence viewing and aggression—a cycle which leads to the development of habitual aggressive behavior.

One argument sometimes leveled against the research linking television violence viewing by children to increased aggressiveness is that "real" aggression was not measured. Boisterousness, hyperactivity, and even some "nastiness" may be related to violence viewing, but these are not the same as the antisocial aggressiveness of youths and adults that concerns society. Certainly, no one would argue that a fight among children can be equated with a fight among adults. As described above, however, there are now numerous longitudinal studies showing that these "childish" types of aggressive behaviors are the precursors of the more serious antisocial aggressive behaviors of adults. For example, Huesmann et al. (1984) have reported that peer-nominated aggressiveness in school at age 8 was predictive of adult criminality 22 years later. These data suggest that one should be greatly concerned with any process that promotes the establishment of aggressive habits in children as these habits may persist in altered forms into adulthood.

The 10- and 22-Year New York State Studies

Perhaps the first longitudinal field study to examine the long-term effects of TV violence on aggression was the Eron, Huesmann, Lefkowitz, and Walder (1972), Lefkowitz, Eron, Walder, and Huesmann (1977)

22-year study of youth in Columbia County, New York. This study, when begun in 1960, was intended primarily to assess the prevalence of aggression in the general population. The original focus was on aggression as a form of psychopathology and how it related to other child, family, and environmental variables. The television viewing habits of the subjects were studied somewhat fortuitously as one of several auxiliary interests.

The subjects of the study constituted the entire 3rd grade population of Columbia County, New York (public and private schools) in 1960—875 children. During that first assessment the children were questioned and tested in their classrooms and 85% of their mothers were interviewed along with 71% of their fathers. The modal age of the subjects was 8 and their mean IQ was 104. Ten years later in 1970 we located 735 of the original subjects and convinced 427 to allow us to reinterview them for $20 payments. An analysis of the sample revealed that those whom we did not succeed in reinterviewing for one reason or another had scored above average on aggression in 1960 and below average on IQ. Thus the sample was somewhat biased toward better adjusted youth. Finally, 12 years later in 1982 we reinterviewed 409 of the original subjects again and collected criminal justice data on 632 of the original subjects.

As described above, one notable result from this study was the finding that early childhood aggression in school is statistically related to adult antisocial and criminal behavior. Numerous other findings from this study have been reported in two books (Eron, Walder, & Lefkowitz, 1971; Lefkowitz, Eron, Walder, & Huesmann, 1977) and many articles (e.g., Huesmann, Eron, Lefkowitz, & Walder, 1984). Of particular interest are the findings concerning the relation between TV violence viewing and later aggression.

In the first wave we found that 8-year-old boys' aggression as determined from peer nominations was correlated with the violence ratings of their favorite shows that they watched most often, as reported by their mothers [$r = .21$, $p < .01$]. We found absolutely no relation at that time between a girl's aggression and her preference for violent TV shows. These findings were particularly notable because different sources of information were used for assessing the children's TV viewing habits (their mothers) and for assessing their social behavior (their classmates).

In the second wave of this study, 10 years later, we did not find any evidence of a relation between and 18-year-old's TV habits and aggressive behavior, either for boys or girls. We found though that the boys' preferences for more violent shows assessed 10 years earlier when they had been in the 3rd grade was also quite predictive of how aggressively they behaved now that they were 18 [$r = .31$, $p < .001$] (Eron et al., 1972).

We conducted an extensive set of longitudinal regression and structural modeling analyses that led us to conclude that it was likely that early exposure to TV violence was stimulating the later aggression. A key analysis in this series is reproduced in Figure 1. It shows that the pattern of correlations obtained for boys at age 8 and 18 can be explained by a path model which incorporates the following components. Aggressive habits are moderately stable over time while TV viewing habits are not. Viewing violent TV regularly at age 8 is related to concurrent aggressive behavior and stimulates aggressive behavior in succeeding years, leading to a stronger longitudinal than concurrent relation. By the midteens, however, the stimulating effect terminates; so there is no concurrent relation in the late teens.

In the third wave of data collected, when the subjects were on the average 30 years old, we also found no relation between these males' current TV viewing habits and any current aggression or antisocial behavior.[2] We again found evidence of a longitudinal effect, this time one that spanned the 22 years from age 8 to age 30. For boys, early TV violence viewing correlated with self-reported aggression at age 30 (especially aggression under the influence of alcohol) and added a significant increment to the prediction of seriousness of criminal arrests accumulated by age 30 (as recorded by New York State) independently of relevant social class, intellectual functioning, and parenting variables (Huesmann, 1986). Figure 2 shows the structural model relating early violence viewing to violence ratings of the crimes for which the males were arrested. Males who were never arrested received a score of 0 on the criterion variable. Males who were arrested received a score for the violence of the crime for which the record showed they were charged on a scale used by the New York State Department of Criminal Justice Records at that time.

The structural model reproduces the observed correlations adequately suggesting that a causal model for TV violence viewing as a stimulant for violent crime is at least plausible. Specifically, a model very

[2] The only exception occurred among the subsample of 87 married males. Within this subsample the males' current frequency of viewing violent programs correlated .22 ($p <$ .05) with their spouses ratings of how aggressive they were. Among the general population of males there was no evidence of such a correlation no matter how aggression was measured. It was also true that the males who had been convicted of crimes of any type reported that they watched TV programs of all kinds more frequently ($r = .20$, $p < .01$), but they did not report watching violent programs more frequently either.

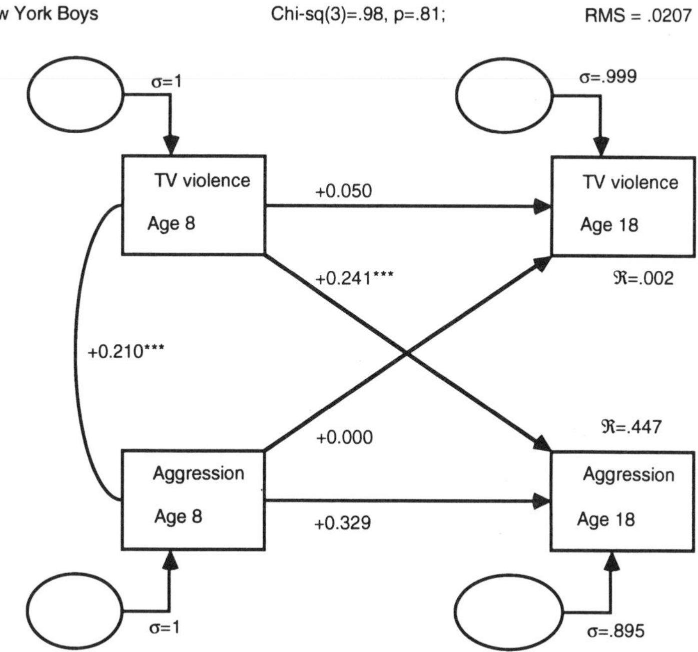

FIGURE 1. A path model showing the relation between TV violence viewing at age 8 and aggression 10 years later at age 18 (Lefkowitz, Eron, Walder, & Huesmann, 1977).

similar to the one derived above for the analysis of the 10-year data is suggested. Early exposure to TV violence stimulates aggression over several years, and early aggression is a statistical precursor of later criminal behavior, leading to the longitudinal relation from habitual childhood exposure to TV violence to adult violent crime.

Unfortunately, the sample on which this conclusion was based was very small because of technical difficulties in locating the original TV data on subjects who were not interviewed at an intermediate point (TV violence was not a focus of major interest when the study was begun). While the results are significant, they mostly reflect the behavior of a few high violence viewers and must be treated very cautiously. Overall, this study strongly supports the conclusions of laboratory experiments that exposure to media violence stimulates aggression and suggests that, as a result, there may well be a relation for males between early violence viewing and adult aggression and criminality. This study provides no evidence of a similar relation for females.

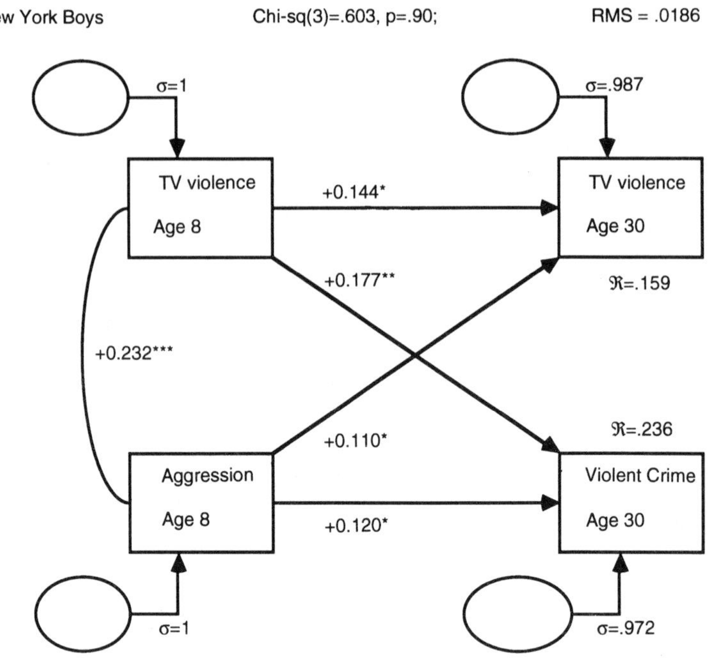

FIGURE 2. A path model showing the relation between TV violence viewing at age 8 and violent criminal behavior 22 years later at age 30 (Huesmann, Eron, Lefkowitz, & Walder, 1984).

A Cross-National Longitudinal Study

In the mid 1970s Huesmann and Eron (1986) began a second longitudinal study. In contrast to the New York study in which the examination of TV viewing behavior was an afterthought, this study was specifically designed in order to explore the relation between children's TV viewing habits and their aggressive behavior. Funded by NIMH and small grants obtained by collaborators in other countries, the study was directed at better understanding the generality of the relation between TV violence viewing and aggression across countries with widely differing TV systems, across genders in countries with differing sex-role expectations, and across the ages 6 to 11. Additionally, specific attention was directed at the role of aggressive fantasy in mediating any effects and in the children's identification with TV characters and perception of TV violence as realistic. Other important familial and environmental variables including parental nurturance, punishment, and rejection, parent's aggressive behavior, parent's TV viewing habits, as well as occupation and socioeconomic status were to be measured as potential moderators of the effect. We were motivated by the conception that the cognitive processes underlying the development of aggression might be strongly affected by environmental and social factors that differ across countries.

In each of five countries—Australia, Finland, Israel, Poland, and the United States—we tested and interviewed substantial samples of 1st and 3rd graders at three one-year intervals as they progressed to the 3rd and 5th grades. The children were interviewed individually (1st graders) or in groups for several sessions. In addition in most countries at least one of their parents was interviewed and tested. The original sample consisted of 1683 children (291 in Australia, 221 in Finland, 186 in Israel, 237 in Poland, and 748 in the United States) about equally divided between boys and girls and 9- and 11-year-olds. By the last year of the study attrition had reduced the total sample to 1297 children. As in most longitudinal studies of aggression there was evidence that the subjects who dropped out of the study had on the average scored higher on initial aggression than those who did not.

The samples in each country were drawn mostly from urban, middle, and lower middle class schools. In the United States about 15% of the sample was drawn from inner city, lower class schools, however; and in Israel about 50% of the sample consisted of kibbutz-raised children. The violent crime rates in these countries varied considerably at the time of this study, with homicides, for example, ranging from about 1 per 100,000 in Poland, to 2 per 100,000 in Israel and Australia, to 3 per 100,000 in Finland, to 10 per 100,000 in the United States. Similarly, the characteristics of the television programming available in each country varied considerably as shown in Table 1. Perhaps the only surprising finding in Table 1 is that the percentage of programming hours with significant violence is more comparable across countries than many would have guessed. One reason for this is the domination of American dramatic TV programs in most of the foreign markets. For example, *Charlie's Angels* was aired in every country in this study during the time of the study.

The collected data from the five countries investigated in the current study clearly indicate that more aggressive children watch more television, prefer more violent programs, identify more with TV characters, and perceive violence as more like real life than do less aggressive children (Huesmann & Bachrach, 1988; Huesmann & Eron, 1986; Huesmann, Lagerspetz, & Eron, 1984). There is substantial variation from

TABLE 1. A Comparison of Violent Television Programming in Five Countries in 1980

TV statistics	Country				
	Australia	Finland	Israel	Poland	United States
TV sets/1000 population[a]	378	374	150	224	624
TV channels in area	4	2	2[b]	2	8[c]
Hours per week in which at least one channel is available	119	60	62[d]	98	154
Estimated hours of programming per week	476	98	106[d]	154	1120
Estimated hours of programming per week with "significant violence"[e]	61	14	11	10.5	188
Estimated percent of programming hours with "significant violence"	12.8%	14.3%	10.4%	6.8%	16.8%

[a]Source is U.S. Bureau of Census, 1982.
[b]One channel actually is based in Jordan.
[c]Excluding cable channels.
[d]Excluding weekday educational TV.
[e]"Significant violence" is defined as that which raters assigned to the highest or second highest category on a 5-category scale.

Source: Huesmann and Eron, 1986.

country to country, but at least some variable relates in each country. For boys the correlations between overall TV violence viewing and aggression were strongest in the United States ($r = .25$, $p < .001$), Finland ($r = .22$, $p < .05$), and among Israeli city boys ($r = .45$, $p < .01$). They were weakest in Poland ($r = .17$, $p < .10$), Australia ($r = .13$), and among Israeli kibbutz boys ($r < .10$). For girls the correlations between overall TV violence viewing and aggression were strongest in the United States ($r = .29$, $p < .001$) and among Israeli city girls ($r = .48$, $p < .01$). They were weakest in Poland ($r = .17$, $p < .10$), Australia ($r = .16$, $p < .10$), Finland ($r = .16$), and among Israeli Kibbutz girls. It is clear from these results that the relation between TV habits and aggression is not limited to countries with large amounts of programming and is no longer limited to boys.

Of course, the correlations obtained are small in terms of variance explained. They account for between 1 and 23% of the variance in aggression. Yet "variance explained" is not necessarily a reasonable measure of the potential importance of these variables. As Abelson (1984) and Rosenthal (1986) have argued, the calculation of "variance explained" may grossly misrepresent the practical and social significance of a variable. According to the developmental model that we have adopted, children in the age range covered in this study are forming cognitive guides for behavior (e.g., scripts, self-regulating internal standards) that may last into adulthood. Small effects on concurrent behavior can accumulate through a cyclical reinforcing process in which TV violence teaches aggressive behavior and aggressive behavior stimulates violence viewing. Furthermore, because aggression is affected by so many uncontrolled situational and characterological factors in natural settings, one should be skeptical if large portions of variance are explained by single variables. The statistical significance of the correlations should be given more importance than the "variance explained."

Nevertheless, in one group of subjects, Israeli kibbutz-raised children (Huesmann & Bachrach, 1988), the effects were particularly weak. Among these kibbutz children, the reasons for small relations between TV habits and aggression seem clear. Such children view TV violence much less frequently. When they do see violent programs, the observation is often followed by a discussion of the social implications of the violence. In addition, the kibbutz child's society is one designed to rebuke children for any aggressive behavior within society. Given such an environment, the lack of a relation between TV violence and aggression is not surprising.

Given that TV habits were related to concurrent aggression in most countries, one can then ask whether the longitudinal patterns of relations suggest the hypothesized cyclical process by which TV viewing stimulates aggression and aggression leads to more exposure to violent TV. To test this hypothesis, we evaluated in each country a regression model relating TV viewing and behavior in the first two waves to TV viewing and behavior in the last wave. In particular we assumed that the effect of either variable on the other would accumulate over the first two years. The resulting model was evaluated with a system of regression equations in each country. The results are shown in Table 2. The key comparison in each column is between the path coefficient in the row labeled *TV(12),* representing the effect of TV viewing in the first two waves on later aggression, and the path coefficient in the row labeled *AGG(12),* representing the effect of aggression in the first two waves on later TV viewing.

Again, there was substantial variation across countries as to which TV habits related most strongly, but a common pattern emerged. For boys in Finland and for both boys and girls in the United States, Poland, and Israeli cities, early TV habits significantly affected the aggressiveness of children at the end of the study even when the children's initial aggressiveness was statistically controlled. Depending on the country,

TABLE 2. A Comparison of Path Coefficients from TV Violence Viewing to Aggression with Coefficients from Aggression to TV Violence Viewing in a Cross-National Comparison

Regression model	Australia	United States	Finland	Israeli cities	Poland
			Girls		
	(N = 107)	(N = 221)	(N = 85)	(N = 39)	(N = 84)
AGG(3)=AGG(1)	.66***	.53***	.65***	.55**	.72***
+TV(12)	.00	.14**	.01	.52**	.14+
TV(3)=TV(1)	.19+	.29***	.41***	.31	.00
+AGG(12)	.08	.26***	.15	.38	.03
			Boys		
	(N = 116)	(N = 200)	(N = 93)	(N = 46)	(N = 95)
AGG(3)=AGG(1)	.71***	.68***	.75***	.58**	.82***
+TV(12)	.08	.15**	.21***	.29*	.14*
TV(3)=TV(1)	.12	.38***	.32***	.45**	.08
+AGG(12)	.10	.10	.18	.10	−.02

+$p < .10$. *$p < .05$. **$p < .01$. ***$p < .001$.
Source: Huesmann and Eron, 1986.

TV violence viewing (girls in the United States, boys and girls in Poland and in Israeli cities), or TV violence viewing coupled with identification with TV characters (boys in the United States and Finland) best predicted changes in aggression. Only in Australia was no longitudinal effect detectable, and only among U.S. girls did early aggression have an effect on later TV violence viewing.

According to our model, once a script for aggressive behavior is stored, whether or not it is ever retrieved may depend on whether it is rehearsed. One form of rehearsal is fantasy. In most countries greater aggressive behavior and more TV violence viewing were associated with more frequent aggressive and heroic fantasies (Huesmann & Eron, 1984, Table 8.4). The strength of the relation varied greatly across samples, but overall the results are consistent with the theory that violent TV (and violent behavior) may stimulate violent fantasies, and violent fantasies may increase the likelihood of violent behavior. Certainly, these data contradict the theory that aggressive fantasies stimulated by aggressive TV might act as a catharsis and reduce the likelihood of aggressive behavior.

What about the possibility that social class or IQ were responsible for the relation between aggression and TV violence viewing? Perhaps less intellectually competent, lower class children behave more aggressively (out of frustration or because they cannot learn nonaggressive scripts) and watch more TV (to obtain the rewards vicariously they are missing in their own lives)? Huesmann and Eron (1986) found that aggression and TV habits were related negatively to the social status of the family and the intellectual competence of the child. However, they also demonstrated with additional regression analyses that early TV habits remained a significant predictor of changes in aggression in most samples even when social class and intellectual competence were controlled statistically. It is worthwhile mentioning at this point an important finding from Huesmann, Eron, and Yarmel's (1987) analyses of the relation between childhood and adult aggression and intellectual competence. On the basis of data spanning the 22 years from age 8 to age 30, it was concluded that childhood aggression interferes with adult intellectual development more than childhood intellectual failure stimulates adult aggression. The implication is clear: A side effect of a child's learning aggressive behavior from violent TV shows might be diminished intellectual achievement by adulthood.

Among the U.S. children, Huesmann and Eron (1986) found that the lower the family's social status, the more aggressive were the children and the more TV violence they watched. This relation was particularly strong for boys. In Israel, it was also true of city boys, but for kibbutz boys and all girls, the relations reversed. Higher status children were more aggressive and watched more violence. In Poland, family income was inversely related to a child's aggression, and girls whose fathers had a higher status job watched less TV violence. In Finland, there was little direct relation between social status or income and aggression. In conjunction with indicators of parental rejection or harsh punishment, however, higher social status was predictive of greater aggression in boys and lesser aggression in girls. These results are puzzling. Part of the problem is undoubtedly that social status was very difficult to measure in Finland, Poland, and Israel. Traditional rankings based on the free-enterprise society of the United States did not apply very well. Moreover, the differences may go deeper. In the United States lower socioeconomic status may both stimulate aggressiveness and be a product of aggression. In societies with greater homogeneity, such effects may not obtain.

On the average, Huesmann and Eron (1986) reported, more aggressive children and children who watched more TV violence had more aggressive parents. Their parents were also more dissatisfied with them (i.e., rejected them more) and punished them more severely. Before one concludes that parental punishment and rejection stimulate a boy's aggression, however, one must examine the longitudinal relation between rejection, punishment, and aggression with the effects of early aggression partialed out. When this is done, the longitudinal relation between rejection, punishment, and aggression disappears completely in the two countries where there were the two waves of parent interviews necessary to test the hypothesis (the United States and Finland). Of course, it is possible that the self-report measures of rejection and punishment may be distorted or that the major detrimental effects of these behaviors occurred earlier in the child's life. Alternatively, it may be that aggression by the child stimulates rejection and punishment by the parents which in turn, while not directly stimulating aggression, isolates the child more and drives him or her to watch more TV and hence, more violent programs. This would be somewhat consistent with the findings of Heath (Heath & Kruttschnitt, 1986) that childhood exposure to TV violence combined with parental rejection and punishment predict violence in a criminal sample.

Finally, Huesmann and Eron (1986) examined the role of popularity as a mediator. In every country (except perhaps Israel) the more aggressive children are the less popular children. Only in the United States, however, was there evidence that the less popular children watched more TV violence.

In the United States a subsample of high violence viewers also participated in a 2-year intervention designed to mitigate the effects of TV violence on aggression (Huesmann, Eron, Klein, Brice, & Fischer, 1983). The 169 high violence viewers were randomly assigned to a treatment or control group. The treatment group received didactic lessons about the unreality of TV violence during the second year of the study and an attitude change treatment during the third year. By the end of that year the treatment subjects were rated as significantly less aggressive than the control subjects on peer nominations, and the relation between their aggressiveness and TV violence viewing was diminished.

A Netherlands Study

At about the same time as the above cross-national study was being conducted in Australia, Finland, Israel, Poland, and the United States, a similar study was being attempted in the Netherlands by Wiegman, Kuttschreuter, and Baarda (1986). Originally intended to duplicate the investigations being conducted in the other countries, the study drew heavily from the work of the other investigators. For a variety of reasons, however, the procedures used in this study eventually deviated substantially from the procedures used in other countries and comparison of exact results is problematic. For example, because they believed that "in the Netherlands the relation between parents and children is less based on authority and more on friendship" (Wiegman et al., 1986, p. 32), they declined to question children or parents about the possibility that any parents might harshly punish their children. A more detailed critique of the methodological problems in this study is presented in Huesmann and Eron (1986). Despite the methodological deficiencies of the Netherlands study, many of the results obtained from that study mirror results in other studies. Very significant positive correlations were obtained for both boys and girls between TV violence viewing and aggression. While the path coefficients from early violence viewing to later aggression were not significant, all of them were in the positive direction. Although the Netherlands' data are generally consistent with other data supporting a longitudinal effect for TV violence, the Netherlands' authors reinterpreted their data and existing data to suggest that low IQ was responsible for the relation. Their reinterpretation was based on a flawed use of structural modeling in their own data, however, and on improper use of partial data taken from preprints issued by the investigators in other countries.

An NBC Study

A more sophisticated use of structural modeling of longitudinal data was undertaken by Milavsky et al. (1982) in their analysis of data collected by NBC during the 1970s. Data on television viewing and peer-nominated aggression were collected on a substantial sample of elementary schoolchildren. Data collection involved repeated assessments, with lags between assessments ranging from a few months to several years.

Milavsky et al.'s findings of positive and mostly significant relations between television violence viewing and aggression (ranging from .13 to .23) are consistent with the findings of the majority of studies in this area. Their study paralleled the findings from the cross-national studies described above in that an equally strong relation between television violence viewing and aggressive behavior was noted for girls compared to boys, and that the relation between overall television viewing and aggression was almost as strong as the relation between violent television viewing and aggression.

Milavsky et al. employed regression analyses similar to those described in the cross-national study above in order to examine longitudinal relations between television habits and aggressive behavior. For each different lag, they constructed a different regression equation yielding a total of 15 different analyses. In each analysis, later aggression was predicted from early television violence viewing and aggression. As previous research suggests, one would expect to find a substantial relation between early and later aggression. The question to be addressed here is whether early television violence viewing increases one's ability to predict to later aggression above what is predicted from early aggression. In the cross-national study described above, among boys and girls from the cities of the United States, Poland, and Israel, and among boys from Finland, it was demonstrated that early television habits significantly predicted later aggression even after the effect of early aggression was statistically controlled in the regression analyses. There was no such effect for the Australian children. In the Netherlands study, positive coefficients were reported; however, they did not reach statistical significance. Similarly, Milavsky et al. found mostly positive coefficients (12 of 15) in the critical analyses, although only a few were significant on their own. The chances of observing 12 positive coefficients in 15 analyses would be less than 1 in 1000. Thus, their results seem reasonably consistent with the hypothesized model that television violence viewing leads to aggressive behavior. The "causal" coefficients observed by Milavsky et al. increase almost monotonically with the duration of the lag between observations. The coefficients are very small for the short lags and larger for the longer lags, which is what one would expect given a cumulative effect, bidirectional model.

Milavsky et al. reject that their data support the theory that repeated exposure to violent television programming leads to increased aggressive behavior. They suggest that the strength of the positive coefficients observed in their study is not sufficient to make such a conclusion. Additionally, they cite several artifacts that they believe contribute to the observed correlations between television violence viewing and aggression. They argue that (1) high aggressive boys exaggerate their violence viewing, and (2) both violence viewing and aggression are correlated with social class. While one would expect that data from more aggressive boys would be least valid due to their poor reading skills and lower IQs, the appropriateness of removing these subjects whether statistically or physically from the analysis is questionable. One should at least first examine the psychological processes that might be represented by this behavior. Furthermore, it is not clear that aggressive boys who underreported their television violence viewing would have been detected and removed. The drop in correlations when social class is partialed out is also much higher than that reported in most other studies. The measure of social class used by Milavsky et al. differs from most other studies in that it includes mother's occupation (or lack of occupation). This may be critical because children of working mothers with relatively low-status jobs may be more aggressive and watch more television. Again, before controlling for such a variable, one would want to understand what psychological processes are involved. For example, the mother's presence in the house may serve as a control that limits the extent to which violence viewing could influence aggression.

Because Milavsky et al. ignore developmental theory in the interpretation of their data, they are forced into making merely descriptive statements: "television exposure leads to increased aggressiveness; or aggressive children tend to select violent television programs or some third variables . . . lead (to) both" (p. 114). Not only do these conclusions neglect developmental theory but they are also not mutually exclusive as presented. Although Milavsky et al. do not come to this conclusion, their data are not inconsistent with the hypothesis that repeated exposure to television violence leads to increased aggressive behavior.

A South African Study

Botha (1990) conducted a longitudinal field study of 856 South African boys and 914 South African girls between 1977 and 1981. This study is particularly interesting because television was not present in South Africa until just before this study began in 1976. The subjects in the study were all white South African youth who were in the 8th grade in 1977. A stratified random sampling approach guaranteed that they were fairly representative of the population of white 8th grade youth in South Africa. The subjects were interviewed in 1977 when they were in the 8th grade and again 4 years later in 1981 when they were in the 12th grade.

Botha, unlike most other researchers, analyzed total amount of TV viewing by the adolescents rather than violence viewing. These and his measures of aggression were all self-report measures. Nevertheless, he did find positive correlations between total amount of TV viewing and aggression in both the boys and the girls. Furthermore, when he constructed structural models to relate TV viewing and aggression, he found statistically significant positive causal coefficients from TV viewing to aggression for both boys and girls. The effects were not large and were smaller than the effects on aggression of some other measured variables; for example, family and social influences. Nevertheless, it is notable that an effect would be found at all with this age children. They are past the age when most habitual forms of social behavior have developed, and one would expect the effect of any external influence on habitual social behavior to be reduced. One can speculate that an even stronger effect would have been found with younger subjects.

META-ANALYTIC REVIEWS

One cannot complete a review of the major studies on this topic without mentioning two meta-analyses that have been recently published which summarize the findings of most of the studies conducted over the past 30 years on media violence and aggression. Comstock and Paik (1991) calculated the obtained effect sizes for over 1000 comparisons derived from 185 different experiments, static field studies, and longitudinal studies. After an extensive set of analyses, they concluded that the association between exposure to television violence and antisocial and aggressive behavior is extremely robust. Furthermore, they conclude, "The data of the past decade and a half strengthens rather than weakens the case that television violence increases aggressive and antisocial behavior" (p. 54). Wood, Wong, and Chachere (1991) analyzed 30 comparisons in 23 studies in which the outcome variable was aggression measured in unstructured social interaction. They concluded that exposure to media violence significantly enhanced viewers' aggressive behavior when the findings were aggregated across studies, though the effect was not uniform across investigations.

SUMMARY

The severe negative outcome for children who display antisocial behavior is costly at both individual and societal levels. As the rates of interpersonal violence remain alarmingly high, researchers continue to investigate the causes of such behavior. It is generally accepted that antisocial behavior results when a number of important factors converge. No one factor is viewed as necessary or sufficient to produce long-term antisocial behavior. It is understood by researchers interested in the development of aggressive behavior that repeated exposure to media violence alone is not enough to account for the development of serious antisocial behavior. Media violence is regarded as one potential contributor to the learning environment of children who eventually go on to develop aggressive patterns of behavior.

In this chapter, we describe a theoretical model that could account for the way in which children might learn to behave aggressively from watching violent television. Huesmann's (1988) script theory posits that social behavior is controlled, to a large extent, by programs for behavior that are established early on in development. These scripts are stored in memory and are accessed as guides for social interactions. The violent scenes that a child observes on television can serve to teach a child to be aggressive through several learning processes as the child not only observes aggressive patterns of behaviors but also witnesses their acceptance and reinforcement.

Several methods for studying the relations between television violence viewing and aggression have been employed. Experimental studies have clearly demonstrated that under well-controlled conditions, the observation of violent scenes observed in the media causes children to behave more aggressively. Static observational studies have demonstrated that the amount of violent television observed by a child is positively related to the child's current aggressivity. Although this relation is not strong compared to the relation between aggression and other salient environmental variables, it is repeatedly observed across studies to be statistically significant and of a magnitude that has been assessed to have real social significance.

The data available from longitudinal studies provide additional support for the hypothesis that television violence viewing leads to the development of aggressive behavior. These longitudinal studies employ a wide range of samples and methodologies. Again, we are not arguing that television violence viewing is the only cause of aggressive behavior. However, the research suggests that the effect of television violence viewing on aggression is relatively independent of other likely influences and of a magnitude great enough to account for socially important differences.

While children are likely to imitate specific behaviors observed on television, we suggest that the long-term effects are likely to be a result of the development of scripts for behavior that are observed on television and enacted by the child who is reinforced in his or her natural environment for displaying such aggressive behavior. We have also argued that not all children who observe a steady diet of violent television go on to display patterns of aggressive behavior. Important environmental, cultural, familial, and cognitive differences may exacerbate or mitigate such long-term effects.

Acknowledgments

The authors gratefully acknowledge the assistance of Leonard Eron in the preparation of this manuscript. Portions of the text have appeared previously in Huesmann and Eron (1986). This research was supported in part by Grant MH47474 from the National Institute of Mental Health to the senior author and by a James McKeen Cattell Foundation fellowship to the senior author.

REFERENCES

Abelson, R. P. (1981). The psychological status of the script concept. *American Psychologist, 36,* 715–729.

Abelson, R. (1984). A variance explanation paradox: When a little is a lot. *Psychological Bulletin, 97,* 129–133.

Andison, F. S. (1977). TV violence and viewer aggression: A cumulation of study results 1956–1976. *Public Opinion Quarterly, 41,* 314–331.

Bachrach, R. S. (1986). The differential effect of observation of violence on Kibbutz and city children in Israel. In: L. R. Huesmann & L. D. Eron (Eds.), *Television and the aggressive child: A cross-national comparison,* (pp. 201–238). Hillsdale, NJ: Lawrence Erlbaum.

Bandura, A. (1973). *Aggression: A social learning analysis.* Englewood Cliffs, NJ: Prentice-Hall.

Bandura, A. (1977). Social learning theory. Englewood Cliffs, NJ: Prentice-Hall.

Bandura, A. (1986). *Social foundations of thought and action: A social cognitive theory.* Englewood Cliffs, NJ: Prentice-Hall.

Bandura, A. (1989). Social cognitive theory. Englewood Cliffs, NJ: Prentice-Hall.

Bell, R. Q. & Harper, L. V. (1977). *Child effects on adults.* Hillsdale, NJ: Lawrence Erlbaum.

Belson, W. (1978). *Television violence and the adolescent boy.* Hampshire, England: Saxon House.

Berkowitz, L. (1974). Some determinants of impulsive aggression: The role of mediated associations with reinforcements for aggression. *Psychological Review, 81,* 165–176.

Berkowitz, L. (1983). Aversively stimulated aggression: Some parallels and differences in research with animals and humans. *American Psychologist, 38,* 1135–1144.

Berkowitz, L. (1984). Some effects of thoughts on anti- and prosocial influences of media events: A cognitive-neoassociation analysis. *Psychological Bulletin, 95,* 3, 410–427.

Berkowitz, L. (1988). Frustrations, appraisals, and aversively stimulated aggression. *Aggressive Behavior, 14,* 3–12.

Bjorkqvist, K. (1985). *Violent films, anxiety and aggression.* Helsinki: Finish Society of Sciences and Letters.

Botha, M. (1990). Television exposure and aggression among adolescents: A follow-up study over 5 years, *Aggressive Behavior.*

Bouchard, T. J. (1984). Twins reared together and apart: What they tell us about human diversity. In: S. W. Fox (Ed.), *Individuality and determinism: Chemical and biological basis* (pp. 147–184). New York: Plenum.

Bushman, B. J., & Geen, R. (1990). Role of cognitive-emotional mediators and individual differences in the effects of media violence on aggression. *Journal of Personality and Social Psychology, 58,* 156–163.

Chaffee, S. H. (1972). Television and adolescent aggressiveness (overview). In: G. A. Comstock & E. A. Rubinstein (Eds.), *Television and social behavior: Vol. 3. Television and adolescent aggressiveness,* (pp. 1–34). Washington, DC: U.S. Government Printing Office.

Cloninger, C. R., & Gottesman, A. (1987). Genetic and environmental factors in antisocial behavior disorders. In: Mednick, S.A., Moffitt, T. E., & Stack, S. A. (Eds.), *The causes of crime: New biological approaches* (pp. 92–109). New York: Cambridge University Press.

Comstock, G. A. (1980). New emphases in research on the effects of television and film violence. In: E. L. Paler & A. Dorr (Eds.), *Children and the faces of television: Teaching, violence, selling*. New York: Academic Press.

Comstock, G. A., & Paik, H. (1990). The effects of television violence on aggressive behavior: A meta-analysis. Unpublished report to the National Academy of Sciences Panel on the Understanding and Control of Violent Behavior. Washington, D.C.

Comstock, G. A., & Paik, H. (1991). The effects of television violence on aggressive behavior: A meta-analysis. In: *A preliminary report to the National Research Council on the understanding and control of violent behavior.* Washington, DC: National Research Council.

Dalton, K. (1977). *The pre-menstrual syndrome and progesterone therapy.* London: Heinemann.

Damon, W. (1983). *Social and personality development.* New York: W.W. Norton.

Eron, L. D. (1963). Relationship of TV viewing habits and aggressive behavior in children. *Journal of Abnormal and Social Psychology, 67*, 193–196.

Eron, L. D., & Huesmann, L. R. (1986). The role of television in the development of prosocial and antisocial behavior. In: D. Olweus, J. Block & M. Radke-Yarrow (Eds.), *Development of antisocial and prosocial behavior*, (pp. 285–314). New York: Academic Press.

Eron, L. D., Huesmann, L. R., Lefkowitz, M. M., & Walder, O. (1972). Does television violence cause aggression? *American Psychologist, 27*, 253–263.

Eron, L. D., Walder, L. O., & Lefkowitz, M. M. (1971). *The learning of aggression in children.* Boston: Little, Brown.

Ensminger, M. E., Kellam, S. G., & Rubin, B. R. (1983). School and family origins of delinquency. In: K. T. Van Dusen & S. A. Mednick (Eds.), *Prospective studies of crime and delinquency* (pp. 73–97). Boston: Kluwer-Nijhoff.

Eysenck, H. J., & Nias, D. K. (1978). *Sex, violence, and he media.* London: Maurice Temple-Smith.

Farrington, D. P. (1982). Longitudinal analyses of criminal violence. In: M. E. Wolfgang & N. E. Weiner (Eds), *Criminal violence* (pp. 171–200). Beverly Hills, CA: Sage.

Farrington, D. P. (1990). Childhood aggression and adult violence: Early precursors and later-life outcomes. In: D. J. Pepler & K. H. Rubin (Eds.), *The development of childhood aggression* (pp. 5–25). Hillsdale, NJ: Lawrence Erlbaum.

Freedman, J. (1984). Effects of television violence on aggressiveness. *Psychological Bulletin, 96*, 227–246.

Geen, R. G. (1983). In: R. G. Geen & E. I. Donnerstein (Eds.), *Aggression: Theoretical and empirical reviews, Vol. 2: Issues and research* (pp. 103–125). New York: Academic Press.

Geen, R. G. (1990). *Human aggression.* Pacific Grove, CA: Brooks Cole Publishing.

Geen, R. G., & Thomas, S. L. (1986). The immediate effects of media violence on behavior, *Journal of Social Issues, 42*, 7–28.

Hearold, S. L. (1979). *Meta-analysis of the effects of television on social behavior.* Unpublished doctoral dissertation, University of Colorado.

Heath, L., & Kruttschnitt, C. (1986). Television and violent criminal behavior: Beyond the bobo doll. *Victim and Violence, 1*, 177–190.

Huesmann, L. R. (1982). Television violence and aggressive behavior. In: D. Perl, L. Bouthilet, & J. Lazar (Eds.), *Television and behavior: Ten years of programs and implications for the 80's* (pp. 126–137). Washington, DC: U.S. Government Printing Office.

Huesmann, L. R. (1986). Psychological processes promoting the relation between exposure to media violence and aggressive behavior by the viewer. *Journal of Social Issues, 42,* 125–139.

Huesmann, L. R. (1988). An information processing model for the development of aggression. *Aggressive Behavior, 14,* 13–24.

Huesmann, L. R., & Bachrach, R. S. (1988). Differential effects of television violence in kibbutz and city children. In: R. Patterson & P. Drummond (Eds.), *Television and its audience: International research perspectives* (pp. 154–176). London: BFI Publishing.

Huesmann, L. R., & Eron, L. D. (1984). Cognitive processes and the persistence of aggressive behavior. *Aggressive Behavior, 10,* 243–251.

Huesmann, L. R., & Eron, L. D. (1986). *Television and the aggressive child: A cross-national comparison.* Hillsdale, NJ: Lawrence Erlbaum.

Huesmann, L. R., Eron, L. D., Berkowitz, L., & Chaffee, S. (1991). The effects of television violence on aggression: A reply to a skeptic. In: P. Suedfeld & P. Tetlock (Eds.), *Psychology and Social Policy* (pp. 191–200). New York: Hemisphere.

Huesmann, L. R., Eron, L. D., Klein, R., Brice, P., & Fischer, P. (1983). Mitigating the imitation of aggressive behaviors by children's attitudes about media violence. *Journal of Personality and Social Psychology, 44,* 899–910.

Huesmann, L. R., Eron, L. D., Lefkowitz, M. M., & Walder, L. O. (1973). Television violence and aggression: The causal effect remains. *American Psychologist,* 28, 617–620.

Huesmann, L. R., Eron, L. D., Lefkowitz, M. M., & Walder, L. O. (1984). The stability of aggression over time and generations. *Developmental Psychology, 20,* 1120–1134.

Huesmann, L. R., Eron, L. D., & Yarmel, P. (1987). Intellectual functioning and aggression. *Journal of Personality and Social Psychology, 50,* 232–240.

Huesmann, L. R., Lagerspetz, K., & Eron, L. D. (1984b). Intervening variables in the TV violence-aggression relation: Evidence from two countries. *Developmental Psychology, 20,* 746–775.

Josephson, W. L. (1987). Television violence and children's aggression: Testing the priming, social script, and disinhibition predictions. *Journal of Personality and Social Psychology, 53,* 882–890.

Kagan, J. (1988). Temperamental contributions to social behavior. *American Psychologist, 44,* 668–674.

Lagerspetz, K., & Lagerspetz, K. M. J. (1971). Changes in aggressiveness of mice resulting from selective breeding, learning and social isolation. *Scandinavian Journal of Psychology, 12,* 241–278.

Lagerspetz, K., & Sandnabba, K. (1982). The decline of aggression in mice during group caging as determined by punishment delivered by cagemates. *Aggressive Behavior, 8,* 319–334.

Lewis, D. O., Moy, E., Jackson, L. D., Aaronson, R., Restifo, N., Serra, S., & Simos, A. (1985). Biopsychological characteristics of children who later murder: A prospective study. *American Journal of Psychiatry, 142,* 1161–1167.

Loeber, R., & Dishion, T. J. (1983). Early predictors of male delinquency: A review. *Psychological Bulletin, 94,* 68–94.

Loehlin, J. C., Willerman, L., & Horn, J. M. (1985). Personality resemblances in adoptive families when the children are late-adolescent or adult. *Journal of Personality and Social Psychology, 48,* 367–392.

Lefkowitz, M. M., Eron, L. D., Walder, L. O., & Huesmann, L. R. (1977). *Growing up to be violent.* New York: Pergamon.

Leyens, J. P., Parke, R. D., Camino, L., & Berkowitz, L. (1975). Effects of movie violence on aggression in a field setting as a function of group dominance and cohesion. *Journal of Personality and Social Psychology, 32,* 346–360.

Loye, D., Gorney, R., & Steele, G. (1977). An experimental field study. *Journal of Communication, 27*, 206–216.

Magnusson, D., Duner, A., & Zetterblom, G. (1975). *Adjustment: A longitudinal study.* Stockholm: Almqvist & Wiksell.

Malamuth, N. M., & Briere, J. (1986). Sexual violence in the media: Indirect effects on aggression against women. *Journal of Social Issues, 42*, 75–92.

Malamuth, N. M., & Donnerstein, E. (1982). the effects of aggressive and pornographic mass media stimuli. In: L. Berkowitz (Ed.), *Advances in experimental social psychology* (Vol. 15, pp. 103–136). New York: Academic Press.

Mednick, S. A., Gabrielli, W. F., & Hutchings, B. (1984). Genetic influences in criminal convictions: Evidence from an adoption cohort. *Science, 224*, 891–894.

Milavsky, J. R., Kessler, R., Sipp, H., & Rubens, W. S. (1982). Television and aggression: Results of a panel study. In: D. Pearl, L. Bouthilet, & J. Lazar (Eds.), *Television and behavior: Ten years of scientific progress and implications for the 80's: Vol 2. Technical reviews.* Washington DC: Government Printing Office.

Moffitt, T. E. (1990). Juvenile delinquency and attention deficit disorder: Boys developmental trajectories from age 3 to age 15. *Child Development, 61*, 893–910.

Moyer, K. E. (1976). *The psychobiology of aggression.* New York: Harper & Row.

Nachson, I., & Denno, D. (1987). Violent behavior and cerebral hemisphere dysfunctions. In: S.A. Mednick, T.E. Moffitt, & S.A. Stack (Eds.), *The causes of crime: New biological approaches* (pp. 185–217). New York: Cambridge University Press.

Olweus, D. (1979). The stability of aggressive reaction patterns in human males: A review. *Psychological Bulletin, 85*, 852–875.

Olweus, D., Mattsson, A., Schalling, D., & Low, H. (1980). Testosterone, aggression, physical, and personality dimensions in normal adolescent males. *Psychosomatic Medicine, 42*, 253–69.

Olweus, D., Mattsson, A., Schalling, D., & Low, H. (1988). Circulating testosterone levels and aggression in adolescent males: A causal analysis. *Psychosomatic Medicine, 50*, 261–272.

Parke, R. D., Berkowitz, L., Leyens, S. P., West, S., & Sebastian, R. S. (1977). Some effects of violent and nonviolent movies on the behavior of juvenile delinquents. In: L. Berkowitz (Ed.), *Advances in experimental social psychology* (Vol. 10, pp. 135–172). New York: Academic Press.

Parke, R. D., & Slaby, R. G. (1983). The development of aggression. In: P. Mussen (Ed.), *Handbook of child psychology* (pp. 547–642). New York: John Wiley.

Pitkannen-Pulkkinen, L. (1979). Self-control as a prerequisite for constructive behavior. In: S. Feshbach & A. Fraczek (Eds.), *Aggression and behavior change* (pp. 20–270). New York: Praeger.

Pontius, A. A. (1984). Specific stimulus-evoked violent action in psychotic trigger reaction: A seizure-like imbalance between frontal lobe and limbic system? *Perceptual and Motor Skills, 59*, 299–333.

Raine, A., & Jones, F. (1987). Attention, autonomic arousal, and personality in behaviorally disordered children. *Journal of Abnormal Child Psychology, 15*, 583–599.

Robins, L. N., & Ratcliff, K. S. (1980). Childhood conduct disorders and later arrest. In: L. N. Robins, P. J. Clayton, & J. K. Wing (Eds.), *The social consequences of psychiatric illness* (pp. 248–263). New York: Brunner/Mazel.

Rosenthal, R. (1986). The social consequences of small effects. *Journal of Social Issues, 42*, 141–154.

Rowe, D. C. (1987). Resolving the person-situation debate: Invitation to an interdisciplinary dialogue, *American Psychologist, 42*, 218–227.

Rule, B. G., & Ferguson, T. J. (1986). The effects of media violence on attitudes, emotions, and cognitions. *Journal of Social Issues, 4,* 29–50.

Rushton, J. P., Fulker, D. W., Neale, M. C., Nias, D. K. B., & Eysenck, H. J. (1986). Altruism and aggression: The heritability of individual differences. *Journal of Personality and Social Psychology, 50,* 1192–1198.

Schneider, W., & Shriffrin, R. (1977). Controlled and automatic human information processing: Detection, search and attention. *Psychological Review, 84,* 1–66.

Singer, J. L., & Singer, D. G. (1981). *Television, imagination, and aggression: A study of preschooler's play.* Hillsdale, NJ: Lawrence Erlbaum.

Spivack, G. (1983). *High risk early behaviors indicating vulnerability to delinquency in the community and school.* Washington, DC: NIMH.

Stein, A. H., & Friedrich, L. K. (1972). Television content and young children's behavior. In: J. P. Murray, E. A. Rubinstein, & G. A. Comstock (Eds.), *Television and social behavior: Vol. 2. Television and social learning.* (pp. 202–317). Washington, DC: U.S. Government Printing Office.

Weigman, O., Kuttschreuter, M., & Baarda, B. (1986). *Television viewing related to aggressive and prosocial behavior.* The Hague, The Netherlands: Stitching voor Onderzoek van het Onderwijs.

Williams, T. M. (1978). *Differential impact of TV on children: A natural experiment in communities with and without TV.* Paper presented at the meeting of the International Society for Research on Aggression, Washington, DC.

Wood, W., Wong, F. Y., & Chachere, G. (1991). Effects of media violence on viewers' aggression in unconstrained social interaction. *Psychological Bulletin, 109,* 371–383.

CHAPTER 8

RISK AND RESOURCE VARIABLES IN CHILDREN'S AGGRESSIVE BEHAVIOR

A Two-Year Longitudinal Study

ERIC F. DUBOW AND GRAHAM J. REID

INTRODUCTION

Interpersonal aggression creates numerous problems for victims, perpetrators, and society in general. The prevalence estimates of conduct disorder in children and adolescents are approximately 5% (e.g., Offord, Boyle, & Racine, 1991). Definitions of aggression are numerous and include aggressive behaviors which vary in levels of severity. Eron (1987) defined aggression as, "an act that injures or irritates another person" (p. 435). This definition subsumes most others and avoids issues related to intentionality, which may be difficult to ascertain in children.

Many studies have identified risk factors for aggression. The strongest risk factor appears to be the presence and pattern of early aggression

ERIC F. DUBOW • Department of Psychology, Bowling Green State University, Bowling Green, Ohio 43403. GRAHAM J. REID • Department of Psychology, Bowling Green State University, Bowling Green, Ohio 43403.

Aggressive Behavior: Current Perspectives, edited by L. Rowell Huesmann. Plenum Press, New York, 1994.

(Huesmann, Eron, Lefkowitz, & Walder, 1984; Moskowitz, Schwartzman, & Ledingham, 1985; Stattin & Magnusson, 1989). In addition, a number of parenting and family variables, such as stress in the parent–child relationship, have also been implicated as risk factors in the development of aggression and delinquency (Eron, Walder, & Lefkowitz, 1971; Lefkowitz, Eron, Walder, & Huesmann, 1977; Patterson, DeBarsyshe, & Ramsey, 1989; Webster-Stratton, 1988).

Recently, increasing attention has been given to variables that promote competence or reduce the potentially negative effects of risk factors in childhood (Rolf, Masten, Cicchetti, Nuechterlein, & Weintraub, 1990). Such resource variables include coping or social problem-solving skills, and sources of social support, both within and outside the family (e.g., Compas, 1987; Cowen & Work, 1988; Rutter, 1979, 1990; Werner, 1989). This paper will examine both risk and resource variables in the development of children's aggression.

RISK FACTORS AND AGGRESSION

Risk factors consist of events, variables, and mechanisms which are associated with maladjustment (Garmezy, 1983; Rutter, 1990). By definition, a risk factor must occur prior to later negative outcomes (Loeber, 1990). Rutter (1990) discussed the notion of a "risk trajectory"; that is, certain turning points in life exist which, unless modified by a protective factor, lead to negative outcomes. Risks factors appear to be cumulative, in that the presence of only a single risk factor may not be associated with increased likelihood of negative outcomes, but two or more risks could potentiate each other leading to significantly higher probabilities of negative outcomes. In addition, the presence of risk factors may increase the likelihood of exposure to multiple acute stressors (Rutter, 1979). Thus, it may be important to examine changes in risk factors over time, rather than view risk factors as static, and how these changes relate to the development of adjustment problems.

One specific risk factor for later aggression appears to be the presence and pattern of early aggressive behavior (see Loeber & Stouthamer-Loeber, 1987, for a meta-analytic review). Using structural equation modeling, Huesmann et al. (1984) reported moderate stability between peer-rated aggression at ages 8 and 19 and multiple indices of aggression (i.e., self-ratings, spouse abuse, punishment of children, traffic violations, and criminal offenses) at age 30 for both boys and girls. In a review article, Loeber (1982) stated that in addition to greater frequency, variety, and early age of onset of behavior problems, the occurrence of behavior difficulties in more than one setting increased the risk for later deviant behavior. In this regard, Pollack, Gilmore, Stewart, and Mattison (1989) found that 8- and 9-year-olds who were rated as high in aggression (above the 90th percentile) in two or three settings (i.e., by self, teacher, peer-ratings) were most likely to also be high in aggression 4 years later. McGee, Silva, and Williams (1983) found that children who were rated by both their parents and teachers as high in aggression were observed to have greater numbers of behavior problems than children rated as aggressive by either their parents or teachers. Thus, one specific risk factor for later aggression appears to be the number of settings in which a child is aggressive early on.

Several studies have identified exposure to family stressors (e.g., death in the family, parents separated or divorced, severe economic difficulties) as a risk factor for the development of behavior problems in general (Cowen, Weissberg, & Guare, 1984; Sterling, Cowen, Weissberg, Lotyczewski, & Boike, 1985), and specifically, aggression (Bennett & Bates, 1990). Rutter (1985) reviewed evidence that higher levels of parental deviance and family discord, and the lack of a secure and stable parent–child relationship were related to the development of children's aggression. Recently, "parenting stress" has also been examined as a risk factor for children's behavior problems. According to Abidin (1990), parenting stress refers to both the child's characteristics that cause stress in the parent–child relationship (e.g., demandingness, negative mood), and aspects of the family context that "influence the parent's ability to respond effectively to her child" (p. 2) (e.g., parent's relationship with spouse, sense of competence in parenting, sense of social isolation, and role restriction imposed by parenting tasks). Webster-Stratton (1988) and Webster-Stratton and Hammond (1988) found that higher levels of maternal parenting stress were related to higher levels of both internalizing and externalizing child behavior problems. It should be noted that a limitation of these studies and many of the other studies of family risk factors is their cross-sectional design which prevents one from drawing implications about the direction of causation between family variables and child behavior problems.

RESOURCE VARIABLES AND AGGRESSION

Garmezy, Masten, and Tellegen (1984) and Rutter (1990) describe certain variables that may play compensatory or, alternatively, protective roles in the development of competence. These variables may be personal resources (e.g., coping skills), or environmental resources (e.g., social support). The resource plays a compensatory role when it operates independently of risk factors; that is, higher levels of the resource relate to higher levels of competence, holding stress constant. Thus, risk and resource variables could have additive, main effects. Alternatively, a resource plays a *protective role* when it operates only in the presence of a risk factor and involves a change from a risk to an adaptive trajectory. Thus, the resource variable may modify (or interact with) the experience of a risk situation in such a manner that there is an increased likelihood of a positive outcome for children with high levels of the resource despite the presence of the risk factor.

Social cognitive abilities have been examined as resources relating to lower levels of aggression (see Dodge & Crick, 1990, for a review). Studies have typically followed a main effects compensatory model. Specifically, aggressive children have been found to generate more aggressive solutions, fewer solutions, and more ineffective solutions to social conflict vignettes than their nonaggressive peers (e.g., Deluty, 1981; Rubin, Bream, & Krasnor, 1991). Dubow, Tisak, Causey, Hryshko, and Reid (1991) found that improvement, over two years, in children's social problem-solving skills (composite measure taking into account the number and effectiveness of solutions) was related to decreases in teacher and parent ratings of children's behavior problems. Thus, there is some suggestion that social problem-solving skills serve a compensatory role in the development of behavior problems.

Only a few studies present evidence that social problem-solving skills serve a protective function. Dubow and Tisak (1989) found that social problem-solving abilities buffered the effects of exposure to stressful life events on teacher- and parent-rated behavior problems and grade-point average; that is, higher levels of social problem-solving abilities moderated the relation between stressful life events and maladjustment. Parker, Cowen, Work, and Wyman (1990) found that highly stressed children who attained adequate behavioral adjustment had higher levels of interpersonal problem-solving skills compared to highly stressed children who were maladjusted. This is *not* complete evidence of a true protective effect, however, because high levels of interpersonal problem-solving skills might similarly differentiate nonstressed adjusted and maladjusted children, indicating a compensatory effect. Also, intervention programs aimed at remediating social cognitive deficits in aggressive children are somewhat consistent with the notion that social problem-solving abilities might serve protective functions, if one views the recipients of these programs as an "at risk" population. Several programs have been effective in reducing children's aggression (e.g., Guerra & Slaby, 1990; Pepler, King, & Byrd, 1991), but other programs have not been successful (see Kendall, Ronan, & Epps, 1991 for review). Nevertheless, attention to children's social problem-solving ability as a potential protective factor is warranted.

Another resource variable that has received substantial attention is social support, a term that refers to feelings of being cared for and loved, esteemed and valued, and belonging to a network of communication and mutual obligation (Cobb, 1976). Warm and supportive relationships both within and/or outside the family have been directly related to competent behaviors and lower levels of aggression in children (e.g., Compas, Wagner, Slavin, & Vannatta, 1986; Dubow & Tisak, 1989; Kashani & Shepperd, 1990; Zelkowitz, 1987), consistent with a compensatory model. Only a few studies have found protective effects for social support. Rutter (1990) found that the presence of a good relationship with one parent was associated with lower levels of maladjustment for children in families with high levels of discord. Dubow and Tisak (1989) found that social support buffered the negative effects of exposure to stressful life events in elementary school children, but this interaction significantly predicted only one of four adjustment measures (teacher-rated behavior problems). Wyman, Cowen, Work, and Parker (1991) reported that a nurturant and close parent–child relationship was characteristic of highly stressed children who exhibited positive adjustment but not highly stressed children who exhibited maladjustment. But, because the authors did not examine the quality of the parent–child relationship in adjusted and maladjusted children *not* under stress, their findings fail to speak to true protective effects.

One recent study examined simultaneously both risk and resource variables in children's aggression in a sample of 8- to 15-year-olds whose mothers were teenagers when the children were born (Dubow & Luster, 1990). A composite index of risk factors (e.g., lack of spouse/partner in home, family in poverty, four or more children in the home, low maternal self-esteem) and a composite index of potential protective factors (e.g., emotional support at home, high child self-worth, at least average IQ) were both related to maternal ratings of children's antisocial behavior problems. For children at risk for antisocial behavior problems (i.e., children who had been exposed to at least one risk factor), those who had higher levels of emotional support at home or higher self-esteem were less likely to have antisocial behavior problems (i.e., were below the 66th percentile) than children who had low levels of emotional support or self-esteem. Moreover, for children at risk, the more protective factors that were present, the lower the likelihood of antisocial behavior problems.

The present study examined both risk and resource variables in children's aggression. Two risk factors (a specific risk for aggression index—the number of early settings in which a child was rated as aggressive, and parenting stress) and two resource variables (social problem-solving skills and social support) were included. Given that the present study was a 2-year longitudinal project, the contributions of changes over time in parenting stress and the resource variables to predicting changes in aggression could be examined. In addition, compensatory and protective roles of the resource variables were of special interest.

METHOD

SUBJECTS

The analyses for this study are based on a subset of elementary school children who participated in a two-year longitudinal study on the contributions of stress and resource variables to predicting adjustment (Dubow & Tisak, 1989; Dubow et al., 1991). In the spring of 1987 (Time 1), the original sample of 361 third through fifth graders (195 girls, 73% white) was recruited from two urban and two suburban lower-middle-class schools. Data were collected from the children, their parents, and their teachers. Two years later, in the spring of 1989 (Time 2), parental consent was obtained for 193 (53%) of the original sample. The two-year time span was selected in order to allow for changes to occur in the variables of interest. Reasons for attrition were: moving out of district (79 subjects), failure to return consent forms (77 subjects), and declining to participate (12 subjects).

The analyses for the current study focus on 102 children for whom complete child, parent, and teacher data were available at both time points. This subsample consists of 36 boys and 66 girls who were in grades 5 ($n = 36$), 6 ($n = 34$), and 7 ($n = 32$) at Time 2; 82 of the children were white. The majority of the parents had at least a high school education (60%), 53% had a household income greater than $30,000, and 80% were currently married. According to Hollingshead's index of social position (Miller, 1977), the average socioeconomic status was 42.69 ($SD = 16.5$), which corresponds to a lower-middle-class status. The mean number of children in the family was 2.37 ($SD = 1.02$).

In terms of the effects of subject attrition, we compared the 102 subjects for whom all data were available at both time points with those who had incomplete data. The subsample for whom all data were available had lower levels of peer-nominated aggression at Time 1, $t(359) = 2.45$, $p < .04$, lower levels of teacher-rated aggression at Time 1, $t(341) =$

1.85, $p < .07$, and came from families with higher levels of socioeconomic status, $t(236) = 2.96$, $p < .01$. In addition, the subsample for whom all data were available was more likely to be composed of girls, $\chi^2(1, N = 102) = 6.88$, $p < .01$, and white children, $\chi^2(1, N = 102) = 3.13$, $p < .08$. Attrition was not related to parent-rated aggression, parenting stress, children's social support and social problem-solving skills, or grade level. In general, the loss of subjects with higher levels of aggression is consistent with other longitudinal studies (e.g., Lefkowitz et al., 1977).

Procedures

At Time 1, the children completed paper-and-pencil measures in their classrooms during three 45-minute sessions. At Time 2, due to the schools' time constraints, the children completed measures during one 60-minute session. The measures were administered by two trained research assistants, one of whom read the questions aloud, while the other checked that the children were following directions, not skipping ahead, and so on. Teachers also provided information on the children's adjustment, and parents were mailed measures of family stress and child adjustment. Ninety-six percent of the parent questionnaires were completed by mothers. Parents and teachers received a $10 honorarium for completing the measures at each time point.

Measures

Demographic Variables

Children reported their gender, grade level, and race. Parents provided demographic information including their education and occupation; based on this information, Hollingshead's two-factor index of social position was used to compute socioeconomic status (SES; Miller, 1977). For each family, the score of the parent with the higher socioeconomic status was used.

Aggression and Risk Variables

Peer-Nominations of Aggression. In each participating classroom, children listed the names of three classmates in response to the following vignette (Coie, Dodge, & Coppotelli, 1982): "This person starts fights. They say mean things to other kids or push them or hit them. Name three children in your class who are like this child." Children were provided with a class roster to help them with this task. Nominations for each child were tallied and standardized within each classroom to control for differences in the number of nominators. Nominations were not restricted to same-sex peers because previous research has found considerable overlap between same-sex and entire-class peers in this peer-rated aggression item (Dubow, 1988). Peer-nominations of aggression were obtained at Time 1 only due to time constraints.

Teacher-Rated Aggression. Teachers completed the Teacher-Child Rating Scale (T-CRS; Hightower, Work, Cowen, Lotyczewski, Spinell, Guare, & Rohrbeck, 1986) which assesses both problem behaviors and competencies. Teachers rate the degree to which the child exhibits each behavior along a 5-point continuum. Of particular interest in this study is the 6-item acting-out subscale which includes such behaviors as disruptive in class, overly aggressive to peers (fights), disturbs others while they are working, and so on. Hightower et al. (1986) reported internal consistencies of .89 and .94 for two different samples of elementary school children, and 10-week test–retest reliabilities ranging from .66 to .88 in three different samples. The authors reported moderate to high correlations between the acting-out subscale and other measures of adjustment. The T-CRS was administered at both Time 1 and Time 2. Internal consistencies of the acting-out subscale were .92 (Time 1) and .94 (Time 2).

Parent-Rated Aggression. Parents completed the Revised Behavior Problem Checklist (Quay & Peterson, 1983), an 89-item measure assessing several types of child behavior problems (e.g., anxiety, aggression). The parent rates the degree to which the child exhibits each behavior along a 3-point continuum (0 = not a problem, 1 = mild problem, 2 = severe problem). Of particular interest in the current study is the 22-item conduct disorder subscale, which includes such behaviors as fights, has temper tantrums, disobedient–difficult to control, impertinent—talks back, blames others, and so on. Quay and Peterson (1983, 1984) present data supporting the reliability and validity of this measure. The Revised Behavior Problem Checklist was administered at both Time 1 and Time 2. The internal consistencies of the conduct disorder subscale were .94 (Time 1) and .93 (Time 2).

All aggression measures were standardized by gender given the consistency of gender differences on these measures in terms of the normative data as well as in the current study. In order to develop an index of *specific risk for later aggression,* a score was computed to indicate the number of settings in which a child was rated as aggressive at Time 1 (by peers, parents, and teachers). Within each gender, the distributions for Time 1 parent-, teacher-, and peer-ratings of aggression were examined. Children were considered to be aggressive, within each context, if their score was above the 67th percentile of the distribution for their gender. Thus, a child could have been rated as aggressive in up to three contexts at Time 1 (by peers, parents, and teachers).

Parenting Stress. Parents completed the Parenting Stress Index (PSI; Abidin, 1990) as a measure of stress in the parent–child relationship. The PSI includes two domains: child domain assesses aspects of the child that the parent perceives as stress-enhancing; parent domain assesses "some of the principal parent characteristics and family context variables which have been identified as impacting upon the parent's ability to function as a competent care-giver" (Abidin, 1990, p. 2). Only the parent domain score was used in the present study. Although there are seven parenting domain subscales (depression, attachment to the child, restriction caused by the parenting role, sense of competence, social isolation, relationship with spouse, parental health), the high internal consistency (.93, Abidin, 1990) of the 57-item parent domain suggests that it is a homogeneous scale. Parents are asked to indicate the extent to which they agree with each item on a 5-point continuum (1 = strongly agree to 5 = strongly disagree). Abidin (1990) reviews several studies showing the validity of the PSI. The parent domain scale was administered at both Time 1 and Time 2. Internal consistencies were .92 at both time points.

Resource Variables

Social Support. The Social Support Appraisals Scale (SSAS; Dubow & Ullman, 1989) was administered at Time 1. This 31-item child self-report measure assesses the child's appraisals of peer, family, and teacher support. Items reflect Cobb's (1976) conceptualization of social support, that is, information indicating to the individual that he or she is valued and esteemed by others. Items include: peer items (e.g., whether the child feels left out by his friends); family items (e.g., whether the child is an important member of his family); and teacher items (e.g., whether the child feels his teachers are good people to ask for help or advice about problems). The child responds to each item on a 5-point continuum (1 = always, 5 = never). Dubow and Ullman (1989) reported an internal consistency reliability (Cronbach's alpha) of .88 and 3 to 4 week test—retest reliability of .75. Although factor analyses supported a 3-factor solution (family, peer, and teacher support), moderate intercorrelations exist among the three subscales. Validity data for this measure include significant correlations with other measures of social support, as well as self-esteem and peer nominations of social preference (Dubow & Ullman, 1989).

At Time 2, a revised version of the SSAS was administered. This 41-item revision included additional teacher and classmate support items, and rewording of some items in the reverse direction to control for response bias. The internal consistency of the total revised scale was .93, and a similar 3-factor solution emerged as with the original version of the scale. Dubow et al. (1991) reported analyses which suggest that the original and revised scales are highly comparable.

Social Problem-Solving Skills. The children's social problem-solving skills were assessed using a procedure developed by Deluty (1981). At Time 1, children were read 10 vignettes depicting conflict situations involving peers and parents. For each vignette, children were given 4 minutes to "Write down all the things you really might say or do if you found yourself in this situation." A sample vignette is, "You're standing in line for a drink of water. A kid your age and size walks over and just shoves you out of line. What would you do?"

Training of raters to score children's responses and details regarding assessment of inter-rater reliability are explained in detail by Dubow and Tisak (1989) and Dubow et al. (1991). Briefly, judges rated the number of solutions given to each vignette, the content category of each solution (e.g., verbal/physical aggression, verbal assertion/direct action), and the effectiveness of each solution (a 4-point rating ranging from 1 = immediate action that escalates the conflict, to 4 = socially appropriate resolution). On a subset of actual study protocols (15%), exact agreement between four raters and a criterion judge on whether each response in fact constituted a scorable solution was 98% for each rater; percent of exact agreement with the criterion judge on the content of each solution ranged from 89 to 91% across raters; and correlations of each rater's effectiveness ratings with those of the criterion judge ranged from r = .87 to r = .90 across judges. Because other investigators (e.g., Fischler & Kendall, 1988) have demonstrated the need to consider simultaneously the number of solutions as well as their effectiveness, a social problem-solving composite score (SPS Composite) was derived as follows: for each of the 10 vignettes, the effectiveness ratings for all of the child's solutions to that vignette were summed, yielding 10 scores; the mean of these 10 scores was the SPS Composite score (coefficient alpha for these 10 scores was .85).

At Time 2, only five of the original 10 vignettes were administered (the odd-numbered items). Similar levels of interrater reliability were obtained, as was reported for the Time 1 social problem-solving data (see Dubow et al., 1991). (Coefficient alpha for the SPS Composite score at Time 2 was .87.) Dubow et al. (1991) reported analyses showing that the original 10-vignette version and the 5-vignette version are comparable.

RESULTS

Relation between Specific Risk for Aggression Index and Later Aggression

Table 1 shows that subjects who were aggressive in an increasing number of settings at Time 1 were more likely to be rated as high in aggression at Time 2 (above the 67th percentile) by teachers, $\chi^2(3, N = 102) = 14.47$, $p < .01$, and by parents, $\chi^2(3, N = 102) = 14.99$, $p < .01$. Of the 40 subjects who were aggressive in zero settings at Time 1, only 10% were rated as high in aggression by teachers at Time 2, and only 13% were rated as high in aggression by parents at Time 2. In contrast, of the 25 subjects rated as aggressive in two or three settings at Time 1, 48% were rated as high in aggression by teachers at Time 2 and 56% were rated as high in aggression by parents at Time 2.

In a second analysis, ANOVAs revealed significant differences in the continuous scores for Time 2 teacher-rated aggression, $F(3, 98) = 6.81$, $p < .001$, and Time 2 parent-rated aggression, $F(3, 98) = 7.78$, $p < .001$, among subjects at different levels of the specific risk factor. Table 1

TABLE 1. Relation between Specific Risk for Aggression (Number of Contexts in Which Subject Was Aggressive at Time 1) and Aggressive Behavior at Time 2

Specific risk for aggression (number of contexts in which subject was aggressive at Time 1)	Time 2 teacher-rated aggression			Time 2 parent-rated aggression		
	High %	Mean	*SD*	High %	Mean	*SD*
0 ($n = 40$)	10	$-.36_a$	(.49)	13	$-.39_a$	(.52)
1 ($n = 37$)	30	$.02_a$	(1.08)	35	$.00_{ab}$	(1.01)
2 ($n = 18$)	39	$.28_a$	(1.10)	50	$.41_b$	(1.08)
3 ($n = 7$)	71	1.23_b	(1.37)	71	1.20_c	(1.52)

Note. Subjects were rated as "high" in Time 2 teacher- or parent-rated aggression if their scores were above the 67th percentile in the respective distributions. Time 2 aggression scores represent *z*-score values. For each Time 2 aggression measure, means with the same subscript are not significantly different from each other ($p < .05$) in a Duncan multiple-range test.

TABLE 2. Correlations among Time 1 Variables (below Diagonal) and among Time 2 Variables (above Diagonal)

	Demographic variables				Risk and resource variables			Aggression variables		
	Sex	Grade	Race	SES	Parenting stress	Social support	Social problem solving	Teacher rated	Parent rated	Peer rated
Demographic variables										
Sex[a]					.05	−.04	−.14	.00	.00	
Grade	.21*				.05	−.14	.23*	−.15	−.05	
Race[b]	−.11	−.01			.10	.10	−.33**	.33**	.08	
SES[c]	−.02	.12	.25*		.32**	−.22*	−.13	.12	.30**	
Risk and resource variables										
Parenting stress	.04	.13	.03	.24*		−.26**	−.23*	.00	.44**	
Social support	−.01	−.02	−.05	−.19+	−.24*		.03	−.16	−.09	
Social problem solving	−.20*	.35**	−.05	.00	−.08	.24*		−.34**	−.36**	
Aggression variables										
Teacher rated	.00	−.08	.15	.22*	.05	−.27**	−.17+		.28**	
Parent rated	.00	−.02	.12	.29**	.44**	−.09	−.11	.32**		
Peer rated	.00	.06	−.01	.16	−.01	.05	.07	.27**	.23*	
Specific risk for aggression (number of contexts)	.02	.03	.12	.26**	.16+	−.13	−.19+	.65**	.59**	.52**

[a]Gender was coded as follows: 0 = females, 1 = males.
[b]Race was coded as follows: 1 = white, 2 = minority.
[c]Higher scores reflect lower levels of socioeconomic status.
$+p < .10$. $^*p < .05$. $^{**}p < .10$.

shows that subjects who were aggressive in all three contexts at Time 1 were rated as more aggressive at Time 2 by both teachers and parents than subjects who were aggressive in fewer than three contexts.

Cross-Sectional Correlations among Risk, Resource, and Aggression Variables

Table 2 shows correlations among all demographic, risk, resource, and aggression variables at Time 1 (below the diagonal) and at Time 2 (above the diagonal). Of particular interest are the correlations of the risk and resource variables with the aggression measures. Specific risk for aggression (measured at Time 1 only) was significantly related to each Time 1 aggression measure (*r*s ranged from .52 to .65). Parenting stress was moderately related to parent-rated aggression ($r = .44$ at each time point). In terms of the resource variables: (1) higher levels of social support (total score; and the teacher and peer support subscales, not shown on (Table 2) were related to lower levels of teacher-rated aggression at Time 1 only ($r = -.27$ for the total social support score); and (2) higher levels of social problem-solving skills were related to lower levels of teacher-rated aggression at Time 1 ($r = -.17$) and at Time 2 ($r = -.34$), and lower levels of parent-rated aggression at Time 2 only ($r \doteq -.36$).

Table 2 also shows that the relations between the risk and resource variables within each time period were not significant or were modest. Thus, each risk and resource variable appears to tap different constructs. Finally, correlations among the aggression measures at each time point were moderate. Of specific note, the two aggression measures that were collected at both time points, teacher- and parent-rated aggression, were correlated only .32 at Time 1, and only .28 at Time 2, suggesting that different informants may have somewhat different perspectives of the child's aggression, and/or that children react differently in different settings. Thus, later analyses will examine separately the predictors of Time 2 teacher- and parent-rated aggression.

Correlations of Time 1 Risk and Resource Variables with Time 2 Aggression

Table 3 shows the correlations between the Time 1 variables and Time 2 teacher- and parent-rated aggression. Of particular interest, the specific risk for aggression index was moderately related to later teacher- ($r = .40$) and parent-rated aggression ($r = .43$). In addition, higher levels of Time 1 parenting stress were related to higher levels of Time 2 parent-rated aggression ($r = .37$), but not to teacher-rated aggression. Of the

TABLE 3. Correlations of Time 1 Variables with Time 2 Aggression

Time 1 predictors	Time 2 teacher-rated aggression	Time 2 parent-rated aggression
Demographic variables		
Sex[a]	.00	.00
Grade	−.15	−.05
Race[b]	.33**	.08
SES[c]	.12	.30**
Risk variables		
Peer-rated aggression	.21*	.25*
Teacher-rated aggression	.47**	.24*
Parent-rated aggression	.26**	.86**
Specific risk for aggression (number of contexts)	.40**	.43**
Parenting stress	.01	.37**
Resource variables		
Social support	−.13	−.10
Social problem solving	−.25*	−.04

[a]Gender was coded as follows: 0 = females, 1 = males.
[b]Race was coded as follows: 1 = white, 2 = minority.
[c]Higher scores reflect lower levels of socioeconomic status.
$+p < .10$. $*p < .05$. $**p < .01$.

resource variables, higher levels of Time 1 social problem-solving skills were related to lower levels of later teacher-rated aggression ($r = -.25$), but not to later parent-rated aggression; Time 1 social support was unrelated to later aggression.

There are limitations to interpreting both cross-sectional and longitudinal correlations. Significant cross-sectional relations are not indicative of direction of causality between variables. For example, it is equally plausible that parenting stress causes child aggression and/or that child aggression causes parenting stress. Although longitudinal relations solve the temporal problem (i.e., parenting stress may be measured two years prior to the assessment of aggression), a significant correlation between Time 1 parenting stress and Time 2 aggression might actually reflect the stability of aggression between Time 1 and Time 2 if Time 1 parenting stress is related to Time 1 aggression. Cohen, Burt, and Bjorck (1987) describe how "prospective analyses" within the stressful life events literature address these limitations. This approach examines the relation between Time 1 stress or risk factors and Time 2 adjustment after controlling for Time 1 adjustment. Thus, one tests the effect of Time 1 stress on change in adjustment over time. However, Dubow et al. (1991) and Rutter (1990) note that exposure to risk is unlikely to be static; changes in the level of risk may be more important in predicting changes over time in adjustment than simply the initial level of risk. A similar argument could be made for studying the contribution of changes in resource variables over time rather than simply the initial level of the resource variables.

Hierarchical Regressions: Time 1 and Time 2 Risk and Resource Variables as Predictors of Aggression

A hierarchical regression model was used to analyze prospective effects for risk and resource variables, whether changes in these variables were predictive of later aggression, and whether the resource variables played compensatory or protective roles. Demographic variables (gender, grade, race, and socioeconomic status) were entered in the first step because these variables were related to some of the risk and resource variables to be entered into the regression equation in later steps (see Tables 2 and 3 for correlations between the demographic variables and all other variables). In the second step, the specific risk for aggression score (number of settings in which the subject was aggressive at Time 1) was entered as a risk factor for later aggression, and as an index of initial level of aggression. In the third step, Time 1 parenting stress and the resource variables were entered to test the prospective effects of these variables; significant effects for the resource variables would suggest compensatory effects for initial levels of resources. In the fourth step, Time 2 parenting stress and the resource variables were entered. Significant findings at this step suggest that changes in these variables over time are related to changes in aggression because significant findings represent the residual effects of the Time 2 variables after controlling for their initial levels in step 3 (see Holahan & Moos, 1981); significant results for the resource variables would indicate that changes in resources compensate for risk effects. In the fifth step, the interaction terms involving specific risk for aggression × Time 2 resources, and Time 2 parenting stress × Time 2 resources were entered to test the protective model regarding the resource variables, that is, whether changes in the resource variables in fact modified the relation between risk variables and later aggression (e.g., does improvement in social problem-solving skills help protect *specifically* those children at risk?). Two sets of hierarchical regressions were computed, one predicting Time 2 teacher-rated aggression and one predicting Time 2 parent-rated aggression. Table 4 presents the findings of these analyses.

TABLE 4. Hierarchical Multiple Regressions of Time 2 Aggression on Demographic Variables, Time 1 Risk and Resource Variables, and Time 2 Risk and Resource Variables

Predictor variables	Time 2 teacher-rated aggression			Time 2 parent-rated aggression		
	Cum R^2	Beta	F (step)	Cum R^2	Beta	F (step)
Step 1: Background variables	.14			.10		
Gender[a]			NS			NS
Grade		−.10	3.12+			NS
Race[b]		.24	10.31**			NS
Socioeconomic status[c]			NS		.07	9.25**
Step 2: Specific risk for aggression (number of contexts)	.26	.34	15.77**	.23	.40	16.17**
Step 3: Time 1 stress and resource variables	.28			.32		
Parenting stress			NS		.11	11.37**
Social support			NS			NS
Social problem solving			NS			NS
Step 4: Time 2 stress and resource variables	.37			.46		
Parenting stress			NS		.26	4.72*
Social support		−.18	5.76*			NS
Social problem solving		−.20	6.02*		−.31	13.49**
Step 5: Interaction terms	.39			.49		
Agg. risk × Time 2 SS[e]			NS			NS
Agg. risk × Time 2 SPS[f]			NS		−.18	5.40*
Time 2 stress[g] × Time 2 SPS			NS			NS
Time 2 stress × Time 2 SPS			NS			NS

Note. All beta values reported in this table are standardized betas obtained for the entire regression rather than those obtained at each step of the hierarchical procedure.
[a]Gender was coded as follows: 0 = females, 1 = males.
[b]Race was coded as follows: 1 = white, 2 = minority.
[c]Higher scores reflect lower levels of socioeconomic status.
[d]Agg. risk = specific risk for aggression (number of contexts).
[e]SS = social support.
[f]SPS = social problem solving.
[g]Time 2 stress = Time 2 parenting stress.
$^{+}p < .10$. $^{*}p < .05$. $^{**}p < .01$.

In step 1, the set of demographic variables accounted for 14% of the variance in teacher-rated aggression and 10% of the variance in parent-rated aggression. In step 2, specific risk for aggression accounted for an additional 12% of the variance in teacher-rated aggression and 13% of the variance in parent-rated aggression. In step 3, only one significant prospective effect was found: Time 1 parenting stress predicted later parent-rated aggression, even after controlling for initial level of aggression in step 2. The initial levels of the resource variables, however, failed to compensate for early risk.

At this point Time 2 variables were introduced as predictors. In step 4, the Time 2 stress and resource variables accounted for an additional 9% of the variance in teacher-rated aggression and 14% of the variance in parent-rated aggression. Specifically, increases in parenting stress were related to an increased likelihood of parent-rated aggression. Also, improvement in social problem-solving was related to a lower likelihood of teacher- and parent-rated aggression; and increases in social support (total score; and teacher support subscale, not shown) were related to a lower likelihood of teacher-rated aggression; thus, changes in the resource variables compensated for risk. Finally, in step 5, the results showed that changes in the resource variables generally failed to interact with the effect of the risk factors (i.e., were not protective) on Time 2 aggression with one exception: the interaction term of specific risk for aggression × Time 2 social problem solving significantly predicted Time 2 parent-rated aggression. Figure 1 shows that children whose social problem-solving skills increased (versus those whose skills decreased) over time were "protected" from the effects of high levels of risk on later parent-rated aggression.

DISCUSSION

This two-year longitudinal study addressed several issues raised in previous studies. The first question sought replication of the findings that the number of settings in which a child was rated as aggressive was a specific risk factor for later aggression. The second question examined whether parental stress could be considered to be a risk factor for later aggression. A final question explored compensatory and protective effects of two resource variables, social support and social problem-solving skills, on the development of aggression.

Risk Factors for Aggression

Children who were initially rated as aggressive in three contexts (i.e., by peers, parents, and teachers) were more likely to be rated as

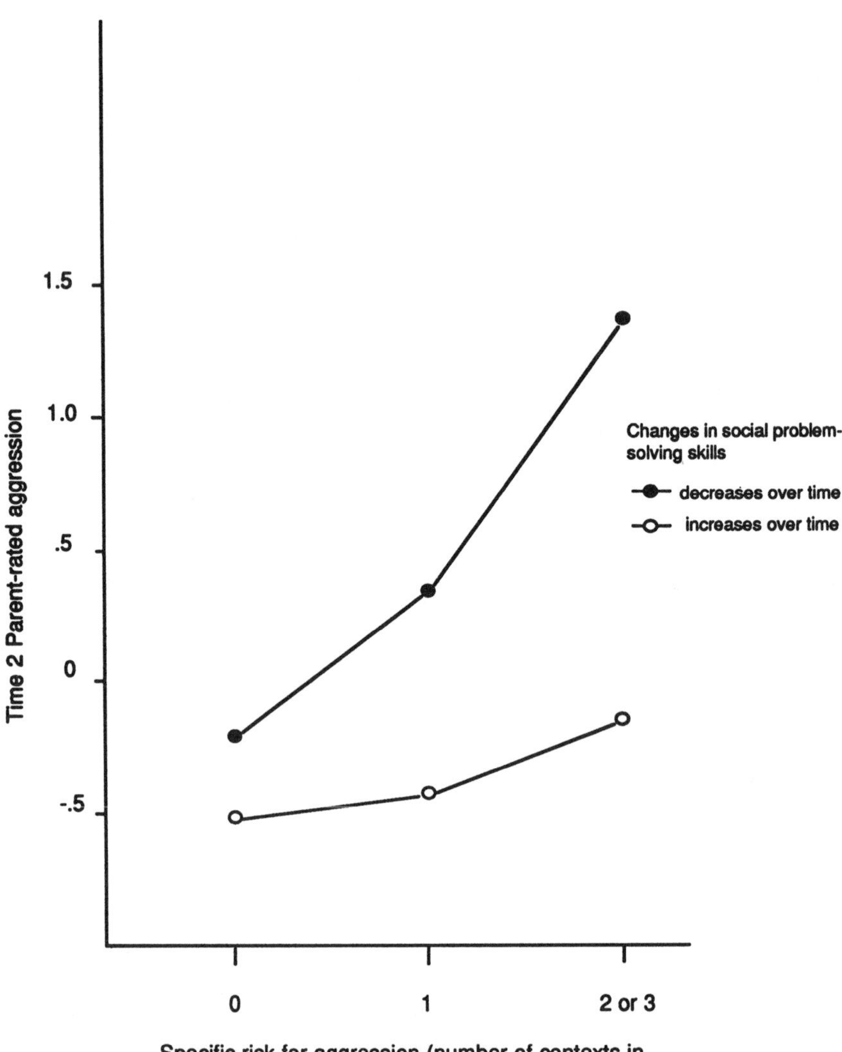

FIGURE 1. Relation between specific risk for aggression (number of contexts in which child was rated as aggressive at Time 1) and Time 2 parent-rated aggression for children whose social problem-solving skills increased and decreased over time.

aggressive by both teachers and parents two years later compared to children who were initially rated as aggressive in two or fewer contexts. These findings are similar to those of other studies predicting similar types of later aggression and even more serious forms of criminal and antisocial behavior (Kirkpatrick, 1978, cited in Loeber, 1982; McGee et al. 1983; Pollack et al. 1989). Huesmann (1988) suggested that the persistence of aggression is influenced by programs for aggressive behavior, or "aggressive scripts," which have been developed following observational and enactive learning. These learning opportunities for the highly aggressive child may take place across multiple settings, leading to the development of aggressive scripts across situations. Aggressive scripts are subsequently strengthened through frequent rehearsal, and thus are easily retrieved from memory whenever the child is confronted with a problematic situation.

Higher initial levels of, and increases in, parenting stress were related to later parent-rated, but not teacher-rated, aggression. Thus, it appears that parenting stress may be a risk factor for later child aggression, but only in the home. These results are congruent with findings relating parenting stress and child behavior problems in general (Webster-Stratton, 1988; Webster-Stratton & Hammond, 1988). Webster-Stratton (1988) found that higher levels of parenting stress were related to a higher incidence of maternal criticism and physical punishment toward the child. According to Patterson's (1976) "family coercion model," such coercive maternal behavior may elicit reciprocal coercive behaviors in the child. The sequence continues to be repeated, escalating to higher intensities of aggressive interactions. Of course, an alternative interpretation of the significant relation between parenting stress and parent-rated child aggression, but not teacher-rated aggression, is that parents under high levels of stress may simply be more likely to perceive a variety of child behaviors in a negative light.

Resource Variables: Compensatory and Protective Effects of Social Support and Social Problem-Solving Skills

With respect to the resource variables, improvements over time in social support had a compensatory effect on teacher-rated aggression. That is, independent of any effects of risk variables, increases in social support were related to lower levels of teacher-rated aggression two years later. These findings are consistent with previous research (Bennett & Bates, 1990; Kashani & Shepperd, 1990; Zelkowitz, 1987). Children whose social support systems improved over time may have been more able to develop adaptive means of coping with their social environments for several reasons. First, children's improved social networks may be providing them with tangible and informational aid that is directly useful in solving interpersonal problems in a prosocial, as opposed to an aggressive, manner. In addition, Sandler, Miller, Short, and Wolchik (1989) note that social support may affect intervening variables such as self-esteem, sense of security, and feelings of mastery over situations; higher levels of these variables could reduce the likelihood of resorting to aggressive and impulsive means to solve social problems. Increased social support might also have increased the child's opportunities to observe prosocial methods of dealing with social situations, encouraging the development of these behaviors in the child's own repertoire. Supplementary analyses revealed that the compensatory effect for social support on teacher-rated aggression was primarily due to increases in teacher support specifically, but not peer or parent support. As suggested by Dubow and Tisak (1989), the beneficial effects of specific sources of social support are likely to be closely related to the setting in which the support was provided. Thus, teacher support would most likely affect behavior within the school setting (e.g., teacher-rated aggression). If the match between the source of support and the setting in which adjustment is being measured is critical, however, then it is unclear why there was no compensatory effect for family support on parent-rated aggression. It is possible that the family support measure, which assesses support from family members in general and not parents specifically, fails to provide a clear test of this hypothesis.

Improvements over time in social problem-solving skills also had a compensatory effect on both teacher- and parent-rated aggression. That is, independent of any effects of risk factors, increases in children's social problem-solving abilities were related to decreases over time in aggression. These findings are consistent with previous research demonstrating positive main effects for social problem solving on children's behavioral competence and grade point averages (e.g., Dubow et al., 1991), and are also consistent with the findings from intervention studies that social problem-solving training leads to decreases in aggression (e.g., Pepler et al., 1991). Social problem-solving skills are personal resources of the child and hence are available across situations. Improvements in the ability to generate a greater number of, and more effective, solutions in the face of social conflict might facilitate more prosocial, and less aggressive, behavior both at home and in the classroom.

In addition to the compensatory effect of social problem-solving skills on parent-rated aggression, social problem-solving skills were found to play a protective role in the relation between early specific risk for aggression and later parent-rated aggression. That is, improvement in social problem-solving skills were beneficial for all children, regardless of early risk status, but were *especially* helpful for children at high levels of risk (i.e., children who were rated as aggressive at Time 1 in two or more contexts). The social problem-solving measure assesses children's abilities to respond specifically to conflict situations. Children who are aggressive in multiple contexts are confronted with a greater number of conflict situations, which require more frequent and effective utilization of their social problem-solving skills if they are to behave less aggressively. It remains unclear, however, why this protective effect was found for parent-rated, but not teacher-rated, aggression.

It is important to note that only *changes* in the resource variables were found to have any compensatory effects. That is, compensatory effects on later aggression were not found for initial levels of either social support or social problem-solving skills. Similarly, the only significant protective effect (social problem solving on parent-rated aggression) involved changes over time in social problem-solving ability. (Supplementary analyses failed to show protective effects for Time 1 levels of social problem solving on parent-rated aggression.) These results suggest that resource variables should be thought of in terms of processes, or attributes that change over time, rather than static variables. Research documenting the relation between resource variables and adjustment measured concurrently cannot address this ongoing process.

Limitations and Conclusions

Several limitations to the present study should be addressed. First, protective effects are often difficult to obtain because relatively few subjects have high levels of both risk and resource variables (Rutter, 1990), and this is the major group of interest in studying protective effects. Thus, research on protective effects must utilize samples with a large number of subjects who are at risk; this might insure an adequate subsample that also has high levels of resource variables. Unfortunately, in longitudinal research, attrition often occurs most among subjects who have higher levels of risk. In the present study, of the 102 subjects for whom data were available at both time points, only 7 subjects were rated as aggressive in all three settings (25 were rated as aggressive in two or three contexts). Subjects who dropped out of the study by Time 2 were more aggressive and came from families of lower socioeconomic status than subjects completing both phases of the study.

The use of a longitudinal design has a number of advantages over cross-sectional research models and more closely approximates the process aspects of risk and resource variables. No correlational study, however, even one with a longitudinal design, can definitively address issues of causality (Cohen et al., 1987). First, even if prospective effects are found, for example, Time 1 parenting stress relates to Time 2 aggression after controlling for Time 1 aggression, it is not clear that parenting stress causes changes in aggression over time because a third unmeasured variable might cause both initial parenting stress and aggression at both time points. Second, if findings relate significant changes in risk and resource variables to changes in aggression, a reverse causal explanation is possible: perhaps changes in aggression lead to changes in risk and/or resource variables. Intervention studies designed to alter risk and resource variables would help to address the direction of causality. For example, mothers at high levels of parenting stress could be taught parenting techniques designed to decrease parenting stress. Improvement in children's aggression, while controlling for levels of resource variables, would clarify the role of parenting stress in children's aggression.

Finally, the present study does not delineate the specific mechanisms by which the risk or resources variables might be operating. For example, how does parenting stress lead to child aggression? Perhaps parenting stress leads to certain child-rearing behaviors that frustrate the child, or instigate the child to behave in aggressive ways (see Eron et al., 1971). How does social support compensate for any negative effects of risk on later aggression? Perhaps, as Sandler et al. (1989) suggest, social support affects intervening variables such as self-esteem and feelings of mastery and self-efficacy, which in turn discourage the development of aggressive behaviors. Interventions designed to prevent aggressive behavior in children at all levels of risk will be more powerful when we gain a better understanding of the mechanisms involved in the influence of risk and resource variables.

Acknowledgments

This research was supported by a State of Ohio Board of Regents Research Challenge Grant awarded to the first author. The authors thank the Toledo and Northwood school systems in Ohio for their support of this research project.

REFERENCES

Abidin, R. R. (1990). *Parenting stress index-manual* (3rd ed.). Charlottesville, VA: Pediatric Psychology Press.

Bennett, D. S., & Bates, J. E. (1990, May). *Attributional style, life stress, and social support as predictors of depressive symptoms and aggressive behaviors in early adolescence.* Paper presented at the annual meeting of the Midwestern Psychological Association, Chicago.

Cobb, S. (1976). Social support as a mediator of life stress. *Psychosomatic Medicine, 38,* 300–314.

Cohen, L. H., Burt, C. E., & Bjorck, J. P. (1987). Life stress and adjustment: Effects of life events experienced by young adolescents and their parents. *Developmental Psychology, 23,* 583–592.

Coie, J. D., Dodge, K. A., & Coppotelli, H. (1982). Dimensions and types of social status: A cross-age perspective. *Developmental Psychology, 18,* 557–570.

Compas, B. E. (1987). Coping with stress during childhood and adolescence. *Psychological Bulletin, 101,* 393–403.

Compas, B. E., Wagner, B. M., Slavin, L. A., & Vannatta, K. (1986). A prospective study of life events, social support, and psychological symptomatology during the transition from high school to college. *American Journal of Community Psychology, 14,* 241–257.

Cowen, E. L., & Work, W. C. (1988). Resilient children, psychological wellness, and primary prevention. *American Journal of Community Psychology, 16,* 591–607.

Cowen, E. L., Weissberg, R. P., & Guare, J. (1984). Differentiating attributes of children referred to a school mental health program. *Journal of Abnormal Child Psychology, 12,* 397–410.

Deluty, R. H. (1981). Alternative-thinking ability of aggressive, assertive, and submissive children. *Cognitive Therapy and Research, 5,* 309–312.

Dodge, K. A., & Crick, N. R. (1990). Social information-processing biases of aggressive behavior in children. *Personality and Social Psychology Bulletin, 16,* 8–22.

Dubow, E. F. (1988). Aggressive behavior and peer social status of elementary school children. *Aggressive Behavior, 14,* 315–324.

Dubow, E. F., & Luster, T. (1990). Adjustment of children born to teenage mothers: The contributions of risk and protective factors. *Journal of Marriage and the Family, 52,* 393–404.

Dubow, E. F., & Tisak, J. (1989). The relation between stressful life events and adjustment in elementary school children: The role of social support and social problem-solving skills. *Child Development, 60,* 1412–1423.

Dubow, E. F., Tisak, J., Causey, D., Hryshko, A., & Reid, G. (1991). A two-year longitudinal study of stressful life events, social support, and social problem-solving skills: Contributions to children's behavioral and academic adjustment. *Child Development, 62,* 583–599.

Dubow, E. F., & Ullman, D. G. (1989). Assessing social support in elementary school children: The survey of children's social support. *Journal of Clinical Child Psychology, 18,* 52–64.

Eron, L. D. (1987). The development of aggressive behavior from the perspective of a developing behaviorism. *American Psychologist, 42,* 435–442.

Eron, L. D., Walder, L. O., & Lefkowitz, M. M. (1971). *Learning of aggression.* Boston: Little, Brown.

Fischler, G. L., & Kendall, P. C. (1988). Social cognitive problem solving and childhood adjustment: Qualitative and topological analyses. *Cognitive Therapy and Research, 12,* 133–153.

Garmezy, N. (1983). Stressors of childhood. In: N. Garmezy, & M. Rutter (Eds.), *Stress, coping, and development in children* (pp. 43–84). New York: McGraw-Hill.

Garmezy, N., Masten, A., & Tellegen, A. (1984). The study of stress and competence in children. *Child Development, 55,* 97–111.

Guerra, N. C., & Slaby, R. G. (1990). Cognitive mediators of aggression in adolescent offenders: 2. Intervention. *Developmental Psychology, 26,* 269–277.

Hightower, A. D., Work, W. C., Cowen, E. L., Lotyczewski, B. S., Spinell, A. P., Guare, J. C., & Rohrbeck, C. A. (1986). The teacher-child rating scale: A brief objective measure of elementary children's school problem behaviors and competencies. *School Psychology Review, 15,* 393–409.

Holahan, C. J., & Moos, R. H. (1981). Social support and psychological distress: A longitudinal analysis. *Journal of Abnormal Psychology, 90,* 365–370.

Huesmann, L. R. (1988). An information-processing model for the development of aggression. *Aggressive Behavior, 14,* 13–24.

Huesmann, L. R., Eron, L. D., Lefkowitz, M. M., & Walder, L. O. (1984). Stability of aggression over time and generations. *Developmental Psychology, 20,* 1120–1134.

Kashani, J. H., & Shepperd, J. A. (1990). Aggression in adolescents: The role of social support and personality. *Canadian Journal of Psychiatry, 35,* 311–315.

Kendall, P. C., Ronan, K. R., & Epps, J. (1991). Aggression in children/adolescents: Cognitive-behavioral treatment perspectives. In: D. J. Pepler & K. H. Rubin (Eds.), *The development and treatment of childhood aggression* (pp. 341–360). Hillsdale, NJ: Lawrence Erlbaum.

Lefkowitz, M. M., Eron, L. D., Walder, L. O., & Huesmann, L. R. (1977). *Growing up to be violent: A longitudinal study of the development of aggression.* New York: Pergamon.

Loeber, R. (1982). The stability of antisocial and delinquent child behavior. A review. *Child Development, 53,* 1431–1446.

Loeber, R. (1990). Development and risk factors of juvenile antisocial behavior and delinquency. *Clinical Psychology Review, 10,* 1–42.

Loeber, R., & Stouthamer-Loeber, M. (1987). Prediction. In: H. C. Quay (Ed.), *Handbook of juvenile delinquency* (pp. 325–382). New York: John Wiley.

McGee, R., Silva, P., & Williams, S. (1983). Parents' and teachers' perceptions of behaviour problems in seven year old children. *The Exceptional Child, 30,* 151–161.

Miller, D. C. (1977). *Handbook of research design and social measurement.* New York: McKay.

Moskowitz, D. S., Schwartzman, A. E., & Ledingham, J. E. (1985). Stability and change in aggression and withdrawal in middle childhood and early adolescence. *Journal of Abnormal Psychology, 94,* 30–41.

Offord, D. R., Boyle, M. C., & Racine, Y. A. (1991). The epidemiology of antisocial behavior in childhood and adolescence. In: D. J. Pepler & K. H. Rubin (Eds.), *The development and treatment of childhood aggression* (pp. 31–54). Hillsdale, NJ: Lawrence Erlbaum.

Parker, G. R., Cowen, E. L., Work, W. C., & Wyman, P. A. (1990). Test correlates of stress affected and stress resilient outcomes among urban children. *Journal of Primary Prevention, 11,* 19–35.

Patterson, G. R. (1976). The aggressive child: Victim and architect of a coercive system. In: E. J. Mash, L. A. Hamerlynck, & L. C. Handy (Eds.), *Behavior modification and families: Vol. 1. Theory and research* (pp. 267–316). New York: Brunner/Masel.

Patterson, G. R., DeBarsyche, B. D., & Ramsey, E. (1989). A developmental perspective on antisocial behavior. *American Psychologist, 44,* 329–335.

Pepler, D. J., King, G., & Byrd, W. (1991). A social-cognitively based social skills training program for aggressive children. In: D. J. Pepler & K. H. Rubin (Eds.), *The development and treatment of childhood aggression,* (pp. 361–379). Hillsdale, NJ: Lawrence Erlbaum.

Pollack, G., Gilmore, C., Stewart, J., & Mattison, S. (1989). A follow-up of aggressive behaviour in children. *Educational Review, 41,* 263–270.

Quay, H. C., & Peterson, D. P. (1983). *Interim manual for the revised behavior problem checklist.* Coral Gables, FL: University of Miami.

Quay, H. C., & Peterson, D. P. (1984). *Appendix I to the interim manual for the revised behavior problem checklist.* Coral Gables, FL: University of Miami.

Rolf, J., Masten, A. E., Cicchetti, D., Nuechterlein, K. H., & Weintraub, S. (Eds.) (1990). *Risk and protective factors in the development of psychopathology.* New York: Cambridge University Press.

Rubin, K. H., Bream, L. A., & Krasnor, L. R. (1991). Social problem solving and aggression in childhood. In: D. Pepler & K. H. Rubin (Eds.), *The development and treatment of childhood aggression* (pp. 219–248). Hillsdale, NJ: Lawrence Erlbaum.

Rutter, M. (1979). Protective factors in children's responses to stress and disadvantage. In: M. W. Kent & J. E. Rolf (Eds.), *Social competence in children,* (pp. 49–74). Hanover, NH: University Press of New England.

Rutter, M. (1985). Aggression and the family. *Series Paedopsychiatric Fasc., 6,* 11–25.

Rutter, M. (1990). Psychosocial resilience and protective mechanisms. In: J. Rolf, A. E. Masten, D. Cicchetti, K. H. Nuechterlein, & S. Weintraub (Eds.), *Risk and protective factors in the development of psychopathology* (pp. 118–214). New York: Cambridge University Press.

Sandler, I. N., Miller, P., Short, J., & Wolchik, S. (1989). Social support as a protective factor for children in stress. In: D. Belle (Ed.), *Children's social networks and social supports* (pp. 277–307). New York: John Wiley.

Stattin, H., & Magnusson, D. (1989). The role of early aggressive behavior in the frequency, seriousness, and types of later crimes. *Journal of Consulting and Clinical Psychology, 57,* 710–718.

Sterling, S., Cowen, E. L., Weissberg, R. P., Lotyczewski, B., & Boike, M. (1985). Recent stressful events and young children's school adjustment. *American Journal of Community Psychology, 13,* 87–98.

Webster-Stratton, C. (1988). Mothers' and fathers' perceptions of child deviance: Roles of parent and child behaviors and parent adjustment. *Journal of Consulting and Clinical Psychology, 56,* 909–915.

Webster-Stratton, C., & Hammond, M. (1988). Maternal depression and its relationship to life stress, perceptions of child behavior problems, parenting behaviors, and child conduct problems. *Journal of Abnormal Child Psychology, 16,* 299–315.

Werner, E. E. (1989). High-risk children in young adulthood: A longitudinal study from birth to 32 years. *American Journal of Orthopsychiatry, 59,* 72–81.

Wyman, P. A., Cowen, E. L., Work, W. C., & Parker, G. R. (1991). Developmental and family milieu correlates of resilience in urban children who have experienced major life stress. *American Journal of Community Psychology, 19,* 405–426.

Zelkowitz, P. (1987). Social support and aggressive behavior in young children. *Family Relations, 36,* 129–134.

PART IV

DEVELOPMENT OF ADULT AGGRESSION

Using data from two of the most famous longitudinal studies of aggression, the two chapters in this part elucidate the processes whereby early childhood factors influence adult aggression.

Farrington, with data from his longitudinal study in England, investigates the extent to which adult aggression such as spouse abuse, fighting, "soccer hooliganism," and violent crime is related to early childhood family variables. He suggests that difficulties in relationships with parents and parental disharmony may stimulate boys to be aggressive.

In her chapter, using data from her Cambridge–Somerville study, McCord reaches similar conclusions about the role of parental disharmony as a predictor of later aggressive behavior by the child. She also theorizes that such parental disharmony may be affected by paternal criminality as well as the child's early troublesome behavior.

Chapter 9

CHILDHOOD, ADOLESCENT, AND ADULT FEATURES OF VIOLENT MALES

David P. Farrington

INTRODUCTION

The primary aim of this chapter is to investigate the predictors and correlates of four groups of violent males:

1. Those involved in violence at professional soccer matches at age 18
2. Those identified as aggressive frequent group fighters at age 18
3. Those who had assaulted their wives or cohabitees at age 32
4. Those who were convicted for violent offenses up to age 32

Soccer violence is a somewhat culturally specific phenomenon, whereas the other three types of violence have more cross-cultural applicability.

A great deal is known about the development of violent offenders, especially among males. In particular, one of the best predictors of later violent offending is aggression in childhood and adolescence. For exam-

---

David P. Farrington • Institute of Criminology, Cambridge University, Cambridge, CB3 9DT, United Kingdom.

Aggressive Behavior: Current Perspectives, edited by L. Rowell Huesmann. Plenum Press, New York, 1994.

ple, in one of the most impressive and longest lasting studies of the continuity of aggression, Huesmann and Eron (1992) in New York State showed that peer-rated aggression at age 8 predicted self-reported aggression and criminal violence at age 30. Similar results were reported by Pulkkinen (1983, 1987) in Finland and by Magnusson, Stattin, and Duner (1983) and Stattin and Magnusson (1989) in Sweden. It is also clear that juvenile violent offenses predict adult violent offenses (e.g., Hamparian, Davis, Jacobson & McGraw, 1985).

The early family precursors of male violent offending have been extensively documented in the important Cambridge-Somerville (Boston) study by McCord, McCord, and Howard (1963). They found that, as children, violent offenders tended to have parents who were in conflict, who supervised them poorly, who were rejecting and punitive, whose discipline was erratic, and who were aggressive, alcoholic, or convicted. Similarly, in her later follow-up, McCord (1979) again showed that males convicted of violent crimes tended to have aggressive, conflicting parents, and McCord (1977) discovered that parents who were convicted for violence tended to have sons who were convicted for violence. Generally, boys who are abused or neglected by their parents have a higher risk than others of committing violent offenses as adults, as the retrospective longitudinal study by Widom (1989) and Rivera and Widom (1990) demonstrates. In their prospective study in New York State, Eron, Huesmann, and Zelli (1991) also reported that males who were physically punished at age 8 tended to commit violent offenses up to age 30 (and indeed, showing an intergenerational link, that they used physical punishment on their own children; see also Eron, Huesmann, Dubow, Romanoff, & Yarmel, 1987).

Violent offenders tend to be frequent offenders, as research in Philadelphia (Piper, 1985) and Copenhagen (Guttridge, Gabrielli, Mednick, & Van Dusen, 1983) has demonstrated. Hence, it is important to study how far different factors are specifically related to violence rather than generally related to offending. One method of investigating this question is to compare violent and nonviolent offenders. For example, McCord (1979) found that they were similar in having poor parental supervision, but different in that parental conflict and parental aggressiveness were more predictive of violence, while maternal affection and parental criminality were more predictive of property crimes.

There have been many other studies of the characteristics of violent offenders. For example, Hogh and Wolf (1983) in Copenhagen showed that they had relatively low intelligence, while Wikstrom (1987) in Stockholm discovered that they were more likely to come from lower-class families than other types of offenders. Brennan, Mednick, and Kandel

(1991) were even able to trace back the determinants of violent offending to delivery complications at the time of birth. In this chapter, it is not possible to provide an extensive review of the predictors and correlates of violent offending; the recent book edited by Pepler and Rubin (1991) yields more extensive information about findings and theories.

Turning to soccer hooliganism, the two most important studies of the characteristics of British hooligans were carried out by Harrington (1968) and Trevizas (1980, 1984). Most of the soccer-related offenses were legally categorized as "threatening behavior." Both found that soccer hooligans were predominantly young working-class males, while Harrington (1968) also reported research showing that most hooligans had been drinking prior to the offenses. The major difference between the two studies was that Harrington (1968) discovered that two-thirds of soccer hooligans had previous convictions, while the corresponding figure was only one-third in Trevizas' research (1980). This difference might possibly be attributable to the fact that Harrington studied convicted hooligans, who might possibly have been more extreme than the arrested hooligans studied by Trevizas. Neither research project compared soccer hooligans with nonarrested or nonconvicted soccer fans (or with nonsoccer fans, for that matter), so there is relatively little firm knowledge about differentiating characteristics of soccer hooligans.

Turning finally to spouse assault, Eron and Huesmann (1990) demonstrated that peer-rated aggression at age 8 predicted spouse assault at age 30 among males. Generally, male spouse assaulters tend to have experienced violent and abusive childhoods, to be frequently unemployed and of low social class, to have low income and low educational attainment, to be impulsive and neurotic, alcohol and drug abusers, and to be child physical abusers (e.g., Gelles, 1982; Gelles & Cornell, 1985; Hotaling & Sugarman, 1986; Hotaling, Strauss, & Lincoln, 1989). A key issue is how far males who are violent within the family also tend to be violent outside it, and how far spouse assaulters are similar to or different from other types of violent offenders. Hotaling et al. (1989) concluded that there was a considerable amount of overlap between spouse assaulters and males who were violent outside the family. For example, in their second National Family Violence Survey carried out in 1985, spouse assaulters were four times as likely to commit violence outside the family as other males. There is some contrary evidence (Shields, McCall, & Hanneke, 1988), however, suggesting that men who were violent only against spouses were different from men who were violent outside the family. It is important to investigate whether there is some kind of developmental progression from teenage violence to spouse assault in the twenties and thirties.

THE CAMBRIDGE STUDY

The present research uses data collected in the Cambridge Study in Delinquent Development, which is a prospective longitudinal survey of 411 males. At the time they were first contacted in 1961 and 1962, they were all living in a working-class area of London, England. The vast majority of the sample was chosen by taking *all* the boys who were then aged 8 and on the registers of six state primary schools within a one-mile radius of a research office that had been established. In addition to 399 boys from these six schools, 12 boys from a local school for educationally subnormal children were included in the sample, in an attempt to make it more representative of the population of boys living in the area. The boys were overwhelmingly white, working-class, and of British origin. Major results obtained in this survey have been reported in four books (West, 1969, 1982; West & Farrington, 1973, 1977) and in more than 60 papers listed by Farrington and West (1990).

The major aim in this survey was to measure as many factors as possible that were alleged to be causes or correlates of offending. The boys were interviewed and tested in their schools when they were aged about 8, 10, and 14, by male or female psychologists. They were interviewed in our research office at about 16, 18, and 21, and in their homes at about 25 and 32, by young male social science graduates. The tests in schools measured individual characteristics such as intelligence, attainment, personality, and psychomotor impulsivity, while information was collected in the interviews about such topics as living circumstances, employment histories, relationships with females, leisure activities, and offending behavior. On all occasions, except at ages 21 and 25, the aim was to interview the whole sample, and it was always possible to trace and interview a high proportion. For example, 389 of the 410 males still alive at 18 (94.9%), and 378 of the 403 males still alive at 32 (93.8%), were interviewed.

In addition to the interviews and tests with the boys, interviews with their parents were carried out by female social workers who visited their homes. These took place about once a year from when the boy was about 8 until when he was aged 14 to 15 and was in his last year of compulsory education. The primary informant was the mother, although many fathers were also seen. The parents provided details about such matters as family income, family size, their employment histories, their child-rearing practices (including attitudes, discipline, and parental agreement), their degree of supervision of the boy, and his temporary or permanent separations from them. Also, when the boy was aged 12, the parents completed questionnaires about their child-rearing attitudes and about the boy's leisure activities.

The boys' teachers completed questionnaires when the boys were aged about 8, 10, 12, and 14. These provided information about the boys' troublesome and aggressive school behavior, their attention deficit, their school attainments, and their truancy. Ratings were also obtained from the boys' peers when they were in their primary schools, about such topics as their dating, dishonesty, troublesomeness, and popularity.

Searches were also carried out in the national Criminal Record Office in London to try to locate findings of guilt of the boys, of their parents, of their brothers and sisters, and (in recent years) of their wives and cohabitees. Convictions were only counted if they were for offenses normally recorded in this office, thereby excluding minor crimes such as common (simple) assault, traffic offenses, and drunkenness. The most common offenses included were thefts, burglaries, and unauthorized taking of motor vehicles. We did not rely on official records for our information about offending, because we also obtained self-reports of offending from the boys themselves at every age from 14 onwards.

For the present analyses, each variable was dichotomized, as far as possible, into the "worst" quarter of boys (e.g., the quarter with lowest income or lowest intelligence) versus the remainder. This was done in order to compare the importance of different variables and also to permit a "risk factor" approach. Because most variables were originally classified into a small number of categories, and because fine distinctions between categories could not be made very accurately, this dichotomizing did not usually involve a great loss of information. The one-quarter/three-quarters split was chosen to match the prior expectation that about one-quarter of the sample would be convicted as juveniles. Variables were not included in the analysis if less than 90% of the sample were identified as them. (For more information about all the variables discussed here, see the books on the Study listed above.)

Summarizing, the Cambridge Study in Delinquent Development has a unique combination of features. Eight face-to-face interviews have been completed with the subjects over a period of 24 years, between ages 8 and 32. The attrition rate is unusually low for such a long-term survey. The main focus of interest is on crime and delinquency, but the survey also provides information about alcohol and drug abuse, educational problems, poverty and poor housing, unemployment, sexual behavior, and other social problems. The sample size of about 400 is large enough for many statistical analyses, but small enough to permit detailed case histories of the males and their families. Information has been obtained from multiple sources, including the subjects themselves, their parents, teachers, peers, and official records. Generally, the information came from parents, teachers, peers, or tests completed by the males between ages 8 and 14, but primarily from interviews with the males between ages 16 and 32. Data has been collected about a wide variety of theoretical constructs at different ages, including biological (e.g., heart rate), psychological (e.g., intelligence), family (e.g., parental discipline), and social (e.g., socioeconomic status) factors.

PREVIOUS ANALYSES OF AGGRESSION AND VIOLENCE

Most of the analyses carried out in the Cambridge Study have focused on offending or antisocial behavior in general (including, recently, Farrington, 1989b, 1989c, 1990a, 1990b, 1991a, 1992; Farrington & Hawkins, 1991; Reiss & Farrington, 1991), but four analyses have focused specifically on aggression and violence. Farrington (1978) found that there was significant continuity over time between teacher-rated aggressiveness at age 8 and self-reported violence at age 18. The best predictors of who, out of all boys rated aggressive at 8 to 10, went on to be rated aggressive at ages 12 to 14 and 16 to 18 were peer-rated unpopularity at 8 to 10 and separation from parents up to age 10. Measures of aggressiveness at all ages between 8 and 18 were significantly correlated with convictions for violence up to age 21. The best predictors of convictions for violence were harsh parental attitude and discipline, poor parental supervision, convicted parents, separation from parents, daring, and low nonverbal intelligence, all measured at ages 8 to 10.

AFG: Aggressive Frequent Group Fighters

Farrington, Berkowitz, and West (1982) analyzed verbatim reports from the boys about the "most vicious" fight in which they had been involved between ages 15 and 18. They concluded that the most important dimension on which these fights differed was whether they were between individuals or between groups. Group fights tended to occur in pubs or streets, and they were more serious—involving weapons, injuries to the combatants, and police intervention—than fights between individuals. The group fighters tended to be involved in more fights and to endorse aggressive attitudes on a questionnaire (e.g., "Anyone who insults me is asking for a fight"). Farrington et al. (1982) identified 40 boys who were among the highest quarter on aggressive attitudes, who had been involved in three or more fights, and whose most vicious fight was in a group, as the "aggressive frequent group (AFG) fighters." They also summarized the most important predictors (including low family income at 8, large family size at 10, and daring at 8 to 10) and correlates (including heavy drinking, an unstable job record, and spending time hanging about on the street, all at 18) of AFG fighters.

More recently, Farrington (1989a) investigated the most important predictors of teacher-rated aggression at 12 to 14, self-reported violence at 16 to 18, self-reported violence at 32, and convictions for violence up to 32. The aggressive boys at 12 to 14 were those whose teachers identified them as having most of the following features: disobedient, difficult to discipline, unduly rough during playtime, quarrelsome and aggressive, overcompetitive with other children, and unduly resentful of criticism or punishment. The violent boys at 16 to 18 were those who most frequently admitted getting into physical fights, starting fights, and carrying and using weapons. The violent men at 32 were those who admitted being involved in physical fights in the previous 5 years. Fights were defined as incidents in which blows were struck; fights in the course of work (e.g., as a police officer, prison officer, or security guard), and men who were victims of mugging, were excluded. Of the 411 Study males, 50 (12.2%) were convicted for at least one violent offense (assault, robbery, or threatening behavior) up to 32.

Farrington (1989a) concluded that the most important predictors at 8 to 10 of these measures of aggression and violence fell into six categories of theoretical constructs: (1) economic deprivation (e.g., low family income, poor housing, large family size); (2) family criminality (convicted parent, delinquent sibling); (3) poor child-rearing (harsh and authoritarian discipline, parental disharmony, poor supervision); (4) school failure (low intelligence and attainment, low parental interest in education); (5) hyperactivity-impulsivity-attention deficit (psychomotor impulsivity, daring, lack of concentration, restlessness); and (6) antisocial child behavior (aggression, troublesomeness).

Farrington (1991b) demonstrated the continuity in measures of aggressiveness from 8 to 32. He also showed that the later life outcomes (at 32) of those who were aggressive as children or adolescents included getting convicted, renting rather than owning accommodation, frequent unemployment, heavy drinking, and drug use. He also found that males convicted of violence tended to be frequent offenders. Importantly, violent offenders were very similar to nonviolent but equally frequent offenders in childhood, adolescent, and adult features. Hence, he concluded that the causes of aggression and violence were essentially the same as the causes of persistent and extreme antisocial, delinquent, and criminal behavior.

MEASURES OF VIOLENCE

Soccer Hooligans

The present research focuses particularly on the characteristics of two groups of males who have not previously been studied in detail: soccer hooligans and spouse assaulters. At age 18, 238 of the males (61.5% of 387 known) said that they had attended a professional soccer match (involving English Football League clubs) in the previous 3 years. Of these 238, 39 (16.4%) said that they had been involved in fights inside or outside soccer grounds, and 17 of these 39 (43.6%) had been apprehended by the police inside or outside soccer grounds. In this chapter, the 39 soccer hooligans are compared with 199 nonviolent soccer fans, to investigate factors associated with violence at soccer matches (as opposed to factors associated with attending soccer matches).

Spouse Assaulters

At age 32, 289 of the males (76.5% of 378 known) were living with a wife or female cohabitee. Of these 289, 42 (14.5%) said that they had struck their wife or cohabitee. In half of these cases (21), the wife or cohabitee had also hit the man. In this chapter, the 42 spouse assaulters are compared with 247 nonassaultive men with spouses, to investigate factors associated with violence against spouses (as opposed to factors associated with having a wife or cohabitee).

The main aim of the present chapter is to investigate the childhood, adolescent, and adult features of soccer hooligans and spouse assaulters. The extensive range of variables measured in the Cambridge Study provides a unique opportunity to establish the predictors and correlates of soccer hooliganism and spouse assault at different ages. In order to assess the characteristics of these two groups of violent males in the context of other groups of violent males, these two groups are also compared with the 40 aggressive frequent group (AFG) fighters at 18 (10.3% of 387 known) and with the 50 males convicted for violence up to age 32 (12.2% of 411). Studies of AFG fighters and violent offenders are based on virtually the whole sample, whereas studies of soccer hooligans and spouse assaulters are based on fewer males. Hence, relationships of any given degree of strength are more likely to be statistically significant with AFG fighters and violent offenders than with soccer hooligans and spouse assaulters.

Table 1 shows the interrelations among these four measures of violence. For example, 25.6% of 39 soccer hooligans at 18 were convicted for violence up to 32, compared with 10.6% of the remaining 199 boys who

TABLE 1. Interrelations among Measures of Violence

Measure 1	Measure 2	% V2 NV1	V1	Chi-squared	p	Odds ratio
Soccer 18	AFG 18	7.5	33.3	18.49	.0001	6.13
Soccer 18	Spouse 32	13.5	9.7	0.08	N.S.	−1.46
Soccer 18	Convicted 32	10.6	25.6	5.29	.01	2.92
AFG 18	Spouse 32	15.8	11.1	0.23	N.S.	−1.50
AFG 18	Convicted 32	12.1	17.5	0.52	N.S.	1.54
Spouse 32	Convicted 32	9.7	26.2	7.67	.003	3.30

Notes: % V2 = % Violent on Measure 2. NV1 = Not violent on Measure 1. V1 = Violent on Measure 1. One-tailed significance tests used in view of directional predictions.

attended soccer matches (chi-squared, corrected for continuity, = 5.29, p = .01, one-tailed tests used in view of directional predictions; all tests in this chapter are similar). The odds ratio for this comparison was 2.92. This statistic is the odds of conviction given a soccer hooligan (10/29) divided by the odds of conviction given a nonhooligan (21/178). The odds ratio (OR) shows the increase in risk associated with each factor or the strength of the relationship, with the chance value being 1. Hence, there was a significant overlap between soccer hooligans and violent offenders.

Table 1 also shows that spouse assaulters at 32 were significantly likely to be convicted for violence up to 32; 26.2% of 42 spouse assaulters were convicted, compared with only 9.7% of the remaining 247 males with wives or cohabitees (chi-squared = 7.67, p = .003, OR = 3.30). There was also a highly significant overlap between soccer hooligans at 18 and AFG fighters at 18. This is not surprising, since fights at soccer matches are likely to involve warring groups and may occur frequently. Soccer hooliganism was, if anything, negatively related to spouse assault; only 9.7% of hooligans were spouse assaulters, compared with 13.5% of nonhooligans (chi-squared = 0.08, N.S., OR = −1.46; for ease of comparison, negative odds ratios are shown, whereas strictly speaking they should be reciprocals). Similarly, AFG fighters were, if anything, negatively related to spouse assaulters. Surprisingly, there was no significant tendency for AFG fighters to be convicted for violence.

CASE HISTORIES OF SOCCER HOOLIGANISM

The reality of soccer hooliganism can be brought home by quoting two case histories. Only one Study male (case 882) was known to have been convicted for this offense (twice) between the ages 15 and 18. It is possible that other males may have been convicted for soccer hooliganism, but the convictions may not have been recorded in the Criminal Record Office because they fell below the threshold of serious violence necessary for recording. For example, case 630 said that he had been convicted for threatening behavior, but this conviction could not be found. No Study male was known to have a conviction for violence against a wife or cohabitee, but one (case 301) was arrested at age 32 and charged with threatening to kill his ex-wife. As the male was not convicted, however, it is likely either that the police declined to proceed with the charge or that he was found not guilty.

Case 882 was a Chelsea supporter who was convicted twice for threatening behavior in connection with soccer matches at age 16. He was recorded by the police as being "skinhead in appearance." He was the first boy in the sample to be convicted for violence (assault occasioning actual bodily harm, at age 10, when he hit a girl with a milk bottle), and he was also convicted for robbery at age 20. Altogether he had 9 juvenile and 11 adult convictions up to age 32, making him one of the most frequent offenders in the sample. However, he was not an AFG fighter at 18 or a spouse assaulter at 32. Here is his (verbatim, tape-recorded) account of the two soccer convictions:

> 1. At football. I got nicked didn't I. Fighting and they nicked us all. There was 9 of us at Crystal Palace. We were all coming back. These geezers starting fighting so the police came and got us. We were coming back down the road and all these Palace supporters come along. So there were about 100 of us. . . . We didn't know if they were Chelsea or Palace or what, they just came up to us and started fighting. So we were all fighting them and then the police came along and we all legged it off and they grabbed us. So we all went to court. I was charged with threatening behavior leading to a breach of the peace or something like that. I pleaded not guilty but I got a 5 pound fine and was bound over for a year.
>
> 2. Once at Chelsea this kid started on me in the street you know. So I was just fighting with him so the police came along and dragged me out. They left him; they just came and nicked me you know. I was standing there one time singing, a bit of a laugh, and this kid kept pushing his way through; he was a really niggly bloke you know. He shouldn't even come to football. The next minute he sort of pushed me one and I pushed him away and the next minute I lost my temper and got him on the floor. I pleaded not guilty but I got a 5 pound fine for threatening behavior.

His other statements about soccer hooliganism were as follows:

> I was thrown out a few times. They just grab you out if there's a big crowd of you there. They just come along and they'll throw you out whether you've paid your money or not. It's ridiculous but there's nothing you can do about

it. [Did you go to away matches?] I went to every away London match like if Chelsea were playing Tottenham or Arsenal or West Ham or those sort of ones, but now and again I would go a long way away. I went to Leicester and I went to Manchester. The police up there, they'll batter you and they'll nick you rather than they'll nick their own. You didn't stand a chance sometimes. You'll stand at the railway station and they'll just pull up and grab about 5 of you for just standing there. I didn't like going there. [Did you get involved in fights at Chelsea?] Sometimes you get Arsenal or West Ham. They'll be up one end and they'll all come down and they'll try to take your end, you know, and you couldn't let them do that. Well, sort of the embarrassment you know. So you just stood there and didn't let them take it.

Case 630 was a London-based Manchester United supporter who said that he had been convicted at age 18 for soccer-related threatening behavior, but his only two recorded convictions were for theft and deception. He was classified as an AFG fighter but not as a spouse assaulter:

I go to all Man United home and away matches. About 15 of us go round together and when we meet up with other supporters there may be as many as 200. We get into fights nearly every other week. [Who usually starts them?] It depends really. Sometimes it's the ones I'm with. It's mainly when they come out of the pub really. Sometimes it's the other lot [rival supporters] as well. Because if there's more of the other lot they all come running over at us sort of thing. [Why are there so many fights at matches?] I dunno. It's just the thing that happens, isn't it? Like one lot trying to prove they're harder than the other lot sort of thing. When City plays United, it's murder—fights then—because you get all the United fans going up to the other end to get the City fans, just to prove they're the hardest in Manchester, you know. City put up a good fight considering there's not that many of them. [Do you go to football for fights or for football?] Oh, no. If I wanted to go for fights I could go to Millwall or somewhere like that, couldn't I? I go to see the football. The United fans always go up to the other end. Like Chelsea's got the Shed, haven't they? United fans always go in the Shed when they play Chelsea to try and take it.

I have been thrown out of 3 matches: from Crystal Palace and Preston for fighting and from Stoke for swearing. At Crystal Palace I thought they was going to nick me but the police took me up to this office, took my name and address. I gave them a false name and address you know and they just chucked me out. They said "You're lucky this time." But I weren't so lucky because later on I got nicked at Leicester Square for fighting. Because all the United fans went over to Leicester Square afterwards and there was this big mob of Arsenal supporters down Leicester Square. It all happened about 9 o'clock at night and I got nicked for threatening behavior. All night the Arsenal fans was coming in, shouting their mouths off outside this pub, you know. When the United fans came out, they'd all run away again sort of thing. Then they'd come back mouthing it off again and all run away again. Well, this kid, he said to me "Let's have a look to see if they're coming back." We walked round the corner and the Arsenal fans was all in front of us. The Scotch kid came running at me and I hit him and he fell on the floor. This

> other kid—who got nicked with me—he jumped on top of me and we both fell on the floor. The next thing I knew I felt this arm on me and I thought "Hello" and it was a copper [a police officer]. I got up and said "Thank you" and started walking away, and he said "Oy, where are you going?" and grabbed me back. They took me to Bow Street police station. I went to court on the Monday and got a 3 pound fine.

Many of the key features identified by writers on soccer hooliganism (e.g., Dunning, Murphy, & Williams, 1986, 1988) are seen in these accounts, such as the aggressive working-class masculinity, the use of alcohol, and the provocative and challenging invasions of "ends" where rival supporters traditionally stand.

PREDICTORS OF VIOLENCE

Table 2 summarizes the strength of relationships between predictor variables and the four measures of violence using odds ratios. For example, in the whole sample, 22.6% of males were from low income families at age 8; 25.5% of these low income males were soccer hooligans, compared with 13.9% of the remainder (chi-squared = 3.13, $p = .039$, $OR = 2.12$); 19.3% of low income males were AFG fighters, compared with 7.7% of the remainder (chi-squared = 8.70, $p = .002$, $OR = 2.87$); 25.0% of low income males were spouse assaulters, compared with 11.6% of the remainder (chi-squared = 6.21, $p = .006$, $OR = 2.55$); and 23.7% of low income males were convicted for violence, compared with 8.8% of the remainder (chi-squared = 13.49, $p = .0001$, $OR = 3.21$). It has to be realized that all these comparisons involve rather small numbers of violent males, so that a few cases going in a different direction could make quite a big difference to the results. Variables measured at ages 12 to 14 were not, strictly speaking, predictors of convictions for violence in all cases; only 4 of the 50 males convicted for violence up to 32 were convicted by 14.

The strongest relationship in Table 2 shows that boys who were regular church attenders at 8 to 10 were unlikely to become soccer hooligans; only one (2.5%) out of 40 church attenders became a soccer hooligan, compared with 20.8% of the remaining 168 boys in this comparison (chi-squared = 6.36, $p = .006$, $OR = -10.26$). Also at 8 to 10, future soccer hooligans tended to have fathers who were not interested in their children, unemployed fathers, poor parental supervision or monitoring, relatively small height, low verbal intelligence, large families (with 4 or more biological siblings), and behavior problem siblings. At ages 12 to 14, future soccer hooligans tended to have high self-reported delinquen-

TABLE 2. Predictors of Violence

Variable (% identified)	Odds ratios			
	Soccer 18	Aggressive Frequent Group 18	Spouse 32	Convicted 32
Ages 8–10				
Low family income (23)	2.12*	2.87*	2.55*	3.21**
Father unemployed (13)	2.72*	2.27*	1.04	2.92*
Low social class (19)	1.13	1.26	1.96*	2.48*
Large family size (24)	2.05*	2.68*	1.25	2.90**
Convicted parent (25)	1.08	1.97*	3.57**	2.94**
Behavior problem sibling (38)	2.07*	1.60	−1.54	2.44*
Poor child-rearing (24)	−1.02	1.44	−1.08	2.31*
Poor supervision (19)	2.68*	2.23*	1.77	2.99**
Separated (22)	1.84	1.38	2.84*	2.50*
Physical neglect (12)	1.65	1.76	2.79*	4.08**
Father not interested (12)	4.80*	1.30	1.10	1.65
Low interest in education (17)	1.31	2.03	−1.12	3.68**
Catholic family (21)	1.54	2.96*	1.33	1.59
Low nonverbal IQ (25)	1.31	1.53	1.46	2.23*
Low verbal IQ (25)	2.19*	1.12	1.64	2.80**
Low attainment (23)	−1.02	1.67	1.77	2.30*
Low school track (29)	1.31	2.17*	1.23	2.08*
Daring (30)	1.15	2.38*	2.21*	3.00**
High impulsivity (25)	−1.61	2.47*	1.40	1.62
Lacks concentration/restless (20)	−1.34	1.39	−1.14	2.10*
Attends church (19)	−10.26*	−1.71	−1.42	−2.20
Unpopular (32)	1.65	2.23*	2.61*	1.53
Small (18)	2.59*	1.24	−1.53	1.17
Vulnerable (15)	1.88	2.80*	3.24*	4.42**
Dishonest (25)	1.12	−1.75	1.63	2.47*
Troublesome (22)	1.41	2.37*	1.88	2.96**
Antisocial (24)	1.34	3.52**	1.63	3.58**
Ages 12–14				
Father unemployed (11)	1.93	1.06	2.78*	4.04**
Large family size (21)	2.41*	3.21**	−1.07	2.42*
Poor child-rearing (29)	1.98*	1.72	−1.31	1.58
Authoritarian parents (24)	2.19*	−2.16	1.91	3.24*
Father not involved (28)	1.44	−1.32	1.80	3.22*
Low nonverbal IQ (29)	1.47	2.00*	2.37*	2.12*
Low verbal IQ (23)	1.29	2.21*	1.59	1.53
Stayed at school (39)	−3.33*	−3.47*	−1.74	−2.90*
Daring (13)	−1.32	−1.38	1.17	3.21**
Lacks concentration/restless (26)	2.09*	1.88*	1.94*	4.12**
Frequent liar (30)	1.34	1.60	2.09*	2.99**

(*continued*)

TABLE 2. *(Continued)*

Variable (% Identified)	Odds ratios Soccer 18	Aggressive Frequent Group 18	Spouse 32	Convicted 32
Ages 12–14 (cont.)				
Frequent truant (18)	2.71*	2.45*	1.06	3.87**
Nervous (28)	−3.30*	−1.32	1.19	1.18
Unpopular (17)	1.60	−1.11	1.39	2.21*
Small (24)	3.68**	−1.29	1.90	1.42
Had sex (29)	3.70**	2.78*	1.28	3.14**
Regular smoker (17)	2.61*	2.28*	1.80	2.44*
Fights outside home (29)	−1.01	2.28*	1.11	1.63
Steals outside home (17)	1.85	1.81	−1.09	4.93**
Hostile to police (27)	2.24*	1.89*	2.29*	3.97**
Delinquent friends (25)	1.71	3.66**	2.60*	3.33**
Self-reported delinquent (20)	3.77**	5.09**	2.73*	6.12**
Antisocial (21)	2.26*	2.69*	2.68*	7.07**
Aggressive (33)	1.99*	2.51*	2.05*	3.71**

*= $p < .05$. **$p < .001$ (one-tailed).

cy scores, early sexual intercourse (by 14), small height, frequent truancy, regular smoking, and large families, but they were unlikely to be rated as nervous by their parents or to stay on at school beyond the minimum leaving age of 15.

The future AFG fighters especially tended to come from Roman Catholic families at age 8, which were often associated with an Irish ethnic background. (The majority of the sample were, at least nominally, Protestant.) At 8 to 10, they also tended to come from large-sized, low-income families, with a convicted parent, unemployed fathers, and poor parental supervision. They were impulsive on psychomotor tests, and tended to be rated as troublesome (by peers and teachers), daring (by parents and peers), and unpopular (by peers). Also, they tended to be placed in low school streams (tracks). The AFG fighters were also identified as vulnerable according to a combination of five background factors (low income, large-sized family, convicted parent, poor parental child-rearing behavior, and low nonverbal IQ), and as antisocial according to a combination of 10 measures of childhood conduct problems (see Farrington, 1991a). At 12 to 14, the future AFG fighters particularly tended to have high self-reported delinquency, many delinquent friends, large-sized families, early sexual intercourse, frequent truancy, and high aggressiveness according to teachers. Like the soccer hooligans, they were unlikely to stay at school beyond the minimum school leaving age.

At 8 to 10, the future spouse assaulters at 32 especially tended to have a convicted parent. In fact, 28.0% of those with a convicted parent by their tenth birthday became spouse assaulters, compared with only 9.8% of the remainder (chi-squared = 13.36, p = .0001, *OR* = 3.57). At 8 to 10, the future spouse assaulters also tended to be separated from a parent (for reasons other than death or hospitalization), physically neglected, unpopular, from low-income families and from low social-class families (according to the occupational prestige of the head of the household). They were also identified as having a vulnerable background on the combined rating. At 12 to 14, they tended to have unemployed fathers, high self-reported delinquency, delinquent friends, low nonverbal intelligence, high hostility to the police, frequent lying, and were lacking in concentration or restless. Also, they were rated as aggressive by teachers and were antisocial according to the combined measure at 12 to 14.

Most of the variables measured at 8 to 10 predicted the males who were convicted for violence. According to the odds ratio, the best predictors were the combined rating of vulnerable background, physical neglect, low parental interest in education, the combined rating of antisocial behavior, daring, poor parental supervision, troublesomeness, convicted parents, unemployed fathers, large-sized families, and low verbal intelligence. The strongest relationships at 12 to 14 were with the combined rating of antisocial behavior, self-reported delinquency, stealing outside home (according to parents), lack of concentration or restlessness, unemployed fathers, a hostile attitude to the police, high aggressiveness (according to teachers), delinquent friends, authoritarian parents (according to a child-rearing questionnaire at 12), the father not involved in the boy's leisure activities (according to a leisure questionnaire at 12), daring, and early sexual intercourse.

At 8 to 14, 64 key predictors were investigated. The proportion of significant relationships was far in excess of the chance expectation of 5%: 23 for soccer hooliganism (36%), 27 for AFG fighting (42%), 17 for spouse assault (27%), and 39 for convictions for violence (61%). In all, 51 variables significantly predicted at least one of the four violence measures, and these are shown in Table 2. The 13 nonsignificant predictors were: at 8 to 10, education of father, education of mother, boy has few or no friends, nervous boy, high neuroticism (on the New Junior Maudsley Inventory), nervousness of father, nervousness of mother, poor housing, high delinquency rate school, low weight; at 12 to 14, high neuroticism, low social class, low weight. At both ages, low weight was nearly significantly predictive of soccer hooliganism.

CORRELATES OF VIOLENCE

The variables measured at ages 18 and 32 are discussed as correlates of violence although, strictly speaking, the 18-year variables were predictors of spouse assault at 32. Table 3 again summarizes the strength of the correlates of violence using odds ratios. An aggressive attitude is not shown as a correlate of AFG fighting because it was one of the 3 components of this measure, and similarly spouse assault was a very small component (part of one factor out of 12) of the measure of antisocial behavior at 32.

At age 18, not surprisingly, the most important correlates of soccer hooliganism were high self-reported violence and high self-reported delinquency (both in the previous 3 years), and going round in antisocial groups (of 4 or more). The soccer hooligans also tended to have been hospitalized because of illness (in the previous 2 years), to have taken no examinations, to be involved in fights after drinking, to have unskilled jobs, to endorse antiestablishment and aggressive attitudes (on a questionnaire), and to use drugs (principally marijuana at this age). They were unlikely to have no girl friend or to have not had sexual intercourse. At age 32, the soccer hooligans especially tended to be marijuana and other drug users (in the previous 5 years), self-reported offenders (in the previous 5 years), antisocial according to the combined measure, heavy drinkers (40 or more units of alcohol per week), and binge drinkers (20 or more units of alcohol in one evening, where one unit equals one half-pint of beer, one glass of wine, or one single measure of spirits). In addition, they tended to have convictions as adults (age 17 or older), to disagree with their wife or cohabitee about child-rearing, to be renting rather than owning their home, to be impulsive on a questionnaire (in response to items such as "I generally do and say things quickly without stopping to think"), and to endorse aggressive attitudes on the same questionnaire.

At 18, the AFG fighters were high on all the other measures of aggression and violence, such as self-reported violence, involvement in fights after drinking, and involvement in antisocial groups. Remarkably, none of these 40 males was still a virgin by age 18, compared with 29.7% of the remaining 344 known (chi-squared = 14.67, p = .0001, OR = −16.44, calculated by assuming that 1 was a virgin). Also, they were unlikely to have no girl friend. At 18, the AFG fighters tended to be drunk

TABLE 3. Correlates of Violence

Variable (% Identified)	Odds ratios			
	Soccer 18	Aggressive Frequent Group 18	Spouse 32	Convicted 32
Age 18				
Unskilled manual job (16)	2.77*	3.34**	2.87*	5.45**
Unstable job record (24)	1.66	3.81**	2.16*	3.13**
No exams taken (51)	3.25*	1.95*	2.25*	3.45**
Poor relation with parents (22)	1.51	1.04	1.66	3.51**
Not living with parents (12)	1.51	−1.27	2.43*	1.22
No girl friend (42)	−2.98*	−3.94**	−1.42	−2.52*
No sex (26)	−2.98*	−16.44**	−1.22	−3.46*
Promiscuous sex (29)	1.94*	2.78*	1.39	1.91*
Irresponsible sex (20)	1.34	1.43	1.41	2.89**
Impulsive (27)	−1.12	1.69	1.63	2.04*
Aggressive attitude (26)	2.37*	—	−1.18	1.83*
Antiestablishment (25)	2.72*	2.43*	1.18	2.83**
Hangs about (16)	1.87	3.00*	1.52	2.20*
Hospitalized for illness (14)	3.27*	−1.15	1.56	1.72
Heavy gambler (22)	1.76	1.55	−1.29	3.43**
Heavy smoker (27)	1.48	2.82*	2.19*	2.82**
Heavy drinker (25)	2.19*	2.19*	1.13	3.81**
Binge drinker (21)	1.82	3.32**	1.35	2.04*
Drunk driver (22)	−1.12	3.91**	2.27*	2.36*
Drug user (31)	2.50*	1.36	1.93*	3.49**
Antisocial group (17)	5.91**	8.64**	−1.56	2.56*
Fights after drinking (32)	3.05*	16.43**	1.26	1.70
Antisocial (23)	4.47**	9.74**	2.42*	12.00**
Self-reported delinquent (25)	6.06**	8.37**	1.44	3.88**
Self-reported violence (20)	12.24**	21.46**	1.11	4.05**
Convicted juvenile (21)	1.78	2.79*	3.18**	—
Age 32				
Not home owner (52)	2.49*	1.44	1.62	2.90*
Poor home conditions (28)	1.90	2.06*	1.31	2.17*
Living in London (52)	1.88	1.26	1.25	1.80*
Area problems (19)	1.81	1.73	2.28*	1.85
Poor relation with wife/cohabitee (8)	2.98	1.55	9.48**	5.08**
Disagrees with wife/cohabitee (18)	3.08*	1.68	1.16	1.27
Poor relation with mother (15)	1.40	2.18	2.55*	2.02
Poor relation with father (20)	1.34	1.88	2.52*	1.44
Child elsewhere (22)	1.17	1.03	1.86	2.94*
Child bully (11)	−1.71	−1.53	2.08	6.31**

(*continued*)

TABLE 3. (*Continued*)

	Odds ratios			
Variable (% Identified)	Soccer 18	Aggressive Frequent Group 18	Spouse 32	Convicted 32
Age 32 (cont.)				
Impulsive (22)	2.46*	1.43	1.26	1.99*
Tattooed (16)	1.95	2.23*	2.48*	3.41**
Unemployed (12)	1.52	1.65	4.49**	3.41**
Frequently out (17)	1.64	−2.02	2.18	2.37*
Aggressive attitude (22)	2.44*	4.17**	2.30*	4.86**
Antiestablishment (29)	1.07	1.90*	1.76	2.70*
Heavy gambler (29)	1.00	1.51	1.45	2.08*
Heavy smoker (32)	−1.25	1.03	1.57	2.03*
Heavy drinker (21)	2.83*	1.88	1.94	3.32**
Binge drinker (20)	2.82*	1.66	3.09*	3.03**
Drunk driver (53)	1.18	1.18	3.67*	2.23*
Alcoholism CAGE (29)	1.74	1.40	2.06*	2.58*
Taken marijuana (18)	3.27*	2.04*	3.72**	5.40**
Taken other drug (10)	4.20*	1.01	10.56**	4.83**
Psychiatric illness GHQ (24)	−1.12	−1.91	2.24*	1.35
Involved in fights (37)	2.19*	1.45	1.85*	5.56**
Antisocial (24)	2.95*	2.55*	—	8.74**
Self-reported offender (22)	3.42**	2.00*	2.59*	4.10**
Stolen from work (24)	1.42	2.30*	−1.20	2.37
Tax evasion (51)	1.67	1.45	2.02*	1.51
Social failure (25)	2.17*	1.14	6.62**	4.87**
Convicted adult (21)	3.78*	2.05	1.91	—
Any conviction (37)	3.10**	2.77*	2.84*	—

* = $p < .05$, ** $p < .001$ (one-tailed). — = Not independent.

drivers, to have an unstable job record, to have an unskilled manual job, to be binge drinkers (defined at this age as over 12 units of alcohol in an evening), to spend time hanging about on the street, to be heavy smokers (20 or more cigarettes per day), and sexually promiscuous (having intercourse with 2 or more girls in the previous 6 months). At 32, the AFG fighters still tended to have relatively aggressive attitudes, and they also tended to be convicted of any offense, antisocial on the combined measure, thieves from their workplace, tattooed (often reflecting risky or daring behavior), marijuana users, self-reported offenders, and living in poor housing conditions.

At 18, the future spouse assaulters tended to be convicted (as juveniles, under age 17), in unskilled manual jobs, not living with their parents, antisocial on the combined measure, drunk drivers, heavy smokers, and drug users, and they also tended to have taken no examinations and to have an unstable job record. At 32, not surprisingly, they tended to have a poor relationship with their wife or cohabitee. The strongest correlate of spouse assault at 32 was taking drugs other than marijuana (principally cocaine, amphetamines, LSD, and heroin; most of these males were multiple drug users); 57.9% of serious drug users were spouse assaulters, compared with 11.5% of the remainder (chi-squared = 27.02, $p < .0001$, $OR = 10.56$). Also at 32, spouse assaulters tended to be social failures according to a combined measure (see Farrington, 1989b), unemployed, marijuana users, drunk drivers, binge drinkers, convicted of any offense, self-reported offenders, tattooed, and living in problem areas (e.g., noisy, dirty, violent). They had aggressive attitudes and poor relationships with their mothers and fathers. They showed signs of alcoholism on the CAGE questionnaire and signs of psychiatric illness on the General Health Questionnaire; however, they did not significantly tend to be heavy drinkers.

As before, the males convicted for violence differed significantly from the remainder in almost every factor measured at 18 and 32. At 18, the strongest relationships were between violent offenders and antisocial behavior, an unskilled manual job, self-reported violence, self-reported delinquency, heavy drinking, a poor relationship with parents, drug use, not being a virgin, no examinations taken, heavy gambling, and an unstable job record. At 32, apart from the combined measure of antisocial behavior, the strongest relationship was with having a child who was a bully. Of the violent offenders, 35.0% had a child who was a bully, compared with 7.9% of the nonviolent offenders who had children aged 3 to 15 (chi-squared = 10.34, $p = .0007$, $OR = 6.31$). Also at 32, the violent offenders tended to be involved in fights, to have a poor relationship with their wife or cohabitee, to have aggressive attitudes, to take maijuana and other drugs, to be social failures on the combined scale, self-reported offenders, tattooed, unemployed, heavy drinkers, and binge drinkers. In addition, they tended to have a child living separately from them, and to be renting rather than owning their homes.

At 18 and 32, 77 key correlates were investigated. The proportion of significant relationships was far in excess of the chance expectation of 5%: 29 for soccer hooliganism (38%), 27 for AFG fighting and spouse assault (35%), and 46 for convictions for violence (60%). In all, 59 variables were significantly correlated with at least one of the four violence measures, and these are shown in Table 3. The 18 nonsignificant correlates were: at 18, living outside London, going out with male friends, high neuroticism (on the Eysenck Personality Inventory), low height, low heart rate, low weight, driving convictions, low take-home pay; at

32, high residential mobility, divorced or separated, low social class job, low take-home pay, hospitalized in the last 5 years, unstable job record, large family size, high debts, accommodation problems (e.g., damp, structural, overcrowding, heating), and frequent arguments with the wife or cohabitee. A poor relationship with the wife or cohabitee was included in Table 3 even though less than 10% of the sample were identified on this variable, because of its importance in relation to spouse assault.

INDEPENDENT EXPLANATORY PREDICTORS

In an attempting to explain the development of soccer hooligans and spouse assaulters, an important first step is to establish which factors are independent predictors of these groups of violent males. In view of the likelihood that violence is one symptom of an antisocial personality, it is essential for explanatory purposes to exclude as predictors any other factors that might also be symptoms of an antisocial personality (such as troublesomeness, delinquency, frequent lying, frequent truancy, and early sexual intercourse). The choice of excluded factors is to some extent a subjective decision, since some factors, such as frequent truancy, might be causal as well as symptomatic of antisocial behavior. The factors included in analyses as possible predictors were those judged clearly to measure theoretical constructs other than antisocial behavior. Obviously, the accuracy of prediction would be greater if measures of antisocial behavior were included as predictors of violence (Amdur, 1989). Only factors measured up to age 14 were included in this analysis as possible predictors.

Table 4 shows that the best independent predictors of soccer hooliganism at 18 were a lack of interest by the father in his children, being relatively small at 14, leaving school at the earliest possible age of 15, not being nervous at 14, having parents with authoritarian child-rearing attitudes at 12, and not attending church at 8. The best independent predictors of AFG fighting at 18 were leaving school at the earliest possible age of 15, coming from a Roman Catholic family at 8, coming from a large family at 8, daring and unpopularity at 8–10.

The best independent predictors of spouse assault at 32 were a convicted parent by the tenth birthday, daring and unpopularity at 8–10, and separation from a parent (usually the father) by the tenth birthday. The best independent predictors of convictions for violence up to 32 were lack of concentration or restlessness at 12–14, parents with authori-

TABLE 4. Logistic Regression Analyses for Violence

	Likelihood ratio chi-squared change	p^a
Soccer 18		
Father not interested 8	10.51	.0006
Small 14	10.26	.0007
Stayed at school 15 (−)	7.84	.003
Nervous 14 (−)	6.87	.004
Authoritarian parents 12	4.39	.018
Attends church 8 (−)	3.46	.031
AFG 18		
Stayed at school 15 (−)	10.10	.0008
Catholic family 8	9.86	.0008
Large family size 14	3.99	.023
Daring 8–10	3.21	.037
Unpopular 8–10	2.35	.06
Spouse 32		
Convicted parent 10	8.59	.002
Daring 8–10	5.29	.011
Unpopular 8–10	5.25	.011
Separated 10	2.56	.055
Convicted 32		
Lacks concentration/restless 12–14	15.25	.0001
Authoritarian parents 12	8.45	.002
Father unemployed 14	6.13	.007
Daring 8–10	5.03	.012
Low interest in education 8	1.91	.08

[a]p values are one-tailed.

tarian child-rearing attitudes at 12, an unemployed father at 14, daring at 8–10, and (non-significantly) low parental interest in education at 8.

The accuracy of prediction in the logistic regression was greatest for soccer hooliganism. Of 42 males with a predicted probability of being a soccer hooligan of .2 or greater, 20 (47.6%) actually were soccer hooligans, compared with only 9 (7.8%) of the remaining 115 in this logistic regression analysis (OR = 10.71; the number of males included in this analysis was small because authoritarian parents was one of the predictors; 24% of parents failed to complete the child-rearing questionnaire when the boy was aged 12). Of 61 males predicted (at .2 or greater) to be spouse assaulters, 19 (31.2%) actually were spouse assaulters, compared with 19 (8.7%) of the remaining 219 males in this analysis (*OR* = 4.76). Of 50 males predicted to be AFG fighters, 16 (32%) actually were AFG fighters, compared with 21 (7.6%) of the remaining 276 males in this analysis (*OR* = 5.71). Of 48 males predicted to be violent offenders, 17 (35.4%) actually were violent offenders, compared with 14 (6.5%) of the remaining 214 males in this analysis (*OR* = 7.83; again, cases were lost primarily because of the inclusion of authoritarian parents as one of the predictors).

CONCLUSIONS

These analyses reveal new findings about soccer hooliganism and spouse assault. In particular, relatively small boys, and those who were not church attenders and not nervous, tended to become soccer hooligans. Perhaps church attendance and nervousness to some extent acted as protective factors against hooliganism. It was less surprising to find that soccer hooligans tended to be drawn from those who left school early (presumably reflecting low school attainment in many cases) and from large families, those with unemployed fathers, and those experiencing poor parental supervision or monitoring. The fact that authoritarian parents (who approved of physical punishment for children) tended to have children who were soccer hooligans may reflect the intergenerational transmission of aggression. It was also not surprising to find that, later on in life, soccer hooligans tended to have unskilled manual jobs and to be impulsive, heavy drinkers, drug users, and sexually promiscuous, like many other antisocial males in this Study.

As children and adolescents, spouse assaulters tended to have convicted parents, to be physically neglected by their parents, to come from low income, low social class families, and to have unemployed fathers. The fact that they tended to be separated from their parents for reasons of disharmony may reflect the intergenerational transmission of family conflict. They also tended to be unpopular, daring, with low intelligence, and lacking in concentration or restless. As teenagers, they tended to have unskilled manual jobs, an unstable job record, and were not living with their parents, probably reflecting conflict with their family of origin. As adults, they were especially likely to be drug abusers, binge drinkers, showed signs of alcoholism and mental illness, tended to be frequently unemployed, and had poor relationships with their fathers and mothers.

The AFG fighters tended to come from large-sized, Roman Catholic families, had low educational attainment, and were daring and unpopular. In addition, they came from low-income families, tended to have a convicted parent, and received poor parental supervision. As teenagers, they had unskilled manual jobs, an unstable job record, were sexually promiscuous, binge drinkers, and generally antisocial. As adults, they were living in poor home conditions and tended to be marijuana users.

The violent offenders were the most deviant and antisocial. As children and adolescents, they tended to be lacking in concentration, restless, and daring, had authoritarian parents, unemployed fathers, and parents who were not interested in their education. As teenagers, they tended to have unskilled manual jobs, an unstable job record, had taken no examinations, were heavy drinkers and drug users, heavy gamblers, and sexually promiscuous. As adults, they had a poor relationship with their wife or cohabitee, tended to be frequently unemployed, drug users and heavy drinkers, and showed signs of alcoholism. In another interesting sign of the intergenerational transmission of aggression, their children tended to be bullies.

Soccer hooligans significantly tended to be AFG fighters and violent offenders. Many of the significant predictors of soccer hooliganism were also significant predictors of AFG fighting and violent offending. However, four of the six most important independent predictors of soccer hooliganism—being relatively small, having a father who was not interested in his children, not attending church, and not being nervous—were not significant predictors of either AFG fighting or violent offending. Consequently, there seem to be important differences between soccer hooligans and other groups of violent males.

Spouse assaulters significantly tended also to be violent offenders. Again, many of the significant predictors of spouse assault were also significant predictors of violent offending. The only exception among the childhood factors was unpopularity, and the only exception among the teenage factors was not living with the parents. Similarly, among the adult correlates, having a poor relationship with the mother and with the father were significantly correlated with spouse assault but not with violent offending. It might be concluded that spouse assaulters and violent offenders are similar in many respects in their antisociality, but that spouse assaulters seem to have specific difficulties in their relationships with other people—peers, parents, and eventually spouses. These difficulties may possibly be connected to their symptoms of psychiatric illness, which again were a significant feature of spouse assaulters but not of violent offenders.

Returning to the six most important predictors of aggression and violence in this study, soccer hooligans had economic deprivation (low income, an unemployed father, large-sized families), poor child-rearing (poor parental supervision, authoritarian parents), and school failure (low verbal IQ, early school leaving). They showed only one sign of hyperactivity-impulsivity-attention deficit (lacking in concentration or restless at 12–14) and did not have family criminality. Like the other groups, they showed many symptoms of aggressive and antisocial behavior at different ages. Spouse assaulters had economic deprivation (low family income, low social class, an unemployed father), family criminality (a convicted parent), poor child-rearing (separation from a parent—usually the father—through disharmony), and hyperactivity-impulsivity-attention deficit (daring, lacking in concentration or restless). They showed only one sign of school failure (low nonverbal IQ at 14), although they had also taken no examinations by 18. Like the other groups, they showed many symptoms of aggressive and antisocial behavior at different ages.

To conclude, there are important similarities and important differences among soccer hooligans and spouse assaulters and other types of violent males. The differences involving soccer hooligans are not easily interpretable. Conceivably, relatively small boys whose fathers pay little attention to them might try to compensate for these handicaps by showing off and being aggressive in soccer crowds, especially if they are not inhibited by nervousness or religious beliefs. The differences involving spouse assaulters suggest that there may be a link between experiencing parental disharmony and early separation from a parent in childhood, difficulties in relationships with peers and parents, and later difficulties in relationships with spouses and cohabitees. Teenage violence may indeed develop into spouse assault in the thirties, but particularly for those aggressive males who have specific and long-lasting difficulties in relationships with other people.

REFERENCES

Amdur, R. L. (1989). Testing causal models of delinquency: A methodological critique. *Criminal Justice and Behavior, 16*, 35–62.

Brennan, P., Mednick, S. A., & Kandel, E. (1991). Congenital determinants of violent and property offending. In D. J. Pepler & K. H. Rubin (Eds.), *The development and treatment of childhood aggression* (pp. 81–92). Hillsdale, NJ: Lawrence Erlbaum.

Dunning, E., Murphy, P., & Williams, J. (1986). Spectator violence at football matches: Towards a sociological explanation. *British Journal of Sociology, 37*, 221–244.

Dunning, E., Murphy, P., & Williams, J. (1988). *The roots of football hooliganism*. London: Routledge & Kegan Paul.

Eron, L. D., & Huesmann, L. R. (1990). The stability of aggressive behavior—Even unto the third generation. In M. Lewis & S. M. Miller (Eds.), *Handbook of developmental psychopathology* (pp. 147–156). New York: Plenum.

Eron, L. D., Huesmann, L. R., Dubow, E., Romanoff, R., & Yarmel, P. W. (1987). Aggression and its correlates over 22 years. In D. H. Crowell, I. M. Evans & C. R. O'Donnell (Eds.), *Childhood aggression and violence* (pp. 249–262). New York: Plenum.

Eron, L. D., Huesmann, L. R. & Zelli, A. (1991). The role of parental variables in the learning of aggression. In D. J. Pepler & K. H. Rubin (Eds.), *The development and treatment of childhood aggression* (pp. 169–188). Hillsdale, NJ: Lawrence Erlbaum.

Farrington, D. P. (1978). The family backgrounds of aggressive youths. In L. Hersov, M. Berger, & D. Shaffer (Eds), *Aggression and antisocial behavior in childhood and adolescence* (pp. 73–93). Oxford: Pergamon.

Farrington, D. P. (1989a). Early predictors of adolescent aggression and adult violence. *Violence and Victims, 4*, 79–100.

Farrington, D. P. (1989b). Later adult life outcomes of offenders and non-offenders. In M. Brambring, F. Losel, & H. Skowronek (Eds.), *Children at risk: Assessment, longitudinal research and intervention* (pp. 220–244). Berlin: De Gruyter.

Farrington, D. P. (1989c). Self-reported and official offending from adolescence to adulthood. In M. W. Klein (Ed.), *Cross-national research in self-reported crime and delinquency* (pp. 399–423). Dordrecht, Netherlands: Kluwer.

Farrington, D. P. (1990a). Age, period, cohort, and offending. In D. M. Gottfredson & R. V. Clarke (Eds.), *Policy and theory in criminal justice: Contributions in honor of Leslie T. Wilkins* (pp. 51–75). Aldershot, U.K.: Gower.

Farrington, D. P. (1990b). Implications of criminal career research for the prevention of offending. *Journal of Adolescence, 13*, 93–113.

Farrington, D. P. (1991a). Antisocial personality from childhood to adulthood. *The Psychologist, 4*, 389–394.

Farrington, D. P. (1991b). Childhood aggression and adult violence: Early precursors and later life outcomes. In D. J. Pepler & K. H. Rubin (Eds.), *The development and treatment of childhood aggression* (pp. 5–29). Hillsdale, NJ: Lawrence Erlbaum.

Farrington, D. P. (1992). Explaining the beginning, progress and ending of antisocial behavior from birth to adulthood. In J. McCord (Ed.), *Facts, frameworks and forecasts: Advances in criminological theory*, Vol. 3, pp. 253–286. New Brunswick, NJ: Transaction.

Farrington, D. P., Berkowitz, L., & West, D. J. (1982). Differences between individual and group fights. *British Journal of Social Psychology, 21*, 323–333.

Farrington, D. P., & Hawkins, J. D. (1991). Predicting participation, early onset, and later persistence in officially recorded offending. *Criminal Behavior and Mental Health, 1*, 1–33.

Farrington, D. P., & West, D. J. (1990). The Cambridge Study in Delinquent Development: A long-term follow-up of 411 London males. In H. J. Kerner & G. Kaiser (Eds.), *Kriminalität: Personlichkeit, lebensgeschichte und verhalten (Criminality: Personality, behavior and life history)* (pp. 115–138). Berlin, Germany: Springer-Verlag.

Gelles, R. J. (1982). Domestic criminal violence. In M. E. Wolfgang & N. A. Weiner (Eds.), *Criminal violence* (pp. 201–235). Beverly Hills, CA: Sage.

Gelles, R. J., & Cornell, C. P. (1985). *Intimate violence in families.* Beverly Hills, CA: Sage.

Guttridge, P., Gabrielli, W. F., Mednick, S. A., & Van Dusen, K. T. (1983). Criminal violence in a birth cohort. In K. T. Van Dusen & S. A. Mednick (Eds.), *Prospective studies of crime and delinquency* (pp. 211–224). Boston: Kluwer-Nijhoff.

Hamparian, D. M., Davis, J. M., Jacobson, J. M., & McGraw, R. E. (1985). *The young criminal years of the violent few.* Washington, DC: National Institute for Juvenile Justice and Delinquency Prevention.

Harrington, J. A. (1968). *Soccer hooliganism.* Bristol: John Wright.

Hogh, E., & Wolf, P. (1983). Violent crimes in a birth cohort: Copenhagen 1953–1977. In

K. T. Van Dusen & S. A. Mednick (Eds.), *Prospective studies of crime and delinquency* (pp. 249–267). Boston: Kluwer-Nijhoff.

Hotaling, G. T. & Sugarman, D. B. (1986). An analysis of risk markers in husband to wife violence: The current state of knowledge. *Violence and Victims, 1,* 101–124.

Hotaling, G. T., Strauss, M. A., & Lincoln, A. J. (1989). Intrafamily violence and crime and violence outside the family. In L. Ohlin & M. Tonry (Eds.), *Family violence* (pp. 315–375). Chicago: University of Chicago Press.

Huesmann, L. R. & Eron, L. D. (1992). Childhood aggression and adult criminality. In J. McCord (Ed.), *Facts, frameworks, and forecasts: Advances in criminological theory,* Vol. 3, pp. 137–156. New Brunswick, NJ: Transaction.

Magnusson, D., Stattin, H., & Duner, A. (1983). Aggression and criminality in a longitudinal perspective. In K. T. Van Dusen & S. A. Mednick (Eds.), *Prospective studies of crime and delinquency* (pp. 277–301). Boston: Kluwer-Nijhoff.

McCord, J. (1977). A comparative study of two generations of native Americans. In R. F. Meier (Ed.), *Theory in criminology* (pp. 83–92). Beverly Hills, CA: Sage.

McCord, J. (1979). Some child-rearing antecedents of criminal behavior in adult men. *Journal of Personality and Social Psychology, 37,* 1477–1486.

McCord, J., McCord W., & Howard, A. (1963). Family interaction as antecedent to the direction of male aggressiveness. *Journal of Abnormal and Social Psychology, 66,* 239–242.

Pepler, D. J., & Rubin, K. H. (1991, Eds.). *The development and treatment of childhood aggression.* Hillsdale, N.J.: Lawrence Erlbaum.

Piper, E. S. (1985). Violent recidivism and chronicity in the 1958 Philadelphia cohort. *Journal of Quantitative Criminology, 1,* 319–344.

Pulkkinen, L. (1983). Finland: The search for alternatives to aggression. In A. P. Goldstein & M. H. Segall (Eds.), *Aggression in global perspective* (pp. 104–144). New York: Pergamon.

Pulkkinen, L. (1987). Offensive and defensive aggression in humans: A longitudinal perspective. *Aggressive Behavior, 13,* 197–212.

Reiss, A. J. & Farrington, D. P. (1991). Advancing knowledge about co-offending: Results from a prospective longitudinal survey of London males. *Journal of Criminal Law and Criminology, 82,* 360–395.

Rivera, B., & Widom, C. S. (1990). Childhood victimization and violent offending. *Violence and Victims, 5,* 19–35.

Shields, N., McCall, G. J., & Hanneke, C. R. (1988). Patterns of family and nonfamily violence: Violent husbands and violent men. *Violence and Victims, 3,* 83–98.

Stattin, H. & Magnusson, D. (1989). The role of early aggressive behavior in the frequency, seriousness, and types of later crime. *Journal of Consulting and Clinical Psychology, 57,* 710–718.

Trevizas, E. (1980). Offenses and offenders in football crowd disorders. *British Journal of Criminology, 20,* 276–288.

Trevizas, E. (1984). Disturbances associated with football matches. *British Journal of Criminology, 24,* 361–383.

West, D. J. (1969). *Present conduct and future delinquency.* London: Heinemann.

West, D. J. (1982). *Delinquency: Its roots, careers, and prospects.* London: Heinemann.

West, D. J., & Farrington, D. P. (1973). *Who becomes delinquent?* London: Heinemann.

West, D. J., & Farrington, D. P. (1977). *The delinquent way of life.* London: Heinemann.

Widom, C. S. (1989). The cycle of violence. *Science, 244,* 160–166.

Wikstrom, P. H. (1987). *Patterns of crime in a birth cohort.* Stockholm: University of Stockholm, Department of Sociology.

CHAPTER 10

AGGRESSION IN TWO GENERATIONS

JOAN MCCORD

INTRODUCTION

Continuities between misbehavior in childhood and subsequent aggression, conduct disorder, and criminal activities have been reported by many researchers studying samples from a variety of backgrounds (Eron, 1987; Farrington, 1978, 1986; McCord, 1983; Robins, 1966; Robins & Ratcliff, 1979; Satterfield, 1987; Stattin & Magnusson, 1989). As an example, in their longitudinal study of a New Zealand birth cohort, White, Moffitt, Earls, Robins, and Silva (1990) found that antisocial behavior at age 11 was related to police contacts at age 15. Furthermore, they concluded that "behavioral problems are the best preschool predictors of antisocial behavior at age 11" (1990, p. 519).

Many studies have also noted intergenerational links of criminality and aggression (e.g., Call, 1984; Egeland & Sroufe, 1981; Farrington, 1978, 1979; Gelles, 1980; Glueck & Glueck, 1950; Herrenkohl & Herrenkohl, 1981; Jouriles, Barling, & O'Leary, 1987; Lewis, Pincus, Lovely, Spitzer, & Moy, 1987; Main & Goldwyn, 1984; McCord, 1979, 1983; Offord, 1982; Pulkkinen, 1983; Robins, 1966; Widom, 1989). Eron and Hues-

---

JOAN MCCORD • Temple University, Philadelphia, Pennsylvania 19122.

Aggressive Behavior: Current Perspectives, edited by L. Rowell Huesmann. Plenum Press, New York, 1994.

mann, in particular, have shown that aggression at age 8 is a good predictor of aggression in offspring 22 years later (Eron, Huesmann, Dubow, Romanoff, & Yarmel, 1987; Huesmann, Eron, Lefkowitz, & Walder, 1984).

Other studies have indicated that parental conflict is highly criminogenic and may be responsible for most of the criminogenic effects of broken homes (Emery, 1982; Farrington, 1978, 1986; Hirschi, 1969; Loeber & Stouthamer-Loeber, 1986; McCord, 1982, 1990, 1991). Typically, these studies have been interpreted as revealing a social cause of crime. Yet if parental conflict were itself caused by children's misbehavior, the parental conflict might be no more than a perturbation in the linkage of aggression between generations.

Person-Environment Interaction

Suggestions that socialization practices are responses to child behaviors are not new. In 1957, for example, Sears, Maccoby, and Levin noted: "What a child does influences his mother, just as what she does influences him" (p. 141). Later, Maccoby and Jacklin (1982) showed that interchanges between effects of a child and effects of a mother begin during infancy when mothers respond to difficult behavior with reductions in pressure to conform, and low levels of pressure to conform increase difficult behavior. Eron, Walder, & Lefkowitz (1971) found that parental rejection and punishment were related to aggression in children who did not identify with parents. These results led Eron, Huesmann, and Zelli (1991) to hypothesize: "Perhaps parental rejection and punishment are reactions to the aggressive behavior that the youngster originally displays and lack of identification then results from the aversive nature of the interactions between parent and child" (p. 179).

Using correlational data Patterson (1986) examined two explanations for why misbehavior of the child might increase inept parental socialization practices. The analyses supported both a view that daily hassles increase the difficulty of coping and the view that misbehavior brings distressing signals to indicate that a mother has failed in her role.

In carrying out a longitudinal study of a Swedish cohort, Magnusson (1988) organized the data to show how "the child is both the creation of and the creator of his or her environment" (p. 33). In particular, he was able to show that age at menarche produced delinquency through friendship patterns that involved interacting with older peers. Lytton (1990) has suggested that "it could well be earlier difficultness in the child that provokes later parental rejection" (p. 685). And Bell (1964, 1968, 1979, 1986), more generally, suggested a variety of interpretations to indicate how child effects might be responsible for some of the relationships attributed to social environments. He noted, for example, that infant crying patterns can keep mothers awake, influencing their child-rearing behaviors; that health differences of children could mistakenly be attributed to social class; and that infants' inadequate communications might produce failures of parental responsiveness.

Rutter and Garmezy (1983) suggested specifically that a child's misbehavior promotes marital discord which, in turn, increases conduct disorder. This hypothesis gained some support in an experimental study in which boys between the ages of 6 and 11 interacted with their own and other mothers (Anderson, Lytton, & Romney, 1986). Half the boys were classified by DSM-III criteria as conduct disordered (APA, 1980). Mothers of both conduct disordered and normal children tended to be more negative toward the conduct disordered children. The authors concluded: "CD children could also elicit greater punitiveness in their parents and even provoke marital discord" (p. 608).

Research showing that methylphenidate-induced changes in behavior of hyperactive children produced changes in their mothers' behavior provided meat to the skeleton of theory regarding the potential direction of effects within the family (Barkley & Cunningham, 1979). Reviewing studies of children's psychiatric disorders, Rutter, Bolton, Harrington, Couteur, Macdonald and Simonoff (1990) concluded that conduct disorder appeared to be a consequence of family discord rather than genetic in origin. Nevertheless, they noted, genetic factors may help to shape the environment as well as influence susceptibilities to its impact.

Two Hypotheses

Two hypotheses about the intergenerational transmission of criminality are investigated in the research reported below. The first hypothesis involves genetic factors, perhaps not fully understood. Evidence of genetic transmission, I assume, would appear through misbehavior of the child during the early years of schooling. If, for example, children of criminals are prone to inherit whatever causes slow autonomic arousal, easy boredom, tolerance for pain, or heightened aggressive reactions, one would expect to find these children responding poorly in terms of school adjustment and getting into fights with their teachers or classmates. Such behavior might also lead to parental conflict which, in turn, could increase the probability of crime.

The second hypothesis involves social environments. Intergenerational transmission of criminality might be brought about through behavior reflecting the personalities of fathers with criminal records.

Criminal fathers would be expected to be relatively inconsiderate and aggressive, thus increasing the risk of parental conflict. Such conflict might be increased as well, of course, by the misbehavior of a son.

A longitudinal study of two generations is used to disentangle the web linking generations in terms of criminality.

METHOD

In order to evaluate the direction of causality, families were selected from the files of a larger longitudinal study. The larger study had been designed to provide assistance to families living in pockets of poverty in the greater Boston area (Powers & Witmer, 1951). Both "difficult" and "average" boys were included in the program, so the boys presented a broad range of behavior.

Between 1936 and 1939, a selection committee identified pairs of boys who were considered similar in terms of conditions thought to be related to becoming delinquent. By tossing a coin, one member of each pair was selected for the treatment program. Those in the treatment program were visited, on average, twice a month between 1939 and 1945. Case records from these visits reported family interactions in detail. The family records were coded in 1957. As part of an evaluation of the program, criminal records for fathers were gathered in 1948. Criminal records for the sons were collected in 1978 and 1979.

The larger study included 253 pairs of boys. Records for the control group had been based largely on interviews with the mothers and the boys. In order to use a strong measure of family conflict, the control families were not included in the present study. To justify treating each case as independent, only one son from a family was included. This restriction resulted in dropping 21 boys with brothers.

Adoption studies have provided evidence that biological father–son pairs are more similar in terms of criminality than are sociological father–son pairs (Bohman, Cloninger, Sigvardsson, & von Knorring, 1982; Crowe, 1975; Mednick, Gabrielli, & Hutchings, 1987; Schulsinger, 1977). To maximize the potential influence of fathers, only those families in which records described the boy's biological father were included. Nineteen families were excluded because the natural father had not been described in the records.

Thirty-seven families had not been coded for parental conflict, and 18 boys had already reached the age of 10 years at the time initial ratings of behavior were collected from their teachers. To maintain a clear perspective on sequencing, a family was dropped also if the father's first conviction occurred after the teacher had described the son ($N = 25$) or if the son had been less than 10 years old at the time of his own first conviction ($N = 11$).

After elimination as noted above, 149 families remained for analyses. A father's criminality was determined by whether or not he had been convicted for a type 1 Index crime. Thirty-one fathers had been convicted for at least one of the following: theft, breaking and entering, assault, murder, rape, attempted murder, or attempted rape.

Children were identified as showing difficult behavior if their teachers selected at least 3 of the following 12 descriptions to characterize them: fights; blames others for his difficulties; secretive, crafty, sly; rude, saucy, impudent; disobeys; refuses to cooperate; cruel; cheats; lies; steals; destroys property; truant. At the time these descriptions were provided, the boys ranged in age from 4 to 9, with a mean age of 7.6 (S.D. = 1.4). One-third of the boys ($N = 50$) were described by none of these terms and one-third ($N = 48$) were described by more than two of them.

Court records were used to evaluate public misbehavior. A boy was considered troublesome if he was convicted for a nontraffic offense between the ages of 10 and when the program ended in 1945. Boys were born between 1926 and 1934, with the mean and mode in 1928. Twenty-five boys met the criterion for being troublesome.

Evaluation of parental conflict was based on reading of the case records. Coders rated the family after looking for counselors' reports of disagreements about the child, values, money, alcohol, or religion. Parents were classified as evidencing or not evidencing considerable conflict. To estimate reliability of the coding, a second rater independently read a 10% random sample of the cases. The Scott (1955) Interrater Reliability Coefficient, Pi, indicated relative improvement over chance agreement between two raters at .55 with 80% agreement.[1] Fifty-seven of the families were classified as evidencing considerable conflict.

Criminal records collected in 1978 and 1979 were used to identify which of the boys had been convicted for Index crimes as adults. Twenty-eight men had been convicted for such crimes as theft, breaking and entering, assault, murder, rape, attempted murder, or attempted rape.

[1] $Pi = (Po\text{-}Pe)/(1\text{-}Pe)$ where Po represents observed agreement between raters and Pe represents percent of agreement expected by chance, computed by summing the squared proportions of the cases in each category.

RESULTS

Relationships among the variables are shown in Table 1. Correlations are Phi coefficients.

As expected, the father's criminality is correlated with his son's public misbehavior and adult criminality. Additionally, there is a significant correlation between paternal criminality and subsequent parental conflicts.

In accord with prior studies, the children who misbehaved early had a tendency to become juvenile delinquents. Parental conflict and public misbehavior were significantly correlated, and both were correlated with adult serious criminality. However, only a weak and insignificant correlation appeared between the child's earlier misbehavior and later parental conflict.

To test the independent contributions of paternal criminality, parental conflict, difficult child behavior, and child's public misbehavior on adult criminality, the dichotomized variables were standardized. Beta weights for regressing adult criminality onto these four antecedent variables showed that only parental conflict and public misbehavior yielded significant direct contributions (see Figure 1).

Both earlier misbehavior and parental conflict contributed to public misbehavior. Paternal criminality, however, contributed meaningfully only through increasing the probability of parental conflict.

It seemed possible that the impact of paternal criminality on parental conflict masked a contribution of child's early misbehavior to later conflict. To check this possibility, parental conflict was regressed on earlier child misbehavior and contemporaneous public misbehavior

TABLE 1. Relations among Variables

	Father's serious criminality	Difficult child	Public misbehavior	Parental conflict
Difficult child	.071			
p =	NS			
Public misbehavior	.168	.229		
p =	.041	.005		
Parental conflict	.345	.078	.349	
p =	.000	NS	.000	
Adult serious criminality	.219	.110	.290	.293
p =	.008	NS	.000	.000

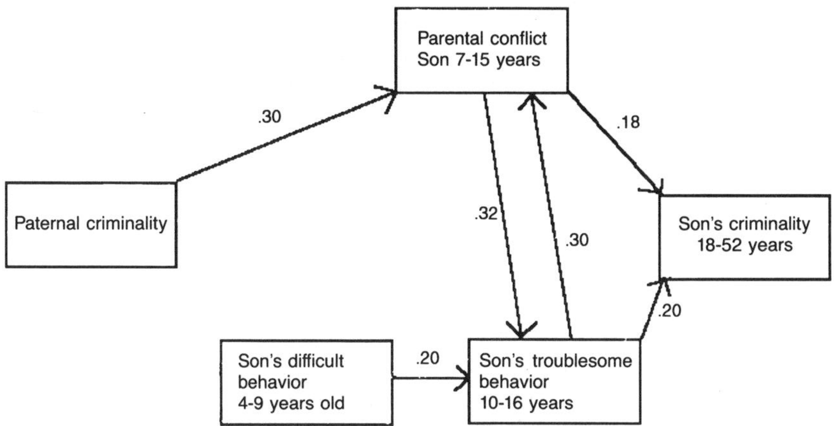

FIGURE 1. Predictors of son's serious adult criminality (beta weights)

among sons of criminals and among sons of noncriminals, separately. Beta weights for the sons of criminals (N = 31) were .09 for earlier troublesomeness and .44 for contemporaneous public misbehavior. Beta weights for the sons of noncriminals (N = 118) were .005 for earlier troublesomeness and .28 for contemporaneous public misbehavior.

In sum, the evidence failed to show that family conflict could be attributed to early child misbehavior, but rather, supported a view that criminogenic effects of paternal criminality depend, at least to some extent, on the fact that male criminals tend to expose their sons to marital discord.

DISCUSSION

Genetic interpretations of generational continuities in antisocial aggression have seemed to gain support through studies of twins and of adoption. In looking at hyperactivity among monozygotic and dizygotic twins, for example, Goodman and Stevenson (1989a,b) reported a considerable amount of heritability. Evidence for heritability of activity level, impulsivity, and desire for excitement has also been reported (e.g., Goldsmith & Gottesman, 1981; Pedersen, Plomin, Mcclearn, & Friberg, 1988).

Evidence shows also that adults are responsive to differences in children's behavior. These effects have been demonstrated for mothers of children medicated to reduce hyperactivity (Barkley & Cunningham, 1979). The study involved use of a placebo, so mothers were not aware of when their children were medicated. When medicated, according to their mothers, the children were less talkative; the mothers became more responsive and less directive toward their children. Differences relevant to socialization have also been demonstrated in relation to experimentally induced child responsiveness, with more responsive children being rewarded by more help and attention (Cantor & Gelfand, 1977) and less negative feedback (Bugental & Shennum, 1984).

If genetically determined characteristics influence parental behavior, then comparing monozygotic with dizygotic twins will not distinguish between environmental and biological determinants. Monozygotic twins will create more similar environments than will dizygotic twins. To the extent that child factors affect interaction, therefore, the degree of social differences will vary concomitantly with the degree of biological differences. This fact suggests that examination of the contributions of biological and social conditions to behavior ought not focus on testing whether biological or social factors contribute to intergenerational transmission of aggression, but rather, on how the transmission occurs.

The son's difficult behavior does not appear to be related directly to the father's criminality. It would be a mistake, however, to conclude that this shows no genetic contribution to misbehavior. Rather, whatever genetic makeup has been passed from father to son ought to be viewed as providing susceptibilities or potentialities which require social conditions for their expression in terms of crime. The data suggest that there are early indications of future trouble and that contemporaneous troublesomeness at least exacerbates parental conflicts. Perhaps most importantly, however, this study suggests that aggression is transmitted intergenerationally at least in part because aggressive, antisocial fathers tend to create the social environments conducive to aggressive, antisocial behavior.

REFERENCES

American Psychiatric Association (1980), *Diagnostic and Statistical Manual of Mental Disorders,* 3rd ed. (DSM-III). Washington, DC: American Psychiatric Press.

Anderson, K. E., Lytton, H., & Romney, D. M. (1986). Mothers' interactions with normal and conduct-disordered boys: Who affects whom? *Developmental Psychology, 22,* 604–609.

Barkley, R. A., & Cunningham, C. E. (1979). The effects of methylphenidate on the mother–child interactions of hyperactive children. *Archives of General Psychiatry, 36,* 201–208.

Bell, R. Q. (1964). The effect on the family of a limitation in coping ability in a child: A research approach and a finding. *Merrill-Palmer Quarterly, 10,* 129–142.

Bell, R. Q. (1968). A reinterpretation of the direction of effects in studies of socialization. *Psychological Review, 75,* 81–95.

Bell, R. Q. (1979). Parent, child, and reciprocal influences. *American Psychologist, 34,* 821–826.

Bell, R. Q. (1986). Age-specific manifestations in changing psychosocial risk. In D. C. Farvan & J. D. McKinney (Eds.), *Risk in intellectual and psychosocial development* (pp. 169–185). Orlando, FL: Academic Press.

Bohman, M., Cloninger, C. R., Sigvardsson, S., & von Knorring, A. (1982). Predisposition to petty criminality in Swedish adoptees. *Archives of General Psychiatry, 39,* 1233–1241.

Bugental, D. B., & Shennum, W. A. (1984). "Difficult" children as elicitors and targets of adult communication patterns: An attributional-behavioral transactional analysis. *Monographs of the Society for Research in Child Development,* Serial No. 205, *49,* 1.

Call, J. D. (1984). Child abuse and neglect in infancy: Sources of hostility within the parent–infant dyad and disorders of attachment in infancy. *Child Abuse & Neglect, 8,* 185–202.

Cantor, N. L., & Gelfand, D. M. (1977). Effects of responsiveness and sex of children on adults' behavior. *Child Development, 48,* 232–238.

Crowe, R. R. (1975). An adoptive study of psychopathy: Preliminary results from arrest records and psychiatric hospital records. In R. R. Fieve, D. Rosenthal, & H. Brill (Eds.), *Genetic research in psychiatry* (pp. 95–103). Baltimore: Johns Hopkins University Press.

Egeland, B., & Sroufe, A. (1981). Developmental sequelae of maltreatment in infancy. In R. Rizley & D. Cicchetti (Eds.), *Developmental perspectives on child maltreatment, new directions for child development* (pp. 77–92). San Francisco: Jossey-Bass.

Emery, R. E. (1982). Interparental conflict and the children of discord and divorce. *Psychological Bulletin, 92,* 310–330.

Eron, L. D. (1987). The development of aggressive behavior from the perspective of a developing behaviorist. *American Psychologist, 42,* 435–442.

Eron, L., Huesmann, R. L., & Zelli, A. (1991). The role of parental variables in the learning of aggression. In D. J. Pepler & K. H. Rubin (Eds.), *The development and treatment of childhood aggression* (pp. 169–188). Hillsdale, NJ: Lawrence Erlbaum.

Eron, L. D., Huesmann, L. R., Dubow, E., Romanoff, R., & Yarmel, P. (1987). Aggression and its correlates over 22 years. In D. H. Crowell, I. M. Evans, & C. R. O'Donnell (Eds.), *Childhood aggression and violence: Sources of influence, prevention, and control* (pp. 249–262). New York: Plenum Press.

Eron, L., Walder, L. O., & Lefkowitz, M. M. (1971). *Learning aggression in children.* Boston: Little, Brown.

Farrington, D. P. (1978). The family backgrounds of aggressive youths. In L. A. Hersov & M. Berger (Eds.), *Aggression and anti-social behaviour in childhood and adolescence* (pp. 73–93). Oxford: Pergamon.

Farrington, D. P. (1979). Environmental stress, delinquent behavior, and convictions. In I. G. Sarason & C. D. Spielberger (Eds.), *Stress and Anxiety* (Vol. 6, pp. 93–106). New York: John Wiley.

Farrington, D. P. (1986). Stepping stones to adult criminal careers. In D. Olweus, J. Block, & M. Radke-Yarrow (Eds.), *Development of antisocial and prosocial behavior* (pp. 359–384). New York: Academic Press.

Gelles, R. J. (1980). Violence in the family: A review of research in the seventies. *Journal of Marriage and the Family, 42,* 873–885.

Glueck, S. & Glueck, E. T. (1950). *Unraveling juvenile delinquency.* New York: Commonwealth Fund.

Goldsmith, H. H., & Gottesman, I. I. (1981). Origins of variation in behavioral style: A longitudinal study of temperament in young twins. *Child Development, 52,* 91–103.

Goodman, R. & Stevenson, J. (1989a). A twin study of hyperactivity. 1. An examination of hyperactivity scores and categories derived from Rutter Teacher and Parent Questionnaires. *Journal of Child Psychology and Psychiatry and Allied Disciplines, 30,* 671–690.

Goodman, R., & Stevenson, J. (1989b). A twin study of hyperactivity. 2. The aetiological role of genes, family relationships and perinatal adversity. *Journal of Child Psychology and Psychiatry and Allied Disciplines, 30,* 691–710.

Harrenkohl, R. C., & Herrenkohl, E. C. (1981). Some antecedents and developmental consequences of child maltreatment. In R. Risley & D. Cicchetti (Eds.), *Developmental perspectives on child maltreatment* (pp. 57–76). San Francisco: Jossey-Bass.

Hirschi, T. (1969). *Causes of delinquency.* Berkeley, CA: University of California Press.

Huesmann, L. R., Eron, L. D., Lefkowitz, M. M. & Walder, L. O. (1984). Stability of aggression over time and generations. *Developmental Psychology, 20,* 1120–1134.

Jouriles, E. N., Barling, J., & O'Leary, K. D. (1987). Predicting child behavior problems in maritally violent families. *Journal of Abnormal Child Psychology, 15,* 165–173.

Lewis, D. O., Pincus, J., Lovely, R., Spitzer, E., & Moy, E. (1987). Biopsychosocial characteristics of matched samples of delinquents and nondelinquents. *Journal of the American Academy of Child and Adolescent Psychiatry, 26,* 744–752.

Loeber, R., & Stouthamer-Loeber, M. (1986). Family factors as correlates and predictors of juvenile conduct problems and delinquency. In M. Tonry & N. Morris (Eds.), *Crime and Justice* (Vol. 7, pp. 29–149). Chicago: University of Chicago Press.

Lytton, H. (1990). Child and parent effects in boy's conduct disorder: A reinterpretation. *Developmental Psychology, 26,* 683–697.

Maccoby, E. E., & Jacklin, C. N. (1982, June). *The "Person" characteristics of children and the family as environment.* Paper presented at the Conference on Interaction of Person and Environment, Stockholm.

Magnusson, D. (1988). *Individual development from an interactional perspective.* Hillsdale, NJ: Lawrence Erlbaum.

Mein, M., & Goldwyn, R. (1984). Predicting rejection of her infant from mother's representation of her own experience: Implications for the abused-abusing intergenerational cycle. *Child Abuse and Neglect, 8,* 203–217.

McCord, J. (1979). Some child-rearing antecedents of criminal behavior in adult men. *Journal of Personality and Social Psychology, 37,* 1477–1486.

McCord, J. (1982). A longitudinal view of the relationship between paternal absence and crime. In J. Gunn & D. P. Farrington (Eds.), *Abnormal offenders, delinquency, and the criminal justice system* (pp. 113–128). Chichester, U.K.: John Wiley.

McCord, J. (1983). A longitudinal study of aggression and antisocial behavior. In K. T. Van Dusen & S. A. Mednick (Eds.), *Prospective studies of crime and delinquency* (pp. 269–275). Boston: Kluwer-Nijhoff.

McCord, J. (1990a). Longterm effects of parental absence. In L. N. Robins & M. Rutter (Eds.), *Straight and devious pathways from childhood to adulthood* (pp. 116–134). Cambridge, U.K.: Cambridge University Press.

McCord, J. (1990b). Crime in moral and social contexts. *Criminology, 28,* 1–26.

McCord, J. (1991). Family relationships, juvenile delinquency, and adult criminality. *Criminology, 29,* 397–417.

Mednick, S. A., Gabrielli, W. F., & Hutchings, B. (1987). Genetic factors in the etiology of criminal behavior. In S. A. Mednick, T. E. Moffitt, & S. A. Stack (Eds.), *The causes of crime: New biological approaches* (pp. 74–91). Cambridge, U.K.: Cambridge University Press.

Offord, D. R. (1982). Family backgrounds of male and female delinquents. In J. Gunn & D. P. Farrington (Eds.), *Abnormal offenders, delinquency, and the criminal justice system* (pp. 129–151). Chichester, U.K.: John Wiley.

Patterson, G. R. (1986). Maternal rejection: Determinant or product for deviant child behavior? In W. Hartup & Z. Rubin (Eds.), *Relationships and development* (pp. 73–92). Hillsdale, NJ: Lawrence Erlbaum.

Pedersen, N. L., Plomin, R., McClearn, G. E., & Friberg, L. (1988). Neuroticism, extraversion, and related traits in adult twins reared apart and reared together. *Journal of Personality and Social Psychology, 55,* 950–957.

Powers, E., & Witmer, H. (1951). *An experiment in the prevention of delinquency: The Cambridge-Somerville Youth Study.* New York: Columbia University Press.

Pulkkinen, L. (1983). Search for alternatives to aggression in Finland. In A. P. Goldstein & M. H. Segall (Eds.), *Aggression in global perspective* (pp. 104–144). Elmsford, NY: Pergamon Press.

Robins, L. N. (1966). *Deviant children grown up.* Baltimore: Williams & Wilkins.

Robins, L. N., & Ratcliff, K. S. (1979). Risk factors in the continuation of childhood antisocial behavior into adulthood. *International Journal of Mental Health, 7,* 96–116.

Rutter, M., & Garmezy, N. (1983). Developmental and psychopathology. In E. M. Hetherington (Ed.), *Handbook of child psychology, Vol. 4: Socialization, personality and social development* (pp. 775–912). New York: John Wiley.

Rutter, M., Bolton, P., Harrington, R., Couteur, A. L., Macdonald, H., & Simonoff, E. (1990). Genetic factors in child psychiatric disorders-I. A review of research strategies. *Journal of Child Psychology and Psychiatry and Allied Disciplines, 31,* 3–37.

Satterfield, J. H. (1987). Childhood diagnostic and neurophysiological predictors of teenage arrest rates: An eight-year prospective study. In S. A. Mednick, T. E. Moffitt, & S. A. Stack (Eds.), *The causes of crime: New biological approaches* (pp. 146–167). Cambridge, U.K.: Cambridge University Press.

Schulsinger, F. (1977). Psychopathy: Heredity and environment. In S. A. Mednick & K. O. Christiansen (Eds.), *Biosocial bases of criminal behavior* (pp. 109–141). New York: Gardner.

Scott, W. A. (1955). Reliability of content analysis: The case of nominal scale coding. *Public Opinion Quarterly, 19,* 321–325.

Sears, R. R., Maccoby, E. E., & Levin, H. (1957). *Patterns of child rearing.* Evanston, IL: Row, Peterson.

Stattin, H., & Magnusson, D. (1989). The role of early aggressive behavior in the frequency, seriousness, and type of later crime. *Journal of Consulting and Clinical Psychology, 57,* 710–718.

White, J. L., Moffitt, T. E., Earls, F., Robins, L., & Silva, P. A. (1990). How early can we tell?: Predictors of childhood conduct disorder and adolescent delinquency. *Criminology, 28,* 507–533.

Widom, C. S. (1989). Child abuse, neglect, and adult behavior: Research design and findings on criminality, violence, and child abuse. *American Journal of Orthopsychiatry, 59,* 355–367.

Part V

GROUP AGGRESSION IN ADOLESCENTS AND ADULTS

This final part includes two chapters that expand researchers' theorizing about individual aggression into the realm of group behavior.

Goldstein summarizes the various theories that have been offered to explain youth gang formation and youth gang violence. First he describes the demographics of gang composition and aggressive behavior. He then argues that current theories can form the basis for comprehensive interventions that could mitigate gang violence.

Feshbach, in the final chapter, addresses the issue of the relation between aggression by whole societies in the form of wars and individual differences in aggressiveness, and attitudes about one's country. Distinguishing formally between "patriotism" and "nationalism," he argues that nationalistic attitudes provide the basis for acceptance of war whereas individual differences in the propensity to aggress against another individual and patriotic attitudes are less important.

CHAPTER 11

DELINQUENT GANGS

ARNOLD P. GOLDSTEIN

WHAT IS A GANG?

Delinquent youth gangs in the United States, as a social (or, better, antisocial) phenomenon, ebb and flow in terms of both their numbers and societal impact. In the early 1990s, there are more of them, more gang youth drug involvement, and greater levels of violence being perpetrated by such youth. The present chapter seeks to describe the sources and substance of this phenomenon and, with a particular focus on gang violence, examine an array of preventative and rehabilitative interventions which have been employed toward delinquency and aggression-reduction ends.

What constitutes a gang has varied with time and place, with political and economic conditions, with community tolerance and community conservatism, with level and nature of police and citizen concern, with cultural and subcultural traditions and mores, and with media-generated sensationalism or indifference to youth groups that violate the law. The answer to the question, What is a gang? has varied chronologically from a play group formed out of unconscious pressures and instinctual need (Puffer, 1912), to an interstitial group derived from conflict with others

---

ARNOLD P. GOLDSTEIN • Department of Special Education, Syracuse University, Syracuse, New York 13244.

Aggressive Behavior: Current Perspectives, edited by L. Rowell Huesmann. Plenum Press, New York, 1994.

(Thrasher, 1936), to an aggregation demarcated as "a gang" via community and then self-labeling processes (Klein, 1971), to singular definitional emphasis on territoriality and delinquent behavior (Gardner, 1983), and, most recently, to a particular definitional focus on violence and drug involvement (Spergel, Curry, Rose, & Chance, 1989).

Spergel et al. (1989) comment with regard to this definitional progression:

> Definitions in the 1950s and 1960s were related to issues of etiology as well as based on liberal, social reform assumptions. Definitions in the 1970s and 1980s are more descriptive, emphasize violent and criminal characteristics, and possibly a more conservative philosophy of social control and deterrence (Klein and Maxson, 1987). The most recent trend may be to view gangs as more pathological than functional and to restrict usage of the term to a narrow set of violent and criminal groups. (p. 13)

The contemporary American juvenile gang may have a structured organization, identifiable leadership, territorial identification, continuous association, specific purpose, and engage in illegal behavior. In the 1990s, these attributes largely characterize many of the gangs in California, Illinois, and elsewhere in America (California Youth Gang Taskforce, 1981). Or, rather less characteristic of the typical, contemporary gang, they may, as is largely the case in New York City, be loosely organized, of changeable leadership, be oriented toward criminal activity rather than territorial issues, associate irregularly, pursue amorphous purposes, and engage in not only illegal, but also legal activities (New York State Taskforce on Junveile Gangs, 1990). Nevertheless, today they are more violent and more drug-involved than in the past, and these two characteristics must also be included when establishing an accurate, contemporary definition of what constitutes a gang in America.

Early theorizing on gangs, reflected heavy reliance on both Darwinian thinking and *instinct* as the core explanatory construct in the behavioral science of the day. It was asserted that one ought to

> look upon the boy's gang as the result of a group of instincts inherited from a distant past. . . . We must suppose that these gang instincts arose in the first because they were useful once, and that they have been preserved to the present day because they are, on the whole, useful still. (Puffer, 1912, p. 83)

Thrasher (1927/1963) looked for causative explanation both within the youths themselves and the greater community of which they were a part. The typical gang member, in his view, was ". . . a rather healthy, well-adjusted, red-blooded American boy seeking an outlet for normal adolescent drives for adventure and expression" (Hardman, 1967, p. 7). Yet, the youth's environment was equally important to Thrasher. Inadequacies in family functioning, schools, housing, sanitation, employment, and other community characteristics combined to help motivate youth to turn to a gang for life satisfactions and rewards. This focus on social causation blossomed fully during the 1930s and early 1940s; Hardman (1967) appropriately, labeled them "the depression studies." It was an era in which social scientists sought an explanation for many of America's ills—including membership in delinquent gangs—in ". . . social causation, social failure, social breakdown" (Hardman, 1967, p. 9). Landesco (1932) emphasized the effects of conflicting immigrant and American cultures. Shaw and McKay (1942) stressed a core complex combination of slum area deterioration, poverty, family dissolution, and organized crime. Tannenbaum (1939) proposed that the gang forms not because of its attractiveness per se, but because "positive sociocultural forces" such as family, school, and church, that might train a youth into more socially acceptable behaviors, are weak or unavailable. Wattenberg and Balistrieri (1950) similarly stressed socioeconomically substandard neighborhoods and lax parental supervision. In the same context, Bogardus (1943), in one of the first West Coast gang studies, emphasized the war and warlike climate in America as underpinning the aggressive gangs forming at that time. Dumpson (1949), more multicausal, but still contextual in his causative thinking, identified the war, racism, and diverse political and economic sources. Over the decades, while the social problems of the day have largely formed the basis for explaining why youths form gangs, Miller (1982) has offered a more fully inclusive perspective, which appears to us to more adequately capture the likely complex determinants of gang formation. He observes:

> Youth gangs persist because they are a product of conditions basic to our social order. Among these are a division of labor between the family and the peer group in the socialization of adolescents, and emphasis on masculinity and collective action in the male subculture; a stress on excitement, congregation, and mating in the adolescent subculture; the importance of toughness and smartness in the subcultures of lower-status populations; and the density conditions and territoriality patterns affecting the subcultures of urban and urbanized locales. (p. 320)

DELINQUENT GANG THEORY

Early interest in delinquent gangs on the part of social scientists was largely descriptive. What gangs were and the societal/familial conditions that were their antecedents and concomitants were the focus of concern. Little emerged during this time in the way of formal gang theory, that is, conceptualizations of the structural and dynamic variables underlying gang formation, organization, and, especially, the delinquent behavior which characterized a substantial amount of gang functioning. These theoretical lacunae began to be filled in the 1950s, and the majority of this theory development was sociological in nature. It focused primarily on seeking to explain the delinquent behavior of individual youth gangs and groups of gangs. Some of the more prominent theories developed during this period were:

Strain Theory

Strain theory emphasized the discrepancy between economic aspiration and opportunity, as well as such discrepancy-induced reactions as frustration, deprivation, and discontent. Cohen's (1955) reactance theory, and Cloward and Ohlin's (1960) differential opportunity theory are both elaborations of strain theory.

Subcultural Theory

Subcultural or cultural deviance theory, holds that delinquent behavior grows from conformity to the prevailing social norms experienced by a young person in his or her particular subcultural group, norms largely at variance with those held by society at large. According to Cohen (1966), these norms include gratuitous hostility, group autonomy, intolerance of restraint, short-run hedonism, the seeking of recognition via antisocial behavior, little interest in planning for long-term goals, and related behavioral preferences. Sutherland's (1937; Sutherland & Cressey, 1974) differential association theory, Miller's (1958) notion of lower-class culture as a "generating milieu" for gang delinquency, differential identification theory (Glaser, 1956), culture conflict theory (Shaw & McKay, 1942), illicit means theory (Shaw & McKay, 1942), and what might be termed structural determinism theory (Clarke, 1977) are the major consolidations of subcultural theory.

Control Theory

While both strain and subcultural theories seek to explain why some youngsters commit delinquent acts, control theory operationalizes its concern with the etiology of delinquency by positing reasons why some youngsters do not become criminals. Everyone, it is assumed, has a predisposition to commit delinquent acts, and the theory concerns itself with how individuals learn not to offend, and suggests that they do so primarily via a process of social bonding (Hirschi, 1969).

Labeling Theory

In 1938, Tannenbaum described an escalating process of stigmatization or labeling which he asserted can occur between the delinquent individual or group and the community of which they are a part. The process by which a person becomes a criminal, accordingly, is a sequence of tagging, defining, identifying, segregating, describing, emphasizing, making conscious, and self-conscious. In labeling theory, a person becomes what he or she is described as being.

Radical Theory

Radical theory is a sociopolitical perspective on crime and delinquency (Abadinsky, 1979; Meier, 1976). Its focus is on the political meanings and motivations underlying society's definitions of crime and its control. In this view, crime is a phenomenon largely created by those who possess wealth and power in the United States. America's laws, it is held, are the laws of the ruling elite, used to subjugate the poor, minorities, and the powerless. Thus, the theory holds as its target for intervention the social and economic structure of American society.

CURRENT GANG DEMOGRAPHICS

Accurate data on the number, nature, structure, and functioning of delinquent gangs are hard to come by. No national-level agency in the United States has assumed responsibility for the systematic collection and reporting of gang-relevant information. Each city or region is free to and does formulate its own definition of what constitutes a gang, and decides what gang-relevant data to collect. Police (who are the major source of gang information in most American cities), public service agencies, schools, the mass media, and others regularly exposed to gang youth not infrequently exaggerate or minimize their numbers and illegal behaviors as a function of political, financial, or other impression management needs. Compounding the difficulty in obtaining adequate, accurate, objective, and relevant information are gang youths themselves, who have their own reasons, real and imagined, for exaggerating or diminishing the purported size, activities, or impact of their gang. Thus, caution in accepting the available data, and conservatism in its interpretation are requisite.

In 1974, Miller conducted a national survey seeking gang-relevant information from a spectrum of public and private service agencies, police departments, probation offices, courts, juvenile bureaus, and other sources. Particular attention was paid to the six American cities reporting the highest levels of gang activity. Philadelphia and Los Angeles reported the highest proportion of gang members to their respective male adolescent populations (6 per 100). Gang members in the surveyed cities were predominantly male; ages 12 to 21; residing in the poorer, usually central-city areas; and came from families at the lower occupational and educational levels. Gang youth were African-American (1/2), Hispanic (1/6), Asian (1/10), and non-Hispanic white (1/10), and tended to form themselves into ethnically homogeneous gangs.

Needle and Stapleton (1982) surveyed police departments in 60 American cities of various sizes. In the early eighties, delinquent youth gangs were no longer to be seen as only a big city problem. Though the popular mythology attributes this spread to smaller cities as being caused by big city gangs or megagangs (especially the Los Angeles Crips and Bloods) intentionally establishing branches, the reality is more complex. While a modest amount of such "franchising," "branching," or "hiving off" may occur, most mid- and smaller city gangs either originate in such locations or are started by nonresident gang members via kinship, alliance, the expansion of turf boundaries, or the movement of gang members' families into new areas (Moore, Vigil, & Garcia, 1983).

By 1989, according to yet another, and particularly extensive, survey conducted by Spergel et al. (1989) delinquent gangs were located in almost all 50 states. As a group, 35 surveyed cities reported the existence of 1439 gangs. California, Illinois, and Florida have substantial gang concentrations. Spergel et al. report that three jurisdictions in particular have especially high numbers of youth gangs: Los Angeles County (600), Los Angeles City (280), and Chicago (128). Of the total of 120,636 gang members reported to exist in all the surveyed cities combined, 70,000 were estimated to be in Los Angeles County, including 26,000 in Los Angeles and 12,000 in Chicago.[1] But it is clearly not only these three jurisdictions that express concern. Spergel et al. (1989) report that while 14 percent of their survey's law enforcement respondents and 8 percent of other respondents believed that the gang situation in their respective jurisdictions had improved since 1980, 56% of the police and 68% of the non-law-enforcement respondents claimed their situation had worsened.

[1] This numerical litany of youth participation in gangs should be tempered with the reminder that most youths, even in areas in which gangs are common, do not join gangs. Vigil (1983), for example, estimated that only 4 to 10 % of Chicago youth are affiliated with gangs.

Males continue to outnumber female gang members at a ratio of approximately 20 to 1. Gang size is a variable function of a number of determinants, including density of the youth population in a given geographical or psychological area (i.e., the pool to draw upon); the nature of the gang's activities; police pressures; season of the year; gang recruitment efforts; relevant agency activity; and additional factors (Spergel, 1965). Only 5% or less of gang crime is committed by females. Females join gangs later than do males, and leave earlier. The age range of gang membership appears to have expanded to from 9 to 30, as gang involvement in drug dealing has increased. Younger members are often used as lookouts or runners, with the knowledge that if caught, judges and juvenile law are more lenient when the perpetrator is 14 years old or younger. Older members tend to remain in the gang as a result of both the profitability of drug dealing, and the paucity of employment opportunities for disadvantaged populations in the legitimate economy. Blacks, Hispanics, Asians, and whites are America's gang members.[2]

Young people join gangs largely to obtain what all adolescents appropriately seek—peer friendship, pride, identity development, self-esteem enhancement, excitement, the acquisition of resources, and in response to family and community tradition. These goals are often not available to young people through legitimate means in the disorganized and low-income environments from which most gang youth derive.

How do they leave? Gang members may marry out, age out, and find employment in the legitimate economy. They may shift to individual or organized crime. Many go to prison. Some die.

What do gang members do? Mostly gang members just "hang out," engaging in the diverse interpersonal behaviors characteristic of almost all adolescents. They may claim and topographically define their territory, and make sometimes extensive use of graffiti. They do this in order to define their turf, challenge rivals, or proclaim the existence of their gang, incorporate distinctive colors or color combinations within their dress, tattoo their bodies, and make use of special hand signs as a means of communicating.

Not infrequently they commit delinquent acts and engage in various forms and levels of aggressive behavior. While the total amount of such behavior is small, its effect on the chain of media response, public

[2] Membership strongly tends to continue, and is often further solidified, when and if the gang youth is incarcerated (Camp & Camp, 1985; Jacobs, 1974; Lane, 1989). Gott (1989), for example, reports that in 1989 approximately 5000 of the 9000 youths incarcerated in California Youth Authority facilities were gang members and that, as other have also observed, gang cohesiveness and activity level appear to be substantially accelerated by and during incarceration.

perception of gang youth behavior, and police and public agency countermeasures is quite substantial.

Through the 1970s and 1980s, the levels and forms of gang violence in the United States substantially increased, along with the levels and forms of violence elsewhere on the American scene.[3] Whereas the Roxbury Project (Miller, 1980), Group Guidance Project (Klein, 1971), and Ladino Hills Project (Klein, 1971) gang intervention programs of the 1950s and 1960s collectively revealed almost no homicides and only modest amounts of other types of gang violence, there were 81 gang-related homicides in Chicago in 1981, 351 such deaths in Los Angeles in 1980, and over 1500 in Los Angeles during the 1985 to 1989 period (Gott, 1989). Spergel et al. (1989) report that only about 1% of all the violent crime committed in Chicago was perpetrated by gang members. The seriousness of such figures, however, resides not only in their relative increase from past years, but also, and especially, in their nature—primarily homicide and aggravated assault. Such violent offenses, Spergel et al. (1989) observe, are three times more likely to be committed by gang members than by nongang delinquents, a finding also reported by Friedman, Mann, & Friedman (1975) and Tracy (1979).

What do they fight over? Drugs, territory, honor, girls, perceived insults, "bad looks," reputation, ethnic tensions.

INTERVENTIONS

Detached Workers

Gang intervention programming may be conveniently described chronologically as shown in Table 1. As can be seen, until approximately 1950, gangs violence was not a major American phenomenon, and thus neither were gang intervention efforts. As the postwar gang problem

[3] The weight of evidence combines to suggest that delinquent gangs in America are indeed behaving in a more violent manner in recent years (Miller 1990; Short, 1990). Nevertheless, it is important to note that such an apparent increase may derive, at least in part, from artifactual sources. Media interest in youth gangs ebbs and flows, and tends to be accentuated in direct proportion to youth violence levels. The contemporary increase in such behaviors may be partially just such a media interest effect. The likelihood of this possibility is enhanced by a second potential artifact, the relative absence of reliable sources of gang-relevant information. As Klein and Maxson (1989) note: "The 1960s gang programs, which permitted detailed description of gang structure and activity patterns, are now largely absent . . . the current picture is based on evidence that is largely hearsay rather than empirical" (p. 209). Finally, following from the fact that by far the majority of the current gang-relevant information which is available comes from police sources, it becomes possible that information regarding increased gang violence is in part also an artifact of more, and more intensive, police department gang intelligence unit activity.

TABLE 1. Gang Intervention Programming

Past	
–1950:	Indifferent or unsystematic
1950–1965:	Detached worker, youth outreach, street gang work
1965–1980:	Social and economic opportunities provision
1980–1990:	Suppression/incarceration, gangbusting, just desserts
Present	
1991–1992:	Suppression/incarceration, gangbusting, just desserts
1991–1992:	Comprehensive programming
Future	
1992–	Comprehensive programming

grew in the United States, so too did intervention programming. In the 1950s, it largely took the form of social workers working where the young gang members themselves were, on the streets.

According to Spergel (1965):

> The practice variously labeled detached work, street club, gang work, area work, extension youth work, corner work, etc., is the systematic effort of an agency worker, through social work or treatment techniques within the neighborhood context, to help a group of young people who are described as delinquent or partially delinquent to achieve a conventional adaptation. (p. 22)
>
> The assumption of youth agencies was that youth gangs were viable or adaptive and could be redirected. Counseling and group activities could be useful in persuading youth gang members to give up unlawful behavior. The small gang group or subgroup was to be the center of attention of the street worker. (p. 145)

Detached work programs grew from a historical context reaching back to the midnineteenth century, in which, as Brace (1872) reported, charity and church groups, as well as Boy Scouts, Boys' Clubs, YMCA's, and settlement houses, sought to establish relationships with and programs for urban youths in trouble or at risk (Brace, 1872, cited in Bremmer, 1976). Thrasher spoke of similar efforts in 1927, and the Chicago Area Projects of the 1930s (Kobrin, 1959) provided much of the procedural prototype for the youth outreach, detached work programs which emerged in force in the 1950s and 1960s. In the fertile context of the social action movements of midcentury America, many U.S. cities developed outreach programs for gang members.

The New York City Youth Board (1960), one of the major early programs (The Street Club Project) during the period, aspired to provide

> group work and recreation services to youngsters previously unable to use the traditional, existing facilities; the opportunity to make referrals of gang

> members for necessary treatment . . . the provision of assistance and guidance in the vocational area; and . . . the education of the community to the fact that . . . members of fighting gangs can be redirected into constructive positive paths. (p. 7)

At a more general level, this and many of the detached work programs which soon followed, also held as their broad goals the reduction of antisocial behavior; friendlier relations with other street gangs, increased participation of a democratic nature within the gang; increased responsibility for self-direction among individual gang members, as well as their improved social and personal adjustment; and better relations with the larger community of which the gang was a part.

Most detached work programs, as the movement evolved, came to the position that their central aspiration was value transformation, a rechanneling of the youths' beliefs and attitudes, and consequently they hoped, his or her behavior, in a less antisocial and more prosocial direction.

Four major evaluations of the effectiveness of detached worker, gang intervention programming were conducted during this era. The programs evaluated were the New York City Youth Board Project (New York City Youth Board, 1960), the Roxbury Project in Boston (Miller, 1970), the Chicago Youth Development Project (Mattick & Caplan, 1962); and the Los Angeles Group Guidance Project (Klein, 1968). Each concluded that such programming was ineffective. Yet in each instance, while both implementation plans, and later evaluation procedures seemed adequate, such was not the case regarding the manner in which worker activities were actually conducted. If this assertion is correct, program effectiveness remains indeterminate and conclusions regarding outcome efficacy must be suspended. There are five reasons why we take this position:

1. Failure of program integrity (i.e., the degree to which the intervention as actually implemented corresponded to or followed the intervention program as planned).
2. Failure of program intensity (i.e., the intervention's amount, level, or dosage).
3. Absence of delinquency-relevant techniques (i.e., lack of direct connections between the intervention's procedures and its hoped-for outcome, delinquency reduction).
4. Failure of program prescriptiveness (i.e., to match technique, worker, and youth in a propitiously differential, tailored, or individualized manner).
5. Failure of program comprehensiveness (i.e., to match the multi-

source, multilevel nature of delinquency causation with a similarly multipronged intervention.

Even given these realities, we must conclude that the demise of detached work programming was premature, and that the relevant evidence, instead of being interpreted as proof of lack of effectiveness, should more parsimoniously be viewed as indeterminate, generally neither adding to nor detracting from a conclusion of effectiveness or ineffectiveness.

Opportunities Provision

Starting in the mid-1960s, and continuing to the late 1970s, gang intervention programming shifted away from primary emphasis on the worker–youth relationship and attempts to alter youth behavior by gang reorientation and value transformation, to a greater concern with *system* change (i.e., the enhancement of work, school, or family opportunities). This shift in gang programming emphasis occurred in, and as part of, the broader context of increased legislation and funding for social programming of many types in the United States during this period. Often described as the era of opportunities provision, Spergel et al. (1989) describe this intervention strategy as:

> A series of large scale social resource infusions and efforts to change institutional structures, including schools, job opportunities, political employment . . . in the solution not only of delinquency, but poverty itself. Youth work strategies were regarded as insufficient. Structural strain, lack of resources, and relative deprivation were the key ideas which explained delinquency, including youth gang behavior. The structures of social and economic means rather than the behavior of gangs and individual youth had to be modified. (p. 147)

The proposed relevance of this strategy to gang youth in particular is captured well by Morales (1981):

> The gang is a symptom of certain noxious conditions found in society. These conditions often include low wages, unemployment, lack of recreational opportunities, inadequate schools, poor health, deteriorated housing and other factors contributing to urban decay and slums. (p. 4)

The need for provision of utilitarian and esteem-enhancing opportunity, of course, was apparent as far back as Thrasher's (1927/1963) work and earlier. What was different in the late 1960s and 1970s was America's willingness to respond to such beliefs with a broad programmatic effort. And indeed, many dozens of varied opportunity-providing programs followed (see Goldstein [1991] for a comprehensive summary).

With very few exceptions (Klein, 1968; Thompson & Jason, 1988), opportunities-provision gang programming has not been systematically evaluated. We do not know with any substantial degree of evaluative rigor whether or to what degree gang youth in general or particular subgroups thereof accept or seek the diverse opportunities provided. Nor do we know whether gang members benefit therefrom in either proximal, opportunity-specific ways, or more distally in terms of termination of gang membership, delinquency reduction, or future life path. There is no shortage of affirming impressionistic and anecdotal support. There has been a major and highly suggestive 45-city survey of both law enforcement and nonlaw enforcement agency views on the effectiveness of opportunity provision and other gang intervention approaches (Spergel et al., 1989). The value of such survey results notwithstanding, the general absence of rigorous evaluation of opportunities-provision gang programming must be emphasized. Klein's (1968) Ladino Hills Project is an important exception; its careful evaluation sets a standard by which other such studies may be judged.

Opportunity Withdrawal and the Rise of Deterrence/Incarceration

As the 1970s drew to a close, America got tough. A combination of the heavy influx of drugs, growing levels of violence, purported failure of rehabilitative programming, and the rise of political and judicial conservatism, all combined to usher in the era of deterrence/incarceration, and begin ushering out the provision of social, economic, and educational opportunity. Opportunity provision is not gone, but it is much less frequently the centerpiece of gang intervention programming. Social control—surveillance, deterrence, arrest, prosecution, incarceration—has largely replaced social improvement as America's preeminent approach to gang youth.

> A philosophy of increased social opportunity was replaced by growing conservatism. The gang was viewed as evil, a collecting place for sociopaths who were beyond the capacity of most social institutions to redirect or rehabilitate them. Protection of the community became the key goal. (Spergel et al., 1989, p. 148)

The deterrence/incarceration strategy came to guide the gang-relevant behavior not only of law enforcement personnel, but others also. In Philadelphia's Crisis Intervention Network program, in the Los Angeles Community Youth Gang Services, and in the other similar gang crisis intervention programs which sprang up across America, the resource worker, who himself had replaced the detached worker, was in turn replaced by the surveillance/deterrence worker. Working out of radio-dispatched automobiles, and assigned to geographical areas rather than to specific gangs, surveillance/deterrence workers responded to crises, their focus was on rumor control, dispute resolution, and, most centrally, violence reduction. Maxson and Klein (1983) capture well the essence of this strategy, as they contrast it with the earlier, value transformation approach:

> The transformation model fostered social group work in the streets with empathic and sympathetic orientations toward gang members as well as acceptance of gang misbehavior as far less of a problem than the alienating response of community residents and officials. By contrast, the deterrence model eschews an interest in minor gang predations and concentrates on the major ones, especially homicide. The worker is, in essence, part of a dramatically energized community control mechanism, a "firefighter" with a more balanced eye on the consequences as well as the cause of gang violence. Success is measured first in violence reduction, not in group or individual change. (p. 151)

Comprehensive Programming

Indeed, it is a primary responsibility of society's officialdom to protect its citizens. Gang violence in its diverse and often intense forms must be surveilled, deterred, punished. But much more must be done. Gang youth are *our* youth. They are among us now and, even if periodically incarcerated, most will be among us in the future. We deserve protection from their predations, but in turn they deserve the opportunity to lead satisfying and contributory lives without resorting to individual or group violence. Punishment may have to be employed, but punishment fails to teach new, alternative means to desired goals. In essence, the implementation of the deterrence/incarceration model may indeed be necessary in today's violence-prone America, but it is far from sufficient. What is needed, and indeed appears to be beginning to emerge, is a less unidimensional and more integrative gang intervention model, one with at least the potential to supplant exclusive employment of deterrence/incarceration. I term it the comprehensive model,[4] one which incorporates and seeks to prescriptively apply major features of detached worker, opportunities provision, and social control programming. It is a multimodal, multilevel strategy requiring substantial resources, of diverse types, employed in a coordinated manner for its success to be realized. I have documented elsewhere the manner in

[4] Similar in spirit and, in large measure, in its particulars to Spergel et al's (1989) model approach.

which aggressive and antisocial behavior derives from complex causality and, hence, will yield most readily when approached with interventions of parallel complexity and targeting (Goldstein, 1983). This is so, too, for gang aggression and antisocial behavior. Both the 1981 California and the earlier New York State Gang Task Force reports give full philosophical and concrete expression to this comprehensive gang intervention strategy.

The California Report (1981) urges adoption and implementation of a broad array of law enforcement, prosecutorial, correctional, probation/parole, judicial, executive department, legislative, federal agency, local government, school programming, community-based, business and industrial, and media recommendations. The (1990) New York Report concurs with this multichannel strategy, and urges further that, whatever the mode, interventions adopted must be preventive and not only rehabilitative in thrust; interventions must seek not only the reduction of antisocial behavior, but also the enhancement of prosocial alternatives. They must be both comprehensive in their coverage, and coordinated in their implementation; locate themselves in school and other community settings; concern themselves with family, school, employment, and recreational domains. Interventions must seek and be responsive to gang youth input in their planning and conduct; reflect program integrity, intensity, and prescriptiveness; recognize that gangs have the potential for, and at times actually have, served in a constructive, socially beneficial manner; and be evaluated rigorously.

In addition to these several, diverse recommendations, there is one further way in which comprehensiveness of gang programming may be profitably conceptualized and operationalized. I refer to greater involvement and utilization of *psychological* knowledge and techniques in helping us better understand the nature of youth gangs, and more effectively reduce their antisocial behavior. Research and intervention with American gangs have primarily been activities conducted by sociologists, criminologists, and criminal justice professionals, and only very rarely by psychologists (e.g., Cartwright, Schwartz & Tomson, 1975; Goldstein, 1991). Nevertheless, I believe psychologists have a great deal to offer as developers of gang-relevant theory (Bandura, 1986; Ellis, 1987; Feldman, 1977; Nietzel, 1979), as developers and evaluators of gang-relevant interventions (Agee, 1979; Goldstein & Glick, 1987; Gottschalk, Davidson, Gensheimer & Mayer, 1987; Grendreau & Ross, 1987) and as extrapolators, as it were, of psychological knowledge from diverse domains of psychology to our understanding of delinquent gangs.

In a recent text (1991), I proposed a series of substantive ways in which clinical, developmental, social, and community psychology might profitably be drawn upon in order to bring about clarification of gang intervention goals. Clinical psychology provides diverse theoretical understanding of gang member delinquency in its personality, social learning, neurohormonal and multicomponent theories. Developmental psychology examines and elucidates qualities of typical adolescents which appear to exist in exaggerated form in many gang youth—marginality, striving for independence, search for identity, challenge of authority, need for self-esteem enhancement, focus on peer relationships. Social psychology offers the gang intervention professional both theory and data concerned with group development, leadership, cohesiveness, communication, conflict and conflict resolution, norm and role development, influence processes, utilization of power, deindividuation, and groupthink. Community psychology adds to the pool of information from which gang-relevant extrapolations may be drawn, via its findings regarding natural communities, neighborhoods, social networks, and social support. All of these several bodies of psychological knowledge hold potential value for adding to our understanding of why gangs form, why they behave as they do, and how to alter much of their behavior. Very few such extrapolatory efforts have yet been made and tested, either in practice or research. It is my feeling that their likely value is especially great, and thus I enthusiastically encourage such attempts.

Finally I would assert that gang intervention of whatever type is likely to fail unless its strategic planning and tactical implementation involve major and sustained, gang member involvement with a serious response to it. An accurate and heuristic understanding of gang structure, motivation, perception, aspiration, and both routine and dramatic behavior cannot be obtained only from the outside looking in. Such understanding will become available if, and only if, substantial input is obtained from gang members themselves. But such input is not easily acquired. Hagedorn and Macon (1988) observe in this regard that

> . . . we are in the absurd position of having very few first hand studies of, but numerous theoretical speculations about, juvenile gangs. . . . One reason is that the vast majority of sociologists and researchers are white, and gangs today are overwhelmingly minority. (pp. 26–27)

African-American, Hispanic, Asian, and other minority youth do indeed constitute a large portion of America's contemporary gang membership. They bring to their gang participation diverse and often culture-specific membership motivations, perceptions, behaviors and beliefs. Cultural traditions and mores substantially shape such things as the meaning of aggression; the perception of gang as family; the gang as an arena for the acquisition of status, honor, or "rep"; the gang's duration, cohesiveness, typical and atypical legal and illegal pursuits; and its place in the community.

A rich literature exists describing in depth the cultural patterns and perspectives of America's ethnic and racial subgroups: *African-American* (Beverly & Stanback, 1986; Brown, 1978; Glasgow, 1980; Helmreich, 1973; Keiser, 1969; Kochman, 1981; Meltzer, 1980; Silverstein & Krate, 1975; White, 1984); *Hispanic* (Horowitz, 1983; Mirande, 1987; Moore, Garcia, Garcia, Cerda & Valencia, 1978; Quicker, 1983; Ramirez, 1983; Vigil, 1983, Vigil & Long, 1990); *Asian* (Bloodworth, 1966; Bresler, 1980; Kaplan & Dubro, 1986; Meltzer, 1980; President's Commission on Organized Crime, 1985; Wilson, 1970), and others (Hagedorn & Macon, 1988; Howard & Scott, 1981; Schwartz & Disch, 1970).

Especially useful in much of this culture-clarifying literature is the opportunity it provides to view the structure, dynamics, and purposes of delinquent gangs through the cultural lenses of their members, and the support it implies for the crucial necessity of gang member inputs for effective gang member programming.

SUMMARY

Gangs in the United States are growing rapidly in number, breadth of location, drug involvement, amount and lethality of aggression, and, more generally, in their impact on citizen awareness and concern. I have described their history, their demographics, the ways in which they serve their members, activities, and the nature and sources of their frequent aggression. Intervention efforts have sought value transformation via the widespread use of street gang or detached worker programming, opportunities provision via social infusion programming, and deterrence/incarceration by means of social control and criminal justice procedures. Most promising, in our view, is the period of gang intervention work we may now be entering, that of comprehensive programming. Such programming draws selectively and prescriptively on the full range of available interventions—street work, social programming, the criminal justice system, and more—in a broad effort to meet the diverse needs and aspirations of both gang youth and the larger society of which they are a part.

REFERENCES

Abadinsky, H. (1979). Social service in criminal justice. Englewood Cliffs, NJ: Prentice-Hall.

Agee, V. L. (1979). *Treatment of the violent, incorrigible adolescent.* Lexington, MA: Lexington.

Bandura, A. (1986). *Social foundations of thought and action*. Englewood Cliffs, N.J.: Prentice-Hall.

Beverly, C. C., & Stanback, H. J. (1986). The Black underclass: Theory and reality. *The Black Scholar, 17*, 24–31.

Bloodworth, D. (1966). *The Chinese looking glass*. New York: Dell.

Bogardus, E. S. (1943). Gangs of Mexican-American Youth. *Sociology and Social Research, 28*, 55–66.

Bremmer, R. H. (1976). Other people's children. *Journal of Social History, 16*, 1–3.

Bresler, F. (1980). *The Chinese mafia*. New York: Stein & Day.

Brown, M. K. (1978). Black gangs as family extensions. International Journal of Offender Therapy and Comparative Criminology, *22*, 39–48.

California Youth Gang Task Force (1981). *Community access team*. Sacramento, CA: Youth Gang Task Force.

Camp, G. M., & Camp, C. G. (1985). *Prison gangs: Their extent, nature and impact on prisons*. South Salem, NY: Criminal Justice Institute.

Cartwright, D. S., Schwartz, H., & Tomson, B. (1975). *Gang delinquency*. Monterey, CA: Brooks/Cole.

Clarke, R. V. G. (1977). Psychology and crime. *Bulletin of the British Psychological Society, 30*, 280–283.

Cloward, R. A., & Ohlin, L. E. (1960). *Delinquency and opportunity: A theory of delinquent gangs*. New York: Free Press.

Cohen, A. K. (1955). *Delinquent boys: The culture of the gang*. New York: Free Press.

Cohen, A. K. (1966). The delinquency subculture. In R. Giallombardo (Eds.), *Juvenile delinquency*. New York: John Wiley.

Dumpson, J. R. (1949). An approach to antisocial street gangs. *Federal Probation, 13*, 22–29.

Ellis, L. (1987). Neurohormonal bases of varying tendencies to learn delinquent and criminal behavior. In E. K. Morris & C. J. Braukman (Eds.), *Behavioral approaches to crime and delinquency*. New York: Plenum.

Feldman, M. P. (1977). *Criminal behavior: A psychological analysis*. London: Wiley.

Friedman, C. J., Mann, F., & Friedman, A. S. (1975). A profile of juvenile street gang members. *Adolescence, 40*, 563–607.

Gardner, S. (1985). *Street gangs*. New York: Franklin Watts.

Glaser, D. (1956). Criminality theories and behavioral images. In D. R. Cressey & D. A. Ward (Eds.). *Delinquency, crime, and social process*. New York: Harper & Row.

Glasgow, D. G. (1980). *The black underclass: Poverty, unemployment, and entrapment of ghetto youth*. San Francisco: Jossey-Bass.

Goldstein, A. P. (1991). *Delinquent gangs: A psychological perspective*. Champaign, IL: Research Press.

Goldstein, A. P., & Glick, B. (1987). *Aggression replacement training*. Champaign, IL: Research Press.

Gott, R. (1989, May). *Juvenile gangs*. Paper presented at Conference on Juvenile Crime, Eastern Kentucky University.

Hagedorn, J., & Macon, P. (1988). *People and folks*. Chicago: Lake View Press.

Hardman, D. G. (1967). Historical perspectives on gang research. *Journal of Research in Crime and Delinquency, 4*, 5–27.

Helmreich, W. B. (1973). Race, sex and gangs. *Society, 11*, 44–50.

Horowitz, R. (1983). *Honor and the American dream*. New Brunswick, NJ: Rutgers University Press.

Howard, A., & Scott, R. A. (1981). The study of minority groups in complex societies. In

R. H. Monroe, R. L. Monroe & B. B. Whiting (Eds.), *Handbook of cross-cultural human development.* New York: Garland STPM Press.

Jacobs, J. B. (1974). Street gangs behind bars. *Social Problems, 21,* 395–408.

Kaplan, D. E., & Dubro, A. (1986). *Yakuza: The explosive account of Japan's criminal underworld.* Reading, MA: Addison-Wesley.

Klein, M. W. (1968). *The Ladino Hills Project. Final report to the Office of Juvenile Delinquency and Youth Development.* Washington, DC.

Klein, M. W. (1971). *Street gangs and street workers.* Englewood Cliffs, NJ: Prentice-Hall.

Klein, M. W., & Maxson, C. L. (1989). Street gang violence. In N. A. Weiner & N. W. Wolfgang (Eds.), *Violent crime, violent criminals.* Newbury Park, CA: Sage.

Kobrin, S. (1959). The Chicago Area Project: A twenty-five year assessment. *Annals of the American Academy of Political and Social Science, 322,* 136–151.

Kochman, T. (1981). *Black and white styles in conflict.* Chicago: University of Chicago Press.

Landesco, J. (1932). Crime and the failure of institutions in Chicago's immigrant areas. *Journal of Criminal Law and Criminology, July,* 238–248.

Lane, M. P. (1989). Inmate gangs. *Corrections Today, July,* 98–99, 126–128.

Mattick, H. W., & Caplan, N. S. (1962). *Chicago Youth Development Project: The Chicago Boys Club.* Ann Arbor, MI: Institute for Social Research.

Maxson, C. L., & Klein, M. W. (1983). Gangs, Why we couldn't stay away. In J. R. Kleugel (Ed.), *Evaluating juvenile justice.* Newbury Park, CA: Sage.

Meier, R. (1976). The new criminology: Continuity in criminological theory. *Journal of Criminal Law and Criminology, 67,* 461–469.

Meltzer, M. (1980). *The Chinese Americans.* New York: Thomas Y. Crowell.

Miller, W. B. (1958). Lower class culture as a generating milieu of gang delinquency. *Journal of Social Issues, 14,* 5–19.

Miller, W. B. (1970). Youth gangs in the urban crisis era. In J. F. Short (Ed.), *Delinquency, crime, and society.* Chicago: University of Chicago Press.

Miller, W. B. (1974). American youth gangs: Past and present. In A. Blumberg (Ed.), *Current perspectives on criminal behavior.* New York: Alfred A. Knopf.

Miller, W. B. (1980). Gangs, groups, and serious youth crime. In D. Shicker & D. H. Kelly (Eds.), *Critical issues in juvenile delinquency.* Lexington, MA: Lexington Books.

Miller, W. B. (1982). *Crime by youth gangs and groups in the United States.* Washington, DC: National Institute of Juvenile Justice and Delinquency Prevention.

Miller, W. B. (1990). Why the United States has failed to solve its youth gang problem. In C. R. Huff (Ed.), *Gangs in America.* Newbury Park, CA: Sage.

Mirande, A. (1987). *Gringo justice.* Notre Dame, IN: University of Notre Dame.

Moore, J. W., Garcia, R., Garcia, C., Cerda, L., & Valencia, F. (1978). *Homeboys, gangs, drugs, and prison in the barrios of Los Angeles.* Philadelphia: Temple University Press.

Moore, J. W., Vigil, D., & Garcia, R. (1983). Residence and territoriality in Chicano gangs. *Social Problems,* 31, 182–194.

Morales, A. (1981). *Treatment of Hispanic gang members.* Los Angeles: Neuropsychiatric Institute, University of California.

Needle, J. A. & Stapleton, W. V. (1982). *Police handling of youth gangs.* Washington, DC: National Juvenile Justice Assessment Center.

New York City Youth Board (1960). *Reaching the fighting gang.* New York: Author.

New York State Task Force on Juvenile Gangs (1990). *Reaffirming prevention.* Albany, NY: Division for Youth.

Nietzel, M. T. (1979). *Crime and its modification.* Elmsford, N.Y.: Pergamon.

President's Commission on Law Enforcement and Administration of Justice (1967). *Juvenile delinquency and youth crime.* Washington, DC: U.S. Government Printing Office.

Puffer, J. A. (1912). *The boy and his gang*. Boston: Houghton Mifflin.
Quicker, J. S. (1983). *Seven decades of gangs*. Sacramento, CA: State of California Commission on Crime Control and Violence Prevention.
Ramirez, M. (1983). *Psychology of the Americas*. New York: Pergamon Press.
Schwartz, B. N., & Disch, R. (1970). *White racism*. New York: Dell.
Shaw, C. R., & McKay, H. D. (1942). *Juvenile delinquency and urban areas: A study of rates of delinquents in relation to differential characteristics of local communities in American cities*. Chicago: University of Chicago Press.
Short, J. F. (1990). New wine in old bottles? Change and continuity in American gangs. In C. R. Huff (Ed.), *Gangs in America*. Newbury Park, CA: Sage.
Silverstein, B., & Krate, R. (1975). *Children of the dark ghetto*. New York: Praeger.
Spergel, I. (1965). *Street gang work: Theory and practice*. New York: Addison Wesley.
Spergel, I. A., Ross, R. E., Curry, G. D., & Chance, R. (1989). *Youth gangs: Problem and response*. Washington, DC: Office of Juvenile Justice and Delinquency Prevention.
Sutherland, E. H. (1937). *Principles of criminology*. Philadelphia: Lippincott.
Sutherland, E. H., & Cressey, D. R. (1974). *Criminology*. New York: Lippincott.
Tannenbaum, F. (1939). *Crime and the community*. New York: Columbia University Press.
Thompson, D. W., & Jason, L. A. (1988). Street gangs and preventive interventions. *Criminal Justice and Behavior, 15*, 323–333.
Thrasher, F. M. (1927/1963). *The gang*. Chicago: University of Chicago Press.
Tracy, P. E. (1979). *Subcultural delinquency: A comparison of the incidence and seriousness of gang and nongang member offensivity*. Philadelphia: University of Pennsylvania Center for Studies in Criminology and Criminal Law.
Vigil, J. D. (1983). Chicano gangs: One response to Mexican urban adaptation in the Los Angeles area. *Urban Anthropology, 12*, 45–75.
Vigil, J. D., & Long, J. M. (1990). Emic and etic perspectives on gang culture: The Chicano case. In C. R. Hutt (Eds.), *Gangs in America*. Newbury Park, Sage.
Wattenberg, W. W., & Balistrieri, J. J. (1950). Gang membership and juvenile misconduct. *American Sociological Review, 15*, December.
White, J. L. (1984). *The Psychology of Blacks*. Englewood Cliffs, NJ: Prentice-Hall.
Wilson, R. W. (1970). *Learning to be Chinese*. Cambridge, MA: The MIT Press.

CHAPTER 12

NATIONALISM, PATRIOTISM, AND AGGRESSION

A Clarification of Functional Differences

SEYMOUR FESHBACH

INTRODUCTION

Human aggression entails a complex set of behaviors that vary markedly in structure, content, context, and consequences. An angry feeling, a thought of revenge, jostling and "horse-play," teasing and derogation, fighting over a contested object, bullying and sadistic actions, murder, and the killing of others in the context of a revolutionary struggle or a conflict between nations, are all considered to be acts of aggression. They are grouped together because they have in common the intent to or actions that have the consequence of inflicting injury and harm to others. A major question that students of human aggression must address regards the functional similarities and differences between these diverse forms of aggression; that is, to what extent they arise from similar antecedents and have similar objectives or goals. A particular question which has been the subject of a number of inquiries that I have carried

SEYMOUR FESHBACH • Department of Psychology, University of California at Los Angeles, Los Angeles, California 90024.

Aggressive Behavior: Current Perspectives, edited by L. Rowell Huesmann. Plenum Press, New York, 1994.

out in recent years is the relationship between individual differences in aggressive disposition and individual differences in readiness to support military ventures.

Wars and Aggression

Participation in wars is probably the most aggressive of all human activities; it is certainly the most destructive. It is not necessary to belabor the extent and degree of injury that can be inflicted during the course of a war—the number of deaths and number of wounded, the destruction of homes, factories, museums, and houses of worship. There is the often indiscriminate killing that takes place—of children and the aged, and helpless civilians, along with combatants. It is without doubt a major form of human aggression. Yet, until relatively recently, there has been surprisingly little information available concerning the psychological bases of war. For the greater part of this century, not to speak of the centuries prior to the development of the discipline of psychology, it was explicitly or implicitly assumed that wars were fundamentally a manifestation of human aggressive instincts or drive, and functionally similar in that basic sense to other interpersonal expressions of human violence. This perspective was given strong credence by psychoanalytic instinct theory and the prominence Freud afforded to aggressive drive in his writings after World War I (Freud, 1927, 1930, 1957). Even Freud, however, recognized some important differences between war and other instances of aggression and violence. He acknowledged that "a whole gamut of human motives" (Nathan & Norden, 1968, p. 198) may be implicated in war and that these motives may be positive, as well as including a drive for aggression and destruction. Thus Freud, despite his pacifistic inclinations and his hatred of war, felt that he could not condemn all wars.

While psychoanalysts, including Freud, have focused on the aggressive drive antecedents of war (Glover, 1935; Storr, 1968) despite Freud's caveats regarding the motivational complexities underlying wars, contemporary analyses of the psychological bases of war have begun to examine the role of a range of other variables besides individual aggressive impulses (Feshbach, 1987; Groebel & Hinde, 1989; Hinde, in press; Kelman & Hamilton, 1989, Tetlock, Husbands, Jervis, Stern, & Tilly, 1989). These variables range from frustration to complex social processes of conformity and group decision making. This is not to say that individual aggressive dispositions are irrelevant to involvement in war but rather that other factors may be more central to the occurrence of war and to the degree to which individuals support decisions to engage in war. Further, the psychological factors contributing to war are not uniform for all wars and may vary markedly, depending upon the context and nature of the war. It is probably the case that individual aggressive factors played a more important role in earlier centuries when wars entailed a greater instance of individual, hand-to-hand combat, and the role of psychological variables will undoubtedly vary with the political structure of a nation and with the role of economic, religious, ethnic, and other social factors that may be contributing to the hostilities.

My own entry into the study of psychological factors entailed in war began with an interest in understanding the basis for individual differences in the degree of support for nuclear armament-disarmament. In particular, I addressed the relationship between measures of individual aggression and an index of attitudes toward nuclear armament-disarmament. The relationship proved to be marginal, much smaller than anticipated. This was the case whether the aggression measure was of overt aggressive tendencies or of covert hostility. Since support for nuclear armament might reflect the belief that nuclear armament strength is necessary to insure peace as well as reflect more militant tendencies, the interrelationships among a measure of attitudes toward war, a measure of attitudes toward nuclear armament, and a scale assessing individual aggressive tendencies were examined. We found a rather surprisingly strong relationship between support for nuclear armament and readiness to engage in war (Feshbach, 1987). The measures of individual aggression proved to be weakly correlated to the index of attitudes toward war as well as the measure of attitudes toward nuclear armament.

Individual Differences in Support for War

In exploring individual differences in degree of support for war and for nuclear armament, it was recognized that other psychological factors such as conformity might play a more central role in determining individual participation in a military action. The degree to which individuals support and advocate a military option, as contrasted to conformity to authority-prescribed policies, is nevertheless an important factor, particularly where the nations involved have a democratic form of government. And even authoritarian regimes cannot ignore the degree to which their citizenry supports military actions. In addition, in the last analysis, war is initiated by a decision of some individual or group of individuals. The factors that influence decision-makers' readiness to take military action undoubtedly vary with the nature of the circumstances involved and may differ from the factors influencing the readiness of nondecision makers to support a military action. Yet, even at the decision-maker level, there appear to be systematic differences in attitudes toward military action. Some decision makers are more "hawkish," while others are more "dovish." Given the lack of substantial correlations between individual aggressiveness and hawkish versus dovish military positions that we have found in various populations in the community, it is unlikely that individual aggressiveness is a very important factor distinguishing hawks and doves among those who make national policy. In our investigations, we have turned to other individual difference variables such as the extent to and manner in which children are valued and attitudes toward one's nation in our efforts to understand individual differences in attitudes toward war. These variables have been shown to be germane to support for military policies in college student populations and also older and well-educated samples (Feshbach, 1987). Whether these other factors will be germane to differences between hawks and doves among policy-makers is a question to be resolved by future research.

Patriotism and Nationalism

The particular individual difference variable on which I would like to focus here pertains to the nature of the relationship between the individual and his or her nation—what are commonly referred to as patriotic and nationalistic sentiments. The connection between war and patriotic–nationalistic attitudes needs little elaboration. Hardly a day passes by without some clash occurring between different ethnic or national groups. Indeed, one of the principal challenges confronting international leaders over the next several decades is the reconciliation of national or ethnic aspirations without resort to military solutions. Patriotism and nationalism have fueled struggles between human societies through recorded history. They are, paradoxically, among the noblest as well as the most destructive of human impulses. They are associated with such positive virtues as heroism and self-sacrifice and such negative attributes as self-aggrandizement and hostility.

Thus, in our efforts to understand the bases for individual differences in support of military options, we have turned to an analysis of the bases for individual differences in patriotic and nationalistic sentiments, variables that both historical and quantitative psychological data have shown to be significantly and substantially related to attitudes toward war. One contemporary analysis of these sentiments, enunciated by Shaw and Wong (1989), contends that these sentiments, with correlated propensities for warfare, are deeply rooted in human nature.

Shaw and Wong maintain, on the basis of genetic and evolutionary principles of inclusive fitness and kinship selection, that individuals have inherited strong tendencies to defend and expand the power of their kinship groups and to be fearful and suspicious of members of nonkin groups. They recognize that nations may consist of diverse kinship groups who are as genetically dissimilar from each other as they are from members of other nations, and invoke psychological mechanisms such as identification to account for patriotic attachment to groups that have little kinship similarity to the individual. The consequence of this identification is that the biological proclivities to expand the interests of one's kinship group through war or other expressions of power become implicated in one's relationship toward larger and genetically dissimilar groups. As an incidental note, the violent tendencies to defend and expand the interest of one's group may be genetically independent of an individually oriented violent tendency to defend and expand one's immediate interests.

There are a number of difficulties in the Shaw and Wong evolutionary model of nationalism. An allusion has already been made to the necessity for proposing a mechanism such as identification to account for nationalism in nations made up of genetically diverse groups. In addition, the violent propensities manifested in civil wars and in religious wars in which aggression is directed toward genetically similar individuals, cannot be easily reconciled with a genetic model that is based on inclusive fitness and kinship selection. Shaw and Wong are not alone in not being able to offer an adequate explanation of internecine wars. There is little in the way of theory and research that helps to account for the intensity and fervor of violence where ideologies rather than territories or kin are at stake. The case of nationalism is especially complex since one's relationship toward one's nation may entail, in varying degrees, elements of ideology, kinship, territory, status, and power, among other factors. Given the upsurge of nationalistic sentiments in recent years, and the conflicts occurring within and between nations as different ethnic groups seek political autonomy and independence, it is a matter of pragmatic as well as theoretical importance to understand the structure and antecedents of national attitudes and feelings and how these may influence the willingness to pursue or support military ventures.

Further complicating our task are the situational factors that enter into conflictful situations and the readiness to support military responses to a source of conflict between nations. In some instances the major parameter may be variations in the "cost" in casualties and in resources involved, or the likelihood of success if a military action was undertaken. In other instances, the principal parameter may be the value that is being threatened or enhanced (i.e., economic wealth, territory, prestige). As a rule, both sources of variation are entailed in situations that may elicit a military response, and these, in turn, interact with variations in the structure and intensity of national attitudes, plus other variations in individual values, in determining individual differences in the degree of willingness to support military actions. Nevertheless, while recognizing the role of situational factors, it is still possible to discern more generalized hawkish and dovish attitudes and to delineate components of one's relationship toward one's nation that are related to these attitudes (Feshbach, 1990). Clearly, there are some situations that will elicit very little variation in degree of individual support for a military response. Thus, except for some few committed pacifists, the great majority of a nation would agree to military resistance to a direct military attack and invasion.

Defense of one's nation is a widely shared value. Problems and individual differences arise when there has been no military attack and when the term *defense* is used more broadly, as in "defense of one's national interests." Here, individual differences may arise in the perception of the nature of the threat (cf. the literature on the perception of the "enemy"), in the value placed on the threat, in the alternatives perceived as available to cope with the threat, and in the willingness to use military options to defend or realize a particular value. For example, there are individual differences in the perception of North Korea as a threat to international security or to United States power and influence in the Far East. North Korea may be perceived as a threat, but there may be individual differences in the value placed upon U.S. power and influence in the Far East. Or there may be consensus about the threat and its importance but there may be differences in the range of alternatives perceived as effective in coping with the threat. Closely related to the latter, are individual differences in the willingness to resort to military action to eliminate the threat. All of these factors contribute to individual differences in the readiness to use military action against North Korea (or some other possible threat). And, I would argue that these factors are germane to the responses of decision makers as well as to those of the ordinary citizen.

As a beginning approach to an examination of the relationship between attitudes toward one's nation and readiness to engage in war in various circumstances, we addressed the structure of these attitudes. I might note that other structural analyses of nationalism have been suggested, most notably by Kelman & Hamilton (1989). Our own approach is distinguished by its focus on the process of attachment, and the importance of the attachment component of one's relationship toward one's nation. We have suggested that there is a similarity between the properties of national attachment and familial attachment. We have further suggested that the roots of national attachment lie in family attachments, and that the attachment component of the relationship toward one's nation should be distinguished from a power component. These considerations led to a series of investigations which are elsewhere described in greater detail (Feshbach, 1987, 1990; Kosterman & Feshbach, 1989). The initial study, the report of a factor analysis (Kosterman & Feshbach, 1989), resulted in several factors, the first two of which corresponded to the attachment component and the power component. These were respectively labeled "patriotism" and "nationalism." Patriotism, as we have conceptualized that construct, entails attachment to one's nation as characterized by love of one's nation and pride in one's national identification. Nationalism, while related to patriotism, entails feelings of national superiority, of competitiveness with other nations, and of the importance of power over other nations. These constructs are differentiated not only factor analytically but also by their relationship to a number of other variables. Patriotism, but not nationalism, has been found to be significantly correlated with a measure of early attachment to one's father. Nationalism has also been found to be more strongly correlated with measures of individual aggression than patriotism and, most importantly, with pronuclear and prowar attitudes. In addition, the correlations of nationalism with the willingness to resort to extreme military options were much higher than those obtained for individual aggressiveness.

MILITANT MUSIC, PATRIOTISM, AND NATIONALISM

The latter part of this chapter is addressed to an additional effort to demonstrate functional differences between the constructs of patriotism and nationalism. Our prior research has been correlational in nature. To buttress further the distinction between patriotism and nationalism, we wish to show that measures of these constructs will be differentially influenced by an experimentally manipulated situational factor. We chose for this purpose variations in exposure to martial music. While our primary interest is in providing further evidence bearing on the functional difference between patriotism and nationalism, there is a secondary interest in the effects of military music and related stimuli upon attitudes and behavior.

It is commonly assumed that music has psychological effects. While there is not an extensive research literature on the effects of music, a number of experiments have been carried out that demonstrate that music has significant effects on mood and, in some instances, on behavior. In an early study in this area, Greenberg and Fisher (1971) found that female subjects exposed to exciting music responded with significantly more power themes on the thematic apperception test (TAT) than subjects who were give calm music to which to listen. In addition, while scores on a questionnaire measure of aggression were unaffected by the variation in music exposure, the exciting music elicited a greater frequency of hostility themes on the TAT. In a subsequent study in which a no music control condition was also employed (Fisher & Greenberg, 1972), they found a significant increase in aggressive mood in response to the exciting music. Since aggression and power orientation are both correlated with nationalism, these findings are particularly germane to the current study. Also relevant is a study by McFarland (1984) in which he used as an exciting stimulus a "militaristic, shrill piece" entitled "Mars: Bringer of War." The strongest effects of exposure to this stimulus were on affective ratings of anger. It should be noted that a musical piece constitutes a complex stimulus and it is often unclear as to what aspect or aspects of the stimulus may be eliciting the increment in aggressive mood—whether it is the rapid tempo, the loudness, any aversive properties, or possible symbolic associations to the music.

Some of these questions were addressed in a study by Fried and Berkowitz (1979) in which the effects of a no music condition, a soothing music piece (a selection from Mendelssohn's "Songs Without Words"), a stimulating piece (Ellington's "One O'Clock Jump"), and an "aversive" musical passage (Coltrane's "Meditations") were compared. Subjects exposed to the stimulating music reported feeling less tired and less depressed and downhearted while those exposed to the soothing music felt more content and peaceful in comparison to the no music controls. In contrast, the aversive music resulted in significant increments in feelings of irritation, annoyance, and anger and decrements in self-reports of joy and happiness. These changes were not restricted to mood alone but, in the case of the soothing music condition, a significant behavioral effect was obtained. Subjects who had been exposed to the soothing music were significantly more responsive to a request for assistance from the experimenter than subjects in each of the other conditions (perhaps negotiations between conflicting parties should be carried out with a background of soothing music!). While the Fried and Berkowitz study helps clarify some of the stimulus properties of music that may foster aggressive and other mood changes, ambiguity still remains as to the parameters of a musical piece that are germane to the stimulation of aggressive feelings. Thus Wanamaker and Reznikoff (1989) found that variations in rock music and in the aggressiveness of rock lyrics had no effect on TAT story content as well as on a self-report measure of aggressiveness.

The research literature indicates that while music can significantly affect moods, there is no simple relationship between attributes of a musical piece and effects on attitudes and behavior. The question of whether martial music will differentially affect indices of nationalism and patriotism remains in considerable part an empirical issue in that negative results will tell us very little. Only positive findings have theoretical import. Although situational stimuli such as music may influence one's sense of comfort, joy distress, or anger, it does not follow that attitudes and belief systems will also be influenced. The dependent measures employed in this study, particularly nationalism, entail complex cognitions in contrast to simple ratings of affect. For example, the following item had the highest loading on the nationalism factor scale: "In view of America's moral and material superiority, it is only right that we should have the biggest say in deciding United Nations policy." In contrast, a number of the patriotism items entail more simple and salient affective elements; for example, "I love my country," "I feel a great pride in the land that is America." Nevertheless, we would anticipate that martial music would have a greater effect on the power, competitive, superiority component of national attitudes than on the attachment component. Martial music, by virtue of its symbolic components as well as formal musical properties, is reflective of and likely to stimulate the power and dominance elements in an individual's national identification and attitudes. While there may be some effect on pride, martial music, in our judgment, is less consonant with the affectionate elements entailed in patriotic attachment. Thus we anticipate that martial music will produce a significant increment in nationalism as compared to patriotism.

Again, it must be emphasized that our focus here is on the differential qualities of patriotism and nationalism, and we are employing variations in music to provide further evidence bearing on these differential qualities. It is our contention that nationalism is a more problematic attribute than patriotism, and is more likely to be associated with "hawkish," prowar attitudes. Martial music, apart from its tempo and sound amplitude properties, is symbolically associated with military functions such as a parade by military units. Given the intimate relationship that we hypothesize between nationalism and the support of the military, music related to the military should stimulate nationalist attitudes. In addition to studying the effects of martial music, we shall also examine the effects of exposure to "patriotic" music such as the national anthem. The effects of the "patriotic" music are more difficult to predict. The tempo of patriotic music is usually much slower than that of martial music. Symbolically, patriotic music is associated with both military and non-military occasions. Also, depending upon the particular patriotic piece, the lyrics may or may not entail martial elements. Consequently, it is difficult to predict differential effects of exposure to patriotic music on the indices of patriotism versus nationalism. We do anticipate though that in comparison to a control condition, exposure to patriotic music should result in a significant increment on the patriotism measure.

Measures of aggression and aggression-anxiety were included in the study in order to determine whether these indices of aggressive disposition were affected by the experimental manipulations. In addition, a third national attitude measure, the third factor obtained in the original factor analysis and labeled "internationalism," was included for exploratory purposes.

Methods

The subjects were 61 undergraduate volunteers, 27 males and 34 females; 13 of the sample were non-U.S. citizens. The subjects were randomly assigned to one of three experimental groups: (1) martial music; (2) patriotic music; (3) control. Half the controls were given passages to read while half heard parts of string quartets. A greater number of subjects were assigned to the control condition in order to determine whether the music-reading variation had any effect on the dependent measures.

An experimental session lasted from 25 to 30 minutes. The number of subjects participating in a session was most commonly three, although a number of sessions were conducted with only one or two subjects. All subjects were told that the study was concerned with national attitudes, personality, and aesthetic judgments. Subjects were either told that they would be asked to complete questionnaires while listening to music or after reading passages. They were instructed to focus on the evaluation of the music or the passages. All subjects were then given a questionnaire titled "National Attitudes, Personality, and Aesthetics." The questionnaire included the 12-item patriotism scale, the 8-item nationalism scale, and the 9-item internationalism scale. These items were interspersed, along with 14 items entailing "aesthetic" ratings. Examples of the latter were: "This particular piece of music being played needed more amplification"; "This is an excellent performance of this particular piece of music" (or for control subjects given readings,

"The author needed to be more descriptive in depicting the characters"; "This is an excellent passage." Each item in the questionnaire was rated, using a 5-point Likert scale, varying from "Strongly Agree" to "Strongly Disagree." Also included as a separate part of the questionnaire were 8 overt aggression items (The Buss-Durkee scale) and 18 Aggression-Anxiety items, the latter being a scale that I have used in a number of prior studies (Feshbach & Singer, 1970; Feshbach, Stiles, & Bitter, 1967). The aggression and aggression–anxiety items were responded to using a true–false format.

Subjects in the experimental and control music conditions completed the questionnaires while listening to the music; subjects in the control reading condition first read passages before completing the questionnaire. For the martial music condition (M music), recordings of "Anchors Aweigh" and "Stars and Stripes Forever" were played while subjects in the patriotic music condition (P music) listened to "America the Beautiful" and "The Star Spangled Banner." In the control condition, subjects either read excerpts from *Tom Sawyer* and *Huckleberry Finn* or heard Marais' *Pièces en Trio in C major.*

Results

Gender by experimental condition analyses of variance were carried out for each of the dependent measures. Since no significant differences were obtained between the control music and the control reading groups, data for these two groups are combined in the presentation of the results. The findings pertaining to the principal hypothesis bearing on the differential effects of martial music on nationalism and patriotism are presented in Tables 1 and 2.

It can be seen from Table 1 that the nationalism scores of the group exposed to martial music are significantly higher than those of the controls and also of the group exposed to patriotic music. In the case of the latter group, the findings may be influenced by the extremely low scores obtained by two noncitizen males in this experimental group. When they are eliminated from the analysis, the mean for the P-music group is elevated and, while still lower than that of the music group and not significantly different from the control mean, is no longer significantly different from that of the M-music group. While the mean male nationalism scores are higher than those for females, the gender difference does not attain statistical significance for the overall sample. For the U.S. sample only, the mean score of males is significantly higher than females at the .05 confidence level (see Table 2). From Table 2 it can be seen that there were no significant effects of martial or patriotic music on the

TABLE 1. Mean Nationalism Scores as a Function of Experimental Condition and Gender

	Martial music (N = 18)	Patriotic music (N = 18)	Control (N = 25)
	26.1a	21.7b	22.9b

(Means with different subscripts are significantly different at $p < .05$ level.)

	Martial music	Patriotic music	Control
Male	27.0 (N = 2)	23.5 (N = 6)	23.4 (N = 13)
Female	25.1 (N = 10)	20.0 (N = 12)	22.5 (N = 12)

patriotism scores. The same two non-U.S. citizen males in the P-music group who had obtained extremely low nationalism scores also had extremely low patriotism scores. When the non-U.S. citizens are removed from the sample, the mean patriotism score of the P-music males becomes substantially higher (47.0) while the other means remain similar to those for the entire sample. The mean for the P-music group is then higher than that for the other groups, the difference between the P-music group and the control attaining the .10 level.

In summary, the findings from these first two tables are consistent with the proposition that there is a functional distinction between the

TABLE 2. Mean Patriotism Scores as a Function of Experimental Condition and Gender

	Martial music (N = 18)	Patriotic music (N = 18)	Control (N = 23)
	44.4	43.9	43.8

(Means with different subscripts are significantly different at $p < .05$ level.)

	Martial music	Patriotic music	Control
Male	46.6 (N = 8)	41.3 (N = 6)	43.7 (N = 13)
Female	43.7 (N = 10)	45.3 (N = 12)	43.9 (N = 12)

constructs of nationalism and patriotism. Martial music has been shown to elevate nationalism but not patriotism. Also, there is some suggestion that patriotic music (anthems as contrasted to marches) affects patriotic but not nationalistic feelings.

In addition to the primary dependent measures of patriotism and nationalism, measures of aggression, aggression-anxiety, and internationalism were also administered. As is normative for these measures (Feshbach, 1970), females obtained higher scores than males on the aggression scale; higher scores on the internationalism scale; and lower scores on the aggression-anxiety scale. There were no significant differences among the different treatment groups in level of aggression or aggression anxiety. Treatment and gender differences were obtained on the internationalism scale, and these are presented in Table 3. It can be seen from Table 3 that while no gender differences were found in nationalism and patriotism scores and while internationalism is inversely correlated with patriotism and especially nationalism, women are significantly higher in internationalist orientation than males. The significant difference in internationalism scores between the martial and patriotic music conditions is of particular interest. It appears that the more martial march music tended to lower internationalism scores while the anthem mode of patriotic music utilized for the P-music condition tended to enhance internationalism. As a secondary note, the internationalism scores of the non-U.S. citizen males in the P-music group were at the average for the group.

TABLE 3. Mean Internationalism Scores as a Function of Experimental Condition and Gender

	Martial music (N = 18)	Patriotic music (N = 18)	Control (N = 25)
	29.3a	33.1b	31.0ab

(Means with different subscripts are significantly different at $p < .05$ level.)

	Martial music	Patriotic music	Control
Male	27.8 (N = 8)	30.5 (N = 6)	28.8 (N = 13)
Female	30.6 (N = 10)	34.4 (N = 12)	33.3 (N = 12)

Male = 28.9, Female = 32.9.
$p < .02$.

DISCUSSION AND CONCLUSIONS

The proposition that there are functional differences between patriotism and nationalism, and that nationalism is more closely linked to a promilitary orientation is supported by the experimental findings. Martial music, as anticipated, significantly elevated nationalism but not patriotism scores. There is also some suggestion that exposure to martial music may lessen internationalistic attitudes while "patriotic" music, which is slower in beat and a national anthem in content, tends to enhance an internationalistic orientation. There is also some suggestion that the latter tends to enhance patriotic but not nationalistic feelings. Finally, further evidence of the functional difference between nationalism and patriotism is provided by the tendency of males to obtain higher nationalism scores than females, a difference which achieves statistical significance for the U.S. sample.

Questions remain as to the exact nature of the difference between the patriotic and nationalistic musical stimuli that is responsible for the difference in the effects of these stimuli. As has been previously noted, the musical selections employed are complex stimuli, and one cannot determine from the experimental design employed in the study what specific features of the variations in musical passages are responsible for the experimental differences obtained. The data also suggest that in future research it would be useful to include a larger sample of non-U.S. citizens. Nevertheless, with regard to the central proposition addressed by the study, the findings provide experimental support for functional differences that have been previously investigated through correlational procedures. Nationalism and patriotism are differentially affected by the independent variables employed in the study, and the variables that influenced nationalism and patriotism did not affect the measures of individual aggression. Martial music may foster nationalistic sentiments but has much less of an effect on feelings of attachment to one's nation or on levels of individual aggressiveness.

The relationship found between martial music and enhanced nationalism further substantiates the interrelationship that has been theoretically postulated, and empirically supported, between nationalism and readiness to support military actions. It is no mere happenstance that soldiers march to the drumbeat of martial airs. The tempo, pitch, and occasional verbal accompaniment of military marches are consonant with the symbolic and instrumental functions of the marches in which soldiers from all armies engage. There are undoubtedly many reasons for military parades and marches. One such function appears to be the sense of power and strength manifested by groups of soldiers, each bearing arms, and walking in unison at a vigorous pace. From the informal observation of one who has both witnessed and participated in such marches, both the soldier participants and observers of the march experience this heightened sense of power. And it is power and dominance that is at the heart of nationalistic sentiments. This is not to say that patriotic feelings are unaffected by military parades; only that they are less intimately related to this manifestation of military presence and power than nationalistic feelings. And, as a further and informal speculative commentary on the effects of military marches, one's sense of personal power in an individual aggressive encounter is not enhanced. Rather, it is a sense of power that stems from association with a larger group. It seems reasonable to conjecture that it is this group context that separates the aggression stemming from nationalistic impulses from the aggression stemming from individual aggressive dispositions. From this perspective as well as social learning models of aggressive behavior, it is not surprising that only modest correlations are found between measures of individual aggressiveness and measures of support for military options.

From a social learning perspective, it is a relatively simple matter to account for differences between individual aggressive behaviors and readiness to engage in the violence associated with military actions. In terms of the social learning theory framework, both are learned patterns of behavior that ensue from particular reinforcements and antecedent stimuli. While in particular social contexts it may occur that there is a substantial overlap in the reinforcements and eliciting stimuli entailed in individual aggression and in military aggression, there is no a priori reason why this need be the case. We would also argue that even if one asserts the importance of aggressive drive or instinctual aggressive behaviors, it does not follow that war is a manifestation of the same drive or instinct that is believed to govern individual aggression. While individual aggressive tendencies may have some influence on readiness to support military actions, there is a qualitative difference between the social context in which war takes place and the context in which individual aggressive acts are carried out. The data reported on here suggests that this difference in context entails differences in motivations and functions of the behaviors.

We have focused on the importance of nationalism, as contrasted to patriotism, as one factor distinguishing the aggression entailed in war from the aggression entailed in more individual interactions. It is our belief that it is possible to differentially socialize patriotic and nationalistic sentiments,and that is it possible to sustain and even reinforce patriotic attachments to one's nation while fostering internationally oriented attitudes that diminish the likelihood of war. There is some suggestion in our data that stimuli that enhance patriotic feelings can also enhance positive feelings toward other nations. But these data are merely suggestive. A great deal of research must be carried to demonstrate that patriotic attachments are compatible with an international orientation and, perhaps more importantly, to demonstrate the socialization mechanisms and social structures that will foster and strengthen this compatibility.

Acknowledgment

The author wishes to express his appreciation to Joseph Hwang for his efforts and skill in helping carry out the study in this chapter.

REFERENCES

Feshbach, S. (1970). Aggression. In P. H . Musser (Ed.), *Carmichael's manual of child psychology* (Vol. 2, pp. 159–259). New York: John Wiley and Sons.

Feshbach, S. (1987). Individual aggression, national attachment and the search for peace: Psychological perspective. *Aggressive Behavior, 13,* 315–325.

Feshbach, S. (1990). Psychology, human violence and the search for peace: Issues in science and social values. *Journal of Social Issues, 46,* 185–198.

Feshbach, S. & Singer, R. (1970). *Television and aggression.* San Francisco: Jossey-Bass.

Feshbach, S., Stiles, W., & Bitter, E. (1967). The reinforcing effect of witnessing aggression. *Journal of Experimental Research in Personality, 2,* 133–139.

Fisher, S., & Greenberg, R. P. (1972). Selective effects upon women of exciting and calm music. *Perceptual and motor skills, 34,* 987–990.

Freud, S. (1927). *Beyond the pleasure principle.* New York: Boni & Liveright.

Freud, S. (1930/1957). *Civilization and its discontents* (2nd ed.). London: Hogarth Press.

Fried, R., & Berkowitz, L. (1979). Music both charms . . . and can influence helpfulness. *Journal of Applied Social Psychology, 913,* 199–208.

Glover, E. (1935). *War, sadism and pacifism: Further essays on group psychology and war.* London: Allen & Unwin.

Greenberg, R. P., & Fisher, S. (1971). Some different effects of music on projective and structured psychological tests. *Psychological Reports, 28,* 817–818.

Groebel, J., & Hinde, R. (Eds.) (1989). *Aggression and war: Their biological and social roots.* Cambridge, U.K.: Cambridge University Press.

Hinde, R. A. (in press). Aggression and war: Individuals, groups and states. In P. E. Tetlock and O'Hare (Eds.), *Behavior, society and nuclear war* (Vol. 3). New York: Oxford University Press.

Kelman, H. C., & Hamilton, V. L. (1989). *Crimes of obedience.* New Haven, CT: Yale University Press.

Kosterman, R., & Feshbach, S. (1989). Toward a measure of patriotic and nationalistic attitudes. *Political Psychology, 10,* 257–274.

McFarland, R. A. (1984). Effects of music upon emotional content of TAT stories. *Journal of Psychology, 116,* 227–234.

Nathan, O., & Norden, H. (1968). *Einstein on peace.* New York: Schocken.

Shaw, P. R., & Wong, Y. (1989). Genetic seeds of warfare. In *Evolution, Nationalism, and Patriotism* (p. 274). Boston: Unwin Hyman.

Storr, A. (1968). *Human aggression.* New York: Atheneum.

Tetlock, P. E., J. L., Husbands, R., Jervis, P. C., Stern, & Tilly, C. (Eds.) (1989). *Behavior, society and nuclear war.* New York: Oxford University Press.

Wanamaker, L., & Reznikoff, M. (1989). Effects of aggressive and nonaggressive rock songs on projective and structured tests. *The Journal of Psychology,* 123, 561–570.

INDEX